W9-CFL-287

Voices of the American Revolution

Withdrawn

Voices of the American Revolution
Stories of Men, Women, and Children
Who Forged Our Nation

Kendall Haven

2000
Libraries Unlimited, Inc.
(and Its Division
Teacher Ideas Press)
Englewood, Colorado

To the many super-sleuths of our common history who have carefully, meticulously, and doggedly ferreted out the hidden clues and evidence to reconstruct the truth of our shared heritage: the past. Historians perform a difficult, demanding, valuable, and vastly underappreciated service for our country.

Copyright © 2000 by Kendall Haven
All Rights Reserved
Printed in the United States of America

No part of this publication may be reproduced, stored in a retrieval system, or transmitted, in any form or by any means, electronic, mechanical, photocopying, recording, or otherwise, without the prior written permission of the publisher. An exception is made for individual librarians and educators, who may make copies of portions of the book for use in a single school or library. Standard citation information should appear on each page.

Libraries Unlimited, Inc.
(and Its Division
Teacher Ideas Press)
P.O. Box 6633
Englewood, CO 80155-6633
1-800-237-6124
www.lu.com

Library of Congress Cataloging-in-Publication Data

Haven, Kendall F.
    Voices of the American Revolution : stories of men, women, and children who forged our nation / Kendall Haven.
        p. cm.
    Includes bibliographical references (p.) and index.
    ISBN 1-56308-856-8
    1. United States--History--Revolution, 1775-1783--Personal narratives. 2. United States--History--Revolution, 1775-1783--Study and teaching. I. Title

E275.A2 H38 2001
973.3'092--dc21

                                                            00-059343

Contents

v

1776 at a Glance:
Drums of Glory; Face of Disaster

1777 at a Glance:
The Best and Worst of Times

1778 at a Glance:
The Armies Are Stalemated While the Frontier Burns

1779 at a Glance:
The Land War Stagnates; the Seas Catch Fire

1780 at a Glance:
Southern Blood Must Flow

1781 Through 1783 at a Glance:
Did We Win?

Introduction

When we think of the American Revolutionary War, certain images naturally flash into our minds—images of angry tea protests in Boston, of Paul Revere's midnight ride, of the signing of the Declaration of Independence in Philadelphia, of stirring bravery by a small band of soldiers making a dangerous night crossing of the Delaware River through swirling floes of ice, of Betsy Ross diligently sewing the first flag, of the bitter deprivation at Valley Forge—and then our minds jump straight to glorious victory in the bright sunshine at Yorktown. But these images don't connect—not with each other and not with the reality of the world around them.

As I began the research for this book, I held strong, vivid images of battles and weary soldiers in winter camps, of defiant Boston Minutemen, and of well-fed politicians arguing in Philadelphia. But I knew that wasn't the whole picture of the Revolution. The more I sought to complete my image, the more questions I bumped up against.

Why did the Colonists protest so violently against tea when the prices were being *lowered*? They were protesting *cheaper* tea, for goodness sake! Who does that? That tea tax was not the first tax levied on the Colonists by Parliament. Import duties and taxes were a well-established, routine part of colonial life. Why protest *that* tax?

Why was the official Continental Army starving at Valley Forge in the midst of a land of plenty, a land with filled granaries and a well-fed civilian population? Why did so little of the plentiful food supplies in Pennsylvania, New Jersey, and New York ever reach Valley Forge that fateful winter of 1777–1778? Whose fault was it? Surely *someone* should be blamed for a bonehead blunder like forgetting to feed and clothe the army! What about the other winters of the war? Was Washington's beleaguered army better cared for in other years?

Why did Washington have to take such a desperate gamble and risk having his army crushed by jagged boulders of churning ice to cross the Delaware River during a terrible night-time winter storm to attack the Hessians at Trenton one day after Christmas? Why not wait for a clear day in January?

If Washington was in such desperate straits—barely able to survive the winter—how did he suddenly leap to victory at Yorktown? What really went on? Why did these snapshot images we have come into being? *Did* the events really occur, or are they myths, stories that writers have invented to make our origins seem stirringly glorious? What made these particular events significant, if they really did happen?

In fact, our Revolutionary War was a civil war as much as it was a war between British and American armies. The fighting was as much American versus American as America versus England. We don't often hear about that part of the struggle for liberty.

Why did the Colonists want to be free in the first place? In 1770 virtually every Colonist was thrilled to be ruled by England. They *were* English—and they were proud to be English. They had plenty of rights and liberty under English law. England was the greatest power on Earth and had done very well by the Colonists for over a century. Colonists used English money, spoke the English language, sent their sons to English schools, traded with English companies, were protected by the English army, and honored English values and traditions. If the Colonists were so satisfied to snuggle up in the arms of mother England in 1770, why did they choose brutal, bloody revolt five short years later?

What was the point of, the purpose of, the Revolution? Our Founding Fathers established a legal system based on English law. They created a parliamentary government based on the English government using English parliamentary rules of order. They chose to continue to use the English language. It seems the only thing they revolted against was having a king. Did they hate King George that much? What had he done to them? Was that the point of the Revolution—just to get away from the king? Parliament made the laws and rules that affected colonial life, not the king. There was probably not one single American—other than Ben Franklin—who had ever met the king. Could they really have hated someone they didn't know *that* much? Could that really be what started the war?

The more I gazed at the images and information we are routinely fed about our national beginnings, the more I realized that that information carried with it not answers, but a flood of pesky questions. The images didn't make sense. I couldn't reconstruct the thinking and logic of the Colonists in my mind based on what we are told today. Yet there had to be a logic hidden in these images somewhere. The Revolution happened.

What did this America look like that rose up to boldly slap the world's most dominant power in the face? It was an agricultural society. Nineteen out of every 20 Americans were farmers. The *doer* was valued over the *thinker*. The population was rural. There were few cities. Philadelphia was biggest, then New York, Charleston, and Boston. But none of these cities was home to more than 40,000 people. Ninety percent of Americans lived in rural areas or in small towns.

Farmers believed in the moon. They planted on a waxing moon and weeded on a waning moon. They dropped European fertilizing practices and crop rotation. It was cheaper and easier to use up the land and simply move on to another spot. Land was plentiful.

In the northern Colonies the major crops were wheat, corn, and rye. Their big exports were furs, whaling products, and rum. In the South, farmers grew tobacco, rice, and indigo. Cotton didn't become a major crop until the early 1800s. Tobacco was the biggest export.

As of 1770, there existed virtually no manufacturing in the Colonies. There was a sizable shipbuilding industry because northern American forests contained plenty of good, hard wood. There was also some wrought iron manufacturing, mostly in the North.

If America lacked manufacturing, it was bubbling over with craftsmen: leather, silver, wood, pewter, printing, and so forth. The Colonies also featured an abundance of mills for fabric making, linen being the most popular and plentiful of our fabrics.

Colonial America was a young country. The average age was 16. Women were scarce. Bachelors outnumbered unmarried women three to one. Girls married young (age 16 to 18) and often had large families—10 to 12 children. Boys became men at 16 and had to start paying taxes—yes, they had taxes to pay. There were few children's books. Most of those that did exist were religious and moralizing, like the New England Primer.

The sweeteners of choice were still maple syrup and molasses, but imported granular sugar was growing rapidly in popularity. American taverns had English names like Blue Anchor or Harp & Crown.

Most important of all, each Colony was a separate, independent entity. Each felt a far stronger bond with England than with other colonies, even their neighboring colonies. Their economic ties were to England, not to each other. There were few roads between the colonies and they were of dismally poor quality. (The one exception was the New England Colonies, where small size made for more interaction and unity.)

Southerners felt that they had nothing in common with New Englanders and vice versa. Their histories, lifestyles, and dialects were different. They lacked direct political, economic, or social ties with each other. Mid-Atlantic Colonists distrusted the folks with the strange accents living north and south of them. There was no continental unity, only colonial suspicion and distrust.

Almost all travel and transportation of goods was funneled along waterways: rivers, bays, and the ocean. The few dirt roads were narrow, rut- and mud-filled, and often overgrown. Few Americans had ever traveled more than 25 miles from their homes. The first coach service from Philadelphia to New York started in 1756. It took three days if weather was good. Four long, jarring days on the coach were required to travel from New York to Boston

The early 1770s in America were a time of work and socializing within the community. Men's lives centered around work and the tavern. (Cards and gambling were very popular in taverns.) Women's lives centered around home, children, and female friends. Only one in eight Colonists actively belonged to any church.

There were few schools—only five in Boston, with a total enrollment of 625. Informal, in-home, neighborhood schools ("Dame Schools") were both more common and more popular, but only accepted children up to the age of nine or ten. For most American boys, an apprenticeship *was* their education.

"English" or "Writing School" existed for wealthy sons and was more popular in New England. A few "Latin" schools were scattered from Boston to Charleston to teach formal education to college-bound young men. All higher education required a trip to England. It was common for the sons of those who could afford it to be shipped off to England for four or five years to be educated before they returned to take over the family business.

Girls had few options other than Dame School and finishing school, if their parents were wealthy enough to afford it. But finishing schools focused on social refinement, and half of a girl's education there was consumed with needlepoint.

Schools ran all year long. Children dropped in and out as the family (and especially crops) mandated.

There were no toothbrushes in America in 1770, and Americans suffered from bad teeth and great need of dental care. The most common folk remedy for toothache was to carry the tooth of a dead man. A common gift was a dead man's tooth on a necklace. Many false teeth were needed, and that's where Paul Revere made his money.

There were no official holidays. Christmas was a minor religious observance with no exchange of presents. Thanksgiving was generally celebrated, but not always on the same day, and it had nothing to do with the pilgrims. Communities literally held solemn gatherings to give thanks for harvests (mostly), successful plantings, rain, and so forth. Theater (stage plays) was popular in the cities. Washington regularly saw 25 or more plays each year.

America before the war was a land bustling with energy and activity. Life was relatively easy. The America of 1775 was bursting at the seams with confidence, enthusiasm, and self-assurance. Limits didn't seem to apply to the Colonists; land and life were here for the grabbing, and opportunity and optimism reigned supreme.

So why did these Americans risk their happily structured existence on a desperate gamble, the Revolution? In her contribution to Hoffman and Albert's book, *Women in the Age of the American Revolution* (Charlottesville, VA: University Press of Virginia, 1979), historian Cynthia Enlow wrote that a successful revolutionary movement establishes new definitions of "what is valued, what is scorned, what is feared, and what is believed to enhance safety and security." Benjamin Rush in 1786 noted that the "first act" of the great drama of the Revolution was a war accomplished on the battlefield by armies. The second act was a "revolution in principles, opinions and manners" so as to accommodate the new forms of government being created.

Maybe that's why our predecessors charged so eagerly into war with Mother England. America's energy and activity needed an organizing ideal, a loftier purpose, a cause of value.

Lofty or not, wise or not, the Revolution took place and, miraculously, it succeeded. In so doing, it created far more problems for America and Americans than it solved. It set the stage for bitter internal hatred and warfare. But it also led to the creation of the United States of America, of us. The real-life drama of the American Revolution belongs to us because it forms an important link in the fabric that is the history of this nation.

I sought the opportunity to write this book so that I could explore that common history and try to break through the myths, the legends, and view it for the long and desperate struggle that it was. I have collected and studied over 400 references in compiling the stories in this book. The events and characters of these stories are historically accurate. Although the dialogue is fictionalized, it is based on most-probable personality traits of the characters and documented outcomes of conversations and events. These stories paint an accurate mosaic of our revolutionary history.

This book contains 30 stories that capture important moments spread throughout the war period. Some focus on famous historical characters. Most focus on common citizens few have ever heard of but who participated in significant events of the revolutionary struggle. These stories, these events, represent the ebb and flow of the entire Revolution.

Literally, there were hundreds of stories I could have chosen to include. Why did I choose the ones I did? Simple. I used five criteria to settle on the stories in this book:

- The event(s) described had to be significant to the overall flow of the war, or at least representative of a larger aspect of the war.

- The central character had to be compelling, fascinating, and worth reading about.

- I had to find enough background information to feel I could report the truth of the event.

- The stories in the book had to be evenly spread over the duration of the conflict.

- The book had to include the viewpoints, voices, and perspectives of as many disparate groups and factions as possible.

Because the Revolutionary War was not a time of great unity, but rather one of great splintering and factionalism, I felt it was important to include voices from as many of these factions as possible. I was not able to include all possible American factions, but have represented a wide variety of viewpoints: soldiers on both sides, civilians on both sides, those committed to one side and those committed to not committing, children and adults, whites, Native Americans and blacks, Patriots, Loyalists, and Redcoats. Each of these voices has something to add to our understanding of the war.

There are also many powerful, important, and inspiring stories not included—those of Benedict Arnold, Nathaniel Hale, Benjamin Franklin's diplomatic efforts, winters at Morristown, the Morristown Mutiny, many of the key battles (Brandywine, Germantown, Cowpens, Kings Mountain, etc.), hundreds of local communities, efforts to build a road network and communication lines across America, the desperate work of Congress to hold the nation together, and so forth. See how many of these other stories you can discover in other sources or research on your own.

This book contains only 30 brief moments out of the thousands that made up the Revolutionary War. Yet they are important moments and collectively paint an accurate picture of the overall flow of the human drama that was our Revolutionary War. Let them stir your interest in other, similar moments in other communities and on other dates. There is much we do not know about our national origin. See how much you can uncover.

I owe a great debt of thanks to Roni Berg, the love of my life, and to May Haven, a sharp and talented editor who also happens to be my mother. They both graciously spent many hours honing these stories and deserve much of the credit for their clarity and flow. I owe great thanks to Barbara Ittner, who was the guiding force behind the design and content of the follow-up questions and activities in this book. I also want to thank the library staff at the Sonoma State University Salizar Library. They performed heroically in helping me identify and locate many of the references I needed to complete my research. Several of the women's stories in this book were based on stories in a previous book of mine, *Amazing American Women* (Libraries Unlimited, 1996). I would refer anyone to that book for additional stories of incredible and unheralded deeds of the women who helped to forge, build, and create this country.

Finally, I owe a great thanks to you, the reader, for allowing these images of our revolutionary origins to enter your thinking. I hope they inflame your curiosity to learn more of the truth of our national beginnings. Such knowledge is surely the stepping stone to wisdom.

How to Use This Book

The stories in this book are organized chronologically through the years of the Revolutionary War. They can be used as sources of information about major events of the war and as kick-off points, or inspirations, to lead students to further research on related or suggested topics.

The stories are appropriate for read-alouds with younger children and for silent reading and research by older students. Whether used for story time or as assigned reading, these stories greatly enhance and enliven the study of history by creating vivid, diverse, close-up perspectives on the many different experiences of the many different groups of Americans during the Revolutionary War.

Each story is self-contained and can be used singly, can be grouped with other stories with a similar theme, or can be part of an extensive study of the revolutionary period. It is recommended that readers review the "At a Glance" summaries that precede the stories as well as the introductory and accompanying material provided with each story. Readers should refer to the glossary to clarify any unfamiliar terms.

A brief summary ("At a Glance") of the major events for each time period precedes the three to five selected stories that take place during that period. The events, places, dates, and characters in these stories are all real and accurately portrayed. Dialogue is fictionalized based on established personality traits of the characters and on the known outcomes of conversations and interactions.

Each unit is divided into five sections:

- **At a Glance.** This section creates background context and perspective for the following story. It includes a brief review of the events and historical figures that led up to, and set the stage for, the events depicted in the story.

- **Meet the Character.** Because most of the viewpoint characters are not well-known historical figures, this section provides a brief biographical sketch of each story's main character to help students better understand the events of the story and place this story within the context of that character's life.

- **The Story.**

- **Aftermath.** This section quickly summarizes the effect, on the war as a whole, of the events described in the story. It also includes a summary of what happened after the story as a direct result of the events described and a summary of what the events in the story meant to the main character's later life.

- **Follow-up Questions and Activities.** Follow-up questions and activities are divided into four sections that provide different types of discussions and activities and different levels of complexity. Few of these activities require equipment or supplies. Teachers should feel free to modify and restructure the activities to best meet their own needs and those of their students.

1. *What Do You Know?*—Factual questions for students to discuss and answer that demonstrate their knowledge and understanding of the story and its major historical events and figures.

2. *Finding Out More.*—Reading and research questions and topics that extend the events and characters of the story into a wider context and expand student understanding beyond the limits of the material presented in the story. These topics can be used as themes for essays or oral reports and presentations.

3. *Make It Real.*—Multidisciplinary learning extension activities for students that provide demonstration of key concepts and themes of the story.

4. *Points to Ponder.*—Advanced discussion questions and essay ideas designed to incorporate student beliefs and values into the discussion of story themes and events. These can be used in student debates or as essay themes.

Loyal Pride Turned to Kindling

After the French and Indian War (which ended in 1765), the American Colonists were proud to be British and delighted they weren't French or Spanish. But the colonial war had been expensive and Britain needed money. Parliament looked for ways to turn the American Colonies into a source of revenue and thought first of taxes.

In 1765, Parliament passed the Stamp Act. Most Colonists were outraged. American supporters in Parliament got the act repealed. Most Americans were thrilled that their distant government in London had heard their pleas and felt even more proud to be British. Only a small handful realized that the Stamp Act was just the beginning.

This small group—described as radicals by the rest of the Colonists—was led by Samuel Adams of Massachusetts. They created Committees of Correspondence in the various Colonies to begin the long, slow work toward gaining independence from England. Virtually no one listened to them in the early 1770s, even after that unfortunate incident in Boston, which Adams's committees successfully blew all out of proportion by calling it the "Boston Massacre."

Then Parliament passed the Tea Act in early 1773, creating a special tax on tea. Sam Adams saw the new tax as an opportunity and hollered loud and long about taxation without representation. (This was certainly not the first tax that Parliament had levied on the Colonies without colonial representation.) Adams's cries were heard and, in December, some Colonists rallied at a giant protest in Boston—the Boston Tea Party.

England was outraged. Parliament passed the Coercive Acts and sent navy ships and troops to close Boston Harbor and strangle the economic life out of these upstarts. The Committees of Correspondence talked each Colony's leaders into sending representatives to a First Continental Congress in early 1774. Harmony and peace between Britain and her colonies began to erode. Raw edges rubbed together, showering sparks of bitter friction.

However, in late 1774 even Benjamin Franklin claimed that no sane man, drunk or sober, was thinking about independence from England. But Sam Adams, his Committees of Correspondence, and his secret freedom group, the Sons of Liberty, were.

In early 1775, Adams's dream began to come true when Redcoats fired on Americans and Americans fired back during a long, bloody day at Lexington and Concord. The Second Continental Congress was convened, volunteer soldiers laid siege to the British army in Boston, and Anthony Wayne led his volunteer band to capture Fort Ticonderoga and steal its cannons to aid in the siege. In the summer of 1775 the first official battle took place on Breeds Hill (called the Battle of Bunker Hill). An undeclared war was on.

Washington was appointed commander of the army and took command in July. In September General Wayne led a small army north to invade Canada. Suddenly this was no longer a simple disagreement with mother England. It looked like, sounded like, and felt like war.

Up until 1775, the conflict could have been settled peacefully by politicians and diplomats. By the end of that year, the all-out war could only be settled with muskets and bloodshed.

Key Events Before 1776

Date	Event
1764	Sugar Act and Currency Acts are passed to levy taxes to help play for the colonial war with France.
1765	French and Indian War is won by British and Americans.
1765, March	Stamp Act is passed.
1765, November	Stamp Act is repealed.
1767	Townshend Act creates import duties.
1770, March	Boston Massacre.
1770, April	Townshend duties limited to only tea.
1773, May	Tea Act creates new tea tax.
1773, December	Boston Tea Party.
1774, January	Tea ship burned in Annapolis, Maryland; 257 crates of tea lie unclaimed on the dock in Charleston.

Date	Event
1774, March	Parliament passes the Coercive Acts.
1774, May	Boston Harbor closed. Occupation Army arrives in Boston.
1774, September	First Continental Congress convenes in Philadelphia.
1775, January	First British raid to capture a Patriot supply depot is turned back without bloodshed in New Hampshire.
1775, March	Bloodshed at Lexington and Concord.
1775, March	Volunteer soldiers surround British in Boston.
1775, May	Second Continental Congress convenes in Philadelphia.
1775, May	General Wayne captures Fort Ticonderoga.
1775, June	Washington named commander-in-chief.
1775, June	Battle of Breeds (Bunker) Hill.
1775, July	Washington arrives in Cambridge, Massachusetts, to take command of the army.
1775, August	General Wayne leaves with a force to attack Quebec.

Liber . . . Tea

The Boston Tea Party, December 17, 1773

Boston Tea Party

Everyone drank tea in America. It was the national drink. Only a few in the bigger cities preferred coffee. Tea and rum—and occasionally a bit of water— that's what colonial Americans drank.

Tea was supplied to America by the British East India Company, a huge commercial venture created by British nobles to exploit the resources of every remote and exotic corner of the far-flung British empire. One of the products the British East India Company exported from India was tea—tons and tons of tea. For the company to make profits and for England to remain solvent, people all over the world needed to drink this tea.

The growing anti-British crowd in the Americas drank *Dutch* East India Company tea smuggled into various ports and sold at great profit because smuggling avoided all British taxes. Dutch tea was illegal because, as an English colony, Americans were required to trade exclusively with British companies. It was all a question of profits for the British East India Company and tax revenue for the British government.

Parliament had been trying for years to squeeze a profit out of the Colonies. But for Americans to cut back on tea consumption would be disastrous. So, clever English politicians (who owned large shares in the British East India Company) devised a scheme to increase American tea drinking: drop the price of tea. Technically, what they did was allow the company to not pay import duties (dropping tea prices) and also increased the colonial tea tax (but not as much as the drop).

4

As long as the price of tea was *lower*, the Colonists wouldn't care if they were paying more tax, right? Wrong!

Samuel Adams's Committees of Correspondence and his Sons of Liberty were desperately searching for a propaganda issue to stir up anti-British sentiments. A new tea tax was perfect! It mattered not that the ultimate price of tea was going down. The taxes of Americans were being increased without any comment or input from the Colonies. Cries of "Taxation without representation!" rang loud and clear from Savannah to Maine.

The agents who contracted to handle tea in most cities saw the drift of public sentiment and refused to accept the initial tea shipments. Not so in Boston, where every one of the chosen tea agents was a close relative of Governor Hutchinson. They wanted the promised profits and refused to back down.

Three ships loaded with the new tea arrived in Boston and tied up at Griffin's Wharf to await their 20-day quarantine period. The Boston mob screamed that the tea had to go. The British navy and the agents just as defiantly said it must stay. As the days ticked toward the December 17, 1773, end of the quarantine period, the stage was set for a first-class show down. Boston was poised to make history with the Boston Tea Party.

Meet Thomas Moore

Thomas Moore was born in Sheffield, a town in southwest Massachusetts. His family moved to a farm near Cambridge when Thomas was five. At age 12 he was apprenticed to Samuel Mosby (a distant cousin of Moore's father) at his cooperage along the docks in Boston. In part, this arrangement was designed to get Thomas away from trouble. Ready to settle any scrap with his fists, he had started a number of fights with local boys. But when he was 14, he slipped into a Sons of Liberty meeting and instantly became a radical supporter of Sam Adams and of liberty from the English, even though his young mind didn't fully understand the concept. Within a year he became one of the "hotheads," a group of young radicals who wanted to push every confrontation as far as possible toward open warfare. Thomas was quick to join the army in 1775 and died in Canada of disease in January 1776, during the ill-fated Canadian invasion.

Liber ... Tea

Bitter rain, low swirling clouds, and gloom covered Boston on Wednesday, December, 15, 1773. Still the air sizzled with electric anticipation. A showdown was brewing over three shiploads of English tea tied up at Griffin's Wharf, and many feared that the streets of Boston would run far bloodier than they had during the Boston Massacre.

As dark of night slowly pushed out the gray of day and twilight shadows tricked the mind and eye, three men walked together up Fort Street heading away from the wharves. The men hunched low in their thick coats, collars turned up about their necks, hats pulled low as rain dripped off their brims onto the dreary street.

In the middle walked Philip Bark, a local merchant, the tallest of the three, whose head sprouted bushy gray hair although he was only 33. Sheltered closest to the row of Fort Street warehouses walked Samuel Mosby—short, stocky, and with thick arms from years of work at his cooperage, or barrel-making shop. The only one who swaggered as he walked was young Thomas Moore, who had just turned 16 and finished his apprenticeship in Mosby's cooperage. All three were members of the secret, illegal organization supporting American independence, the Sons of Liberty.

Four Redcoats walked briskly toward them, hurrying back to warmth and shelter at the end of their rounds. Moore nudged Philip Bark and jerked his head toward the British. Then he edged out into the street so that he could conveniently and "accidentally" bang shoulders with the nearest Redcoat as they passed. Young hotheads had taken to "shoulder banging" as a way to taunt Redcoats and known Tories, egging them on to fight. Thomas Moore, taller and stronger than his years would warrant, seemed more eager than even the hottest of the hotheads to stir up any mischief and confrontation he could.

After staggering for several steps under the jarring shoulder smack, the soldier Moore had banged spun round and lashed out, seizing Moore by the arm. "Apologize, scum." His other hand flashed to the handle of the gleaming bayonet dangling from his belt. His face, grim and angry, seemed to dare Moore to make any kind of additional insult.

Moore twisted his arm to brush off the Redcoat's grip and glared back. Two bitter faces stared, inches apart, as rain dribbled down, forming a feeble dividing line between then.

Another of the soldiers, bearing sergeant stripes on his sleeve, reached over to gently, but firmly, turn the Redcoat back into his original direction. "Let it go Markham. We have orders to avoid confrontation."

"But he . . ."

"Just let it go."

The soldiers continued their march, disappearing into the swirling rain and dark, leaving only the echoing clatter of their boots on the cobblestone street.

"Cowards!" called Thomas Moore after them.

"Caution, young Thomas," said Mosby in a low, soothing tone. "You don't want to see British regulars grow angry enough to fight. They are the best and fiercest bayonet fighters in the world."

Thomas shrugged off his employer's warning. "There are few Redcoats and many of us. We should act now to destroy the tea and send the Redcoats running back to England with their tails between their legs! All Boston is with us."

"Have care, young hothead," added Bark. "Governor Hutchinson has gathered a great number of Loyalists in Boston as well as the ever-present soldiers. If we bite too hard, Britain will bite back. And a Redcoat army has a mean bite."

But Thomas burned with the youthful flame of hateful passion. "I say we burn the ships *now* with their foul tea—and maybe the soldiers' barracks as well. We have to show Parliament that we will *not* be their slaves!"

"They are not British ships." This from Mosby. "The *Dartmouth* and *Beaver* are both owned by a good American Quaker family. He was just hired in good faith to carry a cargo. It is only the cargo of tea and the English taxing policy behind it we are after. Not Francis Roach."

Thomas reached out to grab the shoulders of both older men. His eyes gleamed through the rain and gloom. "Are you saying there's a plan to destroy the tea before it can be legally off-loaded day after tomorrow? Adams is finally ready to strike?"

Both older men glanced warily at each other. Philip Bark nervously coughed. "There is a plan—of sorts."

Mosby added, "Sam Adams has talked of . . . *some* sort of action. . . ."

Thomas shrugged away from both older men. "Will we destroy the ships or not? You sound like cowardly Tories the way you talk in circles!"

Samuel Mosby shook his head. "We are only men who want to live to enjoy the rights we struggle for. I do not want anyone—and especially hotheads like you—to do something foolish that would start a war with mother England."

"No!" hissed Moore, raising clenched fists toward the dripping heavens. "We *do* want a war. England will listen to nothing less!"

"We just want to convince Parliament to repeal the tea tax," insisted Mosby.

Bark added, "As they did with the Stamp Act some years ago."

"You both talk like English diplomats!" Thomas turned away at the first corner and stomped down Hutchinson Street. Over his shoulder he growled, "I'll seek elsewhere for *true* Sons of Liberty."

Before he had stomped out of earshot he overheard Bark mutter, "Wild youth like Thomas could get us all killed. He must be controlled until after the tea has been dealt with."

"Traitors!" Moore yelled back. His voice echoed down the cobbled streets.

The Green Dragon Tavern had become a favorite meeting spot for the radicals in Boston. Many of the men hunched over tables and mugs of beer or rum were secret members of the Sons of Liberty. The long, back corner table had become the meeting spot for the most radical elements of the organization.

It was at this table that Thomas Moore jerked back a chair and plopped into his seat after leaving Mosby and Bark. Four other teenagers already slouched at the table nursing their drinks, all either apprentices or junior craftsmen at local shops and all radical Sons of Liberty members.

Moore still scowled, his eyes blazing with desire for a fight. "It's up to *us*, lads!" He pounded his fists on the worn, wooden table. "The youth must lead the fight to freedom and destroy the tea ourselves!"

One of his friends, Jonas Billings, an apprentice sail maker, sipped his beer and asked, "Why should we be enraged because England *reduced* the price of tea—tea that we have always loved and bought?"

Thomas snapped, "England must be taught to respect our independence!"

Another friend, Billy Slides, a journeyman printer who worked in one of Alexander Hamilton's shops, asked, "Isn't it just the tea tax and British East India Company's monopoly we're against?"

Thomas's forefinger jabbed at each of his comrades. "It's a tea tax today. It will be something else tomorrow. Three years ago they shot and killed Americans right here in Boston. Their soldiers take jobs that should belong to us. They won't allow us to import from anyone else. They squeeze us under their thumb and laugh at us while we beg for crumbs. There will *always* be *something* until we stand up to England, herself. Someone has to *do* something."

"But who?"

"Us," Thomas answered.

"Us? Just us five?" asked Billy Slides, trying to decide if it was supposed to be a joke.

"I just wish we knew how the British would respond to any action we take," said Jonas.

"Why? Are you afraid?" sneered Thomas. "The Redcoats have grown soft. They're even afraid of a fair fight in the street and run back to their barracks claiming they have orders not to provoke us. Ha! Well, I *am* provoked!" Moore rose to his feet as if delivering a fiery sermon. "They have provoked me! And I, for one, am going to do something about it. Are you with me, lads? Are . . . you . . . with . . . me!?"

Men at other tables were beginning to pay close attention. Whispers darted around the room. Thomas's four friends fidgeted and drained their mugs as nervous glances darted across the table.

Thomas bellowed, "Are you cowards and traitors, or do you cherish your liberty?!"

One by one the four grim faces at the table nodded, afraid not to.

Thomas triumphantly sank back into his seat, a beaming smile on his face. "Good. I knew you were stout lads." He leaned across the table before continuing in a low voice. "Gather a dozen others you can trust and meet me at Mosby's cooperage in one hour. We have barrels of tar and plenty of rags. The bay will burn tonight!"

"We're going to *burn* the ships?"

"To the waterline! And then we'll do the same to the Redcoats' barracks."

"Burn out the British?" gulped Jonas, his face noticeably paling.

Billy slid his chair back. "I don't know if that's a smart idea."

"Are you a coward or a Son of Liberty?" interrupted Thomas.

"I'm no coward," his friend answered.

Thomas smacked the table with the palms of each hand. "It's settled then. We'll do it . . . tonight."

He rose to leave and found six stocky men, arms folded across thick chests, blocking his path. One was Samuel Mosby. Robert Sessions, the tallest of the group, quietly said, "There will be no burning tonight."

"Says who?" sneered Thomas.

"Sam Adams has a different plan and he needs your help. You are to meet him at the Old North Church at 6:00 tomorrow evening."

"More talking?" scoffed Thomas.

"Adams has a plan."

"So do I."

Almost before the words were out of Thomas's mouth, three men whipped out pistols. "And if you try *your* plan I will have to kill you. Your plan will start a war that we will lose," said Sessions, his steel-gray eyes locked onto Thomas's. His hand, holding a rock-steady pistol, pointed at Thomas's stomach.

"But we have to do *something*," Thomas pleaded.

Mosby said, "Wait 24 hours and see. Adams's plan will bring us victory."

Billy Slides said, "I think we should listen to them, Thomas."

Jonas was quick to agree. "Maybe we should wait."

"We don't want to destroy good American ships," added a third of Thomas's gang of five.

"Old North Church tomorrow at 6:00 tomorrow evening. Don't be late," repeated Sessions. "Oh, and tonight, the ships are guarded."

"By Redcoats?" asked Thomas. "I am not afraid of Redcoats."

"No. By faithful Sons of Liberty, and you had best be afraid of us."

"Important task, he says," muttered Thomas to himself as his horse trotted through the wintry night-time chill on Thursday, December 16. It was a clear night but cold enough to make Thomas bundle up in a heavy coat, hat, and two thick scarves before mounting for this ride Sam Adams was sending him on, which would take him well beyond Cambridge.

"Vital to our success, he says," continued Thomas, his breath crystallizing into mini-clouds as he spoke. "But why me? Why does Sam Adams have to send *me* riding out *tonight* with a secret letter? . . . I should be at the meeting tonight. I should be shouting out for liberty and revenge! But, no. I'm riding through the freezing cold to deliver a secret letter. . . ."

Thomas slowed his horse to a walk, these thoughts buzzing through his mind. The distant lights of Boston twinkled through the trees and marsh grass lining this side of the back bay.

Thomas jolted straight up in his saddle. "There's *no* reason to send me on this ride. . . . No reason, unless Adams wanted to get me out of Boston. But why? So he could turn Tory coward and permit the tea to be unloaded!"

Thomas wheeled his mount around and dug his heels hard into the horse's flanks.

The horse whinnied and bucked once before beginning the long gallop back to town. Thomas reached into his coat pocket and fished out the secret letter, sealed in an envelope. Angrily he crumpled it into a wad and threw it into the bushes as he raced back. "No secret is worth missing this night's events!"

At 9:45 P.M. Thomas slid off his horse and dashed into the Old North Church. The building stood empty and graveyard quiet. The first twinges of panic pounded in Thomas's chest. Something important must have happened here, and he had missed it. The ships! The tea! A deep fire began to burn in the pit of his stomach. What was happening to the tea?

Thomas galloped down Milk Street and turned onto Hutchinson Street for the six-block ride to Griffin's Wharf. The wharves were lit as bright as day. Lamps and lanterns blazed in every window. An immense crowd squeezed into every street, wharf, and pier, trying to see. The sea of humanity was almost too thick for Thomas to worm through.

"Are the ships burning yet?" Thomas asked one man as he squeezed past.

"No," he answered.

"Have the Redcoats been beaten yet?" Thomas asked another.

"No fighting at all yet."

"What about the ships' crews?" Thomas demanded.

"Volunteered to stay out of the way below decks. Didn't want to take sides, I guess."

This wasn't right. There was supposed to be confrontation. There was supposed to be fighting. There was supposed to be battle and victory! Thomas realized there was also supposed to be noise—yelling, screaming, cursing. And yet the waterfront was as quiet as a church sermon except for the chopping of axes and hatchets on wood.

Thomas shoved his way to the front row and saw, not proud Sons of Liberty destroying the three tea ships, but what appeared to be a band of Mohawk Indians. Blankets were wrapped over their shoulders. Their faces were covered with ashes and paint. Most had a feather or two stuffed into their hair and were wielding hatchets and axes to act as tomahawks.

Wait! These weren't real Indians. Their skin was white. Then Thomas saw through the makeup and began to recognize one or two of the "Indians." They *were* Sons of Liberty, local Patriots dressed up to look like Indians.

One by one the "Indians" hauled 200-pound tea crates from the hold by ropes and smashed them open in the eerie silence that blanketed the wharf. The huge crowd stared, the "Indians" worked, both without a word or cry.

"Why the costumes?" Thomas asked a woman standing next to him.

"To disguise the men so they won't be arrested tomorrow."

"Why as Mohawks?"

"Mohawks are fierce fighters and defeated the British several times during the French and Indian War."

"Then let the new war begin!" cried Thomas. With a pretend Indian war whoop, he yelled, "Everything English burns tonight!" and sprinted onto the nearest ship, the *Dartmouth*. Thomas grabbed an ax from one astonished "Mohawk" and swung at the ship's center mast, hoping to bring it and its lanterns crashing to the deck.

Thomas was flattened mid-swing by a half-empty crate of tea thrown at him from behind. He sprawled across the deck. A dozen beefy hands pinned him there.

Through clenched teeth Robert Sessions hissed, "We do not damage good American ships, boy."

Struggling against the men's iron grip, Thomas cried, "But we have to burn the tea."

"We burn nothing, boy. We will destroy the tea and nothing more."

Samuel Mosby was one of the "Indians" working on the *Dartmouth*. He leaned over Thomas and said, "Your goal, Thomas, is to *start* a brawl, ours is to avoid one and to still protest the tea tax and monopoly."

Sessions added, "If you are to survive and leave this ship alive, tonight you will abide by our plan."

Sullenly Thomas half-heartedly dumped tea overboard into the bay, hoping all the while that Redcoats would arrive in firing lines with muskets loaded and bayonets fixed. "Then," he thought, "we could start a real protest!"

Almost 400 crates were smashed and poured overboard so that hills of tea built up on the incoming tide. Young boys climbed down to the mud with rakes and pushed mounds of tea leaves out into the water. Some mounds grew so high that leaves blew back onto deck and dock in the light breeze. Some watchers scooped great handfuls of the precious leaves and stuffed them into their pockets. Neighbors scowled and stared until they dumped them back into the harbor.

Although the night was cold, the "Indians" poured sweat from their hard labor, black ash and red paint streaking down their necks and backs with the dribbling perspiration. Lookouts nervously peered down all approach roads for the clatter and sight of Redcoats, but none could be seen on the streets of Boston.

The "Indians" had reached the wharf a little before 9:00. By midnight the work was done, a rolling landscape of tea leaves sloshed in the gentle waves, a brown stain spread to cover the harbor waters, and the decks and docks had been swept clean. An officer from each ship was brought back on deck to confirm that no damage had been done to the vessels. The British garrison had intentionally stayed in their barracks, ordered to avoid a confrontation that would surely turn violent.

The "Indians" removed their boots to ensure that no tea was smuggled off the dock. One man was found with fistfuls of tea leaves stuffed in his shirt. He was thrown overboard into the bay and was forever after disgraced.

Then, as silently as they had arrived, the Indians melted back into the streets of Boston.

It was over. The tea was gone. The protest was complete. Radicals like Thomas Moore grumbled that they should have burned the ships and forced a scrap with the Redcoats and Tories. But wiser men, like Samuel Mosby and Philip Bark, breathed a sigh of relief that no blood had been spilled and felt the icy tremble of fear as they wondered what England would do in response.

Leaving the wharves, Thomas sought out Robert Sessions. "What was so important in that secret letter I carried out of town?"

As other men laughed, Sessions muttered, "You were sent away, young powder keg, to make sure the harbor tonight was stained tea brown and not blood red."

Storming back to his room, Thomas hissed to the sky, "All of them are traitors to liberty. Why can't they see that we will never be free until the streets run red with English blood!"

 Aftermath

"The die is now cast," bellowed King George upon hearing of Boston's Tea Party. "The Colonists must either submit or triumph." It was more the slap in the face to British authority than the tea that steamed the king.

In Annapolis, a tea brigantine was burned to waterline, tea and all. In Charleston, 257 crates of tea were off-loaded but no one dared claim them for fear of Sons of Liberty reprisals. The tea sat rotting for over three years before it was dumped into the harbor in the dead of night. In Philadelphia, two ships with 697 crates of tea turned back because no one would off-load them. In New York, shiploads of tea were similarly refused and sent back to England to the British East India Company's bulging warehouses.

But the Boston protest seemed more deliberate and defiant,so it got all the attention. Samuel Adams's Committee of Correspondence expanded the boycott to include all British manufactured goods with a "Solemn League and Covenant."

Parliament responded by passing the Coercive Acts, which closed Boston Harbor; moved the Colony's capital to Salem; revised the Colony's charter to give far more power to the appointed governor; and, for the first the time in British history, sent an army of occupation under General Gage to control and oppress British colonists.

Open conflict could not be far behind.

Follow-up Questions and Activities

1. **What Do You Know?**

   - What was the Stamp Act? The Tea Act? The Coercive Acts? Who passed them? What were they designed to do?

   - Who were the Sons of Liberty? How were they different from an army or a police force?

   - What was a Committee of Correspondence? Were the members Loyalist or Patriot? With whom did they correspond? What did they correspond about?

   - Why did the Patriots protest the tea tax so strongly?

   - Why did the Patriots dress like Mohawk Indians during the Boston Tea Party?

2. **Finding Out More**. Following are four important topics from this story for you to research in the library and on the Internet. The reference sources at the back of this book will help you get started.

   - Why were the British East India Company (and the Dutch East India Company) called "East India?" What did they do? Who owned them? Why were they created? Why were they so important?

   - When did the Boston Massacre happen? Who massacred whom? Why did it happen? Why was it important?

   - Who was Samuel Adams, the man who led the early Patriot opposition to British rule and who created the Committees of Correspondence? Many call him the architect of American liberty. Where did he come from? How did he find himself in the dangerous position of leading the opposition to Britain?

   - The Boston Tea Party was a protest. Research major American protests throughout U.S. history. Include both violent and nonviolent protests. Why were they staged? Who was protesting? Against what? Against whom? Were they successful?

3. **Make It Real**

- How much tea was destroyed the night of December 17, 1773, in Boston? A total of 352 crates of tea were stored on the three ships. Each of the crates stood three feet long by four feet wide by three feet high and carried about 190 pounds of tea when filled. On the retail market, each crate was worth about 90 English pounds. Calculate how many tons of tea went into the harbor. Compare the volume of this tea to that of your classroom. How much money did the British East India Company lose as the tea was dumped into the harbor?

- Tea was private property. Do you think it is acceptable to destroy someone's private property to protest a government policy? What kinds of public protest do you think are acceptable? Hold a class debate on whether it was right for the Patriots to destroy that tea.

- Was the Boston Tea Party an effective protest? Why? Did it work? That is, did it get the desired results? What were its desired results? Write an essay arguing that the Boston Tea Party was either effective or ineffective as a protest. As a class, debate the topic based on students' individual essays.

- If you were to design a protest as a class, what would you protest? How would you protest without creating an over-reaction (as the Bostonians did)? You want your protest to be big enough to be noticed, but not so big that it causes real trouble. How would you decide how big to make it?

4. **Points to Ponder**

- Do you think it's fair for a few to dictate what everyone can or cannot do? Very few Americans favored liberty in 1773. Should those few who did have kept quiet and gone along with the majority? Can you find modern examples of the same kind of situation at your school, in your community, or in the country?

- Why do you think the British military didn't do anything to stop the Boston Tea Party? Certainly a company of regulars could have broken up the protest and protected the tea. Why do you think the soldiers were kept in their barracks? What could the British commanders in Boston gain by allowing the protest to happen? What was their motive for not stopping it?

- The Boston Tea Party has often been described as a clash of wants (in this case tea) and principles (no taxation without representation). As a class, make a list of six principles you think are important to the quality of your daily lives. Now make a list of 30 material wants that you share (TV, music, radio, potato chips, pizza, bicycles, hair dryers, sports, video games, computers, etc.). How many, and which, of these wants would you be willing to sacrifice to maintain each of the chosen principles? Boston Colonists gave up tea to make their point. What would you be willing to give up to fight for your principles?

- Do you think there is a legitimate and rightful role for radicals ("hotheads") ? Are there always some people more eager to fight than others? Are they always dangerous? Are they ever beneficial? Search for modern examples of both dangerous and beneficial radicals.

A War of Words Becomes a War of Bullets

Confrontation at Lexington and Concord, April 19, 1775

British retreat from Lexington

At a Glance

In late 1774, Parliament ordered General Gage to round up the American Rebels around Boston and seize their war-making equipment. His problem was that there was no organized, uniformed Rebel army to seize and no Rebel forts where equipment was stored. The "rebels" were ordinary citizens and he couldn't arrest *everyone*.

Tensions increased daily along with taunts, jeers, and minor scuffles. It was clear to all that something would have to happen soon.

Gage wanted to intimidate the Rebels and decided to raid a strongly suspected supply point—Concord—and show the might of British troops. His spies hinted that a great horde of cannon, muskets, powder, cartridge paper, axes, shovels, blankets, candles, dishes, spoons, tons of pork, beef and flour, etc., was stored there.

Of course, the Rebels also had a spy network (made more effective because British officers were quartered in American houses). Grooms at stables, chambermaids, Patriot women who employed the wives of British soldiers as maids, men who hired British soldiers as part-time laborers—all filtered information through the network to a group of riders called the Mechanics (messengers) led by Paul Revere.

On Sunday, April 16, 1775, Revere rode to Concord to warn locals that they were the target of a planned British raid. On the night of April 18, Revere got his friend Robert Newman to hang lanterns briefly in North Church tower to signal the Charlestown militia about British troops departing Boston by boat. (Newman was arrested the next day as a spy and jailed.)

The lanterns were a backup, in case neither of the scheduled riders was able to make it out of Boston. One rider did: Richard Dawes (an actor), who was the first to reach Lexington and warn that town. Lexington locals, however, had seen small groups of British officers riding the roads as road blocks and already knew something was up.

Revere decided on his own to cross the bay by boat and assist the Charlestown militia in spreading the alarm. He borrowed a horse, was stopped but escaped, reached Lexington (well after the town had been alerted), and was stopped again before he could reach Concord. His horse was confiscated (stolen) by British officers and he walked back to Lexington.

Dr. Prescott, who had been staying at Lexington, was the one who carried the warning message to Concord through British road blocks.

Meanwhile four Tories, lead by John Howe, were doing the same for the other side—riding into the countryside to alert Tories that regulars were moving and that the Rebels were being roused. By dawn, all factions of the countryside were awake and alert. The stage was set for a first-class British-Rebel showdown.

There had been confrontations before. Everyone assumed there would be angry words and muttered threats as officers debated a reasonable settlement to the confrontation. As dawn broke on the morning of April 19, 1775, no one dreamed that, by nightfall, previously inconceivable events at the sleepy Massachusetts towns of Lexington and Concord would forever close the door on a peaceful settlement between the British and Americans.

Meet Reuben Brown

Twenty-three-year-old Reuben Brown was a saddle maker who worked out of a Concord, Massachusetts, stable. He also owned a small family farm just outside of Concord that he had inherited when his father died in 1773. The farm produced hay, dairy, chickens, and apples. Reuben had a wife, an infant son, and an even temper. He was considered a good shot and had been in the militia since he turned 15. He had been a volunteer "Minuteman" for the past 18 months.

Meet Lt. James Sutherland

James Sutherland came from a solid, wealthy merchant family just out of reach of nobility. Much of the family's recent fortune came from their shares in the British East India Company. The Sutherlands had money and good aristocratic breeding, but not title. The family purchased James's commission (a common practice at the time) and was saving to purchase the rank of colonel for him at some appropriate future date.

James had not wanted to come to America. He thought it would be too dull. He wanted an active assignment where he could make a name for himself. He had little regard for Colonists, considering them lower-class peasants—good workers, but not anyone you would want to socialize with.

James served four years in the American Colonies until he was wounded at the Battle of Monmouth and shipped home. Sutherland always blamed Generals Gage and Howe for the disaster in the Colonies and grew increasingly bitter as he aged. In his mid-30s Sutherland made it to major, but never beyond.

A War of Words Becomes a War of Bullets: Reuben Brown's Story

It couldn't have been much past 4:00 A.M. when the bells clanged me awake. Still I could feel the ripples of excitement spreading with the insistent church bells. By first light the pounding hooves of a rider's horse clattered past. His cry of "The regulars are out!" echoed through the hills. As a Minuteman, I had no choice but to respond.

Back during the French and Indian War, the British insisted that each man between 16 and 50 own a musket and join one of the local militia units they created. Many of these militia units were now decidedly anti-British and had become the backbone and muscle of the resistance to English rule. Minutemen were all members of these local militia. Today the Redcoats would feel the bite of this scruffy dog they had created when it turned upon the master.

I gobbled a quick breakfast of pork pudding with sweet plum sauce and left the farm with my musket, ten rounds, a little powder, and three apples from our straw-filled storage bins. The pre-dawn air held a sharp, wintry bite even though spring buds glowed on apple trees in the moonlight and the fuzz of a new crop of hay was beginning to cover the fields, turning them green as all Ireland.

I felt an urgent tension as I reached the town of Concord, Massachusetts. Some said the Redcoats had already reached Lexington. Most agreed they were on their way here and that we'd have to face them. Women and children huddled in doorways, gazed at the clump of us men milling about the green, and wondered if this motley crew could stop the mighty British Redcoats. These were friends, husbands, fathers, farmers, carpenters, and clerks, not soldiers.

Paul Revere had ridden out on Sunday to warn us that a raid was likely, so the bulk of our military supplies was now scattered and hidden—cannon, powder, shovels, axes, food, extra muskets, sailcloth for tents, coats and blankets, etc. Still, frantic final preparations were busily under way. Almont Jacobs was out plowing his field to cover the spot where most of our cannon had been buried yesterday. Ephraim Jones, both tavern owner and jail proprietor, hid the last two cannons in a jail cell. The town clerk, fat Elisah Woods, hustled out of town with a final wagonload of shot and gunpowder. Mary Broadrick dumped the church pewter and silver into a barrel of soft soap. The last of our flour barrels were hidden behind private grain sacks at the mill.

Dr. Prescott thundered down the road from Lexington like he was being chased by ghosts, his horse covered with foam and sweat, and tried to shout out the news as each of us pelted him with questions. Yes, 800 or more Redcoats were on the way here. Yes, about 80 Minutemen had gathered to face the British outside Buckman's Tavern on the village green in Lexington. No, the Minutemen never fired. They tried to scatter on the first British warning shot. Still the Redcoats had fired again and killed eight and wounded ten more.

Shock rumbled like an earthquake through me. Redcoats had fired on Americans! They had intentionally killed our American Minutemen! This was beginning to sound like war.

Excitement, anger, and fear churned in my stomach. Like many others, I was too nervous to sit and wait on the Concord green for what might come. One hundred fifty of us marched south toward Lexington to see what we could see.

Half a mile from town we heard fifes and stopped. Through the trees we caught the first glints of gleaming bayonet points. Marching feet made the ground vibrate under me. Then orderly ranks of scarlet filled the winding road. Every button sewn in place, every belt and cartridge box an exact match of every other. Endless ranks of gleaming perfection with early morning sun glistening off steel bayonets.

My mouth and throat turned parched and painfully dry. It was hard to swallow. We traded nervous smiles and pretend-brave nods. But with the Redcoats still 300 yards away, we decided to retreat and double-quick marched back into Concord, mocking the British with our fifes and songs as we went.

Some Minutemen decided to head home and live to fight another day. Many more arrived to take their place. The rest of us hustled through town and stopped just past the North Bridge. Four hundred of us milled around in a wide field, wondering what we should do—what we *could* do.

I felt silly and frustrated like a scolded child ordered to sulk in private, on this hill just out of town. The lads around me claimed to be eager for a scrap, but we were each trembling, hoping no one else could see. My stomach was tied up in knots. I dreaded to think what the British were doing in town. I felt ashamed that we weren't doing anything to stop them. Yet I was terrified of marching back into Concord to face battle-hardened Redcoats.

We were opposed at the bridge by only 100 or so British regulars. They stood rock-solid at the bridge as our ranks swelled to over 600, with more Patriot militia units arriving every minute. Maybe we could *at least* take the bridge. Maybe we *should* take the bridge! But did we dare to march into British fire?

Then we saw smoke curling black and ominous over town and everything changed. Now we had a cause. Smoke meant fire, and fire was the sworn enemy of every community. We had to save our town. There was no more room for hesitation.

Major Buttrick ordered us to load up and lined us into columns. We advanced downhill toward the bridge and waiting Redcoats, most of whom hustled into a firing line just behind the bridge. Twenty or so remained on the span, trying to rip up planks and destroy the bridge.

The Redcoats fired a warning volley high over our heads. We advanced, muskets and flintlocks at the ready, one eye on the smoke, one on the ranks of red.

Again they fired—at us this time. Abner Hosner, a young friend and our fife player, fell dead near me.

Major B. yelled, "Fire, for God's sake, fire!"

My heart thundered up in my throat. I yelled and I fired. I'm not even sure I took time to aim. We let 'em have it with all we had. A sheet of flame and a thunderclap exploded from our ranks. An acrid cloud of smoke billowed around us. Musket balls whistled like banshees as they tore through the air.

A dozen British fell. We poured it on, almost four rounds a minute, but couldn't fire very effectively 'cause we were jammed into narrow columns and because we were still too far off (almost 100 yards).

More scarlet coats crumpled to the dusty ground. The rest turned and fled back into town. We surged onto the bridge, howling our triumph.

My heart pounded with the rush of battle and the thrill of victory. We had taken the bridge!

It was only 9:00 A.M., but it felt like we'd been fighting all day. The fight only lasted five minutes—it felt like hours.

Slowly reality sank in. We had fired on the king's troops. We had killed 20 and wounded 30 more. That made us outlaws. What would happen to us now? They were sure to hear about *this* all the way to Parliament!

Throughout the late morning Patriots swarmed around Concord as if all roads led only there. Ministers laid down their Bibles and grabbed a musket. Old Indian fighters grabbed flintlocks and powder horns. Fields were left half-plowed. Shops were closed as clerks abandoned their counters for a spot in our swelling ranks.

General William Heath arrived to take command of the Patriot mob and moved us east of town to set ambushes along the road back to Lexington, beginning at Meriam's Corner. We were so spread out it was hard to tell, but there must have been over 2,000 of us by now. I felt that we had somehow changed in an hour from farmers and Minutemen into an army.

By noon the Redcoats started their march along the twisting, winding, up-and-down road right past us to get back to Lexington. It was easy for us to hide, spring up, fire, and run back under cover. Local Minutemen crouched behind every wall, woodshed, barn, house, and tree. Men hid along river banks and in thick bushes.

We could have—should have—slaughtered them at every turn and narrow pass, but most of us lads were too frightened of facing regulars and fired way too soon—just so we'd have plenty of time to skedaddle before the Brits fired back.

Mentomy (two miles from Lexington) was to be the biggest ambush. Eighteen hundred of us hit them from all sides, from the ground, second-story windows, and trees. Instead of surrendering, the Redcoats went berserk, wild as rabid dogs, burning houses, killing innocents, destroying everything they could reach. It was close-in, hand-to-hand fighting. If fire came from a house, Redcoats rushed in to kill every person inside and burn the place. Most of Mentomy was ablaze before the British staggered on toward Lexington.

In Lexington Redcoat reinforcements arrived. Now they were a fierce mass of over 2,000. But we had swelled to over 3,000. Many of the lads fired a few rounds and left. Some fired 'til they ran out of ammo and ambled back home to finish chores. But most of us hounded the Redcoats from Concord all the way to Cambridge. General Heath was more or less in charge, but every man was really on his own to find a good spot, wait, fire, and run before return fire could find him.

I had run out of ammo by early afternoon but still couldn't make myself leave. I scampered with hundreds of others through fields and woods to get ahead of the British column just so I could stand and shout out my anger when they marched by, as if to kill them with words since I had no more musket balls.

The road from Concord to Cambridge, littered with death and destruction on both sides, was a terrible sight to see and a terrible weight to bear. We hadn't planned to attack the British, or even to fire on them at all. We just meant to show the Redcoats they couldn't bully us any longer.

As the gray of evening signaled an end to this frightful day, the sobs of new widows and the groans of wounded and homeless filled the twilight. Almost 50 men, women, and children had been killed by Redcoats. We had cut down well over six times that number. The bodies littered the road like bread crumbs scattered to mark the trail back toward Boston.

I sat trembling in my darkened house. What had we done? Without a vote, or even a serious discussion, we had killed hundreds of the King's finest. It just . . . happened. What would they do to us in return? How long before a full army of Redcoats marched out to squash us like bugs? How easy it had been to start a war . . . how difficult it would be to stop it. This was surely a day no one could ever forget.

A War of Words Becomes a War of Bullets: Lt. James Sutherland's Story

Even I, a lowly infantry lieutenant, of the 8th Light Infantry, know it is impossible to keep a secret in Boston, especially because officers and sergeants are forcibly quartered in the houses of local citizens. I was not one of the eight hand-picked officers who rode quietly out on the evening of Tuesday, April 18, to block the roads and prevent messengers from reaching Concord. But I am sure a thousand secret eyes watched their every twitch and sniff, and that a thousand secret voices murmured their travel far faster than they could cover the 12-mile ride.

We received orders to assemble the troops at 10:00 P.M. that Tuesday evening, a sure sign of a night march and a morning raid. Still, I gladly preferred a raid to sitting cooped up in Boston having to swallow the jeers and taunts of the Rebels. The kinder we try to be, the more we struggle to avoid confrontation, the bolder and more brazen they become. Well, tomorrow they would see that we have sharp teeth that bite quick and deep into all who oppose legal British rule.

We loaded from the Boston Commons into longboats in front of a growing crowd and were ferried across the back bay, where we had to wade through knee-deep marsh and slime to reach shore near Cambridge. Then we skirted town by slogging through a waist-deep swamp—all the idiotic plan of our general to keep us from being seen as we left Boston. But a great crowd saw us leave and watched our boats paddle across the bay. They each seemed already to know that our mission was to capture the Rebel supplies at Concord.

We then waited in the dark—cold, wet and tired, stamping numb feet, blowing on stiff fingers—for over two hours while our supplies were ferried up from the boats. Around 2:00 A.M. we began our road march—all without proper drums or flags, or food—and covered the 12 miles by back roads to Lexington, reaching that village just about dawn.

All through the grueling pitch-black march we could hear warning bells and occasional warning shots. We could hear the hoofbeats of horses galloping along unseen nearby roads. It was with bitter frustration that I realized the countryside was alerted and watching our every move.

Six companies of Light Infantry (including my own) under Major Pitcairn had been assigned to speed ahead to Lexington to see what kind of force the whispered warnings had gathered. I suddenly feared we would face a sea of ruffian Rebels.

Instead of a formidable force, we found only a laughably pitiful, rag-tag rabble of farmers lined up on the grass-covered Lexington town square they call a "green" to oppose us, a mere handful of brazen scum seemingly asking to be slaughtered. I could feel that the lads itched, burned, to give back some of the abuse they had taken over the past months.

I felt the same yearning and was about to draw my sword and turn my company loose. But the major ordered the front platoons to load with powder only (no musket balls), trying to scare the Rebels without hurting anyone.

I say a few should be hurt—maybe a great number—then they'd come to their senses. Besides, after marching all night, wet and miserable most of the way, we deserved to spill some blood to make the trip worth our misery. We flanked smartly out of columns into ranks. The major ordered those with musket balls to fire. The Rebels turned to flee like dogs at this harmless warning shot.

Someone—I thought from behind a tree to our right, others say from a second floor window in the same direction—fired at us, at the King's appointed troops! And that was more than we could stand.

Without order or hesitation two additional companies (including mine) fired at the scattering rabble. Eight dropped, the rest fled in panic. The lads were so frustrated and stuffed so full of bitter resentment that many rushed after the Rebels to finish the job with bayonets without waiting for orders. It was my duty as an officer to help control the troops and reestablish order. But in my heart I wanted to join them and let several Rebels taste the tip of my sword!

Order restored, we marched quickly and grimly on to Concord, four miles distant and our real destination. We were thirsty, famished, and bitterly tired. Also, we burned for a chance to thrash an actual Rebel force and show these outlaws that British regulars would not tolerate abuse of us, British law, or the Crown.

A band of about 100 Rebels confronted us half-a-mile south of town, but (like their cowardly brothers in Lexington) they turned tail and scurried back toward Concord, throwing insults over their shoulders as they ran. We reached the town center without incident and distributed orders for the men to search for the supposed weapons cache. To many, this seemed fair license to steal and loot with abandon—school books, church Bibles, quilts, silverware—but mostly food. I was not of a mind to hinder them. These Rebels deserved whatever they got.

It was clear to me that we would not get our fight this day. The Rebels were too cowardly to stand against us. We would have to console ourselves with sacking the town.

The men found little of the Rebel weapons cache. I was not at all surprised. The Rebels had obviously been warned of our coming. One company broke open 60 barrels of flour and smashed the jail yard after two cannons were discovered. Another found 500 musket balls and cartridges in one basement and decided to burn them—and the house. They started a brisk fire with furniture as kindling as an elderly couple pleaded with them to spare their dwelling. They should have thought of that before they joined the Rebel cause. The fire threatened to spread. Thick smoke curled into the morning sky.

We officers were served an adequate, but uninspired, meal in lawn chairs on the green while our men scoured the town. Major Pitcairn calmly stirred a brandy and water with one finger as if he were on a pleasant picnic.

A messenger raced back from the North Bridge, requesting reinforcements. Why would even a platoon of British regulars possibly need reinforcements against this scum? "Just say 'boo!' and they will run away like spineless children," I scoffed.

Still, Pitcairn was concerned enough to dispatch me and my company to reinforce Captain Walter Laurie's efforts to secure the North Bridge while some of his company searched nearby estates. I was tired and in no mood to stand watch over a meaningless bridge while I could—and should—be lounging on the green with the other officers.

Laurie's men were agitated and nervous, watching a growing mob of 400 or 500 Rebels gather on a nearby hill. A rumor spread through the ranks that the Rebels were scalping captured soldiers. An air of danger hung over the bridge. A grim determination to survive settled over the company. Each soldier had started the day carrying 36 rounds. Now most wished they had brought twice that number.

The Rebels advanced in well-organized columns. Laurie ordered a warning volley from one platoon.

The Rebels continued unwaveringly to advance. Suddenly this encounter felt completely different than our first two of the day. These men would not turn tail and run at the first whine of musket balls. These men meant to fight.

We fired again, this time in deadly earnest. Two Rebels dropped. The rest marched forward undeterred. On command, they paused to fire, their side of the river erupting in a sheet of flame and smoke. Twelve of Laurie's men dropped instantly. One badly wounded private near me reached in terror for his head as if to hold onto his scalp.

The Rebels rushed the bridge, keeping up a steady stream of fire as they advanced. It was clear that we must yield to this superior force. The men flew in disgraceful panic back to the safety of town, thankful to have their scalps still firmly attached.

I lingered behind to shepherd three wounded soldiers in their retreat and to see what the Rebels would do once they had the bridge.

As I had suspected, they stopped, afraid to advance into the teeth of the main British force. The exchange on that bridge was an insignificant skirmish that the Rebels later tried to make famous by calling it "the shot heard round the world." Rubbish. Nothing was there to be heard except a handful of cowardly traitors.

Colonel Smith hemmed and hawed for over an hour while we sat idle on the Concord green. Scouts reported that new Rebel forces were gathering just beyond our reach. Finally Smith gave the command to march and we headed eagerly back toward Boston. I, for one, had had more than enough of this dingy town and this meaningless march.

That five-hour march from Concord to Charlestown became pure hell and nightmare torment. No one stood in line to oppose us as commanded by the rules of warfare. Rather they hid and fired from behind every tree, stone wall, barn, and farmhouse window. They fired from where we couldn't see them and scampered off like cowardly dogs before we could return fire.

The Americans seemed like phantoms, like ghosts appearing from thin air. Most often they sprang up behind us, materializing on the road after we had passed to fire and run. It was as if they came down from the clouds to shoot and kill.

Always they refused to stand and fight a decent battle and give us a chance. In rage and frustration as friends and comrades fell around them, our troops fired at anything and everything just to have something to do other than march and die. We were not fighting an organized Rebel army. We were attacked by the entire countryside, as if even the trees, rivers, and flies were American allies.

Loot claimed in Concord was abandoned like parade rubbish beside the crumpled bodies of our dead along the 16-mile march of torment. It was a horrid, bloody, and unfair gauntlet. Our faces blackened from tearing open cartridges with our teeth. Many were soon out of rounds and had to march defenseless through the continuous Rebel fire. The lads went wild, attacking any house from which a shot had been fired—burning, destroying, killing, lashing out in agony and frustration.

Some officers—myself included—joined in several of these attacks, hoping to skewer any living or dead Rebel on our swords. Once I led a charge into a road-side farmhouse from which someone had fired on us. In an upstairs bedroom I stabbed and killed an old, unarmed woman and realized with a dreadful shock that I felt no regret or remorse. In fact I laughed and ordered the house burned to the ground!

So terrible was that endless march that it had stripped away all my sense of decency and honor. A British officer does not butcher unarmed, white-haired women! And yet I did and was, at that moment, glad of it. Instantly, my honor as an officer and a gentleman was destroyed; my name will forever be ruined. For *that*, I have vowed to forever hate all Americans!

We staggered into the safety of Charlestown well after dark. Over a third of our column was dead or wounded. All stared at the beckoning lights of Boston with vacant, shell-shocked eyes. How could a simple raid have gone so terribly wrong? How could we have guessed that the entire countryside would erupt against us?

The echoes of this day will ring loud and clear in our minds for years. These Americans will not get off lightly with a simple apology by diplomatic negotiators after this day. They must *pay*. We will *make* them pay ten times over for their bitter efforts on this terrible April day.

Aftermath

Little of physical or military significance happened on April 19. A few Patriot supplies and a few houses were destroyed. The British sustained only several hundred casualties, the Patriots less than 70.

Yet this one day changed everything. A war of words had become a war of bullets. What had been a dispute became a war.

Furthermore, Americans had cracked the myth of British invincibility. An unorganized mob had routed Britain's finest. The first time a real call had gone out for armed action against the British, great masses of the countryside had responded.

General Gage became much sterner in his ruling of Boston, but was terrified to venture outside Boston. He adopted a siege mentality. Boston was his fort and the infidel hordes were gathering at the gates.

Boston, itself, changed. Whigs streamed out (if they stayed, the British would arrest them) and Tories streamed in. Boston became a pro-British enclave surrounded by American patriots.

Blood had been spilled on both sides. There was no turning back. Sam Adams exclaimed, "What a glorious morning this is!" The war he had schemed for was now on.

Follow-up Questions and Activities

1. **What Do You Know?**

   - Who were the Minutemen? Where did they come from? Why were they called "Minutemen?"

   - Why were the battles (skirmishes, really) at Lexington and Concord important?

   - Why did the British feel that the Americans "cheated" during the battle along the road back from Concord?

   - What is a bayonet? A fife? A musket?

   - Why did the British attack Concord? What were they after? What were the Americans protecting?

2. **Finding Out More**. Following are four important topics from this story for you to research in the library and on the Internet. The reference sources at the back of this book will help you get started.

   - The Patriots gathered quickly in force at Concord. Why didn't the area Tory militia units gather, too? What did the American Patriots have at the beginning of the war that the Loyalist Americans did not posses? Does the existence of organized Committees of Correspondence and Sons of Liberty in every colony and in almost every major town and city figure into your answer?

   - Richard Dawes first brought the news of British movement to Lexington. He was a Son of Liberty and in Paul Revere's group of message riders, the Mechanics. What can you find out about Richard Dawes? What did he do for a living? Did he do anything later in the war?

- What was the French and Indian War? When, where, and why was it fought? What was the outcome of that war? How did it affect relations between the Native American tribes and the British Colonists?

- Generals Gage and Howe were the British commanders at Boston. Research their military careers. Where else had they been stationed? What else had they done? What did they do in the war after Boston was abandoned by the British in April 1776?

3. **Make It Real**

- Hold a class debate on the merit of the issues that started the Revolution. As a class, list the major grievances that split the Colonists from England. Appoint teams to prepare arguments on each side of each grievance. Use tangible evidence and facts to support each of your arguments. As a class, listen to each team argue the merit of each grievance, then vote on whether these issues were worth fighting a long and bloody war for.

- Create a population profile of the American Colonies at the beginning of the war. How many people lived in each colony? How many lived in cities? How many were farmers? How many were white? How many were black? How many of the blacks were slaves? How many were free blacks? How many people owned land? How many were considered rich? How many were poor? Make a chart that shows these demographics.

- Draw a time line of the events that led up to the fighting at Lexington and Concord. Start with the Boston Tea Party. Remember to include British actions and plans and Tory actions as well as American patriotic actions and plans.

4. **Points to Ponder**

- Why do you think we hear mostly about Paul Revere and not Billy Dawes, Dr. Prescott, or the other six men (mostly from the Charlestown militia) who rode warning routes that night? Why don't we hear of the over 50 other volunteers in the rest of the nation—including at least five girls—who rode similar warning routes whenever British forces went on the march? Why do you think we don't know the names of Captain Parker (Minuteman commander at Lexington) or Major Buttrick (who commanded the Patriots at Concord's North Bridge)? Does this show you something about how we learn history?

- Did the Patriots "cheat" in their tactics during the British retreat from Concord to Charlestown? Did they break the existing rules for the conduct of warfare? Is that okay to do? Did the Patriots act in a cruel, inhumane, and excessively brutal way? Today our armies conduct wars according to the Geneva Convention. Would it be okay to break those rules when it suited our purpose?

Staring into the Whites of Their Eyes
The Battle of Bunker Hill,
June 17, 1775

**British storm the
Breeds Hill fort**

At a Glance

Following the battles of Lexington and Concord, farmers and millers, sailors and shepherds, clerks and merchants all flooded toward Boston, forming a great ring of almost 10,000 citizen soldiers armed with muskets and clubs. For 10,000 soldiers there should have been hundreds of trained officers. There existed only a half-dozen, and those were instantly promoted to colonel and general rank. There was no pay, no established chain of command, no overall commanding general. These ordinary citizens were there as volunteers to shout out their anger and resentment against a mother country that seemed to have turned against her favorite son.

No war had been declared. Fighting had not yet erupted between Patriot and Loyalist. Armies had not marched across the fields in formal campaigns. This was a deadly earnest scrap between the Patriot people of Massachusetts (supported by their neighboring New Englanders) and the British army, a scrap that would drag the rest of America behind it.

Trapped in Boston were 5,000 British soldiers protected by the mighty guns of the British fleet anchored in the harbor. Boston was a tadpole-shaped blob of land connected to the mainland at its skinny tail at Boston Narrows. The British fortified and heavily manned the narrows. That narrows controlled all land entry and exit from Boston. The guns of the British ships controlled all entry and exit by water.

However, fortified artillery on the high ground north and south of Boston could control the city. Those heights to the north, on Charlestown peninsula, were named Bunker Hill (the taller of the two hills) and Breeds Hill (the hill closest to Boston). General Gage realized full well the danger if rebels gained control of either set of hills and aimed cannon from the heights down into Boston. He planned to send large expeditions out to seize and fortify both hills.

Rebel spies heard of these plans and decided to quickly claim Bunker Hill before the British could post troops there. This was a bold move for an unorganized mob.

Everyone knew the British would have to counter such a move, that they couldn't tolerate Patriots glaring down into their stronghold of Boston.

The two and one-half hours of fighting on Breeds Hill during the afternoon of Saturday, June 17, 1775, were the bloodiest and most violent fighting of the entire Revolutionary War. Massed American muskets created mighty sheets of flame when they fired. The sloping grass was slippery with blood. The battle on Breeds Hill (later named the Battle of Bunker Hill because Bunker Hill was higher) settled nothing and proved only that the Americans—even as disorganized mobs—were willing and able to stand and slug it out with the greatest army on Earth. It was a terrifying lesson for the British.

Just imagine how terrifying those two and one-half hours would have been for a 12-year-old boy crouching in the American trenches. That is exactly what happened to young Robert Ballard.

Meet Robert Ballard

Robert Ballard, the oldest of four children, was born in 1763 on a farm just outside Medford, Massachusetts. As of his twelfth birthday, he had lived, worked, and played his whole life without ever traveling farther from home than the 3.5 miles into the town of Medford. He lived in a sheltered, friendly, safe world.

Then he marched off to war with his father in June 1775 and his world turned upside town. After the Battle of Bunker Hill, Robert returned home and refused to join any military unit or to participate in the war in any way. He was terrified of armies and guns and, at age 18, moved west to central Pennsylvania, where he married and raised six children on a farm, dying at the age of 53 in 1816. (He had refused to even allow the War of 1812 to be discussed in his house and was heartbroken when two of his sons enlisted during that war, one of whom was killed in action.)

Staring into the Whites of Their Eyes

James Ballard, a third-generation American farmer of Welsh decent living in Medford, Massachusetts, joined the local militia in March 1775. His 11-year-old son, Robert, attended every militia meeting with his father and used a rake to pretend to shoot when the militia scrounged enough powder and ball to hold a firing drill. Robert strutted between house and barn each evening after farm chores were done, shouting drill orders to himself as he marched.

James Ballard felt that, as a patriotic American, he was obligated to join the militia and—if necessary—to fight for the Colonists' rights. But he dreamed of a quiet life on his farm. Robert dreamed of the glories of a soldier's life, slashing his way across the continent and around the world.

On June 10, 1775, a galloping courier delivered a letter to the Medford militia summoning them to march in great haste to the camp outside Cambridge, near Boston. They were to join the Massachusetts regiment commanded by famed, broad-shouldered Colonel Prescott, hero of the French and Indian War.

Robert trembled with excitement as his father packed kit, bedroll, musket, powder, and lead balls. "I want to go with you, father."

"No, son. There could be a scrap. Your place is at home."

"But father. I'm almost 12. I want to show that I can be a man—a soldier."

"Army camp is no place for a boy."

"There will be other boys. I can do work and help at camp. It will be good training. Please, father."

Mrs. Ballard sided with her son. "It will be for just a few days, James, and the boy's never seen a city. Besides—you'll see—this will all simmer down right quick. The British have always been reasonable and good to the Colonies. They'll correct their mistakes and we'll be happy brothers again before mid-summer. You'll see."

James Ballard relented, and Robert swaggered proud as a newly appointed general at the head of the line as the Medford militia shuffled along the dusty dirt road toward Boston. The 80-man unit arrived hot and tired on the afternoon of June 13. The helter-skelter Patriot camp sprawled for miles through meadows and woods and buzzed with fighting fervor. In every direction, Robert faced clusters of grim-faced men in the afternoon light eager to pick a brawl with the Red-coats. But in hushed tones around flickering campfires at night, each man admitted his secret terror at facing the pounding power, the training and experience of regular British army and navy units—the fiercest fighting force on Earth.

At 6:00 P.M. on Friday, June 16, Colonel Prescott's regiment was called out for parade (assembly). Each man was to carry a blanket, whatever ammunition he had, and one day's rations. They heard prayers at 8:00 and, through dusky mists of twilight, marched like gray ghosts down Cambridge neck onto Charlestown peninsula, sandwiched between the Mystic River and the Charles River. The lamps of Boston glowed from across the Charles. Having been warned to stay in camp by his father, Robert Ballard and two other boys crept behind the regiment like shadowy wraiths as they marched into history.

Connecticut's aging General Israel Putnam ("Old Put") had been scouting ahead and thundered back to meet the Massachusetts regiment as they toiled up the hundred-foot-tall slope of Bunker Hill. "Shift to Breeds Hill!" he shouted. "It's closer to Boston. From there we can shove our muzzles right down General Gage's redcoated gullet."

Prescott shook his head. "Breeds Hill is lower and harder to defend."

"We will not win this war thinking of defense, Colonel. I tell you, Breeds Hill!"

At 10:30 P.M. the regiment crossed the extra half-mile of dark and climbed 75-foot-high Breeds Hill. Officers feverishly laid out lines for the walls of a fort through the inky blackness, shovels were dispensed, and Prescott ordered all to dig.

The Medford militia dug on the right side of Prescott's dirt fort. Robert and his friends crept into the trench on the far left side to take their turn with shovel and pick.

Straight through the night the men toiled, hot, grimy, and caked with flying dirt that turned to streaking mud in the trickles of their sweat. By first light it was clear that they had the makings of a sturdy, if not fashionable, fort, 160 feet on a side, with dirt walls eight feet high and two feet thick.

British lookouts on the warships in the harbor could now see what night had hidden: the fresh-turned earth and gleaming shovels. Furiously digging Patriots could also see what darkness had covered: a line of eight deadly British warships in the Charles River. Before 6:00 A.M. billows of red flashed and plumes of gray-white smoke erupted from the first of the ships. Cannon balls whined overhead as Prescott marched along the line, urging bone-weary and now terrified men to "Dig! Dig as if your life depended on it!"

A banshee-screeching shell crashed into the earthen wall near Robert's spot in the line. The ground shook, the air roared, and dirt erupted all around him. Robert cried out, dropped his shovel, and turned to run. Then he stopped. No one else had even slowed the furious digging.

Ashamed of his fright—even though he believed they would all be slaughtered by this rain of cannon-ball death—Robert threw himself into a frenzy of digging as the rising sun shimmered over sparkling water and under a dome of breathtakingly flawless blue sky.

Saturday, June 17 had begun.

The navy bombardment continued all morning and was joined by shore batteries on Copp's Hill in Boston. Red-hot cannon balls spewed dirt over the diggers when they hit. Although the British shells tore down the fort's walls almost as fast as diggers could rebuild them, they only struck and killed one man.

Throughout the morning Robert could see other units making the quick march through Charlestown neck. A few joined the digging on Breeds Hill. Some raced to fortify a fence and wall that angled from Breeds Hill down to the Mystic River. But many units milled aimlessly near the base of Bunker Hill, either unsure of what to do or unwilling to venture nearer to the screaming bite of the British bombardment.

The diggers had grown frightfully parched and famished. No water had been carried in and what little food was brought on the march had been gobbled up during the night. Jugs of rum were passed through the thirsty ranks. Wanting to look like his comrades, Robert sucked a great gulp. His throat erupted in fire as hot as if struck by a cannon ball. He wheezed and gasped for breath. The man who had handed him the jug laughed once and then turned back to his digging.

Thick throngs of spectators now lined every shore around Boston and crowded onto each elevated spot. People clung to roofs, hung on church steeples, and climbed the masts of ships tied to the wharves to watch this spectacular show.

At 12:30 a lookout down the line cried, "They're coming!" Over 40 long transport boats shoved off from Boston piers in neat precision, with 2,500 hardened Redcoats sitting in orderly rows in them. Eight hundred oars flashed in the sunlight and dipped in unison into the calm blue water of Boston Bay. Rank after red rank off-loaded on the beach to form a sea of red coats and white breeches and a forest of gleaming bayonets.

Robert's heart dropped. His imaginary picture of war had not included back-breaking work and the terror of seeing endless rows of better-armed enemies intent on his destruction.

Patriot couriers on horseback raced from point to point exchanging news and battle plans, making requests, offering aid. But Robert noticed none of it. He saw only the sea of dragon-fire red that was intent on killing every man in his fort. He heard only the pounding drums and shrill English fifes. He stared at the rows of snapping banners announcing that doom had arrived for the foolish rabble on the hill.

Suddenly Robert felt like a helpless little boy snared in a deadly man's world. This was no game and he did not belong here.

"Dig!" growled the man next to Robert. Mechanically, he returned to his shoveling as the hot sun beat down overhead, as cannon balls screeched past, and as the terror of the pounding drums beat deep in his soul.

"Here they come!" cried a lookout, and the endless red lines, that unstoppable English war machine, a glittering host of red, white, gold, and steel, advanced steadily up the unmowed grass of Breeds Hill to slaughter any fool who stood in their path.

The ground vibrated with the tramping of their countless feet. The air was shattered by the dreadful noise of their drums. With all the pomp and ceremony of a royal wedding, death marched toward the rebel lines.

Shovels were cast aside. Muskets were hurriedly loaded. A tense hush fell over the freshly dug fort.

Patriot snipers using long-range Pennsylvania rifles fired volley upon volley into the red ranks from roofs and steeples in the village of Charlestown, nestled at the side of Breeds Hill. Redcoats crumpled to the grass, but the unstoppable red ranks rolled steadily forward, seeming to be no more bothered by snipers than they would be by pesky flies.

Almost immediately the navy guns responded to the snipers. Exploding fire shells and burning pitch rained down on Charlestown like meteors. In a blink the entire town was engulfed in a billowing, thunderous volcano of flame. Houses and churches collapsed in a screeching roar. Steeple bells clanged as they bounced and rolled toward the bay. Smoke blackened the sky above Breeds Hill like a death shroud. Women and children ran screaming from flaming homes to seek shelter beyond the boundaries of the battle.

And still the scarlet ranks and pounding drums marched steadily up the hill like a gathering wave.

With no musket, Robert clutched his shovel and pressed into the cool, fresh-smelling dirt. Old Put galloped along the trench line of waiting volunteers crying, "Hold your fire, lads! Don't fire 'til you see the whites of their eyes."

An eerie silence fell on the hill as the distance closed between defenders and Redcoats. Robert glanced over the dirt wall and saw a sea of deadly red and gleaming steel.

One hundred feet separated the armies; then 70; then 50; then 30. Robert could scarcely breathe, the tension lay so thick and heavy on him.

Someone yelled, "Fire!" Flame and smoke erupted from Patriot muskets. The British ranks melted, their stiff lines disintegrating as if mowed down by a heavenly scythe. A solid sheet of flame and a wall of raging musket balls ripped across the open space as Patriot musketeers feverishly reloaded, pouring round after round into the grim sea of attackers.

The gleaming British ranks staggered and faltered. Their momentum turned to liquid red flowing out to stain the grass. Like a spent wave, the British ranks stumbled backward in retreat.

Cheers erupted all along the Patriot line. Hats were tossed in the air. Jeers were shouted down the hill. "We beat 'em!" "We won!"

Robert opened his eyes and raised his head. "We won? They're gone?" A euphoric wave of relief swept over him. A feeling of power and glory surged through his body. He shouted, "We won! We won!"

"Wait. Here they come again," called someone down the line. The red ranks had reformed at the bottom of Breeds Hill. Again the drums pounded. Again the rows of British cannon spit fire and screaming shells at the fort. The mighty red war engine rewound for another push up the deadly slope.

"Reload!" cried Colonel Prescott. The man next to Robert muttered that he was low on ammo. So was everyone else.

Suddenly Colonel Prescott hauled Robert up by his collar and pointed toward the milling units standing idle at the base and rear of Bunker Hill. "Boy, we need reinforcements and more ammo! Get those units up here! Go!"

Robert tore like the wind across the ragged dirt of the fort and down the back slope of Breeds Hill. Gasping for breath, he tumbled to a stop before a group of over 100 men sitting in a huddled mass and frantically pointed toward the smoke-shrouded summit. "Quick. Get to the fort."

The men actually laughed. "Don't order us about, boy. You're not our commander."

Robert was stunned. "But . . . but they need you. The Redcoats are attacking."

"We move when our commander tells us to."

Tears of frustration welled into Robert's eyes. "Well, where's your commander?"

His only answer was a series of indifferent shrugs. From group after group the answer was the same. There they and their ammo sat, and there they would stay.

Then Breeds Hill erupted in fire again. The thunder of a thousand muskets tore through the air. Robert sped back up the slope, arriving just as a mighty cheer roared down the Patriot line. "They're falling back again!" Hats flew. Flags were waved from behind the fence and walls.

The dense sulfur smoke of gunpowder made Robert choke as he scrambled back into his spot in the trench. He couldn't make himself jump and cheer with the others. He could see a dozen Patriots sprawled dead in the soft dirt. Many more groaned with the agony of wounds as comrades offered aid. Two of the dead were men Robert had spoken to earlier that day. One had shown him how to hold his shovel so as to not get blisters. How could he cheer while they lay forever still?

Then he gazed over the wall—and felt sick. The slope was littered with hundreds of fallen Redcoats. Some tried to crawl. The screams of the wounded filled the air. Most lay as crumpled lumps on the field. The trampled grass was coated thick and slick with blood. So many dead who, an hour ago had laughed and chatted with friends, who, an hour ago, had had wives and families. So many dead who were now only memories.

Robert sank to his knees, gasping to catch his breath, head spinning with the awful vision of that sloping field. At least the terrible fight was over and they could go home. At least they had won.

"Here they come again!" cried several lookouts on the wall. Cries of "Ammo! Ammo!" echoed up and down the line. "Who's got ammo?" The man next to Robert stared blankly at his empty musket. "How can I drive them off without any powder cartridges and musket balls?"

Colonel Prescott snatched Robert up by the collar. "Where are the reinforcements, boy? Where's the ammo?"

Tears flowed from Robert's eyes. "They wouldn't come, sir. I told them but they wouldn't come."

Prescott cursed and turned away. Then he breathed deep and sprang to the top of the wall. "Hold back until they're right on top of us, lads. Make every shot count!"

He jumped down just as British musket balls began to thud into the dirt wall and to whine overhead. A farmer, turned volunteer soldier, sagged backward with a surprised yelp when he edged up too high and a British musket ball abruptly ended his life. Robert snatched the farmer's loaded musket and cradled it to his chest as he trembled in the trench.

"Steady, boys. . . . Steady. . . ."

Robert sneaked a peek and stared into the very face of the oncoming British. Grim faces, red coats, and gleaming steel were upon them.

"Steady. . . ."

They were no more than five long paces away, their faces as clear as the men around him in the trench.

"Steady. . . ."

"Fire!"

For a third time, a sheet of flame and musket ball exploded from the fort. For a third time the British line staggered and faltered as a new crop of dead sprawled to the ground.

But the wall of Patriot fire could not continue as before. As soon as it had started, the Patriot fire dimmed from a ferocious roar to an occasional pop, and then fell silent. Their ammo was gone.

The Redcoats charged. Men on both sides of Robert fell dead from a British volley as the first wave stormed over the wall. Robert pointed his musket at the surging red tide and squeezed the trigger. Fire and smoke belched from its mouth. The musket recoiled, twisting out of Robert's hands. He screamed and fled, sprinting like a jack rabbit away from the terror on Breeds Hill, one tiny dot in the stream of fleeing Patriot defenders.

Back in camp that night, Robert could not stop trembling. All was in turmoil and confusion. Some were disgusted because the battle could have been won if reinforcements and ammo had moved forward instead of cowardly halting in the rear. Some were elated because twice the mighty British army had been turned back and because English dead numbered triple that of the Patriots. Almost half of the British force had been killed or wounded. Some were disappointed that the hill had been lost but proud to have stood so bravely and firmly against the best army on Earth.

Robert Ballard couldn't focus on philosophical debate. His head still throbbed with the grizzly sights of the dead and with the terror of the final attack. He searched for an hour for his father before learning that he had been killed defending the fort. Robert stumbled into the bushes, dropped to his knees, and wept.

Aftermath

Robert Ballard forever turned against war and refused to ever set foot near Boston. The British were badly frightened by the fighting on Breeds Hill. They had expected the untrained rabble to break and run on the first advance. It was terrifying to learn that the American volunteers (who outnumbered the British army in Boston three to one) would—and could—stand rock-solid and destroy a trained British force. Bunker Hill made the British very cautious and fearful of American attack. General Gage never again dared to venture outside of Boston.

Patriot forces were rousingly encouraged by the battle. They had fought and survived, and they hadn't been routed or destroyed. This "success" led to the Canada Expedition of late 1775 and kept a steady stream of new recruits pouring in. Patriot forces would never again feel totally terrified about facing British regulars.

Follow-up Questions and Activities

1. **What Do You Know?**

    • How did British forces differ from American Patriot forces at the beginning of the war?

    • What were the Patriots trying to do when they built a stronghold on Breeds Hill?

    • Why could the Patriots claim to have won the Battle of Bunker Hill? Why could the British claim victory?

2. **Finding Out More**. Following are three important topics from this story for you to research in the library and on the Internet. The reference sources at the back of this book will help you get started.

    • How many Patriots died during the Battle of Bunker Hill? How many were wounded? How many British were killed? What percentage of each force was killed or wounded? Compare these numbers with the losses at the battles of Saratoga, Germantown, Monmouth, Cowpens, and Yorktown. Where were the losses the greatest?

    • Colonel Prescott of Massachusetts and General Israel Putman (Old Put) of Connecticut commanded the Americans during the Battle of Bunker Hill. Where did they come from? Find out the history of these two men. What military service had they performed before the Revolution? What did they do during the rest of the war?

    • Robert Ballard was 12 and was allowed to be in the trenches during the Battle of Bunker Hill. Did other children fight during the Revolution? Research "children at war." Have children always been allowed to fight during wars? Are they allowed to fight in any other countries today?

3. **Make It Real**

    • Draw a map of the Boston area, including Boston Harbor, Cambridge, Concord and Lexington, and Charlestown peninsula. Include the location of Breeds Hill and Bunker Hill. Draw the position of the American troops and the movements of the British troops for the Battle of Bunker Hill.

- The defenders at Breeds Hill felt the ground vibrate as the British regulars began to march up the hill toward them. How many marching feet does it take to make the ground shake? Do some experiments at your school to find out. First try making the ground shake in the school hallway. How many students have to march (walk in perfect unison) down the hall to make the floor vibrate in another part of the hall? Next try this experiment outside. How many marching students does it take to make the ground vibrate 100 yards way? Does it matter what kind of ground they march over? See if your local newspaper and television stations will be interested in your experiments and your results.

- Imagine that you are a defender in the fort on Breeds Hill. Write a letter home describing the sights, sounds, smells, and feel of the battle.

4. **Points to Ponder**

- Do you think it is acceptable for one group to start an undeclared war that commits everyone else in the society to join their fight? Why do you think 12,000 Patriot militiamen volunteered to gather around Boston without pay or benefits of military service and protection?

- At Breeds Hill a disciplined, trained, uniformed military attacked a gathering of civilians. Was this a wise thing for the British to do? Why or why not? What else could the British have done? When do you think it is justifiable for a group of civilians to rise up in arms against a legitimate ruler without creating a formal army?

Cordial George

Washington Becomes America's First Commander-in-Chief, July 2, 1775

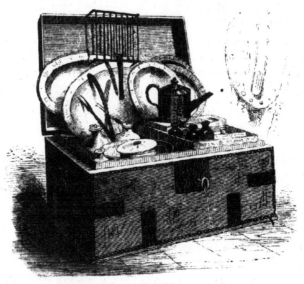

George Washington's camp chest

At a Glance

After skirmishes at Lexington and Concord, an American "army" of 12,000 to 17,000 volunteers surrounded Boston. Patriotic spirit and righteous indignation bristled from Maine to the Carolinas. Every member of the Virginia House of Burgesses swore loyalty to the "Liberty or Death" motto. Even so, "liberty" for these politicians still meant "liberty as part of the British empire." They still assumed things would be patched up with mother England.

In Philadelphia, the Second Continental Congress struggled to form a basic consensus. Most delegates insisted that they had no aggressive intent but rather were acting in a spirit of self-defense. Only a few radicals—like Sam Adams—called for total independence.

How could Congress advance its cause with Britain while an unplanned, unauthorized army of citizens surrounded Boston, following their own, self-defined goals and brand of military conduct? How could Congress claim to speak for the Colonies if it couldn't even control its own army?

Each militia unit elected its own officers, and troops took orders only when they wanted to. They left for home when they needed to visit the family or had work to do. There existed no central command, no supply system for any of the essentials of maintaining an army.

Even more worrisome for Congress, the army around Boston seemed determined to push the British into a real war. How could Congress sue for terms of continued peace if an army using its name rampaged about killing British soldiers? Congress had to find a way to take control of this military defense if America was ever to speak with a unified national voice.

What Congress needed was a general to take command of the army. It had to be someone with enough military experience so that the various state militias would accept his authority. It had to be someone that all 13 colonial legislatures and all 13 sets of congressional delegates would accept and support. It had to be someone with enough experience to quickly create a sense of order and discipline in the makeshift army. It was a tall order. To fill it, Congress found quiet George Washington.

Meet George Washington

George Washington was born sixth of 10 children on a Virginia farm along the Potomac River in 1731. His ancestors had owned and farmed the land since first arriving from England in 1657. The family added milling, iron works, and very successful land trading to their basic farming, rising in wealth and social stature. By the time of his father's death, when George was 11, he owned six sprawling farms. (Mt. Vernon was one of these.)

George received little (if any) formal education, but showed a natural talent for mathematics and became a surveyor by age 15. His mother had wanted him to join the British navy, but was dissuaded when told that "an obscure colonial youth could expect no more at the hands of the British than a job as a common sailor."

While working for the governor of Virginia to protect English claims along the upper Ohio and Allegheny Rivers in 1754, Washington led a small unit in a successful ambush of a French detachment. That one incident ignited the entire French and Indian War. During that war, Washington commanded several small militia units serving under the British, but had little, if any, military success. During this period, however, he lost all affection for the British army, blaming them for most of the problems and losses that beset the Virginia militia.

After the French and Indian War, George married Martha, settled into plantation life at Mt. Vernon, and became an innovative, progressive farmer. This bucolic life was disrupted when Washington was elected as a Virginia delegate to the First Continental Congress. His rise to the level of American hero was set to begin.

Cordial George

The dawn of a sizzling day in June 1775 found the American 8th Massachusetts Infantry manning a flimsy series of fortifications on Cobble Hill near Charlestown neck and the road past Bunker Hill to Charlestown. One hundred fifty strong, the 8th was a tiny gang in the 10,000- to 15,000-man mob that had streamed in a great arc around Boston after the killings at Lexington and Concord, to bottle up the British in the crowded city.

As evening on June 10 slid through muggy deep blues and grays, the regiment lounged restlessly in camp back by Prospect Hill—as it had every evening for the past five weeks—with little to do and virtually no equipment and supplies with which to do it. The eight-man watch for that night slouched behind the Cobble Hill earthen walls, assigned to keep a wary eye on the back bay, on the British fleet of ships, and for any sign of British troop movement by boat.

David Howe, a short, thick leather worker and shrewd Yankee trader, scratched at his matted hair and then rubbed his back on a wood post to reach an itch under his ragged shirt. "I haven't had a change of shirt for three weeks. A man could make a handsome shilling running a bath and laundry around this place."

Lieutenant Jabez Fitch, an old Indian campaigner who still used a flintlock rifle and who sprouted great tufts of snow-white hair in the corners of his beard, laughed. "Too much work, David. I joined 'cause this is the easy life. We sit out here. The Redcoats sit in there, and no one has to do a bloody thing. Besides, we've never been paid. So who's got any shillings to give you for your bath and laundry?"

"Ten thousand men and not a scrap of decent food or material worth bartering and trading for. . . . " Then Howe's eyes brightened. "Say, how would a few pulls on a rum jar interest you?"

Fitch nodded. "*There's* something the lads *would* scrape a few pence together for. But every rum bottle within 10 miles has been licked dry."

"I know of a rum factory out by Wheaton. With you, an officer, to salute fancy-like and give orders, we could slide past the guard posts and make it out there and back with the goods in a day and a half and be rich by sunset."

Again Fitch nodded. "Done. Let's go."

Amos Farnsworth, a pious young corporal from Groton, Massachusetts, said, "We're supposed to be on guard duty 'til relieved at dawn."

David Howe eyed the serious young soldier. "Look, Amos. This army lacks everything else—food, tents, blankets, pay, clothing. So why not lack a couple of guards? Besides, you're still here and nothing is going to happen."

"It's our duty. We're soldiers."

"You do our duty, Amos. Half the regiment has already headed home for a few days here and there to take care of business. Now it's my turn. Be a good lad and watch my musket 'til I get back."

Scrambling over the back wall of the small fort, Fitch and Howe met their company commander making his evening rounds. "Leaving a guard post could get you flogged!"

David Howe leaned close to the captain and grinned. "Now, Cap'n. Talk like that might make a couple of the lads change their vote and then you won't be the captain, just another stiff in the mud like us."

Turning bright red, the captain blustered, "Well . . . ah . . . that is, I was only looking out for your best interests . . . . Don't be gone long. . . . "

As Lieutenant Fitch and Private David Howe scampered into the night, Captain Mathews muttered, "This is no army. It's a filthy squalor and a bunch of hoodlums out for a lark. What will we ever do if the British attack?"

On that same evening of June 10, John Adams, country lawyer and Massachusetts delegate to the Continental Congress, huddled in the doorway of a Philadelphia tavern with Mr. Edmund Pendleton, a tall and stately plantation owner and Virginia delegate, to escape the persistent light rain. Pendleton had to stoop so that their heads could lean close and prevent passers-by from overhearing the urgent tone in their whispered words.

"The army needs a general, someone who can take charge and make them into a true fighting force," insisted Adams.

"I'm not sure we should even have an army. If we don't have an army we can't have a war."

"But we *do* have an army. It's camped all around Boston."

Pendleton's voice began to rise. "That uncontrolled mob of New Englanders you call an army will make negotiations with the King more difficult. It is essential that we stay part of the British Empire."

Adams countered, "Maybe if King George thinks we have an army, it will make negotiations *easier*."

Adams reached out a hand to quiet Pendleton as two known Tories hurried past, boots splashing on the wet street. Glancing up and down the street, Adams hissed, "Think on it. We'll talk again." And he disappeared into the dreary night.

Near midnight Adams hunched over a small table in the sitting room of his boarding house with Robert Paine, another congressional delegate from New England. "We're not a government if we can't control our own army."

Light blazed through the wide windows from glowing lamps. Paine seemed mostly uninterested as he read a packet of correspondence that had arrived that afternoon. "We have 30 companies of uniformed militia in Philadelphia. Isn't that enough?"

"No. A country needs an army. We need a Continental Army that represents *all* the colonies. And that army needs a commander-in-chief—a commander-in-chief *Congress* appoints if we are going to be the governing body of this new nation."

Paine's eyebrows rose as he flopped the stack of letters into his lap and leaned forward. "Commander-in-chief, you say? You mean to nominate John Hancock?" (Hancock had been unanimously elected president of the Continental Congress.) "I believe he wants the position."

Adams recoiled. "Hancock? Egad, no." He waved his hands as if to erase Paine's words from the air. "Hancock is a New Englander. It must be a southern general to make the army seem like a Continental Army." He paused, excitement twinkling in his gray eyes. "I'm thinking of George Washington."

"Washington?" Paine wrinkled up his face as if the word left a bad taste in his mouth. "That quiet man from Virginia?"

"He had command experience during the French and Indian War."

"Washington?!"

Adams reached out to pat Paine's forearm as he said, "Just think on it. We'll talk again tomorrow."

Every conversation over the next two days went the same way.

"Washington? He lost three battles during the French and Indian War, and he never won any."

"Yes, but he has command experience."

"Washington? He's never been in charge of supplies, logistics, the wounded, engineering, or artillery. He has never commanded groups larger than 100 men."

"Yes, but he *has* commanded men in a fight, and afterwards they called him brave."

"Washington? He never studied military strategy or tactics beyond wilderness fighting."

"Yes, but he *does* have command experience and he was educated in America instead of England."

"Washington? But what of Hancock? He has done more for the country. He is the political leader. He wants the nomination. Shouldn't we give it to him? Besides, not even all the Virginia delegates will support Washington."

"The commander-in-chief *must* be a southerner because most of the army is northern, and it must be someone with military experience."

"Washington? He's ambitious. Shouldn't we be afraid of an ambitious general?"

"He's also modest and sensible. Besides, we need that ambition to mold an army and hold it together while we in Congress negotiate with Parliament to secure our rights."

Adams ended each conversation with a sigh and a "Just think on it. We'll talk again tomorrow." The skeptical looks he saw gave him little hope that he had swayed many of those he spoke to even though he was convinced that Washington was the best man Congress could appoint to the position.

As the days of early June melted into memories, John Adams felt he could waste no more time gathering support in secret conversations. He harbored a deep foreboding—almost a premonition—that disaster would surely strike if the army were not brought under proper control.

As Congress convened on that rainy, cool day, June 10, 1775, John Adams rose to make his nomination. After explaining the importance of the position, Adams said, "I have but one gentleman in mind. . . . A gentleman already among us whom you know well. . . . A man with skills as a leader and officer, independent fortune, excellent character. . . . A man who can lead all America to unite under his cordial exertions. . . . The one man who can lead a grand American army."

Sitting on his raised president's dais (raised platform), John Hancock, assuming his fellow New Englander was referring to him, actually blushed as he smiled broadly and nodded as if to adoring subjects.

Adams continued, "I nominate Mr. George Washington of Virginia."

There were scattered murmurs of surprise. The uncommitted Virginia delegates squirmed, feeling they couldn't vote against a fellow Virginian, but not sure they wanted to vote *for* Washington. Hancock paled. His eyes widened in shock and then hardened to a scowl.

Sam Adams quickly seconded the motion. Hancock openly glared at him, appalled that a second fellow New Englander would stab him in the back. After a stunned moment of silence, seemingly every delegate erupted into passionate talk, except for tall, modest George Washington, who quietly slid out the door to sit in an empty adjacent room.

Some still opposed the idea of declaring a national army at all. Some wanted a New England general to lead this New England army. Some wanted more time to consider other possible nominees. Hancock pounded his gavel for order and postponed further discussion for one day.

On the next day Thomas Johnson of Maryland repeated the nomination, Sam Adams again seconded, and others quickly called for a vote to avoid lengthy debate. Yea's and nay's were counted and recorded and, by a narrow margin—and to the dismay of Hancock and many other Congressmen—Washington became the commander-in-chief of the fledgling American army.

Three weeks later, on July 2, 1775, Washington and a tiny general staff arrived at Cambridge, Massachusetts, the army's headquarters, during a rain storm. There were no parades. No bands played. A corporal on duty at headquarters even wrote in the log that nothing of note happened that day.

Washington couldn't simply take over the reins of command. He had to first create those reins. Each militia unit from each state followed its own commander, who was free to do whatever he wanted. It took Washington eight days to collect basic status reports that should have taken no more than two hours.

Washington was appalled by what he read and saw. The army was much smaller than he had been told. Too many men had simply wandered back home and left. Units often weren't sure how many men they were supposed to have, much less where they all were.

There was not one trained engineer in the entire army, no one who knew how to properly build forts, roads, and redoubts. What fortifications there were, were poorly made and were in the wrong places to repel British attacks. Neither were there any trained artillery men or officers. The 28 cannons the army possessed were stacked near headquarters because no one knew how to fire them. Worse, there wasn't enough powder to supply the muskets, let alone the cannons.

The army was worse than undersupplied; it wasn't supplied at all. No one was in charge of procuring food, clothes, tents, gunpowder, or other necessities. Each unit scrounged on its own. Most men carried no more than three rounds of ammo. Every yard of sail cloth within 30 miles had been turned into tents, but still half the army slept in the open. There was no money with which to buy supplies and no way to order or demand them.

Angry local citizens yelled at Washington about the filth and squalor in the army camps, which could be smelled for miles; about the soldiers' stealing and trampling of lands and crops; about how the ragged-looking soldiers frightened women and children. Washington called in his senior officers to discuss these problems and found that his senior officers were consumed with petty squabbles and that each senior officer felt he shouldn't have to take orders from anyone.

New Yorkers distrusted Connecticut units and vice versa. Pennsylvania units didn't want to work with those from Massachusetts. Worse, few of the soldiers respected officers and orders and would follow only those that they chose to follow.

This was not an army; it was a mob. It was a disaster. Washington was shocked. He had never dreamed conditions could be so bad. After one week in Cambridge, Washington wrote to his wife, "Could I have foreseen what I have experienced in the last week, no consideration on Earth would have induced me to accept this command."

"Is there anything this army *does* have?" he asked one of his senior officers.

"Spirit, sir. The lads have plenty of spirit."

What his army needed most was discipline. Washington fired several senior officers. He issued strict general orders. He began to hold courts marshal for all violators for any offense.

David Howe, Lieutenant Jabez Fitch, and Amos Farnsworth were again on guard duty for the 8th Massachusetts on the evening of July 20. Howe had grumbled continuously since arriving at their guard post. "Did you know I was almost arrested *twice* today? Some fancy-dressed major says, 'Why don't you have a decent shirt on?' So I says real smart like, 'Because I forgot to bring my full wardrobe from home. If you'd like I'll scamper home to fetch it.' And he says '20,000 new shirts arrived from Pennsylvania. Go to headquarters and get one.' So I honestly and rightly says, 'Sorry, major, but no shirt from Pennsylvania goes over these Massachusetts shoulders,' figuring that'll rightly explain the situation. But he says 'Get one or I'll have you arrested by noon!' Now can you believe the likes of that? What is this army coming to?"

Jabez Fitch laughed, "You'll look fine in one of them frilly Pennsylvania shirts. What was the second time you were almost arrested?"

"Some Colonel orders me to take a bath. So I says, 'I'd love to oblige ya' colonel, but yesterday's orders said we weren't allowed to swim nude in the river anymore for fear of frightening sensitive local ladies.' So he says, 'Don't talk back to officers and take that bath or you'll be in double trouble!' "

Even serious Amos Farnsworth had to agree that it was no longer the same army they had joined three months earlier. Howe rubbed his back against a post and sighed as a knot scratched just the right spot. "You are exactly right, Amos. This is not the army I joined. So I'm going home. I quit."

"You can't quit," hissed Farnsworth. "You signed up to be a soldier."

"There are too many orders for me. It's been good to know you, Amos."

Fitch scratched his graying beard. "I'll go with you, David. These orders are going to make this into a work, work, work army. Better to leave now while the getting's good."

As the two crept from the trench to make their escape, they met Captain Mathews. "Back in the trench both of you, or you'll be court marshaled for sure!"

"Now Cap'n," cooed David Howe. "Talk like that could get you unelected as our captain."

"Officers aren't elected anymore. We're appointed. Talk back to one and you're court marshaled."

"Says who?" demanded Howe.

"Says General Washington. And if you leave, you'll be hunted down and brought back to face court marshal."

"Says who?" repeated Howe.

"Says General Washington."

"Says Washington. Says Washington. I'd like to say something to this Washington."

They heard the soft clomp of a horse's hooves. A tall, stately man on a magnificent white horse quietly passed. His face was serious and stern. Still, he radiated confidence and authority. All three men turned and automatically saluted.

"That was him—Washington, I mean—wasn't it?" whispered Lieutenant Fitch.

"I never saluted nobody before," groused Howe.

Back in their assigned trench for the night, Howe grumpily slumped onto a log seat. "All right. Tomorrow I'll get my Pennsylvania shirt."

"I guess it's a brand new army," agreed Lieutenant Fitch.

Both men sighed.

"I already miss the old one," added Fitch.

The mob was beginning to act like an army.

Aftermath

In the spring of 1776, Washington proudly proclaimed that this same army contained the finest troops in the world. Even the rowdy riflemen redeemed themselves. "A valuable and brave body of men . . . indeed a very useful corps," Washington called them.

Even after thousands of desertions by those who didn't want any part of Washington's military discipline and order, Washington had 17,000 men he could count as soldiers in each morning's muster in March 1776. He used the worthiness of this great force representing the "United Colonies" to justify raising a new flag: 13 stripes (6 red, 7 white) with the crosses of St. Andrew and St. George in the upper left corner. America finally had both a real army and a real general.

Follow-up Questions and Activities

1. **What Do You Know?**

   • Why did Congress want to elect a general for the volunteer army gathered around Boston? Why did they pick Washington over Hancock?

   • Did everyone in Congress and the colonial legislatures want to elect Washington? How did he get elected to the position of General of the Army?

   • How did Washington establish order and discipline in the army around Boston? Why did he have to create a sense of order and discipline there?

   • After he had spent several weeks with his new "army," Washington wrote his wife that he would have refused the post if he had known the real state of affairs. Why did he say that? What conditions did he find that were worse than he had been led to believe?

2. **Finding Out More.** Following are six important topics from this story for you to research in the library and on the Internet. The reference sources at the back of this book will help you get started.

   • Many myths and legends have grown up around George Washington. See how many you can find. Why do you think so many fictional stories have been created about this man?

   • What is the real history of George Washington? What jobs did he have? How did his family become wealthy land owners? What did he do before the Revolutionary War began?

- What was the Continental Congress? When was it first formed? Why? By whom? How many Continental Congresses were there? What did they do?

- John Hancock was a most important figure in the Continental Congress. What did he do before the war? Why and how was he elected president of the Congress? What did he do after the war? What signature is he most famous for?

- Two Adamses were in Congress, cousins John and Sam, both from Massachusetts. Research these two important men. What contribution to the Revolution did each make? What did they do before the Revolution and after it?

- Many soldiers deserted (ran away from the army) during the winter of 1775 to 1776. Did Washington's army suffer from desertions every winter?

3. **Make It Real**

- In the 1700s few people ever traveled more than 25 miles from their homes during their entire lives. How far from home have you been? As a class, make a list of how far each student in the class has been from home. Why do you think travel was so difficult then and is so easy now?

- The Patriot army around Boston was made up of small, independent units, responsible only to their individual colonial legislatures. There was no overall army commander. Units didn't have to cooperate with each other if they didn't want to. What would that situation be like? You can actually imagine something very close to it at your school with the following exercise:

  Each class at your school follows the lead and direction of its teacher. If there were no principal, teachers could do whatever they wanted. How would the various classes decide who goes to lunch when, who gets physical education when, or when each class gets a turn to use the library? How would school-wide decisions be made? Would they *ever* be made, or would each class act independently? Interview several teachers and the principal and then conduct a class discussion to envision how the school would work if there were no central administration at all. Then write individual essays describing what your school would be like without any administrators (army commanders). How closely do you think that situation would match that of the Patriot army around Boston in mid-1775?

4. **Points to Ponder**

- Was Washington a good general? He lost almost all the battles he fought—even the ones he was supposed to win. His army almost starved every winter. He couldn't even get enough shoes to cover his men's feet. In the winter of 1780–1781 many of his officers and units mutinied against his leadership. Hold a class debate on Washington's ability as a general. Have teams research each side of the question.

- Why is Washington considered the American hero of the Revolutionary War? Did he accomplish all that Congress asked him to do? How? Were congressional requests unreasonable or sometimes even impossible?

- What motivated ordinary people to volunteer to join the Continental Army during the Revolutionary War? What made men stay in the army even though they weren't paid and often had no way to support their families back home?

Friend to Foe

The Alienation of British Soldiers and Boston Residents, 1770–1775

Angry Boston crowds confront the British

At a Glance

The American Colonies were settled primarily by people from England. They were created by England. They had always been a part of England. They *wanted* to be English and couldn't imagine being Dutch, French, or—God forbid—Spanish. They had fought side-by-side with England and supported English troops. Americans cheered English soldiers during the French and Indian War. The Colonists swelled with pride when that war was won and the western territories were swept clear of French influence and made safe for the English Colonists to continue their westward march and domination of the continent unimpeded.

That was 1765.

Then the Stamp Act sent a tremor of doubt through the Colonies. They protested. The vile act was repealed, seeming to reaffirm their faith in, and love of, the English and the English system. At the end of the 1760s Americans felt even more English than before. Everyone bought British goods. Everyone of significance was sent to England for an education. American merchants traded exclusively with English merchants. American farmers and plantation owners sold their produce exclusively to England.

But as Britain peered with a sharper eye at its need for income and at these Colonies that were a net financial loss rather than a profit center, the relationship began to change—slowly. Members of Parliament began to resent the freedoms of the Colonies and to feel that it was England's right and duty to make the Colonists pay for their privileges. The Colonists began to see Parliament as a cruel master trying to suck them dry of all their enterprise and independence.

Still, such a great change of attitude happens slowly. In 1774 Benjamin Franklin said, "No man, drunk or sober, is thinking of separating from Great Britain." But in truth, a great number of Colonists by that year *were* thinking very hard about how to protect their independence and their rights while still being part of the British Empire, and a small, active group of men was actively maneuvering the Colonies toward total independence. The average citizen felt the change of attitude very slowly, grudgingly, and reluctantly.

In 1770, British officers like Lieutenant Montgomery Loftsly were heroes in Boston and in great social demand. By 1775 even children sneered when he walked past. No one could remember exactly how those attitudes had changed so drastically. They just knew that they had.

Meet Lieutenant Montgomery Loftsly

Born near Dover, England, in early 1751, Montgomery Loftsly, at age 26 (1776) rose to the rank of captain and division adjutant for one of the divisions under General Howe. He had previously been a favorite of General Gage in Boston and, before Gage took over command of the Boston military, of Governor Hutchinson.

Both of Loftsly's grandfathers reached the rank of colonel. He was named for one of them. His father, a prosperous London merchant, never entered military service. Loftsly was expected to rise quickly through the ranks even though he was slight and non-athletic. Eager to make a name for himself, Loftsly volunteered for service in America and fell in love with Boston.

That was 1771. By 1775, Loftsly felt dumbfounded and betrayed by the Colonists who had so viciously turned against England. Loftsly fought well and bravely during the battles of Long Island and White Plains before he was fatally wounded during the British assault on Fort Washington in November 1776.

Loftsly wrote regular, lengthy letters to several family members and to several British political figures he knew. Many of these people saved Loftsly's letters. A number were later published, in five different books that included first-hand documentation of British and Tory activity during the Revolutionary War. The letters Loftsly wrote to his uncle, which are quoted in this story, are from Balderston and Syrett, *The Lost War: Letters from British Officers during the American Revolution* (New York: Horizon Press, 1979).

Friend to Foe

On the breezy afternoon of September 24, 1771, Lieutenant Montgomery Loftsly arrived in Boston as part of a small military detachment to serve under the colonial governor to protect His Majesty's Massachusetts colony. He was greeted by cheers as he marched stiffly down the gangplank of the Frigate, *Bristol*, onto Griffin's Wharf. The early fall air of Boston seemed alive with the smells of the sea, fish, chimney smoke, and busy industry. It vibrated with the sounds of ships and ropes creaking, gulls screeching for a handout, the clatter of feet and hooves on cobblestones, and eager voices engaged in bustling trade. Maples and elms offered an early display of brilliant colors seemingly just to please the newly arrived officer. Lieutenant Loftsly instantly declared Boston "as fair and pleasant a port as ever I had entered."

Loftsly, only 21, volunteered for service in the American Colonies. He was neither athletic nor a fierce fighter (nor, as he discovered on the five-week voyage across the Atlantic, was his stomach compatible with ocean travel), but he was sure he possessed the aristocratic bearing to make a fine officer. His family, as was common, had bought his commission as an infantry officer for him.

A splendid reception was held for him at Governor Hutchinson's house, the ballroom ablaze with glowing candles. City and colony leaders shook his hand. For one week, Loftsly slept on board the *Bristol*. Then he was quartered with a courteous family on Hanover Street, James and Sarah Thatcher. It was common for Britain to require that local families house and feed officers stationed in her colonies.

The Thatchers felt it an honor to host a dashing British infantry officer. It gave them an excuse to host parties and took them up a peg on the Boston social ladder. Thatcher owned a warehouse and half-interest in a cooperage on Fish Street. The couple had no children but had a live-in, permanently smiling housekeeper, Mrs. Potters, the wife of a sailor on a whaling ship out just over four months.

Loftsly quickly settled into leisurely colonial life. After performing minor duties for the colonial governor each morning, he had seemingly endless hours in which to socialize, eat, sip tea in public houses during afternoon talks of weather, social, and local matters, and swig ale and American rum (which he truly enjoyed) in the evenings at taverns where the talk turned political.

By December, Loftsly had become a welcome, cash-paying regular at the Green Dragon and the Golden Crown. He bought more than his share of rounds of rum and loved leisurely chats with these friendly, loyal, straightforward Colonists. He enjoyed every slap on the back by a jovial local in thanks for the rum he provided. Wandering home, he glowed in the happy memory of the evening's laughter.

Luckily, Loftsly came from a moneyed family and so didn't have to survive on the meager lieutenant's pay alone. It was worse for the common soldiers, who earned only two pence a day and had to take second jobs to meet their basic expenses.

By the time the first hints of spring buds crept onto tree limbs in 1772, Loftsly had forgotten that there had ever been any other life than this. In the mornings Mrs. Potters baked delicious rolls. She drank American coffee to honor the boycott on British goods; Loftsly sipped tea and they talked for an hour or more in the Thatchers' kitchen. Then Loftsly spent several hours cramming himself into his uniform. As an officer, his uniform was expected to be always picture perfect, yet it was tiresomely uncomfortable. Regulations required that his hair be worn in clubbed pigtails, which were difficult and time consuming to create and pulled at his scalp. Were he not an officer, and thus expected to set a example, he would have ripped them out and happily scratched his scalp for hours on end.

Properly dressed, Loftsly checked in at the governor's office and held inspection at the military barracks for the 50-plus troops assigned to the governor's office. A good officer, Loftsly insisted that the men maintain a perfect appearance. All infractions were immediately punished, not because Loftsly thought appearance was that important, but because discipline was all-important. Discipline was the key to British success. If the men were allowed to grow lax in *one* area, they would surely grow lax in *every* area. And that could not be allowed to happen.

After inspection, Loftsly picked a tea house for a leisurely lunch, even though these establishments no longer served tea. Certainly the juvenile, misdirected boycott against British goods (especially tea) was senseless and irksome. Coffee was a disgusting abomination of a liquid, fit only to terrorize demons and witches. Still, Loftsly tried to avoid creating friction by quietly drinking his tea in private instead of touting the superiority of British wares. The Colonists were slitting their own throats with this foolishness. What irritated Loftsly most was that they seemed to blame Parliament for their own decision to ruin their lives by not using superior British goods.

The afternoons became Loftsly's favorite time of day. He met with Rebecca and Jeremiah Thompson, two neighbor children. The Thompsons lived around the corner on Sudbury Street. Jeremiah was five, Rebecca was seven. Loftsly was happily teaching them world geography and how to read. Rebecca was exceedingly bright and learned quickly. Jeremiah would rather play, and thought reading and letters a silly waste of time. Loftsly delighted in their giggles, how they fawned over his uniform, and how Jeremiah loved to wear his hat, which flopped down almost to his shoulders while he pretended to be a British officer.

Loftsly also delighted in how the children peered out the window, waiting for him to cross the intersection and how they hung on his every word. Rebecca begged for stories of adventures in far-off lands and for detailed descriptions of Loftsly's home in a country town south of London.

Jeremiah loved to fish, and he and Loftsly found a secret fishing spot at the far end of the Mill Dam separating Mill Pond from the back bay. Loftsly delighted in Jeremiah's concentration when he flung his baited hook into the dark waters and the eagerness with which he reeled it in.

By summer Loftsly felt like a doting uncle and saved two months' pay to buy Rebecca a rocking horse for her eighth birthday. He felt more proud that he was the only non-family member invited to this party than he had been when his unit passed inspection with no demerits or whippings. He was overjoyed when Rebecca announced that the rocking horse was her favorite birthday gift.

True, the brightly painted rocking horse raised some murmurs of resentment from the Thompsons. There was a growing undercurrent of anger spreading among the Colonists. For some inexplicable reason, they blamed England for their lack of money. Of course the charge was totally unfounded. Life in America was too easy to develop ambition and a hard-nosed work ethic. That was the problem. These Colonists were a pleasant people, but soft and not particularly intelligent. It could never be expected that they would rise out of the lower classes of any civilized society.

During a bleak February in 1773, Lieutenant Loftsly sat alone musing over a cup of tea (which the owner of the Blue Swallow had almost refused to serve) about how the Colonists were poisoning their own lives. It was the work of those evil Sons of Liberty, whispering their slanderous lies everywhere. They and the shadowy group called "the Mechanics" were creating all the problems.

"Not so shadowy," chuckled Loftsly. The governor had a file on Paul Revere and the other known members of this supposedly secret gang. But somehow it didn't matter that they had incriminating evidence. Rumors carried more weight than evidence in this new, suspicious Boston.

Almost overnight, Boston had become a town driven by rumors and shadowy half-truths. Such whispered beasts seemed to come alive and creep down the darkened night streets into every house, ear, heart, and mind. Like a sorcerer's poison, the unending rumors seemed to have turned friendly smiles to stone.

Loftsly couldn't go to the Green Dragon any more. The same patrons who had eagerly lapped up the rounds he had hosted last year now sneered, turned a cold shoulder when he stepped inside the door, and seemed to resent his very existence. Whispers followed him down the street. Pairs of the Sons of Liberty shadowed his movements. Loftsly was suddenly excluded from even social conversation.

The practice of shoulder banging had begun. Ordinary citizens would smack shoulders with soldiers as they passed each other on the street, pretending it was an accident, but really conveying their new-found scorn for everything British. Were these the same Colonists who had greeted Loftsly with cheers 18 short months earlier? Anger seemed to seep up from the streets and permeate every heart.

Lieutenant Loftsly shrugged off the change until Mr. Thompson requested that he no longer visit the children. Thompson was polite about it and claimed it was nothing personal but rather just a sign of the times. But it *was* personal, as personal as a broken heart can be. Loftsly still hoped to bump into the children on the street. But the streets of Boston had lost their cheery, welcoming bustle and were no longer a place for a British soldier to linger.

Loftsly sat with Mrs. Potters over cinnamon rolls one morning in August. "I have done nothing to these people. The Governor has done nothing. The soldiers have done nothing. And yet the smiles are gone, replaced by sneers and angry glares."

"Do you support Parliament?" asked Mrs. Potters, munching a fragrant roll.

"Certainly. Parliament passes the legal and legitimate laws of the empire."

"Do you support the King?"

"Of course. I am the King's servant."

"Then you have done quite enough to deserve the scorn of every Bostonian," concluded Mrs. Potters, slurping her American coffee.

Loftsly poured out his frustration to Governor Hutchinson. "Nothing has physically changed, and yet everything in this city has changed for the worse."

"We know who's behind it," answered Hutchinson, wearily rubbing his forehead. "Sam Adams and John Hancock. They are fanning a bitter flame of resentment all across New England."

"Arrest them!"

Hutchinson shrugged helplessly. "We are ordered to avoid confrontation. And believe me, Lieutenant, arresting those two would create a bigger confrontation than your troops could handle."

It was understandable that Hancock would be part of this movement. He was a businessman and his business was being hurt by the boycott and by the current set of taxes—even though they were fair and just. Of course *he* would look for some way to improve his advantage in the marketplace.

"But Adams," continued Lieutenant Loftsly. "He scares me. He's a wild radical with nothing to lose. He's willing to gamble everything for his wild ideas."

On the lonely night walk back to the Thatchers' house, where he now felt about as welcome as the pox, Loftsly groused that resentment seemed to be more common (and more bitter) than disgusting American coffee. The clatter of two pairs of hobnailed boots followed him down the street as the Sons of Liberty spies who had been assigned to tail him flitted through the shadows.

Loftsly muttered, "These Colonists are making my life miserable. And yet, I still feel that, if I were to strike an American, I would wound a brother." He turned and said loudly to the shadows following behind him, "Can't you understand that?"

There was no reply other than the soft clicking of hobnail boots on the cobblestones.

In a letter to his uncle, Loftsly wrote, "I fear that the radicals are looking only for an excuse for a fight, for pointless war. I fear that they have picked the tea as the focal point of their lies and propaganda. If cooler heads do not prevail, Adams will surely turn tea into a nasty business."

Two months later the Boston Tea Party galvanized anti-British sentiment across the continent. Throughout 1774 Boston slowly polarized into armed camps, Loyalist and Patriot. The gulf between them grew too wide for words to bridge. Lieutenant Loftsly again wrote to his uncle:

I feel like a foreigner in my own rooms. The world is now ruled by spies and their rumors—rumors of what we are about to do, of what the rebels are about to do. The rumors lead to division, to distrust, to hate.

I am treated like an evil invader instead of noble protector. The rabble and scum on the street show no respect for uniform, rank or crown. These dogs need to be taught a lesson. More troops are arriving soon and we shall shut the port. That is a small pittance of what we *should* do to these vile Sons of Liberty.

Virtually all soldiers have lost local jobs and live in abject poverty. They grow resentful, bitter, and angry. Soon they shall want to take out their aggressions on someone, and I fear for the safety of all.

Shoulder banging and taunts had become daily occurrences. Loftsly rarely ventured out except on official business. He regularly ate and drank alone, locked in his own rooms.

Daily it grew harder for him to control his troops. They yearned for permission to knock the Sons of Liberty about and let their blood show them the folly of their rebellious ways. Daily Loftsly wavered. He yearned to look the other way and allow his soldiers to attack. He agreed with his troops that these nasty Bostonians had invented resentment and hatred all on their own. They had grown mean and no longer listened to reason. Some evil gripped their minds. Best to knock it out of them with the butt of a musket.

Only the firm, steady hand of Governor Hutchinson held Loftsly and his troops in check.

One afternoon in September 1774, Jeremiah passed Loftsly on the street and spit at him. Eight years old and he spit! His face was filled with rage and scorn that he could not possibly understand. Loftsly yelled, "I taught you to juggle and to fish. You held my hand as we walked to our secret fishing spot."

Jeremiah curled his lips back like an angry dog and then spit again as if he could see only Loftsly's uniform and had forgotten there was a person inside.

Rebecca was with him. Loftsly smiled and reached out to her. "Hello, Rebecca. How have you been?" She glared hard and cold and tried to shoulder bang him.

"Rebecca!" he cried. "I taught you to read. I went to your birthday. You called me uncle!"

She sneered and looked at him as if he were a demon. Loftsly numbly stumbled home, feeling as if he had been stabbed in the back, and that love and kindness were no longer possible in that cursed place.

Loftsly wrote to his uncle:

There is a foul poison that has settled over these people as if by a sorcerer's spell. Sam Adams is, I am convinced, the name of the evil sorcerer. General Gage's sources have just learned that Mrs. Potters, the Thatchers' house keeper, has been spying on me for the Sons of Liberty for over a year! I helped her with wash and carried fire wood for her. I glee-fully ate even her most burned biscuits and rolls, and this is the thanks I get!

These are evil times and this has become an evil colony. They are nothing without British protection and rule. They need us, but they have abused and taken advantage of us. They have consistently refused to support the Empire that shelters and civilizes them and pay their fair share. And yet they act as if I, personally, was the source of all their misery, as if I had per-sonally insulted each of them by my mere existence.

I hate this assignment and cannot wait to leave.

By April 1775 the smoldering fire had erupted into the flames of musket ex-plosions and a thousand army campfires that shone bright and hot each night until they paled with the growing dawn. And now it was war. Boston was an armed camp, surrounded by a hostile army.

Lieutenant Loftsly commanded one section of the evening watch on the for-tifications guarding Boston neck. Standing next to Major Pitcairn, he glared across the earth and log ramparts at the shadowy figures that huddled around the flickering light of the fires.

"I despise their twisted, sneaky, underhanded ways."

"They are just simple-minded, misguided farmers," answered Pitcairn.

"They are evil, devious, cowardly, and loathsome."

Pitcairn shook his head. In the brisk night air he could see his own breath. "Capture a dozen of the leaders and the rest will simply go back home to their farms. It is only Adams, Hancock, and the like we need worry about."

Loftsly pointed an angry finger across the no-man's land between the ar-mies. "No! They are *all* the enemy. Their spits, slurs, and bangs have earned them the title of traitor and enemy. I want to conquer and, if necessary, kill them all."

"Soften your anger, Loftsly," cautioned Pitcairn. "A commander must lead by cool logic, not by passion."

That night Loftsly wrote:

Passion is all I have left—passion to revenge these spiteful traitors for filling me with anger and hate. We arrest Whigs at the drop of a hat. I care not anymore if they are guilty or innocent so long as they rot in jail. Our animals are starving in the midst of the world's most powerful army in the midst of the most plentiful country on Earth. It infuriates me and confirms what cold-hearted cowards these Americans are. How did the happy Boston of three years ago disappear? Where did it go?

I saw Rebecca Thompson on the street yesterday and yelled at her to explain where she was going. Two soldiers cornered and threatened her. I laughed and felt no remorse as a look of fear and dread spread across her face. Then I turned away and wept for the friendships and pleasures that have been destroyed by this cruel and unexplainable hatred of the Americans. Rebecca is hard and cold. I saw none of the excitement, wonder, and eager joy that used to spill out from her countenance. I am equally hard and cold. Is there no way to stop this madness?

The hungry drums of war could not, would not, be silenced. Lieutenant Loftsly was killed in November 1776, during the attack to conquer Ft. Washington in New York.

Aftermath

The polarization of the New England community surrounding Boston between 1771 and 1775 became a model for how the entire country would fracture between 1773 and 1778. Although anti-British sentiment peaked early in and around Boston, the bitter and often brutal conflicts between Patriot and Tory factions did not develop there as they did in many other parts of the country. After the British forces evacuated Boston in March 1776, that original hotbed of revolutionary fervor remained surprisingly quiet and peaceful throughout the remainder of the war. Boston was the spark that lit the fires of war, but the war itself burned elsewhere in the Colonies. Boston remained uneventful—even peaceful—during the long Revolutionary War.

Follow-up Questions and Activities

1. **What Do You Know?**
   - What is a frigate? Is a frigate different from a schooner or a navy ship-of-the-line?
   - Who was Governor Hutchinson? What power did he have? What did colonial governors do? Did every Colony have a British governor?
   - Why did British soldiers have to dress so neatly and perfectly every day? Why were officers so concerned with how their troops looked?
   - Why were British officers popular social figures in 1770? Why were they so despised five years later?

2. **Finding Out More.** Following are three important topics from this story for you to research in the library and on the Internet. The reference sources at the back of this book will help you get started.
   - Research the British military hierarchy in the 1700s. What were the enlisted ranks? Did soldiers volunteer, or were they drafted? What were the officer ranks? How did someone become an officer? How did an officer advance in rank? How many soldiers and officers were there in the British army?

- Identify another British officer who kept a journal that has been published or who wrote extensive letters back to Britain that were saved and later published. Research his experiences and compare them with those of Lieutenant Loftsly.

- Research Boston at the beginning of the Revolutionary War. What was life like? What kinds of jobs and industry existed in Boston in 1775? How many and what kind of people lived there? What did they do? How many were educated? Were there restaurants? Did most people eat out a lot? What did they do for fun?

3. **Make It Real**

- It took a minimum of three months for a letter to cross the Atlantic Ocean to London and for the reply to return to America. Think back over the past three months and make a chart of things that have happened to you during those months. Have any of your feelings or attitudes changed? Are the questions you asked three months ago still the most important to you now? Does this exercise help you to understand how difficult it was for the British commanders in America to make requests of Parliament and to follow their orders?

- Often the Colonists had no more than rumors on which to base their decisions about other people. Why are rumors so powerful and believable? Start a rumor at school and see how fast it spreads through the whole school. What kind of rumor will you start? Rumors can be malicious and damaging. Make sure you choose a rumor that won't hurt anyone. As suggestions, start a rumor that Christmas break will be three days longer (or shorter) than originally scheduled, or that a favorite movie star will visit the school. Avoid rumors that involve anyone in the school community or their families.

  How will you make sure that other students believe your rumor? Chart how far and fast the rumor spreads. What keeps it alive? What destroys the rumor?

- Keep a journal. Write in it every day about your feelings, friends, and family. At the end of three months, read it and notice any changes that have occurred over that short period.

- Find out how much of the world was under British control in 1770. Make a map of each continent and color areas under British control red. Where else besides America were British officers likely to be stationed?

4. **Points to Ponder**

- Have you ever had a friend who, over time, changed into an enemy? Why did it happen? How? Whose fault was it? Can you imagine this happening to whole groups of people as it did during the years preceding the Revolutionary War? What role do you think a lack of communication between groups plays in creating the alienation and mistrust that dissolve the bonds of friendship?

- Why do you think communication between the Colonies and London was so poor? Why was it so difficult for the British in America to get clear directions from London?

- Why was Boston such a hotbed of revolutionary fervor at the beginning of the war? Why did conflict erupt there instead of in the south or in the mid-Atlantic states?

1776 at a Glance

Drums of Glory; Face of Disaster

The year 1776 began on a thrilling crescendo for the Patriots. America had risen up against the tyrant Britain. Although the invasion force in Canada was faltering, disease was at fault more than battle losses. Patriots throughout the full length of the Colonies heard the stirring beat of the drums of liberty, and the ranks of Patriot militia and army swelled. Washington had the British penned up in Boston. Congress was trying to organize a country. Thomas Paine's *Common Sense* had been published and stirred the blood of every continental soul. In the south, Redcoats and Loyalists were soundly defeated at Moore's Creek Bridge.

Finally, in March British General Howe gave up on Boston and evacuated. It seemed that the Patriot cause was destined for an easy and swift victory. This feeling was confirmed when the British attack on Charleston was repulsed in June. America felt invincible, even though the invasion of Canada had failed and the survivors had limped home in defeat.

To top it all off, Congress passed a Declaration of Independence. It felt like a time to celebrate.

Then the war began in earnest. British forces gathered 30,000 strong in New York harbor. The Battle of Long Island (August) was a complete disaster; American forces were routed. Suddenly Washington's army seemed to dissolve. They lost Manhattan and battles at Harlem Heights and White Plains. The supposedly unconquerable twin forts along the Hudson River, Forts Washington and Lee, both fell. Washington's rag-tag rabble seemed to sprint in retreat across New Jersey to hide from the unstoppable British.

America reeled in shock. What had seemed to be certain triumph in early August appeared to be disastrous defeat four short months later.

In mid-December Thomas Paine wrote *American Crisis*. ("These are the times that try men's souls. . . .") Everyone grimly nodded and muttered, "You've got that right!" The fire had left the revolutionary spirit of the country, the wind had dropped from her sails. It was a desperate time when the Revolution hung by the thinnest of threads. A victory—any victory—was needed to rally the hopes of soldiers and the support of the people.

Washington, to his great credit, found just such a triumphant note to play when he attacked Trenton the day after Christmas and Princeton six days later. The roller coaster year of 1776 closed with a ray of hope.

Key Events in 1776

Date	Event
January 1	British Lord Dunmore burns Norfolk to punish rebels.
January 10	Thomas Paine publishes *Common Sense*.
February 27	Patriot victory at Moore's Creek Bridge, Virginia.
March 15	Washington mounts cannons on Bemis Heights overlooking Boston.
March 17	British evacuate Boston.
May 6	Americans' final attack on British at Quebec fails, ending the invasion of Canada.
Early June	Washington moves his army to New York to defend the all-important Hudson River.
June 12	Virginia becomes the first independent state by adopting a state constitution.
June 28	British attack on Charleston fails.
July 2	Declaration of Independence is passed.
July 4	Declaration of Independence is announced to the public.
August 27	Battle of Long Island (New York).
September 16	Battle of Harlem Heights (New York).
October 28	Battle of White Plains (New York).
November 16	Fort Washington (New York) surrenders.
November 23	Fort Lee (New Jersey) surrenders.
December 13	The retreating Continental Army abandons New Jersey.
December 26	Attack on Trenton.
January 3, 1777	Attack on Princeton.

Children Choose
Friends Torn Apart by Political Loyalties, 1776

Angry colonial mob

At a Glance

A small but passionate and vocal minority of Colonists actively favored independence. Approximately an equal number were adamantly against independence. The vast majority lay in the middle. They felt loyalty to both sides, but did not passionately support either. They had always been British citizens and part of the British system. They had also always been Americans. How could they choose between country and mother?

But choose they must. That was where the real revolution occurred, in the minds and hearts of ordinary American citizens. In many respects, the "real war" wasn't fought on battlefields, but in small towns across the continent. This war was fought not with soldiers, but between ordinary citizens who had to wrestle with their own consciences and then with their loved and trusted neighbors in the public squares of their towns. This struggle tore apart communities and entire colonies, but somehow in the process forged a new nation. Even in small, rural towns, childhood friends often found themselves divided by a burning conflict and hatred they could not fully understand.

Meet Rebecca Vandermeer

Rebecca Vandermeer was born in late 1766 in Poughkeepsie, New York, into a life of ease and comfort. Her father was a wealthy local merchant and an ardent supporter of Britain who became an active Tory during the war. Her mother came from a family with great land holdings in western Connecticut. Rebecca never took to the refined life her father laid out for her. She would rather romp barefoot with the local boys than attend finishing classes after school.

Rebecca's father was forced to abandon his businesses in 1779 after repeated Patriot threats to both the businesses and his family's lives, and fled with his family to England.

In 1786, Rebecca (then 19) returned to America and settled in Albany, New York, where she taught school for four years before marrying the owner of a timber company. She was killed in an accident at the lumber mill in 1809 (at the age of 43), leaving a husband and two daughters.

Children Choose

"Jeremy Schlister! You are the dumbest person in the world!"

Eleven-year-old Rebecca Vandermeer was so mad she screamed it out for the entire world to hear—well, at least for the entire town of Poughkeepsie, New York, nestled along the Hudson River almost 60 miles up river from Manhattan—as she stood barefoot in the dirt street, carrying her expensive English shoes and stockings in one hand.

Twelve-year-old Jeremy just laughed, "What's the matter, Becky? You scared to race me?"

Rebecca shook her free fist in Jeremy's face. She was taller, but he was compact and quicker. "I most certainly am not! It's just a dumb bet and . . . and you still have to apologize to the King."

"Never! You're just scared. My father says all Tories are scaredy-cats."

Two other boys paused to watch, and both laughed and pointed at Rebecca.

Rebecca felt so angry at her lifelong friend, she trembled bright red. A warm breeze pushed cotton-ball clouds through a crystal blue sky on this gorgeous day of Tuesday, August 6, 1776, as Rebecca spun round and, not knowing what else to do, ran home before tears flooded into her eyes. All the way she could hear Jeremy's cruel laughter ringing in her ears.

Rebecca's mother found her crying on the front steps of the Vandermeer's spacious wood frame house. "What's wrong, dear?"

Rebecca wiped her eyes with the backs of her hands and sucked in a long slow breath to calm herself. "We were just talking . . . "

"We?"

"Jeremy and me."

Mrs. Vandermeer smiled. "You two have played together since you were three. What happened?"

"I said something about the King and Jeremy spit on the King's name!"

"He actually *spit*?"

Rebecca solemnly nodded. "Said his father told him that's what he *should* do. But of course it isn't. Is it?"

Mrs. Vandermeer's mouth and jaw tightened. Her eyes lost their sparkle. "The Schlisters *would* say something crude like that. Is that what this is all about?"

"Well, that . . . and then Jeremy bragged that he could swim across the Hudson faster than me. Well, he can't."

"I know dear. You're a good swimmer," said Mrs. Vandermeer, sinking onto the step beside her daughter.

"Jeremy can barely swim. But he wouldn't give up. Just kept harping and taunting me."

" 'Taunting.' That's a nice word, Rebecca. One of your new vocabulary words?"

"Yes mother. One of eight I learned yesterday. But it fits Jeremy Schlister all over—taunting and teasing. He probably would have drowned halfway across and I'd have to save him."

"Don't swim across the Hudson, Rebecca. The current is too strong."

"That's not the point, mother. The point is how stubborn Jeremy is. And . . . and . . . why would he . . . "

"Spit on the King's name?" Mrs. Vandermeer paused and looked away as if deciding whether or not to answer. Then she turned back, her face set cold and hard. "Because his parents are common rebels. He farms a stingy little plot."

"It's a nice farm," interrupted Rebecca. "They even have a pig."

"*One* pig," said her mother. "They wear rags and the children have to go barefoot. She has to take in sewing on the side to make ends meet. And then they blame the King and Parliament for the troubles they have brought upon themselves."

"This world has gone mad!" Mr. Vandermeer bellowed on entering his house that night.

"What now?" asked his wife.

Mr. Vandermeer was a trim man who wore fashionable English stockings, breeches, and coats. To some he appeared frail and prissy. "A self-appointed Committee of Safety paid me a visit today and insisted I wear American-made clothes. I replied, 'When Americans learn how to make decent clothes I will gladly wear them.' "

"How many were there, father?" This from Rebecca.

"Six. I'm sure they meant to intimidate me."

Mrs. Vandermeer recoiled in fear. "You actually said that?"

Chuckling, Mr. Vandermeer said, "I certainly did. They can't bully me. I own two very profitable stores in this town. Then they said I'd have to stop carrying English goods. I said, 'When there is something else I can legally import and sell at a decent profit, I will.' "

"Oh, dear. I hope you didn't make them angry."

Vandermeer's faced reddened as he bellowed, "One of them was waving a copy of that damnable Declaration of Independence as if one worthless piece of paper gave them the right to order decent, law-abiding citizens around. They even threatened to burn down my stores! They call themselves Patriots. Phooey! I spit on the word! They're nothing but common thugs and vandals!"

"That's what Jeremy did today," added Rebecca in a quiet, solemn voice.

"*What* is? Burn down a store?"

"No, father. He spit . . . on the King's name."

Vandermeer's thin forefinger wagged at his daughter. "His father was one of this committee of hoodlums. They are rotten, evil people. You shouldn't play with their kind anymore."

"But father! Jeremy has *always* been my best friend. He's not a hoodlum. Who else can I play with?"

"Find someone of our own kind. But don't play with him."

"But . . . but, why isn't *Jeremy* my kind?"

"The Schlisters are rebels, out to poison the natural order of the world."

"Jeremy isn't a rebel. He's just a boy."

Mr. Vandermeer's lips tightened as he scowled. "No! If I allow you to associate with a rebel child, some in this town will assume that we have rebel leanings."

Rebecca pleaded, "I just want to play with him. . . . Well, most of the time I do."

"No. Now that that Declaration has been passed, we each have to make our position and loyalties clear and consistent."

"But . . ."

"Enough! You will not play with, or like, that rebel boy any further. I'm sorry, Rebecca, but that is the way it is going to have to be."

Mr. Vandermeer pointed angrily at Rebecca's bare feet. "And why don't you have on the proper shoes of a young lady?"

"I hate shoes."

"I will not have you romping through town like an uneducated commoner. Wear your shoes or I'll never be able to place you in a fine English finishing school."

In an almost inaudibly small voice, Rebecca said to her father's back as he marched toward the kitchen, "I still like Jeremy. . . . And I still hate shoes."

Late the next morning Rebecca and Jeremy awkwardly circled toward each other in the school yard.

"Where you been?" Jeremy demanded.

"Learning new vocabulary words so I won't be *ignorant.*"

"Be what?" Jeremy squealed.

Rebecca proudly smiled. "That's one of my new words for today. And it's what you'll be if you don't study more."

Jeremy shrugged. "Who cares about school? It won't help grow food."

"*I* care," Rebecca snapped.

Eyes downcast onto his bare feet, Jeremy started, "Sorry 'bout yesterday."

She also looked down. "That's okay." Rebecca carried her shoes and stockings in one hand so she could run barefoot through the thick summer grass.

"I know you're a better swimmer," he continued. "I just . . . "

She interrupted. "I said it was okay."

He pawed at the grass, searching for the right words. "My parents said we can't play together any more."

"Just because I'm a better swimmer?"

"Because you're a stinking Tory who hates America."

Rebecca instinctively lashed out, pushing Jeremy back. "You take that back, Jeremy Schlister! I love America and I don't stink!"

Jeremy made no move to retaliate for the shove. His eyes were still locked onto his feet, which continued to paw at the grass. "I know. But that's what my Dad says."

"Well, he's wrong!"

"I know . . . I guess."

Rebecca's eyes bored into her friend's face. "My parents said the same about you."

"That I'm a Tory? I am not! I . . ."

"No. That you hate America and are trying to ruin it."

"Oh. . . . Well, they're wrong!"

"I know. . . . I guess."

Jeremy flopped onto the grass. "This war has made my parents crazy. It's all they talk about anymore . . . "

Rebecca nodded. "My parents think who I choose for friends will make them turn into rebels."

"They mean, *me*. Don't they?"

Rebecca lowered her eyes and sadly nodded.

Jeremy shook his head. "But I don't care what they say. *We're* not at war."

"Agreed. Friends?" Rebecca asked, beginning to smile.

"Friends," concluded Jeremy. "And I'm still faster than you!" He sprang to his feet and dashed toward a distant tree. "First one to the school house tree wins!"

"You cheated!" screamed Rebecca, tossing her shoes aside as she raced after him.

By early afternoon Jeremy had to head back home to finish his farm chores.

"I'll help," Rebecca offered. "I like your farm."

Jeremy hesitated. "You better not. If my father caught you out there . . . "

Both children paused and cocked their heads as the sound of a rumbling commotion back near the center of town drifted toward the school yard. They raced to see what was afoot and found a thick crowd packed onto Williams Street, blocking their view. The outer rows of adults also strained to see, leaning this way and that, rising onto tiptoes. Nearer the center they could hear shouting—angry, vicious, and mean.

The thunderclap of a musket shot made the crowd gasp and squeal. Screams rose from the center along with frantic shouts and threats.

Rebecca and Jeremy were stuck behind a wall of adults packed sardine-tight and couldn't see a thing. But the threats and growls made them both shiver. "Come on," whispered Jeremy, grasping Rebecca's hand. "I gotta see this." Ducking, crawling, wiggling, he led her, threading their way to the inside.

Two packs of angry, glaring men faced each other on the street like miniature armies on a battlefield. Bricks, knives, and clubs were held high in the air. Several men held muskets. One of the guns was still smoking. Each man stared, dumbstruck, like the frozen tableau of a painting.

"He was going to throw that knife at me, I swear it," stammered the man holding the smoking musket.

"You've killed him!" hissed a man who was cradling the head and shoulders of another man lying in a growing pool of his own blood.

Rebecca stood, rooted to the rut-filled road, and stared wide-eyed at the growing pool of blood. Human blood had been spilled in Poughkeepsie! She could scarcely make herself breathe. Jeremy stared at the man holding the smoking gun. It was his father's cousin and best friend.

"I swear. It was self-defense."

A uniformed constable arrived, blowing frantically on his whistle, and muscled his way through the crowd. "What's all this now?" he demanded, trying to restore calm and order.

Mr. Vandermeer, standing beside the fallen man, shook an angry finger at the opposing mob of men. His voice squeaked out high and tight. "Those . . . thugs of the rebel Committee of Safety started this—pushing and shoving elderly Mr. Balkner just because he properly supports the King and Parliament. We came to his defense and tried to break it up . . . "

"Tryin' to drive us out of town by raising prices 'til we bleed is what you do," shouted one of the opposing men.

"Not true," bellowed Mr. Vandermeer. "I charge a fair . . . "

"This town will be better off when the likes of you are run out on a rail!" shouted another. All the men on that side growled their agreement.

"This is America," shouted another man, whom Rebecca recognized as Jeremy's father. "Crawl back to England if you want to kiss the King's toesies."

The rebel side laughed.

The constable raised his hands and scowled in turn at both mobs of men. "Order! Order! I will have order here! This is not a war . . . "

"Yes it is," shouted one of the rebels, shaking a copy of the Declaration of Independence in his clenched fist. "A war for our liberty!"

"Not here it's not!" shouted the constable. "There's no war in Poughkeepsie. Let's be civil and put down the weapons."

There followed much grumbling from both sides and painfully slow compliance as those in the front rows lowered guns, re-sheathed knives, and dropped bricks, clubs, and stones.

Rebecca's heart pounded at the deadly tension of this drama. It terrified her to see adults from her very own community turn on each other like savage animals. She felt that every shred of safety had been stripped away and that Poughkeepsie had turned into a wild jungle.

A heavy brick sailed from the back of the rebel side and struck Mr. Vandermeer over his left eye. He collapsed on the street. Thick streams of blood flowed across his face and hair to mix with the dust of Williams Street.

Rebecca screamed and, still clutching Jeremy's hand, raced to her father.

A shot rang out from a rooftop and the rebel who had thrown the brick spun like a scarecrow and dropped.

Again the mob froze, feeling the sobering chill of musket fire and blood.

"Cease this firing!" screamed the constable as a police squad of reinforcements raced in, blowing their shrill whistles, cheeks puffed out, elbowing through the crowd.

Jeremy's father saw him still standing with Rebecca as she knelt, trembling, next to her father. "Get over here, boy. What are you doin' on the stinkin' Tories' side?"

Embarrassed at suddenly being the center of attention, Jeremy dropped his head and scurried to his father. Mr. Schlister whacked Jeremy's ear hard with his open hand. "I tole you not to play with her no more, boy!" Mr. Schlister actually lifted Jeremy off the ground by his shoulders and shook him violently like a rag doll before slamming him back down.

"But father . . . " Jeremy began. Whap! Mr. Schlister's fist slammed into the side of his son's head, making Jeremy's knees wobble.

The crowd slowly dissipated as a line of police separated Patriot and Loyalist. Each side hurled angry taunts and threats as they retreated. An eerie calm and three pools of blood were left to mark the spot of Poughkeepsie's entry into the Revolutionary War.

Rebecca and Jeremy met the next day at school. As accusingly as if he had done it himself, Rebecca said to him, "Your father's friends almost killed my father."

He lashed back, "My uncle was shot by your father's Tories."

She replied, "My father says there will be a lot more rebel blood spilled around here unless certain people stop trying to ruin things with a *rebellion*—That's one of my new words for today."

He answered, "My father says everyone has to choose. And either you're *for* the revolution and liberty or you're *against* it."

Rebecca slapped her hands against her sides in frustration. "I don't care about the *war*, Jeremy Schlister! I care about my father getting hit with bricks and about being safe when I walk to school."

Jeremy insisted, "You *can't* say you don't care. My parents said everyone *has* to care."

"Well, *my* parents said America is—or *was*—just fine the way it was until rebels began to invent problems."

Two older boys (with a young girl tagging along beside them) watched from across the street. One yelled at Jeremy, "Why are you talking to a *Tory*?" The other sneered, "You must be one yerself! You're probably a King lover. Think I'll go tell your father." He continued in a whiny, sing-song voice, "Jeremy is a Tory. . . . Jeremy is a Tory."

"I am not!" Jeremy yelled back, turning beet red.

"Don't let them *taunt* you. They're just *ignorant*," Rebecca whispered.

Jeremy angrily shrank away from her. "I'm not a Tory!"

The boys swaggered across the street. The young girl followed at their heels. "Then why are you talking to *her*?"

One of the boys shoved Rebecca. She sprawled onto the grass, only to bound back to her feet. "You stop that, Miles Hoffman!"

Jeremy looked at her, and then at the two boys glaring at her. Miles sneered, "My dad said she loves the King, so *she's* the enemy!" and pushed Rebecca again. She was ready for it and only rocked back with the blow. Miles turned to Jeremy. "And if you talk to her, then my dad says you're the enemy, too." And he shoved Jeremy on the shoulder.

The young girl darted out from behind her brother's legs and kicked Rebecca. When Rebecca doubled over to grab her shin, the girl spit on her.

The older boys laughed. One pushed Rebecca again, hard. She crashed down, tearing her dress and grinding her face into the dirt. Almost as fast as she fell, Rebecca scrambled back to her feet, eyes filled with fury, fists clenched.

Jeremy looked from Rebecca—dress ripped and stained with smears of dirt and grass, nose trickling blood—to the two boys. Back to Rebecca. Back to the boys.

Miles Hoffman turned to Jeremy and demanded, "Should I tell everyone that you're a Tory lover, or are you going to stand up for your liberty like a man?"

All eyes turned to Jeremy as his gaze flitted from Rebecca to the boys and back. He slowly stepped to Rebecca.

She tried to hide a smile as she whispered, "Whew! For a minute I thought . . . "

He whispered, "Sorry," and shoved her viciously into a row of bushes along the edge of the school yard. Rebecca sprawled through the thorny hedge and tumbled across the grass.

Jeremy shouted, "I choose America!" With arms around the shoulders of the older boys, he laughed and pointed at Rebecca's mud-smeared face and ruined dress.

Rage burned deep inside Rebecca. She snatched up a rock, glared at Jeremy, and reached back to take aim. The bitterness of the Revolutionary War had settled on Poughkeepsie, New York. Rebecca had never felt such anger and loss in all her life.

Aftermath

This story, this scene, or scenes very much like it, were repeated hundreds of times up and down the Colonies until the war ended in late 1782. This "real war" created much of the heartbreak and anguish that accompanied our Revolutionary War. Yet it was through these intra-community struggles that the conviction, values, and principles of a new nation were forged.

Follow-up Questions and Activities

1. **What Do You Know?**

   - How many Colonists supported the Revolution in 1770? In 1775? In 1778? How many supported it at the end of the war? What caused the change in attitude?

   - What was a Committee of Safety, and what did its members do? Did they have strong links to the Committees of Correspondence?

   - What was a constable? What would we call someone in that position today? Where did the title "constable" come from?

   - What type of people tended to be Tories and what type tended to be Patriots? Can you name any general characteristics? Did wealth, social standing, or profession tend to affect a person's persuasions?

2. **Finding Out More.** Following are three important topics from this story for you to research in the library and on the Internet. The reference sources at the back of this book will help you get started.

   - What were the population demographics in America during the Revolutionary War? Where did people live? How spread out were they? On average, how many lived in each colony? In cities? What occupations did they have?

   - Public schools, which provide you with a strong, general education, were not available to colonial children. What kinds of school were available in the mid-1700s? Who was able to go? How much did schools cost? Which schools allowed girls? Which were for boys only? What did each kind of school teach? What did children your age learn at school in 1770?

   - The vast majority of Americans were farmers. What did they grow? What equipment did they use? How big were their farms? Research farming practices in the mid-1770s. How would a typical farm at that time differ from a typical American farm today?

3. **Make It Real**

- Pretend to be either a Patriot or a Tory child of your own age in the summer of 1776. In as much detail as possible, describe your daily life: activities, friends, chores, what you do with your free time, who you see, what you own, your worries, views, fears, and hopes, and so forth.

- Make a chart showing "average" male and female people in the Colonies. How old is each average person? What did he or she do? Where did the average person live? How much education did men get? Women? How long did they live? How many children would they eventually have?

- Make a chart showing the various professions practiced in the American Colonies. How many people worked at each profession? Were there significant differences in occupations among the Colonies?

- Make a chart showing the possible levels of colonial education and how many people achieved each level. Compile your information by colony. How many attended dame schools? How many traveled overseas to attend college? How many reached each level of schooling between these two?

- What was daily life like for an average American in 1775? Pretend to be this average American and write a detailed journal entry describing everything you did on a typical day.

4. **Points to Ponder**

- What types of political issues have separated friends and next door neighbors in the past and turned them against each other? What issues do it today? What issues tore American communities apart during the Revolutionary War? See how many examples of such issues you can find in American and world history.

- What *really* turned a dispute between the Colonies and the British Parliament into war and revolution? One dispute over tea couldn't have done it. "Taxation without representation" couldn't have done it. (The Colonies had been taxed—without representation—for decades.) Why weren't the individual disputes peacefully resolved? Why did they end up in a war?

- The last paragraph of this story says that Rebecca felt "anger and loss." Why loss? What did she lose? Do you think most citizens "lost" something during the Revolutionary War? What? How? Why?

- How do children get caught up in the conflicts of war? Have you ever been ridiculed or hurt because of your parents' beliefs or actions?

"United" States

Passing the Declaration of Independence, July 2, 1776*

Signing the Declaration of Independence

At a Glance

To what date or event would you trace the origin, the founding of the United States? To the Boston Tea Party? To the first shots fired at Lexington and Concord? To the first real battle, the Battle of Bunker Hill? To the moment when the Continental Congress resolved to become an independent nation? To the date the Declaration of Independence was signed?

Our July 4 celebration honors none of these events. The great vote was taken on the stormy afternoon of July 2, 1776, in Philadelphia, by the Continental Congress. That is when the Colonies decided to break away from England and become the United States of America. July 2 is the first time the words "United States" were officially spoken or written.

However, it took two more days for the delegates to agree on the specific wording of the declaration announcing their decision to the world. The final document, the Declaration of Independence, was presented to the public on the afternoon of July 4, 1776. The document wasn't brought back to Congress for signatures until August 4.

* Excerpted from Kendall Haven's story, "United States Independence Day," in *New Years to Kwanzaa: Original Stories of Celebration*, Fulcrum Publishing, 1999, 800-992-2908, www.fulcrum-resources.com. Used here with the publisher's permission.

John Adams predicted that future generations would honor and cherish the date July 2, when the decision to become a free nation was made. He was wrong. We chose to honor and celebrate the date of the completion of the document. But the truly interesting story is how close that vote on July 2 was, and by what a razor-thin margin we agreed to become a unified country of 13 states.

Meet Andrew McNair

Andrew McNair, a soft-spoken Philadelphia native, turned 56 in 1776. An immediate supporter of independence, McNair had worked for the Pennsylvania legislature as a scribe and doorman for well over a decade before he, along with the meeting hall, was loaned to the First Continental Congress. He was the only official doorman for both the first and and second Continental Congresses. McNair, at 63, was one of the men allowed to ring the liberty bell after the signing of the Paris Peace Treaty, officially ending the war in September 1783. He continued to serve as a congressional doorman until health problems (probably arthritis) forced him to retire at age 66. He died quietly in his Philadelphia home two years later.

"United" States

Unanimous. . . . Why did Mr. Adams say it had to be unanimous?

My name is Andrew McNair. I've been the one and only doorman for the First and Second Continental Congresses. Some say I'm too old for an important job like this. But then they see what happens when someone tries to sneak past me without proper credentials, and they don't say that anymore. No, I don't just open the door. My real job is to make sure no one gets into the red brick State House here in Philadelphia without proper credentials. No assistants, pages, messengers, or visitors. *No one* gets in except the delegates themselves, and they have to have proper credentials from their states.

Now, it's always exciting, listening to official Congress business, watching President John Hancock with his aristocratic airs run the debates from his raised presidential platform. But in early July the vote on independence got me in such a lather I could scarcely sleep!

When the vote on independence first came up on June 10, it was defeated—couldn't even get a simple majority. Many wanted another "humble and dutiful appeal" for discussions to resolve the "unhappy disputes" between Colonies and Crown. Some said it was too late to turn back. Blood had been spilled at Lexington and Concord, at Bunker and Breeds Hills, during the unsuccessful Canadian Campaign. Some argued that Washington's army had already driven the British out of Boston and that maybe they could win a war.

Others said an unbeatable British force was gathering at New York and we had better stop the fighting before it was too late. Others said it was already too late. It looked like a war, felt like a war, and killed like a war. Therefore it was war! Some said "No, no. Just a misunderstanding which can—and should—be diplomatically resolved before any more provocations are issued."

No one could agree on anything. So Hancock postponed the vote for three weeks.

Then, on Monday, July 1, 1776, it came up again. And Mr. John Adams went and declared that it had to be a *unanimous* vote for independence! Ha! A month before they couldn't even win a majority of the 13 Colonies and 56 delegates! But if it lost again, I feared the tide of freedom would be lost for ever.

Oh, I understood Mr. Adams's reasoning. If the 13 Colonies weren't united, he was afraid they would tear apart from within. We'd wind up in a civil war instead of a united fight against England. But how could he hope to get a unanimous vote of all thirteen colonies when he couldn't get seven to vote "yes" a month before?

I couldn't lie in bed past 5:00 that morning. I walked the five blocks down Chestnut to the meeting house and arrived by 7:00, a full hour early. Sessions start at 9:00. I am usually here by 8:00. I check the Congress meeting room, loaned to Congress by the Pennsylvania legislature. I open the curtains to flood light across the white-paneled walls. I make sure the high-ceilinged room is ready. If there is a chill, I light the fireplaces. Then I take my post by the heavy, carved door to greet and admit the delegates.

But every action seemed charged and extra-significant that Monday. Even the weather seemed to feel the tension. By 8:00 the thermometer had reached 78 degrees. It was frightfully muggy. Swirling clouds were gathering. A summer storm was brewing—as if even the sky knew the significance of the day—either we would commit to freedom (and war), or we would remain forever a servant of England!

Such a momentous decision for 56 men to make all on their own, isolated here in this room. One way or the other they would commit the lives of a million Americans!

It would be hard enough to get a majority. But John Adams insisted on a unanimous vote!

After the previous Friday's session I overheard Adams and Benjamin Franklin talking outside the meeting hall while Dr. Franklin waited for his "sedan chair." He suffers from gout and can't walk much, so has hired two stout men to carry him around Philadelphia in a chair mounted on poles.

As I passed by, I heard Adams mutter as he rummaged through his green cloth satchel, "The four New England colonies are solid. So are Virginia and Georgia."

"That's only six," cautioned Franklin, peering through his spectacles.

"Two weeks ago New Jersey appointed new delegates. The new group is solidly for independence."

"That's seven," answered Franklin.

"Both North and South Carolina are wavering. I think they could be talked into voting 'yes'."

"That's nine."

Adams rubbed his forehead for a moment. "The Delaware delegates are split. Maryland delegates are in favor. But their legislature back home won't allow them to vote yes."

Franklin's chair arrived and he climbed in, his long, gray hair straggling across his shoulders. "That still leaves New York and Pennsylvania's 'cool considerate men'."

[New York was thick with Tories, supporters of English rule in America. No one believed New York would ever vote to split from England. Pennsylvania delegates, led by the tall, bean-pole thin Quaker, John Dickinson, were opposed to any drastic action, and especially to war. They *were* in favor of pressing the Colonies' case with England, but firmly against anything so radical as a declaration of independence. They were now called the "cool considerate men." Those favoring independence and war were dubbed "the violent men." Most of these were rash New Englanders.]

As two thick, seaman-looking porters hoisted Franklin's chair and started toward his home, Adams called out, "Has your committee of five finished the Declaration yet?"

Franklin shook his head. "It's really a committee of one. Tom Jefferson's doing all the writing. He has a wonderful start on the first two sections based on the Virginia resolution. But the last two sections are going slowly."

"Tell him to hurry. If the vote goes for independence on Monday, we'll need a document on Tuesday to present to the delegates for their approval."

After hearing *that* conversation, how could I sleep over the weekend? So much depended on one roll call of the delegates. Each colony would cast one vote. If a colony's delegates disagreed on an issue, that colony's vote went with the majority of its delegates.

By 8:30 delegates began to file in, wigs carefully combed, wearing knee breeches and white hose, satin waistcoats, broadcloth over coats, and stylish pumps. Southern drawls mingled with Yankee twangs. A subdued rumble grew across the room as delegates in small groups discussed the day's decision in urgent tones.

I had cleared every delegate through the great front door by 8:50, a record. Outside the temperature climbed past 84 degrees. The first rumblings of a distant storm crept down Chestnut Street and made me shudder.

I closed the big front door and slipped inside the congessional chamber as President Hancock gaveled the meeting to order exactly at 9:00. Delegates expectantly slid into their seats. Hancock raised a stack of mundane business that needed attention before bigger matters could be addressed. There were two letters from General Washington concerning new British troop ship arrivals in New York harbor. There were army supply requests, mostly for food and shoes. Many groaned openly. How could they deal with smaller issues when a vote on freedom waited in the wings? I felt like joining them but didn't dare make a sound.

On and on the business of Congress droned until 12:30 P.M., when Hancock announced that Congress would now consider the proposal by Richard Henry Lee. This was it! Richard Henry Lee was the Virginian who first moved to declare independence back in June. An electric tingle surged through the room, matching the growing rumble of thunder from gathering clouds outside. Delegates straightened in their chairs. Attention focused on every word of the debate. I had to force myself to breathe.

John Dickinson, the Pennsylvania Quaker and leader of the "cool considerate men," leapt to his feet asking to be heard. Apparently he had been up most of the night preparing for this plea. The other delegates used to consider him the leader of Congress, but his power had fallen away in recent weeks as independence gained support. Besides pleading to defeat this measure (which he called "far too extreme") , it seemed to me that he was making a final plea for his own position of authority in Congress.

Dickinson spoke for over four hours. Through his impassioned speech we again and again heard the arguments against independence. Mutters of support drifted through the chamber as he spoke and re-spoke each one. So did louder grumbles of disagreement.

"A lack of prudence will cost the lives of thousands of Americans."

"France's friendship and support are still unknown. But we cannot hope to win a war without them."

"We can still make gains through negotiation."

"Declaring independence now is rash and is a blind and precipitous measure!"

"We are in a wretched state of preparation for war."

At 5:00 an unofficial straw vote was taken as the first jagged lightning bolt knifed to the ground nearby. Hancock wanted to see how the votes would fall. Thunder rattled the windows as New Hampshire, the first colony, shouted "yes!"

The declaration for independence won that straw pole, but only by a vote of nine to four. New York, Pennsylvania, Delaware, and South Carolina voted "no." Edward Rutledge of South Carolina, a supporter of independence, quickly called for a one-day postponement of the official vote.

John Dickinson paled and seemed to shrink. His lengthy plea hadn't swayed anyone. Independence won the day. He was defeated.

I glanced at John Adams. He looked, if not defeated, worried. Only one day left until the official vote, and still four colonies to convert if the vote was to be unanimous.

Before I could lock the doors, rumors were flying. Hasty, tense side conversations filled the hall and spread into the street. One of Delaware's delegates, Caesar Rodney, was absent, but had been sent for. If he arrived in time, Delaware would swing to the "yes" side. New York voted no because their delegates had not received new instructions from the colony's legislature, even though they had repeatedly requested them. Early on the evening of July 1, the New York delegates had agreed to abstain from voting at all unless they received new orders from home. South Carolina delegates agreed to vote "yes" for the sake of unity if no one else voted "no."

That left Pennsylvania. The Pennsylvania delegates had voted five to two against independence. But I heard John Dickinson say he would not even attend the session on Tuesday as a protest against losing the unofficial independence vote. One of his strongest supporters decided to do the same. That meant that their vote tomorrow would be *three* to two against. But one of the three, John Morton, was wavering. I heard Sam Adams tell Hancock that he planned to take Morton out for dinner and a talk that night.

Suddenly quiet John Morton of Pennsylvania was the key. How this one man voted on Tuesday would decide the fate of all 13 colonies! If he voted "no," Pennsylvania, followed by South Carolina, New York, and possibly North Carolina, would also vote "no." Any thought of a united front of colonies would be destroyed. But if he voted "yes," everyone else would fall in behind.

Morton had long been a supporter of John Dickinson. His family, friends, and colleagues were all "cool considerate men." Although he had lately begun to see the value of independence, could he possibly vote against family, friends, and his own history, when so much rode on his one vote?

I shuddered as I walked back home. What an awesome responsibility for one delegate! Then I shuddered again. Independence seemed to hang on a thin and tenuous thread of "if's." IF Rodney of Delaware arrived in time, and IF no new instructions arrived from New York, and IF South Carolina held true to their word, then, IF Morton voted "yes," independence would be declared.

What a day the 2nd of July would be!

I arrived by 6:30 on the hot, rainy morning of July 2. Somber delegates also arrived early. Hancock gaveled the session to order exactly at 9:00. Several bits of congressional business had piled up overnight. It was after 11:00 when Hancock turned back to the final vote on Richard Henry Lee's motion to declare independence.

After final debate the roll call began. Massachusetts, Rhode Island, New Hampshire, and Connecticut all voted "yes," as expected. New York abstained, having received no new instructions overnight. I nervously scanned the room. Caesar Rodney had not yet arrived. I stood by the front door, looking into rain-soaked Chestnut Street, listening to the voting inside.

New Jersey voted "yes." So did Maryland. The clerk called, "How does Delaware vote?" My heart sank. Rodney hadn't made it. Just as fast my heart bounced back into my throat. I heard the hard clatter of pounding hooves on the cobbled street.

"A rider approaches!" I yelled into the meeting room.

Splattered with mud, soaked with rain, gaunt and pale from having ridden all night through the storm, Caesar Rodney slid from his horse and handed me his credentials. One minute later Delaware officially voted "yes."

I sagged, panting, against the great front door. We think such drama only happens in stories. But here it was in real life. Rodney arrived with only seconds to spare! And all our independence had hung in that narrow balance.

But the drama was not over yet. The clerk called, "How does Pennsylvania vote?"

Of the first four delegates, two voted "no" and two voted "yes," as expected. All eyes turned to John Morton. John remained seated for over a minute, eyes on the floor. He neither moved nor uttered a sound. I could see the doubts, the uncertainty, the inner conflict written across his face. Slowly, ashen-faced, he rose and said simply, "I vote yes," and slumped back into his chair.

Quickly Virginia, Georgia, South Carolina, and North Carolina added their "yes" votes. The clerk reported the vote, "twelve for, one abstention, none opposed."

Adams had done it! I expected cheers to explode across the room, and for delegates to jump and dance, tossing papers into the air.

Instead there was silence. The moment was too solemn, too important for cheering. The delegates simply sat in silence, almost stunned.

Hancock adjourned the session with an agreement to take up the wording of Mr. Jefferson's Declaration of Independence in the morning.

The delegates filed quietly out into the late afternoon as the rain faded to drizzle and streaks of golden sunlight broke through from the west.

As he pulled his broadcloth coat over his shoulders, Mr. Adams said, "The second of July will be the most memorable date in the history of America. It will be celebrated by generations to come as the day of deliverance for our new nation."

I smiled and nodded in agreement as I locked the door. The 2nd of July. What a day! I was sure Americans would celebrate this date as long as there was an America.

Aftermath

Passing the Declaration of Independence had little effect on America's relations with England. The King had already declared war (after the events at Lexington and Concord). We had already fought two vicious battles (Bunker Hill and the defense of Charleston Harbor). An American army had already tried to invade and conquer Canada. An American army had already besieged the British garrison at Boston. No, America and England were already at war when the Declaration became just one more insult hurled at an already infuriated king.

But the Declaration had a profound effect in America. It electrified and galvanized the population. American morale skyrocketed. American patriotism became fashionabe.

Passing the Declaration also put Congress back in apparent control of the war effort. It made them appear to be doing something to lead the country, rather than appearing to be a major impediment to progress and action.

Follow-up Questions and Activities

1. **What Do You Know?**
   - When was the term "United States" first spoken, and in what place and context?
   - How many delegates sat in Congress? How many delegates did each colony get to send, and who were they?
   - Where did Congress meet? Why was that place chosen?
   - What differences existed between the Colonies other than their accents?
   - What is pacifism? What is a Quaker? What other groups in America were pacifists?

2. **Finding Out More**. Following are five important topics from this story for you to research in the library and on the Internet. The reference sources at the back of this book will help you get started.

- Our national Declaration of Independence is remarkably similar to a declaration passed in the Virginia House of Burgesses more than six months previously. Research the Declaration and its history. Who in Virginia first created the basic form and structure of the document? Who worked on it? Who in Congress contributed to the rough draft? What parts did Congress change most during the debate over the Declaration's exact wording?

- The Liberty Bell was rung to announce the passage of the Declaration. Where did this bell come from? Did it really get cracked? How Why? When? What happened to it during the war?

- Benjamin Franklin of Pennsylvania and Thomas Jefferson of Virginia were two well-known members of the Continental Congress. Jefferson was extremely quiet and hardly ever said a word during congressional deliberations. Franklin was a powerful and influential man who worked best behind the scenes. Research these two men who were so prominent in the drama of the Declaration. How did others perceive them? What did they do before and after the war? What special contributions did they make during the war?

- Quakers are the best known of the pacifist groups in America. Research pacifist groups. What similarities did they share? What made each group unique? Where did they come from? Where were they concentrated in America? What did they do? What happened to each group over time?

- The Continental Congress was the first attempt at a national government. When did the First Continental Congress meet? How many were there? How long did the Congress function? What replaced it? Who served in Congress? How long could delegates serve? How were they elected? What did Congress do? What powers did it have? What powers did the individual states retain and not grant to the national Congress?

3. **Make It Real**

- As a class, create your own declaration of student rights. What rights do you believe students should automatically have? Write a document clearly stating these rights and your justification for claiming them.

- What do you do to celebrate our independence? Why? Make a list of what you typically do on the 4th of July. Compare your answers to those of your classmates. What else *could* you do? Are there more "patriotic" things you could do? If so, what are they? Make as extensive a list as you can. Search for people who do these patriotic activities and find out why they do them.

4. **Points to Ponder**.

- Why do you think we celebrate independence on July 4 instead of on July 2?

- John Dickinson of Pennsylvania refused to sign the Declaration when all the other congressional delegates did. Can you find out why?

Disaster by Any Other Name . . .

The Battle of Long Island,
August 27, 1776

Battle of Long Island

At a Glance

American confidence was riding high in the early summer of 1776. Washington had turned the mob of individual militia units outside Boston into a real army, had forced the British to evacuate Boston, and had sent most Massachusetts Tories fleeing to Nova Scotia. General Clinton's attempt to take Charleston had been repulsed. The Declaration of Independence had been passed. The attempted American invasion of Quebec had failed, but it was never really authorized, anyway.

Maybe one more quick military success and the British would give up and go home. But where to gather for that all-important battle?

The Hudson River and Lake Champlain formed a natural highway that both cut the American Colonies in two by splitting the hothead New England Colonies from the rest of the continent and linked the Eastern seaboard with British-held Canada. New York City was the gateway to that north-south highway.

In April 1776, Washington moved his headquarters to New York and began preparations for its defense. Surely this was where the big battle would occur.

In May, British Redcoats and German (Hessian) troops (hired by Britain to fight in America) landed on Staten Island. During June additional British forces sailed in from other regions, so that a forest of British masts crowded outer New York Harbor and the bays around Staten Island.

Would they come by land through New Jersey, attempt a landing straight on Manhattan (a patriot stronghold), or attack first on Long Island (which boasted a strong concentration of Tories and Loyalists)? Washington split his army to be better able to respond to British advances in any of these three areas.

The British Parliament demanded quick, decisive victory from the new commander in America, Lord Howe, and gave him 30,000 troops (the largest British army ever to set foot on foreign soil) to do it with. The stage was set for the first real battle between armies of the American Revolution, the test to see if the American forces could really stand up in traditional battle against the mighty British war machine.

Washington waited in New York, not knowing if the British would attack through New Jersey, directly at Manhattan, or by striking at Long Island. The British chose Long Island, with its large population of Tories, to make their move. The question was: Would American commanders be able to meet the challenge of decisive battle with seasoned British troops?

Meet Colonel Samuel Atlee

Born in Carlisle, Pennsylvania, in 1740 of German-American immigrants, Samuel Atlee was a 36-year-old senior commander in 1776 for the Battle of Long Island. Samuel was raised on a family farm and attended an American "Latin" school run by Quakers for seven years before sailing to England for three years of college.

Atlee cut his studies short to return to America so he could serve as an infantry lieutenant during the French and Indian War. He received good reviews by his British superior officers but saw no real action.

After the war Atlee married and, by 1774, had five children when he emerged as a fervent Patriot supporter. He helped form the 8th Pennsylvania Infantry and was elected to command it by the officer corps of the unit. His confidence was shattered by the battle at Long Island and other defeats over the next three months. He grew frightened and ineffective as a field commander, so he served as staff officer for three years before being wounded and discharged in 1779. During his remaining years, he managed the series of dockside warehouses and shops he owned along the waterfront in Baltimore. He died in Baltimore in 1796 at the age of 56.

Most of the quotes from Colonel Atlee's journal included in this story come from Christopher Herbert's book, *Redcoats and Rebels* (New York: Avon Books, 1990).

Disaster by Any Other Name . . .

"Look at us! We tattered remnants of the proud force that greeted the dawn—wild eyed, shivering, huddled together like hunted animals." Colonel Samuel Atlee, commander of the 8th Regiment of Pennsylvania Infantry, clutched his overcoat around him like a protective cocoon as if to hide from this terrible day. But Atlee's heart told him nothing could protect them anymore. Tomorrow or the next day, the British would charge over the Americans' puny walls and mow them down like helpless wheat lying in the field.

One short day ago he had eagerly awaited the chance for battle. What a difference one day can make!

Colonel Atlee's 8th Regiment of 400 Pennsylvania backwoods recruits was assigned under General William Alexander, called Lord Stirling because of his Scottish claim to a title. Stirling's command of 1,600 men spread across part of the American defensive line in front of Brooklyn, Long Island. Atlee's regiment was shoved up against the East River and New York Harbor just ahead of Gowanus Bay and its mire of small creeks and swamps.

"The men are nervous, but eager to get their first battle over with," wrote Atlee in his journal. "We have no officers with battle experience—myself included—but how can such proud and eager enthusiasm ever be defeated?"

He continued, "Scouts who daily ventured the four miles to Gravesend point, the southwest corner of Long Island, report a dozen new masts in the British fleet each day. No one in camp can imagine so great a force as would require such a mighty armada of ships. A few of our lads were at Boston and have had a taste of fighting Redcoat regulars and have shared stories of their triumphs with the rest of us who have never felt the thrill of battle.

"This camp and this effort feel important. Our dear America is being invaded and it feels that we were chosen to stand up and say, 'No! You may not come here and do this. Get out!' Pride and eager excitement permeates our ranks and camp. We will surely triumph if the British dare attack."

Scouts rushed back on the evening of August 22. Eight hundred flat boats had landed on Long Island. More troops than they could count off-loaded and started the march toward Flatbush. The great red line stretched over four miles.

It was only three miles from Flatbush to the lines of the 8th Regiment. Lord Stirling's command numbered only 1,600. All American forces on Long Island numbered under 8,000. Whispered rumors spread at the speed of fear. Some said 20,000 British and barbaric Hessians had landed. Some said 50,000.

Colonel Atlee wrote, "I notice that the men wipe their palms more now and talk in hushed tones. Muskets are clutched tight instead of being loosely slung or carried as before. We double our efforts to dig adequate redoubts to anchor our position. Guards and scout patrols are redoubled and keep a much more attentive eye than before. The easy laughter I so enjoyed hearing throughout our camp has disappeared."

On the brisk morning of August 27, Colonel Atlee was awakened before dawn by one of the forward scouts. British troops were on the move, advancing through an apple orchard in their immediate front. Alarms were sounded, the regiment rushed to their positions. All could hear scattered musket and cannon fire off to the left.

The battle—*their* battle—had started!

Three ranks of Redcoats containing more than 1,000 men marched like machines out of a tree line, emerging through thin wisps of mist like endless red ghosts, Brown Bess muskets held forward, bayonets gleaming. They paused to fire at about 100 yards. Waving his sword above his head, Colonel Atlee held the regiment in check and then returned fire.

The Redcoats advanced, marching slowly, indifferently, as if the Colonists posed no significant threat. Slowly, grudgingly, the 8th gave way as the British pressed in on them. Atlee sent a messenger back to Lord Stirling for reinforcements. Step by step, volley by volley, the 8th retreated across an open field toward a thick tree line. The colonel felt proud of his lads, standing rock-solid in the line even when a wall of fire and whining musket balls exploded from the British.

The Pennsylvanians halted their retreat just inside the line of trees. Two new companies of eager Delaware lads joined them. On Atlee's command, the regiment fired twice and then advanced, the first advance ever by an American force against a British battle line!

"Give 'em hell, boys!" cried the Colonel as they marched stiffly toward the waiting red line. Bodies on both sides began to fall as the two lines closed on each other.

Atlee wrote, "What a rush! What a thrill! They paused, wavered, and slowly fell back! The fire was hot and thick, the morning air filled with smoke and the racket of musket and cannon. And still we advanced and still they retreated! We were shoving the mighty British off the field of battle. What joy! What bliss!"

Scattered fire off to the left attested to the size and importance of this encounter. America was winning!

By 7:00 A.M. the British had reformed with a force of almost 2,000 men about 500 yards beyond the American position and began firing five six-pounders at the 8th, with little effect. Atlee halted, awaiting new orders from Lord Stirling before continuing his giddy advance.

Rumors began to flash through the ranks like lightning bolts. A great force of British had circled around their left flank to cross through undefended Jamaica Pass four miles off to Lord Stirling's left. They were smashing through the rear of the American lines, crumpling American units like paper.

Colonel Atlee told his men to ignore such malicious rumors. "How could it be true?" he called. "We are winning! We are beating the British."

At 7:30, everyone heard three mighty cannon blasts from the area of Bedford far in the rear. Fear gripped the American forces. It was true. British forces were behind the American lines!

In a flash Atlee understood that these cannon blasts were a signal and that now the real attack would begin. Not 1,000, but almost 6,000 British and green-clad Hessians emerged from the cover of woods and advanced toward Colonel Atlee's position.

In a sickening flash he realized that his glorious early victory was a sham. The early British attack had been a feint, a fake. With overwhelming British power both in front and behind, the real battle would now begin—a battle for their very lives.

Three thousand Redcoats swept up along the shore to force past the 8th on the right. Barbaric Hessians, numbering 2,500, uttering animal cries and bearing long bayonets, axes, and clubs, rushed at their center. The hopelessness of his position hit Colonel Atlee like a crushing cannon ball.

The 8th turned to retreat in orderly fashion, only to face new British units that had materialized out of the woods and paths between the front lines and the safety of Brooklyn.

They were surrounded. They were alone. And they were cut off from all American aid. In their first battle they would have to endure the worst possible battlefield nightmare. Confusion and panic rippled through the 500 men under Colonel Atlee's command. Some rushed blindly one way, some rushed the other. All met stiff lines of the enemy and raced back to the central body of the regiment. Only the sound of raging cannon and musket fire up and down the American line kept the regiment from thinking that the rest of the army had ceased to exist and that the entire British force had turned its brutal power upon them.

The regiment massed and tried to smash through one of the British lines but were repulsed by heavy fire. Again they massed and charged . . . and again . . . and again. The British lines were too strong, their flashing bayonets were too deadly to overcome.

Green-clad Hessians, supported by several companies of local Tory militia, rushed into the field, slashing and hacking at the rear of the 8th regiment.

Order dissolved. Chaos and panic reigned. The men scattered for the swamp and creeks and woods, running like wild animals, terror in their hearts, fearing that a line of red would appear around every tree, bush, and turn.

Gowans Creek bulged with high-tide water. The men of the 8th plunged in anyway, hundreds of them wading through water up to their necks, through slime, muck, and thick nettles. Some held their muskets above their heads. Most cast them aside in their desperate scramble for survival. Some swam; some drowned. All felt as if they were moving through thick molasses while the British dashed freely along the bank.

British musket balls thudded into the water all around them, creating a sea of mini-geysers. Many hit their mark and the bodies floated thick on the water. Atlee saw three Maryland boys sprint into a muddy slough at the end of the tidal creek, their feet getting stuck in the thick goo. They were each slashed by a dozen bayonets where they stood, unarmed and defenseless, as the wild Hessians roared through.

The battle was over before noon. The American forces had been routed. The forward units had been destroyed with no more effort than a bully would need to humiliate and torment a young child. Of the original 500 in Colonel Atlee's 8th regiment, only 150 made it back to the shelter of the American forts that ringed Brooklyn. Among the losses were 120 killed and 130 captured and chained in hideous dungeons and prison ships like slaves.

Colonel Atlee wrote, "The illusion of American military strength and power has burst. We are like foolish children playing at war. How can we ever hold up against a British charge? Will they attack tomorrow or the next day? Will they wait until their navy can sail up the east river and bombard our forts into dust? It matters little. When they come I am now convinced that we will surely die. When we do, the revolution will surely die with us."

The bleak night of August 27, 1776, was a very gloomy moment in America's long struggle for independence.

Aftermath

Washington successfully (some say almost magically) extracted the remaining shreds of his shell-shocked army from Long Island and began a long series of retreats—first up Manhattan, then (when Forts Lee and Washington fell) into New Jersey and down into Pennsylvania. American forces ran from the British Redcoats almost before the Redcoats could fire. Positions were lost almost faster than they could be identified. The last three months of 1776 were an endless string of disastrous routs for the American forces.

New York was lost to the British and would not be reclaimed until the peace treaty was signed in 1783. New York and Long Island became the center of Loyalist and Tory strength and activity.

Washington was forced to admit that his officer corps was too weak and inexperienced to create a powerful fighting force. Without extensive officer and enlisted training, he would never defeat the British army. He also knew that the Revolution would collapse if he were defeated in a decisive battle. His forces would have to become like the shadow of an army—always present, and yet always dancing just out of British reach—and he must never allow his flimsy force to be trapped into a major confrontation.

The confidence of American citizens was deeply shaken after Long Island. Over half of the population of New Jersey assumed that the Revolution had collapsed and signed Loyalty Papers pledging to support the King.

The British government and people rejoiced and assumed the rebellion would quickly collapse. The situation *did* appear exceedingly bleak for the rebels, but that only brought out the cunning best of the Patriot resistance. A five-year cat and mouse game began—one the British were not prepared to play.

Follow-up Questions and Activities

1. **What Do You Know?**

   - The Battle of Long Island was considered extremely important because it was the first "real" battle between the Continental Army and the British army. Why didn't the leaders think that Lexington and Concord, or Breeds Hill, counted as *real* battles between armies? What was different about the Continental Army by the summer of 1776, when the Battle of Long Island took place? Why was the *first* battle felt to be extra important? What information did it give American leaders about their chances of success in the Revolution?

   - Lord Howe was not the first British commander in America during the Revolutionary War, nor was he the last. Can you name the other British commanders? The first two were stationed in Boston. Then came Howe. How long did he command? Who followed Howe?

   - Why did soldiers in the eighteenth century stand in open, tight-packed lines and fire at each other? Does that tell you something about how accurate their muskets were?

2. **Finding Out More.** Following are three important topics from this story for you to research in the library and on the Internet. The reference sources at the back of this book will help you get started.

   - Who was Lord Howe? How did he become a lord? What had he done before taking command of the largest British expeditionary force in history? What happened to him after he left America?

   - Long Island was considered a Tory stronghold. How many Tories were there in America during the war? Where did they live? Were they organized into militia units like the Patriots? Did any Tory militia units fight in any of the battles?

   - Research muskets and flintlocks. What was the difference between a musket and a flintlock? How did they each fire? Why weren't muskets very accurate? When did soldiers stop using muskets? Draw a picture of a Revolutionary War era musket and of a flintlock rifle.

3. **Make It Real**

   - Imagine you are in an eighteenth-century battle in your school, with 500 students acting as British and attacking 200 Americans (or numbers in that same ratio). As the "action" occurs, write the numbers on the board or an overhead projector. Each student commanding officer would have to coordinate four kinds of weapons:

     Cannon. The British would typically have two six-pound field pieces for that regimental-sized unit. They can fire accurately for 500 yards and can fire once every 45 seconds if using solid shot cannon balls. Such a cannon ball would be expected to kill three defenders if a shot landed among the soldiers. If the defenders are entrenched behind earthen walls, cannon balls would create more fear than real damage, because few if any cannon balls would clear the walls and not also sail over the defenders' heads. The British cannons would aim primarily for the American cannons. The Americans would probably have one cannon, also a six-pound field piece. Firing into close-packed advancing troops, that cannon could kill eight to twelve men per shot.

Rifles. Rifles were accurate to 275 yards, but could only fire once every 35 to 45 seconds. The Americans would typically have ten in a 200-man unit, deployed as sharp-shooters out in front of the main line. They would fire several times and fall back to keep from being shot or captured, winding up as a reserve force behind the action. The British probably wouldn't have any rifles. They tended to concentrate their rifles in larger units that stayed with divisions and armies instead of something as small as a regiment.

Muskets. Virtually everyone else had a musket. They were reasonably accurate at 100 yards and could be reloaded and fired once every 20 seconds. At 100 yards, figure that one out of every four of the defenders' muskets fired would cause a casualty. (Some would miss; some attackers would be struck by more than one shot.) At 70 yards, one out of three would put an attacker out of action; at 40 yards, one out of two;, and at 20 yards, two out of three. The British guns wouldn't fare nearly as well if the defenders hid behind protective barricades. Figure that they would score hits about one-quarter as often as the Americans.

Bayonets. The British were better at bayonet fighting than were the Americans. Figure that, in hand-to-hand fighting, 40 British soldiers could defeat 60 Americans, and that for every two British killed, three Americans will be killed.

Now figure that the attacking British can cross a 500-yard field in five minutes while marching in formation. If they start 530 yards away from the Americans and pause twice along the way to fire and reload (20 seconds added for each) and charge at a sprint from 30 yards away (six seconds to close and engage the Americans with bayonets), who will win?

Imagine holding the battle. Have each commander decide when the troops will fire. Assess the "kills" for each volley and appropriately "thin" the opposing lines. Also thin ranks to account for cannon fire. How many British are left for the final charge? Enough to defeat the Americans? How many British and Americans lie dead on the field? Can you see now why Revolutionary War forces were quick to surrender (and stop the killing) once they could clearly see who was going to win?

- What did American soldiers carry as they marched through the summer campaign? Research what each soldier had to pack. Remember to include powder, bullets, and wadding in a cartouche box and camp equipment (cook pot, tents, etc.) as well as clothes, blanket, and musket. Can you estimate how many pounds each soldier had to lug? Using books and other readily available objects, build a pack of similar weight. How does the extra weight affect your ability to walk?

- Make a map showing the date and location of every Revolutionary War battle. Can you see the general flow of the war from north to mid-Atlantic to south? Did you have trouble locating all the battles? Did you have trouble deciding which were *battles* and which were skirmishes and local fights? How did *you* distinguish battles from smaller fights?

4. **Points to Ponder**

- The Battle of Long Island was a disastrous defeat for the Continental Army. They were completely outmaneuvered and out-generaled by the British. Is defeat always bad? Can disaster ever be good for an army? Can you find any benefit to the American Army from this defeat? Search for examples of when disaster turned out to be beneficial.

- Long Island was a command failure for the Continental Army. It was a failure of senior officers, not of the rank and file soldiers. If you were in charge, how could you tell if your officers were capable of doing their job? Why didn't Washington know that he didn't have a capable corps of senior officers? Why didn't he do anything about it? What could he have done?

Revolution or Redcoats?
New Jersey Indecision, 1776

War news comes to a colonial family

At a Glance

Events beginning the Revolutionary War took place in and around Boston (the Boston Massacre, the Boston Tea Party, Lexington and Concord, Bunker Hill, and the Siege of Boston). Colonists outside New England felt somewhat like outside observers. In 1776 the war shifted its central focus to New York and to the area between New York and Philadelphia: New Jersey. For the next three years armies tramped across New Jersey, either in hasty retreat or in advance.

New Jersey citizens were caught in the middle. Most (as was true of all the Colonies) supported American liberty and the Declaration of Independence. They also supported the early war efforts in Boston and Canada. It was easy to support a cause being fought somewhere else.

Then, in the summer and fall of 1776, Washington's army disintegrated into ineffective tatters and fled south, abandoning New Jersey. Suddenly British Redcoats controlled the colony. British victory seemed inevitable. Revolution and liberty looked like a foolish pipe-dream hatched by radicals in far-off Boston.

Over half the New Jersey inhabitants lined up to sign Loyalty Papers offered by General Howe in the late fall of 1776 and re-entered the good graces of England. By signing, each person pledged to loyally support the King, Parliament, British rule, and the British army. On paper, New Jersey looked like a great concentration of faithful Loyalists.

However, after Washington's victory at the Battles of Trenton and Princeton, most of those who had signed such papers renounced them and again supported the Revolution.

New Jersey was inhabited by neither vast plantation owners nor the powerful merchants who were most affected by the taxing and domination policies of Parliament. New Jersians were ordinary citizens trying to make ends meet. For such people, 1776 was a year when it was difficult to sort out loyalties and the murky issues of personal and family safety, tradition, and ideology. It was a confused and confusing time for New Jersey residents, a time when what appeared "right" one day might not look right at all the next. As the tide of war shifted back and forth through the summer and fall of 1776, so too did the loyalties expressed by many of the citizens of New Jersey. This is a story of one of those citizens, his daughter, and his friends.

Meet Charity Kosterman

Charity Kosterman was born in Freehold, New Jersey, in the spring of 1764, the second of the two children in the family. Charity's childhood was typical for the times and, except for the excitement of the Revolutionary War, remained relatively uneventful. She was assigned household chores when she turned six and attended neighborhood Dame School for five years. There she fought for the chance to learn to read instead of concentrating on needlepoint, etiquette, and sewing (the normal subjects for girls).

Charity possessed all the intellectual curiosity and drive her older brother, Israel, lacked. Still, she was never able to further her education. At age 18 she married a man who apprenticed to her father and moved with him to Wilmington, Delaware, where he set up his own pewter shop after completing his training.

Charity raised seven children, was a lifelong avid reader, and was active in the Wilmington community and in efforts to improve local educational opportunities.

Revolution or Redcoats?

Twelve-year-old Charity Kosterman hung the broom, dust pan, and dust cloth on their assigned hooks in the small closet at the back of her father's pewter shop and smiled, not because she had done a good job of cleaning the shop before another day's work, but because she had managed to finish a full 15 minutes early. That gave her 15 minutes of solitude to curl up on the wooden floor behind the counter and read before her father arrived from the family house next door to begin his day's work sculpting magnificent pewter plates, goblets, bowls, forks, knives, spoons, and other utensils.

It was early July 1776, and the Kostermans lived in Freehold, New Jersey, a small, sleepy farming town. Certainly they had discussed the growing war with England. A few Freehold boys were part of a militia unit that had marched off to Boston to join Washington's army. But Boston and Philadelphia seemed like other worlds. The struggles of war seemed like someone else's problem. They didn't seem to have anything to do with daily life in Freehold. Charity was much more concerned with finding time to read than with either Revolution or Redcoats.

Entering the shop precisely at 9:00—as he did every morning—Charity's father, Joseph Kosterman, eagerly rubbed his hands together with a great "Ahhhhh!"—as he did every morning—as if he already knew that this day would be the best day of his life.

Joseph Kosterman was a thick, rock-solid man of 31—thick chest, thick arms, thick mop of curly brown hair, and thick, beefy hands. Yet he had spent 20 years training those massive hands to produce the colony's—and maybe the continent's—most delicate and elegant pewter ware.

But this day's "Ahhhh" caught Charity's ear, made her pull her mind out of a good story to peak up over the counter. This "Ahhhh" boomed across the room like a dozen regular "Ahhhh's" all piled on top of each other. Her father so gushed with dazzling enthusiasm that it frightened Charity.

"What's wrong, father?"

"Wrong? What could possibly be wrong on such a glorious day, Charity? Why even the air smells freer on *this* fine day!"

Charity still knelt behind the work counter, almost afraid to move.

"We're free!" cried Mr. Kosterman, dancing his way across the small shop toward his daughter.

Charity's eyes, resting just above the counter and work bench, were like soft, dark pools that soaked everything in. The girl behind those eyes was thoughtful and studious. "Weren't we free before, father?"

"Not from the British," he snorted. "But now Congress has passed a Declaration of Independence. *Now* we're an independent country and free!"

Charity's eyebrows knitted as she turned her father's words over and over in her mind. "But, father, you've always told me that we *were* free and that only slaves weren't."

"How could we be free when we were stuck under English tyranny without any representation? We were no better than dogs to the British."

Charity stood and rubbed her forehead as she thought. "But father, you've always said we were *lucky* to be English and that being English was the best thing in the world."

"I never!" he spluttered.

"Last Christmas," answered Charity, "when I got to meet my cousins and we were counting our blessings, that's what you said."

Suddenly flustered and embarrassed, Mr. Kosterman said, "A lot of people *used* to say that, Charity. But that was before we realized the British aim all along was to make us English slaves, not free and equal partners."

"*And*," she continued, "you've said it several times in here with customers."

"I probably knew they were Tories and had to appease them to make a sale," he muttered. "I've *always* wanted freedom and basic human rights," he explained. "But the lobster-back dogs won't give it to us. So we're going to *take* it." He rubbed his thick hands together and chuckled. "Washington has a grand army digging in to defend New York. Mark my words, Charity, those Redcoats are going to be sorry they ever set foot in this country."

"I'm still confused, father. Didn't you join a *British* militia unit?"

"Charity!" Mr. Kosterman snapped, frowning. "You obviously don't understand politics! We all *had* to join. It doesn't mean a thing." He cocked his head, peering around his daughter. "What's that behind you? A book?"

Her eyes lowered to the floor. "A science book, father." She defiantly raised her dark eyes to gaze into her father's face. "I want to study science and go to school."

"You mean to learn needlepoint and etiquette? You already know them."

"No. *Book* learning. Science and math. *Real* school."

"Why would a smart girl like you want to waste her time on something she will never be able to use?" he demanded.

"Because . . . " she began, but was interrupted when the shop door clanged open. A tall, thin man with a droopy, hound-dog face entered.

Kosterman slowly tore his eyes away from his daughter. "Ahh, Mr. Gunter. Welcome." Kosterman pumped the hound dog's hand so hard the thin man looked as if he feared his arm would be torn out by the roots. "What can I do for you?"

Gunter's voice was thin and precise. "Goblets, dinner plates and silverware."

Kosterman scowled as he stepped behind the counter. "*Place ware*, Mr. Gunter."

"That is what I said."

"You said *silver*ware. This is a pewter shop. No silver crosses my doorstep. I make *place* ware."

Charity slid the book back behind her and eased toward the back door of the shop, planning to escape with her book and dream both intact.

"Would you like an independence theme on the scroll work?" Mr. Kosterman asked, dipping a quill pen and preparing to take notes.

"You mean that disaster of a Declaration of Independence?" replied Gunter, wrinkling up his nose in disgust.

"Disaster?" bellowed Kosterman. "It is a glorious triumph."

Mr. Gunter dabbed a handkerchief at the corner of his mouth and rolled his eyes as he said, "If you say so."

"I do!"

"Personally, I thought it was just those New England radicals letting off steam. I thought it would end with that tea business, which I never fully understood. Why argue about tea when the price is going down? Wouldn't it make more sense to protest when the price goes up?"

Kosterman nodded. "I must admit I never quite understood why cheaper tea suddenly meant we were being taxed without representation." He quickly added, "Though I agreed with the Bostonians' principles, of course."

Gunter nodded in agreement. "As did I. But things got so rapidly out of hand. One day we are arguing about tea. Next day everyone's yelling 'Liberty! Liberty!' and men line up to kill each other." He wrinkled his eyebrows as his droopy, hound-dog eyes gazed at the pewter smith. "I never understood how being offered cheaper tea meant we weren't free. Did you?"

"Well . . . it's more complicated than *that*," Kosterman spluttered.

Gunter shrugged and waved his handkerchief through the air. "It always is. Could I see some samples of your plates, please?"

Charity stood rooted in the doorway, fascinated by this political debate, soaking in every word.

"Just a moment," Kosterman insisted. He sucked in a deep breath to regain his enthusiasm. "You must admit that *now* we are definitely free! We can decide our own future, make our own decisions."

Mr. Gunter frowned. "I say it's dangerous to slap the hand that feeds us."

"Feeds us?" bellowed Kosterman. "That *crushes* us. Liberty or death—isn't that the motto they're using? We'll spin those Redcoats around so fast they won't know what hit them!'

"I wouldn't be so sure of your revolution, Joseph. And I would like to see some samples."

Kosterman pulled back with a look of shocked surprise. "Don't you support the revolution?"

"I support New Jersey. I don't give a fig for the other colonies and they don't give a fig for New Jersey. All I'm saying is that it will be very uncomfortable around here for anyone who supported this independence business if the British win. How heavy are your forks?"

"But the British can't win," laughed Mr. Kosterman.

"Yes they can," Gunter insisted. "They beat the French and they have a real, trained army. Washington has to fight the greatest army in the world and with no trained officers and no soldiers with combat experience."

"But . . . but our freedom," stammered Kosterman. "We need to fight for our freedom."

"You've always made a decent living for your family doing exactly what you wanted to do under British rule. Haven't you?" Gunter demanded.

"Well, I guess . . . "

"How much freer than that can you be? And *please* let me see your samples!"

"We need the right to govern ourselves!" Kosterman argued, ignoring the request.

"Why? I don't see anyone except British governors in these colonies who know the first thing about governing a country."

"You sound like a Loyalist," insisted Kosterman.

Gunter tapped a long, thin finger on the counter. "I'm just saying, principles are fine, but be smart, Joseph. Make sure you are on the side that wins. That's where freedom and privilege will come from."

"You aim to side with the British, then?" Kosterman asked, almost spitting the words.

"I 'aim'," Gunter barked, "to be standing proudly with which ever side is on top in the end. And now I think I 'aim' to purchase my *silver*ware from someone who will show me samples! Good day!" And he stomped out of the shop, leaving Joseph Kosterman angrily attacking a pewter pitcher with a polishing rag to work off his frustration.

The noise of Charity opening the back door to sneak out drew Mr. Kosterman's attention. His finger jabbed at the air toward her. "And you. Why waste your time with nonsense you can't possibly use when you could do useful chores around the house and shop?"

"I *want* to learn. And I'm smarter than Israel."

Her father snorted and shook his head. "Girls have no practical use for learning. Your brother goes to school because he will be a man. He'll *need* to be educated."

"At least let me be your apprentice and learn how to make pewter."

"This is a man's trade, Charity. Besides, you're already part of the business. You sweep and clean. Now, no more nonsense. You'll be a fine, lovely woman. But Charity, try to behave like a woman. Now run inside and help your mother with chores. I have a business to run here."

Charity fumed as she walked, quiet and ladylike, back to the house, wondering all over again who was, and who was not, free.

The morning of November 26, 1776, found Joseph Kosterman slumped on a stool behind his workbench, puttering nervously and idly with a dull lump of pewter. His hands were covered with a sheen of oil and gray shavings. His eyes were locked on the counter before him, but his mind seemed to wander a thousand miles away. Charity silently finished her morning cleaning, sensing her father would not tolerate the interruption of her questions.

Steven Karcoff, a bearded local farmer with callused hands that looked like they hadn't been out of the dirt in years, pushed open the door and stepped in. The silent, brooding entry of her father's lifelong friend redoubled the worry building in Charity. Something must be very wrong. Mr. Karcoff *always* laughed and joked like a refreshing spring breeze when he entered the shop. It was one thing for father to brood; that happened a lot. But if Mr. Karcoff was worried . . .

Kosterman kneaded his ball of pewter. "I told you those idiot New Englanders would drag us all down. And for what?"

Karcoff nodded solemnly in agreement. "Washington's army has completely disintegrated."

"The army is made up of idiots," grumbled Kosterman, rumbling like distant thunder. "The officers can't lead. The soldiers are cowards who run away when anyone says 'boo'!"

Charity thought both men seemed nervous and fidgety. Their talk both confused and frightened her. "But, father, you said Washington was going to pound the tar and feathers out of the Redcoats."

His eyebrows arched in surprise, then wrinkled in anger. "Don't argue with your father, young lady. . . . And I'll not having you using that kind of language! It's not lady-like."

Charity's cheeks reddened in shame. She whispered, "I'm sorry, father."

Mr. Kosterman went back to pounding his lump of pewter. "Who were we to think we could conquer the greatest army on Earth? How can we beat the Redcoats with a bunch of disorganized amateurs? You mark my words, Steven. This whole business is turning into a disaster."

Again Karcoff solemnly nodded. "There was nothing for us to gain and everything to lose from siding with those New England rebels. No one on Earth is freer than citizens in the British Empire."

"Exactly!" exclaimed Kosterman, slamming his pewter ball onto the counter. "England has always supplied the manufactured goods we need. *England* is the future."

Karcoff slowly rubbed his chin with his thick stub of a hand and watched his friend out of the corner of one eye. "Having second thoughts about backing the Revolution?"

"Nothing wrong with thinking things through again," Kosterman defensively answered.

Karcoff lowered his voice. "So you're going to sign a Loyalty Paper, then?"

"I'm *thinking* about it . . . ." Mr. Kosterman tried to sound casual, but Charity could tell he was tense and worried.

Karcoff jabbed a thick finger on the counter and leaned forward as if to make sure no one overheard him. "We both openly declared support for the Patriot cause and the Revolution. You think they don't know that?"

Mr. Kosterman answered, "General Howe said they would forgive if we signed the papers now."

But his voice didn't sound as if even he were convinced. Charity could no longer stand not knowing what they were talking about. "The *what* papers?" she blurted.

Both men turned to glare at young Charity. Her face reddened.

"The Loyalty Papers, Charity," repeated her father. "General Howe has given New Jersey citizens a chance to again pledge the loyalty of our families to King George."

"But . . . " began Charity.

Her father raised his voice to cut her off. "The British are obviously going to win this fight. They have always treated us well, and if we are among the first to show our renewed support to the King, our position will be substantially improved once the rebels are crushed."

The dark pools of Charity's eyes clouded as she found it impossible to make any sense of her father's words. "But don't we still want our freedom and independence from English tyranny, father?"

Irritated by having his daughter bring back his own words to haunt him, Kosterman snapped, "Freedom, Charity, will come from being trusted by the British once this meaningless rebellion is crushed and they are looking for solid citizens to put in responsible positions in the colony."

Steven Karcoff nervously shifted his feet and wiped his face. "It could be a trick to lure former rebels into the open. We were both signed up to join a Patriot militia unit in the spring. Why would they believe us now if we signed?"

"It's a chance we have to take," answered Kosterman. "We need to be on the winning side if we are to live comfortably after the war."

Steven Karcoff still looked edgy, nervous, and unconvinced. "What if Washington rallies?"

"Not a chance," Kosterman sadly snorted. "The British are professional soldiers. Washington is powerless because he is surrounded by cowards. They lost on Long Island. They lost on Manhattan. They lost at White Plains. They lost Forts Washington and Lee!" Kosterman chuckled and jabbed a thumb toward his daughter. "*Charity* could rout Washington's army, the way they're fighting!"

"Did you know, Gunter already signed?" asked Karcoff.

"Of course *he* would. He always leaned British, anyway."

Karcoff frowned and shook his head. "No. Gunter doesn't care about anyone except Gunter. He's only acting British because he's convinced the Revolution has collapsed."

"Maybe he's right," answered Mr. Kosterman. "Maybe we should sign, too."

"Maybe . . . " echoed Karcoff.

To distract himself while he wrestled with this great decision, Kosterman wiped his hands and furiously attacked a new pewter bowl with a polishing rag, trying to punish the metal with his soft cloth.

Karcoff was still unconvinced. "What if Congress convinces the French to enter the war? What if public support turns in favor of the rebels?"

Kosterman snorted. "Congress is a bunch of fools who couldn't argue their way out of a burning building. And without victories, the public will never turn in favor of the rebels. Nor will the French."

Karcoff laughed. His usual sparkle appeared in his eyes. "I suppose you're right. The 'war' is over. The English are here to stay and we had better make the best of it. I'll sign this afternoon for my family."

Joseph Kosterman sucked in a deep breath and nodded. "I'll go and sign with you."

He seemed greatly relieved, but Charity was not. "But father, you said the British were tyrants who wanted to crush us."

"Of course they want to crush their *enemies*, daughter. But *we* are not the enemy. We are part of the British family."

"But what if *I* don't want to be British anymore?"

Kosterman raised his voice like booming cannon fire. "And we will not doubt the King, our British loyalty, or our own father again. Nor will we ask any more senseless questions. Understood?"

Charity clenched her teeth to dutifully shut in her flood of concerns, lowered her eyes, and silently nodded her head. Loyal to the British she would be. What she really wanted to ask was: Do the British allow girls to go to *real* school and learn science?

As light snows swirled past the shop windows in a biting wind on January 4, 1777, Charity stoked the shop's wood stove to warm it enough for her father to work comfortably. It was 13 minutes after 9:00 A.M. and it was not like her father to be late for work. Six days a week, rain, sleet, heat, or snow, Joseph Kosterman worked from exactly 9:00 A.M. to exactly 4:00 P.M. Filled with foreboding, Charity stared at the corner clock as it tocked slowly past 9:14 and headed toward 9:15.

The door was flung open. Beaming like Christmas, itself, her father sprang in, arms spread wide to hug the world. "Ahhhh! They did it, Charity! It was a total rout!"

Charity stammered, "Was there a battle, father?"

"Of course there was, Charity. A glorious victory!" He actually danced his way into the shop.

"The British have won?" asked Charity.

Joseph Kosterman stopped, his face scrunched up as if he had bitten sour lemons. "The British? Whatever could you be thinking, Charity? Washington has crushed the lobster backs at Trenton and at Princeton. General Howe's Redcoats are retreating toward New York as fast as they can run! I *knew* the British couldn't sustain a war this far from their home base. It was obvious that Washington would cut them down when he was ready to."

Charity asked, "Does this mean we aren't British anymore?"

"We never were, daughter. Don't you see? We are Americans! *This* is our home. *This* is where our loyalties lie."

"But you signed a Loyalty Paper for the British. You pledged our oath to be loyal to the British and gave it to General Howe."

"That doesn't matter, Charity. They are the enemy and nothing I say to them really counts. Any oath that *might* have been pledged is totally invalid. I even wrote a note saying it was a lie. No, daughter, we are pure Americans and have always supported General Washington and the Revolution."

Charity's dark eyes soaked in her father's boyish enthusiasm. She slowly nodded. "If we're going to be revolutionaries again, father, and seek our liberty, I'd like to talk to you about going to school."

Aftermath

New Jersey followed its year of indecision with seven years of solid support for the Continental Army and the War for Independence. The colony remained rock-solid in its support even though it sat under the shadow of British naval power in New York harbor and under the threat of General Howe's massive British army housed next door in New York City. The Colonists remained loyal even though Howe's soldiers regularly foraged across New Jersey to plunder the land and threaten the residents. In the end, the solid strength of New Jersey support was a major factor in making General Clinton afraid to venture out of his sheltered New York fortress for any offensive campaigns from 1779 through 1782.

Follow-up Questions and Activities

1. **What Do You Know?**

   • Charity said that she wanted to be an apprentice to her father. What does that mean? What is an apprenticeship? Why have apprenticeships? Do we still use apprentices and apprenticeships in America today? For what trades and fields? How else do young workers get their training now? If you could be an apprentice, what field of work would it be in?

   • Why was the Battle of Long Island important? Why did the British win and the Americans lose?

- Why did patriotic Americans feel confident in August 1776 as they watched Washington's great army prepare to defend New York and await British attack?

- After the Battle of Long Island, Washington was able to sneak his army across to Manhattan. Why did the British think that the army would surrender instead? How was Washington able to sneak them out without being seen?

2. **Finding Out More**. Following are four important topics from this story for you to research in the library and on the Internet. The reference sources at the back of this book will help you get started.

- Make a list of the key ideals of the Revolution that the Founding Fathers fought to attain. Then trace the history of each of these ideals in American life. Which ones have been the easiest to achieve? Which have been the most difficult to fulfill? Why?

- Events in 1776 ranged from glorious successes to unbelievable disaster for the Continental Army. Research the early successes (Boston, Moore's Creek Bridge, Charleston, and the Declaration of Independence) that created such enthusiasm for and confidence in the Patriot cause. How were the Patriot forces able to win these victories? Describe the size and strength of the British forces the Continentals had to face in each of these battles.

- Research the string of disasters from August through early December 1776 (Long Island, Manhattan, Ft. Lee, Ft. Washington, abandoning New Jersey) that had most people thinking that Washington's army and the Revolution were about to collapse. Why did Washington's army fare so badly in the last half of 1776 when it had seemed to do so well against the British during the previous year?

- Research the role and position of an apprentice. When did the practice of apprenticeship begin? Typically, how old were beginning apprentices? What did they do? What did they have to learn? How long did an apprenticeship last? What happened to an apprentice when he or she finished his or her apprenticeship?

3. **Make It Real**

- Research the kinds of schools that existed in 1776. Who attended them? What did girls study? What did boys study? What did the children do who couldn't afford Latin Schools? Create a one-day schedule for what someone your own age would do in school in 1776.

- Pretend that you are your own age, living in Brooklyn, Long Island, in the summer of 1776. You may decide to be either a Patriot or a Loyalist. Write a letter to a friend describing your experience of the Battle of Long Island: the appearance and emotions of the soldiers; the sounds and sights of preparation; and the sights, sounds, and feel of the battle. Describe the change in the Continental soldiers after the battle. How did their complete collapse make you feel? How did you feel as the British moved in to occupy your town?

4. **Points to Ponder**.

- Why do you think so many New Jersey citizens first supported the Revolution, then signed Loyalty Papers, then went back to supporting the Revolution? Do you think it had anything to do with military events during the nine months in question?

- In this story, do you see any parallel between Charity's discussion with her father about her freedom and the freedom of the Colonists in relation to England? Reread the story and try to build the case that there are similarities between these two struggles, that they are both the struggle for personal independence. Does this same kind of disagreement happen in your family? How? Over what issues?

- Did you ever change your mind on an issue, then later change your mind back to your original position after you received new information? Were you a little embarrassed by your changing back and forth? Did you feel defensive about it?

Victory or Death
Battle of Trenton, December 26, 1776

Crossing the Delaware in ice and sleet

At a Glance

The first half of 1776 was full of successes for the Revolution. The second half saw terrifying disaster. Long Island was lost. Manhattan was lost. The Hudson River was lost. Ft. Washington—lost. Ft. Lee—lost. General Lee had been captured. The army was in tatters and total disarray.

Conditions were more dismal than anyone could have imagined. Men were deserting faster than they could be counted. Twelve thousand troops had become 6,000 or less. Common citizens were convinced that Washington was going to lose. No one would accept Continental paper money for supplies. The army was disintegrating; morale was nonexistent. The men were lethargic, energyless, and beaten, and couldn't wait to leave.

To make matters even worse, the enlistments for many—if not most—of the army would be up on December, 31, 1776. At the stroke of midnight, most of the army, like Cinderella, would revert back to ordinary citizens and would walk out of camp, leaving Washington with fewer than 2,000 men in tattered uniforms.

A French observer said, "There is more energy and passion for your Revolution in one coffee house in Paris than in your entire army!" Washington was described as "depressed."

British General Howe, on the other hand, felt quite content. The Revolution was disintegrating all on its own and he could take the credit. He established a string of posts throughout New Jersey to keep Washington bottled up during the winter, assuming there would be no Continental Army left by spring and he could go home a hero. General Cornwallis (the British second in command) packed for a vacation trip to England. Howe retired to New York for an endless string of winter parties and balls. General Clinton settled in Newport, Rhode Island, dreaming of his next assignment.

Colonel Rahl, the Hessian in charge of the garrison at Trenton, New Jersey, felt so confident he didn't order redoubts (small fortifications) built and scheduled no distant sentry routes or scouts. What was the point when Washington's army was afraid to fight? Rather than plan for Trenton's defense, he planned luxurious Christmas parties, seizing supplies and goods from locals in New Jersey.

Washington needed a victory, any victory, or he would have no army left with which to fight come spring. The Delaware River was both his sole protection from the advancing British and a major obstacle if he were to make some aggressive move.

Late in that December of 1776 there was a warm spell quickly followed by a brutal cold snap. The Delaware roared at near flood levels, with thick ice floes drifting and twirling in a strong current. Everyone thought it was impassable.

But Washington needed a victory . . . fast. He couldn't wait for spring. He couldn't wait for better conditions, or for the British and their hired Hessians to attack. If he didn't fight and win now, the army and the Revolution would collapse. Even though his army had been decimated in six straight battles and was in shambles, Washington would have to attack, now, before the end of the year, in the worst imaginable conditions.

Meet Marcus Raymond Stanton and Oliver Cromwell

Marcus Raymond Stanton was born a South Carolina slave in 1757. His mother also had been born on the Stanton plantation northwest of Charleston. His father had been purchased as a teenager. Marcus, a field worker, had never set foot outside the boundaries of the modest Stanton plantation when he was shoved into a recruiter's wagon and hustled 1,500 miles north to join the army, taking the place of Mr. Stanton's son, who didn't want to serve.

Marcus didn't know what an army was, that there was a war in progress, or even that there were other countries and colonies when he climbed out of that wagon and found himself thrown into the chaos surrounding Washington's retreat up Manhattan just after the battle of White Plains. Marcus survived the war and then drifted west, settling first in Kentucky and then in Ohio. He never returned to South Carolina for fear of again being made a slave.

Oliver Cromwell was born a free black in a ghetto on the south side of Philadelphia in 1752. His father died of disease when Oliver was a young boy. His mother and her three surviving children worked their way to New York and then to Boston, arriving when Oliver was 12. His mother died when he was 14. His older brother and younger sister moved west to start a farm. Farming held no attraction for Oliver, who stayed in the city to scrounge whatever work he could. Over the years, he always found enough work to survive but never enough to climb far ahead of starvation.

Oliver jumped at the chance to join the army, thinking it meant a steady source of food, clothes, and income. He held no ideological leanings one way or the other during the war, seeing it only as a practical way to survive. After the war he headed west, planning to meet up with his brother and sister. However, there is no record of him after his split from Marcus Stanton.

Victory or Death

Three soldiers huddled around a puny fire in the dark. Patches of bare dirt and dead grass peeked through the crusted snow. Stars sparkled crystal-clear in the bitter-cold sky above. Many in Washington's Continental Army had already crawled into tents to shiver under threadbare blankets. Others sat huddled around meager fires, unable to sleep.

Some, since this was the night of Tuesday, December 24, 1776, thought of Christmas at home. Some thought of Thomas Paine's stirring words ("These are the times that try men's souls. The summer soldier and the sunshine patriot will, in this crisis, shrink from the service of their country. . . ."), which had been read to every soldier that afternoon. Some thought only of the cold.

Two of the three soldiers huddled close to this particular fire were black: Marcus Raymond Stanton, a 19-year-old slave sent up from South Carolina, who joined the army in September just after the Battle of Long Island, and Oliver Cromwell, a 24-year-old Massachusetts free black who had been with the army since before the Battle of Bunker Hill. The third soldier, 17-year-old Joseph Martin, was fresh off his family's Pennsylvania farm. He had waited until all the crops were in to enlist and had only been in the army for a month. This was the first time in his life he had been more than 10 miles from home.

Joseph still glowed from the emotion of Paine's words read by their company commander. "Wasn't that a wonderful paper?"

Oliver said, "Nothing is wonderful when I'm cold, hungry, and tired."

Marcus added, "I'm too cold to sleep." He shivered, trembling through every part of his body. "I am so cold I don't think my bones will ever warm up again. There were nights in South Carolina we thought were cold, but they were like sweetest honey compared to the cold up here in this frozen North."

Joseph's mind couldn't leave Paine's stirring words. "Paine must be a great man to write like that. Just remembering the words still makes me excited."

"A coat would make me excited," interrupted Marcus. "How come we can't get coats? They should give us coats . . . and more fire wood."

"I had a coat last summer," said Oliver. "Hated lugging the thing around in the heat. I thought I would *never* need that mass of wool while we sweltered on Long Island. Didn't mind at all when I lost it when we ran at Gowanus Bay. Now I sure do miss that coat."

"You really been in all them battles?" asked Joseph.

"I was there—and don't you even hint I weren't. Breeds Hill I was under Colonel Prescott from Massachusetts. Fought next to Peter Salem and Salem Poor—now *there* was two amazing black fighters, sure enough!—both won theirselfs medals that day! For Long Island I was in Lord Stirling's Command. Man, was that one awful day. I was at Ft. Lee . . . "

"*I* was even at Ft. Lee and Ft. Washington," interrupted Marcus. "Those losses was just last month—only four weeks after I was joined up."

"You volunteered, too?" asked Joseph.

Marcus rocked back and laughed, white teeth flashing in the dark. "*Volunteer*? Naw. I'm a slave. My master had to send somebody. It was either one of us or his son. So here I am."

Oliver asked, "Why don't you run away?"

"Naw! Then I'm a run-away slave. Ain't nothin' lower than that. I'd be lynched for sure."

"Plenty of soldiers are running away," added Joseph. "I hear if we stay we're all going to die—killed in battle or hung once the British win. I hear this army is only one more defeat away from total collapse. But still we have to try to win the war to gain our freedom."

"Naw, I *ain't* runnin' away. And this here war is for white man's freedom, not mine—which is mighty peculiar since they already seem plenty free to me. No, I figure it this way. All I gots to do is not get shot and I win. I'm free. If the Americans win, I get my freedom 'cause I served in the army. If the British win, they ain't gonna hang a poor black slave ordered to fight, and since they don't believe in slavery, they'll make me free. 'These are the times that try men's souls. . . .' Phooey! This is the best of all 'times' for me. I stay alive and I am no longer a slave! I ain't goin' anywhere."

Oliver shook his head and laughed, "Man, you make me almost wish I was a slave instead of a free black who join up 'cause I was starvin' to death without a job in the city."

Joseph fidgeted, staring at the glowing embers of their fire, before he asked, "Do they treat you different because you're . . . you know, black?"

"Mostly, naw," answered Oliver. "Black or white we all march the same, eat the same slop, carry the same . . . "

Marcus interrupted, "Not me. I gots to carry the cook pot for our unit. That thing must weigh 20 pounds."

"Yeah, but plenty of whites are carryin' cook pots, too. I say it's only the few Southern whites who hate blacks that make it hard."

"Speakin' of whites that hates blacks," hissed Marcus leaning in toward the fire and his comrades, "here comes Captain Herfanger."

Oliver groaned. Joseph asked, "What's wrong with Captain Herfanger? He's helped me whenever I need it."

"That's because you're white," muttered Oliver.

Captain Sherman Herfanger was a blacksmith from North Carolina. He had been elected captain just after the Battle of Long Island. "You two," he growled, jabbing a cigar butt toward Marcus and Oliver, "on guard duty tonight."

"Again?" whined Marcus.

"Don't sass me, boy. Just do it."

"I'll think on it, Captain," answered Oliver, leaning back to gaze up at the stars as if he had all the time in the world. "Maybe if you was to make it worth my while . . . "

"You do it!" spluttered Herfanger, now red faced. "I'm an officer and I got privileges—like giving orders."

"Yeah," muttered Oliver. "And like stealing blankets and shoes from supply and selling them."

"I got expenses."

"Yeah, like bribing half the company so he can get reelected captain."

"He never bribed me," interrupted Marcus.

"You're black," answered Oliver.

"I never got a bribe, either," said Joseph.

"It ain't time for elections again. You just wait."

Herfanger hissed, "You two stop yer bellyachin' and get out there or you'll get 100 lashes in the morning!"

By noon on Christmas Day the camp buzzed with the certainty that something was up. Campfires were stoked and each unit was ordered to prepare three days' rations. Kits were packed. Powder and musket balls were distributed so that cartouche boxes bulged.

During supper the password was whispered to each company: "Victory or Death." Joseph Martin paled. "Oh, no. It's gonna be death. I just know it."

Almost 5,000 soldiers in ragged groups began a two-mile march to the Delaware River just after sunset. An icy wind had swirled through camp all afternoon. Now it was filled with sleet and howled out of the northeast, straight into the men's face as they trudged toward the river.

Joseph still had shoes because he had only been with the army a month and his hadn't worn out yet. Marcus's and Oliver's bare feet were both wrapped in slowly disintegrating rags that were stained a dark red from where their feet had bled through tender cracks between thick calluses.

They reached the bank of the Delaware River at 10:00 P.M. Snow and sleet drove into their faces, making it difficult to see. The river current ran hard, with jagged boulders of ice swirling ominously through the eddies.

Oliver sighed, "Too bad the weather and river are so mean and nasty tonight. They'll cancel the fight for sure."

Marcus scoffed, "You *want* to fight on a night like this?"

"Better to fight than just sit around and freeze."

Young Joseph's eyes filled with terror. "Look at that river! We're gonna freeze or drown if we try to cross. We'll never make it!"

A fleet of 60-foot Durham boats, manned by John Glover's Marblehead, Massachusetts, fishermen volunteers, began to ferry the troops, horses, and cannons across the river. Oarsmen slowly picked their way between raging chunks of ice, many big enough to crush a boat. Fighting wind, snow, current, and ice, the crossing bogged down, tedious and frightfully slow.

Troops waiting on each bank were ordered not to smoke, drink, or talk for fear of being heard by British scouts and pickets. The night grew fearfully cold and raw for men shivering without coats or shoes in the drifting snow, ice forming in their hair and on their skin. The air was wet and bitter cold and stung the face. The snow thickened into blinding clouds.

The crossing was supposed to be completed by midnight, but it was after 3:30 A.M.when the last of the artillery rolled off the battered boats and back onto New Jersey soil. Still Washington stood wrapped in his cloak at the river's edge, calm and unruffled, as if his desperate timetable weren't beginning to unravel.

In these bleak, dark hours of the frozen night, the weary army began the nine-mile march to Trenton. No rest halts were allowed for fear that some men would freeze to death if allowed to sink into the snow to doze. Washington issued orders to maintain strictest silence. Wheels on cannons were wrapped in cloth to muffle their sound.

Hail and sleet tore at their faces as Marcus, Oliver, and Joseph stumbled forward. The roads grew slick with ice. Unshod horses pulling cannons were unable to stand or walk on the ice and slid in every direction. Many bucked and stomped in fright. Two men had to walk beside each horse to hold it up and keep it moving.

When someone fell with a clatter of equipment, 10 others would fall over him, unable to stop in time in the dark. Officers hissed curses for everyone to be quiet. The fallen would have to be forced back up to their feet.

Ice built thick on eyelashes, closing eyes. Blood soaked through rags wrapped around feet and stained the new-fallen snow. Yet these injured feet were too cold to feel the pain, so soldiers numbly marched toward dawn and Trenton.

The snow turned to freezing rain and then back to sleet that cut through a man like a knife. Many drifted to sleep while they shuffled forward. Sergeants hissed and prodded them back awake for fear that, if they drifted off, they would never wake up again.

Still no one complained. Each soldier agreed that even this torment was better than running backwards away from the British. All seemed to know that the Revolution itself was on the line. The army couldn't afford to lose again.

Washington's plan called for the attack to begin before dawn. The wintry sky began to lighten to pale blue in the eastern sky while the lead units were still three miles from Trenton. The army staggered into a long trot over the slick ground, trying to reach Trenton before surprise was lost.

The hundred scattered houses of Trenton, New Jersey, were quiet and shut under the pounding of the storm. Ice glinted off picket fences and covered every tree branch in the wide apple orchards surrounding the town. The German soldiers of the Hessian regiment stationed by General Gage at Trenton were still fast asleep after their wild Christmas parties as the sun rose behind slate-gray clouds.

The units under General Nathaniel Greene were the first to reach Trenton, arriving just after 7:30 A.M. Captain Herfanger's company was second in line. The snow and sleet had stopped at first light, only to be replaced by dancing mists that swirled through the gray twilight.

A Hessian lieutenant, whose uniform coat was still unbuttoned, stepped out of the first house with a great yawn to gather his sentries for the day and post them around town. He froze, thunderstruck, staring at the mists. At first he thought his eyes were playing tricks on him. Then he thought he was seeing ghosts. The ranks of ragged Continentals shuffled out of the mists, and he screamed, "Der Deind! Heraus! Heraus!"

Neither Marcus nor Oliver could understand the words, but they both knew their meaning. They had been seen. Precious surprise was lost. Several in the lead company fired to scatter the lieutenant and the few soldiers who staggered in disbelief out of the door behind him.

The lead company rushed forward. Without waiting for a command, Captain Herfanger's company followed, almost at a sprint. Surges of battle-induced excitement shattered their frozen weariness.

They heard drums and bugles call the Hessians to arms, but the German mercenaries were too slow. The Continentals rushed forward, scattering the German units before they could form. Powder was too wet to ignite, so the charge was made in an eerie silence, broken only by drums, the clanking of bayonets, and an occasional shouted order.

Captain Herfanger screamed a command to halt so he could reorganize his company before their ranks were lost in the chaos of a mad charge. He hesitated, glaring at Marcus, Oliver, and the five other blacks in his command, unsure of where to place them—in front to get killed first, or in the rear because he didn't think them capable of carrying out an effective attack and he wanted his company to do well.

The sight of a Hessian unit hastily forming a hay-bale blockade across the road before them settled the question. The soldiers galloped forward as they were, not waiting for any orders from their captain. Maybe some hand-to-hand action would warm their chilled blood. The company leapt upon the barricade and the Hessians. Bayonets gleamed and flashed in the misty light. The first rank of green-coated Hessians crumpled to the dirt. The rest dissolved into a rout.

Two German cannons set up on Princeton road to sweep the flank of General Sullivan's men. Colonel Scott rallied Herfanger's and two other companies and led a charge across open fields of ice that crunched under their feet to capture the cannons and Princeton Road.

By 8:00 the powder began to dry and the crackle of gunfire erupted like popcorn across the town. The Hessians were almost surrounded, jabbering to each other and running this way and that. Riflemen mowed down German troops trying to find their units and stay out of American fire. The German colonel was shot leading a retreat into an ice-covered apple orchard. Within minutes, the Hessians surrendered.

The whole battle lasted less than one hour. Whereas 900 Hessians had been captured, 80 killed, and 150 wounded, only two Americans had died and only three were wounded. Panting, his breath snorting out as clouds of steam in the cold, Joseph shouted, "We did it! We won! We're alive!"

Oliver smacked his lips as if savoring the sweetest of desserts. "This winning surely feels better than losing and running!"

Captain Herfanger grudgingly nodded, acknowledging Marcus's and Oliver's performance during the battle.

Marcus elbowed Oliver in the side. "He smiled! Now *that* is a victory." Then his thoughts turned back to the gnawing hunger in his stomach and the numbed pain in his raw and bleeding feet. One smile was a start, but it would take a lot more than that to survive this winter and this war.

Aftermath

Militarily and strategically, the battles at Trenton and Princeton meant little. Psychologically, they meant everything. Both were victories for America. Both were offensive (not defensive) fights for the Continentals. Both were won by bayonet charges. (Americans weren't supposed to be any good with the bayonet.)

Trenton and Princeton made the Americans look like a real army. They made the citizens *believe* that they had a real army, and they made the *British* believe that Washington had a real army. Howe drew his tentacles in close to New York and refused to venture out until reinforcements arrived from England in the spring.

Washington was a hero again. Some of the short-term enlistees re-upped for another term, but most still left. The army dropped to as few as 1,500 souls. But Washington was able to hide his weakness from British view until new recruits (encouraged by the Trenton and Princeton victories) joined during the winter and spring.

The Trenton and Princeton battles didn't win the war, but single-handedly they kept Washington from losing the war. Washington was given credit for baffling the enemy. He had "pounced like an eagle" and was elevated to the status of national hero. With beaming smiles of relief, many in Congress said, "If he does nothing more, he will live in history as a great military leader."

Over 10,000 free blacks and slaves—sent in place of their masters—fought for the Continental Army during the Revolutionary War. Over 1,100 fought with British forces. Blacks made up as much as 20 percent of Washington's army near the end of the war. The Continental Army was the most integrated American Army ever fielded until World War II.

Follow-up Questions and Activities

1. **What Do You Know?**

   - This story describes men trudging through snow and ice barefoot. Why didn't they freeze? How dangerous is it to march barefoot through snow, ice, and sleet?

   - At Trenton, the Continental Army fought Hessian mercenary soldiers. What are mercenaries? Why would one country "rent" soldiers from another? Why would a country "rent out" its own army? Has the use of mercenaries been a common practice throughout history? Is it still practiced today? How? Where?

   - Did blacks live in all 13 of the Colonies at the beginning of the Revolutionary War? Were there slaves in each of the 13 Colonies?

   - How could a black slave gain freedom? List as many ways for slaves to become free as you can. How did they prove they were free when they needed to?

   - Why were the Hessians so lax in their security at Trenton? What did they expect to happen?

2. **Finding Out More.** Following are three important topics from this story for you to research in the library and on the Internet. The reference sources at the back of this book will help you get started.

   - How many blacks lived in each colony? How many were free? How many were slaves? What percentage of the total population did blacks represent? What jobs did slaves perform? Who does similar types of jobs in this country today?

   - Washington's soldiers were already dressed in rags by December 1776. Why didn't they have new shoes and uniforms? Who was supposed to supply them, and how? Why didn't those supplies ever get to the soldiers who needed them? Research the funding and supply of the Continental Army. Where did the real problems with supplying the army lie?

   - During the early stages of the Battle of Trenton, no soldiers could fire their weapons because their powder was too damp. How did early muskets fire? How were they loaded? Research the use of muzzle-loading muskets to see how slow and awkward they were.

3. **Make It Real**

   - Prepare a chart showing the population of free blacks and slaves in each colony at the beginning of the war. Compare life for free blacks and black slaves in the mid-1770s.

   - Research the writer Thomas Paine. Why were the two books he printed in 1776 so powerful and effective? What did he do before and after 1776? What else did he write?

4.   **Points to Ponder**

- The Continental Army enlisted more blacks than any American army until World War II. Why do you think the Continental Army was so integrated? What was the benefit to the army of recruiting blacks? Search for as many benefits as you can to opening the army to minority races. Then search for reasons why whites might not have wanted to arm blacks and place them in the army.

- Do you think Washington's attack on Trenton was a military *campaign* or just a bluff, a meaningless show? How close to defeat was Washington in late December 1776? Do you think the attack on Trenton was a last, desperate gamble to keep the army from total collapse?

1777
at a
Glance

The Best and Worst of Times

The year 1777 dawned on notes both of cautious optimism and of dread for the American cause. Would events follow from the glorious closing triumphs of Trenton and Princeton, or would the great surge of British military might reassert itself as it had the previous summer and fall?

The year started slowly for the Americans, waiting for the British to make a move. General Burgoyne devised a grand, three-pronged plan to slice the Colonies in two along the Hudson River and Lake Champlain. London approved, but apparently General Howe never cared much for the plan.

In early summer, Burgoyne started south from Canada with his army. Howe was supposed to move north up the Hudson from New York with his troops. Colonel Le-Gare, with a smaller force, was to sweep east from Lake Ontario through the Mohawk Valley in upstate New York. All three forces were to meet at Albany, New York, in the fall.

Burgoyne progressed slowly, hampered by his ponderous line of soldiers and supply wagons. Howe decided to attack Philadelphia instead of marching up the Hudson to meet Burgoyne.

Washington moved toward Philadelphia to follow Howe. With the Continental Army moving south, a volunteer army of militia groups gathered in upstate New York to meet Burgoyne. Burgoyne's force was destroyed; he surrendered his entire army. LeGare was crushed. Triumphant town bells announcing these great victories were rung from Maine to Georgia.

At the same time, Howe and Cornwallis outmaneuvered and outfought Washington's army at every encounter. Just as victory was declared in the North, defeat was realized in Pennsylvania. Howe took the Patriot capital and Washington limped off into the country, afraid to face another major battle with the British.

Just when it looked like America had something to cheer about (Burgoyne's defeat), it appeared that Washington's Continental Army might once again utterly collapse and disintegrate as the disillusioned, lifeless, ragamuffin band shuffled (more barefoot than not) into winter camp at Valley Forge, seemingly incapable of defeating any British armed force.

Key Events in 1777

Date	Event
May 20	Cherokees sign Treaty of DeWitts Corner, giving up all land in South Carolina.
Early June	Burgoyne begins his move south from Canada.
June 14	United States flag adopted by Congress (Flag Day).
July 6	Burgoyne captures Ft. Ticonderoga.
Mid-August	Howe swings his army by ship south from New York to capture Philadelphia.
August 16	Battle of Bennington, New York. Burgoyne pushes farther south to the Hudson.
September 2	Battle of Brandywine, Pennsylvania. Howe outmaneuvers and defeats Washington.
September 19	Battle of Freeman's Farm (New York). Burgoyne is halted.
September 20	Paoli Massacre. British, Tory, and Mohawk force is destroyed in western New York.
September 26	Howe occupies Philadelphia.
October 4	Battle of Germantown. Washington muffs a chance for victory.
October 17	Burgoyne surrenders at Saratoga.
December 11	Washington limps into winter quarters at Valley Forge.

You Go, Girl!

Women Take up the War, Groton, Massachusetts, 1777

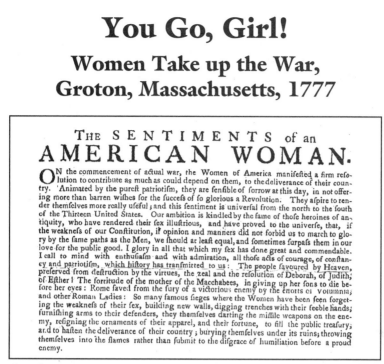

THE SENTIMENTS of an

AMERICAN WOMAN.

ON the commencement of actual war, the Women of America manifested a firm refolution to contribute as much as could depend on them, to the deliverance of their country. Animated by the pureft patriotifm, they are fenfible of forrow at this day, in not offering more than barren wifhes for the fuccefs of fo glorious a Revolution. They afpire to render themfelves more really ufeful; and this fentiment is univerfal from the north to the fouth of the Thirteen United States. Our ambition is kindled by the fame of thofe heroines of antiquity, who have rendered their fex illuftrious, and have proved to the univerfe, that, if the weaknefs of our Conftitution, if opinion and manners did not forbid us to march to glory by the fame paths as the Men, we fhould at leaft equal, and fometimes furpafs them in our love for the public good. I glory in all that which my fex has done great and commendable. I call to mind with enthufiafm and with admiration, all thofe acts of courage, of conftancy and patriotifm, which hiftory has tranfmitted to us: The people favoured by Heaven, preferved from deftruction by the virtues, the zeal and the refolution of Deborah, of Judith, of Efther! The forritude of the mother of the Macchabees, in giving up her fons to die before her eyes: Rome faved from the fury of a victorious enemy by the efforts of Volumnia; and other Roman Ladies: So many famous fieges where the Women have been feen forgetting the weaknefs of their fex, building new walls, digging trenches with their feeble hands; furnifhing arms to their defenders, they themfelves darting the miffile weapons on the enemy, refigning the ornaments of their apparel, and their fortune, to fill the public treafury; and to haften the deliverance of their country; burying themfelves under its ruins; throwing themfelves into the flames rather than fubmit to the difgrace of humiliation before a proud enemy.

Opening paragraph of a famous statement of women's view of the war

At a Glance

Fighting had always been men's business. In colony after colony men left the farm unplanted, or unharvested, the live stock untended, the grain unthreshed and unmilled, the hides untanned, and rushed to join armies and militia units. Fishing boats were tied to docks, stores were locked, and men raced to war.

Women were left at home to do their own work *plus* care for the children *plus* do the men's work that supported the family *plus* support the war by making clothes, blankets, and gunpowder and by collecting food. It was a crushing burden.

But many women took on even more. Many formed local committees and militia of their own under the general banner of "Daughters of Liberty." If the war could not have been won without the brave efforts of many men, neither could it have been won without the equally courageous, usually more arduous, and mostly unheralded efforts of an army of women. This is a small part of the story of one such group.

Meet Virginia Wright

Virginia Haverall was born in 1737 in England. Her parents immigrated to America for better economic opportunities when she was five and settled in Providence, Rhode Island. Her father worked in a sail-making shop, eventually becoming foreman. Virginia worked with her mother as a seamstress from the age of eight. She attended a

Dame School for six years in Providence and traveled to Boston for finishing school, staying there with an aunt. In Boston she met David Wright, whose father owned three fishing boats in Groton, Massachusetts. They married and settled in Groton when Virginia was 17.

David Wright took over the family fishing business and was able to double the size of their fishing fleet and add a whaling schooner, partly because Virginia helped run the business. She was a tall and powerful woman who could easily intimidate most merchants and dealers.

Virginia was a pillar of Groton society and the recognized leader of the local Patriot (Whig) women. Mr. Wright was wounded during the war. He was carried home with a bad limp and was never able to put out to sea again. Virginia lived comfortably in Groton until she died in 1807.

The rainy Tuesday afternoon of February 10, 1777, lo~
ter day in the seaport town of Groton, Massachusetts. ~
were tied thick and tight in the harbor, some because of the ga~
had kicked the sea into a wild toss of whitecaps and driving foam and spray, ~
because owners and crew were off fighting the war and had abandoned their trad~
until national freedom should be won.

One by one, the women of the town braved the driving storm to struggle
down Harbor Street and around the corner onto tree-shaded Maple Road to the
generous house of Mrs. David Wright. (Mr. Wright, the owner of a fleet of five
fishing boats and one whaling boat, was off at the war as a colonel of militia.) The
porch offered a grand view of the usually quiet marshes that surrounded the inland sides of Groton. As was true at every spot in town, visitors to the porch could
smell the pungent scent of salt water and hear the sound of buoy bells, of screeching gulls, and of clanging ropes against masts in addition to this afternoon's driving rain and pesky wind. Groton was a town that lived by the rhythms of the sea.

One by one the women mounted the stairs to the wide sitting porch and
shook off their coats and shoes in the sheltered safety. Every Tuesday afternoon
and evening were reserved for the Daughters of Liberty sewing and knitting bee.
The women of Groton were more obviously divided into Loyalist and Rebel by
who attended these bees than had been the men of the town before they rushed off
to join Patriot and Tory militia units.

"Mrs. Parsons! Welcome," said Mrs. Wright, holding the door and extending a greeting hand. Virginia Wright was a tall, heavyset woman with fashionable
chestnut hair and sea-blue eyes that blazed with patriotic zeal like shimmers of
sunlight off a calm ocean.

"Good afternoon, Virginia," replied Susan Parsons, wife of Henry Parsons,
prosperous local merchant, whose bad leg kept him from joining the military.
"Will the rain *ever* let up?" She leaned close and whispered, "Will I be in the
basement today?" Susan Parsons appeared thin and frail, with willowy blond
hair. Her eyes always appeared as if she were about to cry. But she was a tough,
dependable worker and a mainstay of the Patriot community.

"No, Susan. We are well stocked on gunpowder, but there has been a desperate call for blankets. So we will all be working upstairs on knitting today."

...n Parsons settled into her work in the spacious Wright living room next ...be Henshaw (wife of Parson Henshaw, who was chaplain for three Mas-...setts regiments camped with Washington at Morristown, New Jersey) and ...ng Charity Plummer (wife of William Plummer, first mate on a whaling ship ...w serving the army as a boatman to ferry supplies and soldiers across rivers and lakes).

Although pleasant conversation rippled around the room, all were focused on their work. "Ladies," announced Virginia Wright in a commanding voice, "I have just received the final casualty lists from the sterling victories at Trenton and Princeton. A total of 30 dead. Two were from Massachusetts, but from the western end of our fair state. None of the wounded were from Groton."

A cheer arose throughout the room and the women seemed to redouble their efforts to produce an overwhelming abundance of blankets for their soldiers.

Mrs. Wright's servants brought out carts of tea and coffee to refresh the workers.

"Tea?" asked Phoebe Henshaw, more as an accusation than a question. With callused hands, patched and faded clothes, and tousled hair, Phoebe looked more like a washer woman than a parson's wife. On a parson's meager salary, she had to work more like a washer woman than a society lady.

"Apricot leaf tea from good Massachusetts trees," answered Virginia Wright with relish and pride. "The coffee is wheat coffee. Weak and poor of taste, but very patriotic!"

Again everyone clapped and paused long enough to crowd around the cart for a cup. As they settled back into their work, Phoebe Henshaw brushed back her hair with rough fingers. "Why has real coffee become so expensive? It isn't banned or blockaded by British ships."

"Need I remind thee that there is a war on?" answered trim Mary Titus, a gi-ant Quaker woman who stood well over six feet tall and towered over everyone else in the community. Her dark, thoughtful eyes always appeared grave and stern against her pale, alabaster skin. But she really possessed a quick wit and was free with her friendly smile.

Young Charity Plummer batted her long lashes as she said, "Phoebe is right. There is no reason for the price of coffee to have tripled in the last year." Chari-ty's red hair fell in curls across her shoulders, but it was her deep green eyes that drew attention—maybe because she loved to bat her eyelashes when she spoke. "My cousin wrote that they caught a merchant in Boston hoarding coffee just to raise the price and gouge extra profits."

Virginia Wright rose with a commanding scowl. "Ladies, that is positively un-American and unacceptable! If it is happening here we must stop it!"

Mary Titus asked, "And how exactly will thee find out and do that, Virginia?"

After an awkward pause, Susan Parsons added, "And why are Tory messen-gers allowed to roam freely up and down the coast, and in and out of town?"

Again it was Mary Titus who responded. "Because the men of the militia who could stop them are off at war, Susan."

Virginia's considerable bulk seemed to swell; she looked like a general posturing before his troops. "Ladies, the Daughters of Liberty must do more than knit (and make gunpowder)."

Weary Phoebe Henshaw said, "We are already overburdened. With the men gone, we have to plant, make hay, husk and garner corn, care for livestock, butcher and clean meats, make flour and breads, make rum, make linen and woolens, blankets and bedding, do the weekly wash, care for the house and the sick and needy, and raise the children. What more can we do?"

Virginia snapped back, "We must do what needs to be done! If we do not win the war *here*, there will be no point in our husbands and sons winning the war on the battlefield."

Charity laughed, "Groton's not important, Virginia. There's nothing that needs to be won here."

Virginia's voice rose as she answered like a preacher rising to the climax of a fiery sermon. She shook her finger. "Groton is important to us. It is our home. It is where we are. It must be where we fight as needed to win the war."

Mary calmly said, "That is fine talk, Virginia Wright, but what does thee propose to do?"

Again there was an awkward pause before Virginia answered. "For today, I propose to think upon the matter. But know this. We must *do* something. Liberty depends on it!"

As the clicking of knitting needles swung into high gear at the beginning of the next week's knitting circle, Virginia Wright rose and politely coughed to draw everyone's attention. "Ladies, the Groton Daughters of Liberty must become the women's militia in the absence of our husbands."

Looks of surprise and horror were exchanged around the room. "But I don't know how to shoot."

"We don't have a musket. My husband and son took our only two when they marched to war."

"There is already too much to do. We have no time to drill and practice."

Mary Titus smiled, "Would thee have us become the Groton Minute-Women, Virginia?"

"Precisely! We have been plundered several times by British ships confiscating supplies for their army. Other towns have been stripped bare by the thieving Redcoats. Churches have been taken over as British granaries and stables. Tory units have terrorized decent, law-abiding citizens. Loyalist merchants see the war as a chance to gouge extra profits from their communities. We must make sure it never again happens here!"

"How?" demanded Mary.

"First, we will post armed guards at the bridge to disrupt Tory communications. No foe to freedom shall pass over our town's bridge! Next we will inspect the stores and records of the town's merchants to ensure they make only a fair profit on grains and coffee."

Again Mary demanded, "How? What if they will not show us their ledgers?"

"With a force of 30 armed women, we will not ask, we will demand!"

A rush of empowering energy ran through the room and erupted in spontaneous cheers. Heady with excitement, the women agreed to scrounge whatever arms they could muster—musket, pistol, pitchfork, or club—and become the Women's Army of Groton.

The next afternoon frail Susan Parsons and towering Mary Titus were on guard duty. Susan carried an old family musket. Mary carried only a pitchfork. They stood by a tree at the Groton end of the bridge over the Nashua River and the road to Pepperell. At the sounds of an approaching rider, both women raced to the middle of the road. Mary also carried the large drum that was the signaling device for reinforcements.

The rider approached at a fast trot but reigned in his horse in mid-stride while he sized up the women blocking his path. "Good afternoon, ladies," he said with a sweeping bow of body and hat.

"It's Captain Leonard Whiting," hissed Mary.

"He's a known Tory," whispered Susan, priming and cocking her musket. "Hit the drum."

Mary began to beat the booming drum. Gulls screeched and flapped into the air in response.

"Is there a problem, ladies?" inquired the captain, glancing nervously at the road to town beyond the bridge guards.

"Step down, Captain Whiting, or I will fire."

"Are you bandits?" he demanded. "This is robbery. This is an outrage!"

"Dismount, Tory spy," repeated Mary.

Too late Captain Whiting saw the flood of armed women racing down the street toward him. Too late he realized his danger. He tried to wheel his horse and make a run for it. Susan's gun exploded in flame and smoke. A thunderclap report echoed across the landscape.

Captain Whiting's horse bucked and whinnied. Whiting sprawled on the bridge's deck, a neat musket ball hole ripped through the hem of his coat.

Almost before he could scramble to his feet, he was surrounded by an army of women wielding guns, knives, cleavers, and pitchforks. Slowly he raised his hands and the search began. In his left boot Virginia Wright found the folded messages from the British in Canada to Tory units throughout Massachusetts.

"To the jail!" bellowed Virginia Wright, and Whiting was prodded and hustled through town by his women captors while Groton men laughed and pointed.

With Whiting locked in irons, Virginia cried, "To Milikin's store. Let's find out the truth about coffee prices!"

The army of women cheered and, waving their weapons, stormed down Market Street toward Milikin's general store. A crowd of onlookers—some amused, some horrified, some shocked—followed behind the militia, determined not to miss one word of the coming confrontation.

Hearing the clattering commotion tearing down the street towards him, Mr. Samuel Milikin met the women's militia on the boardwalk outside his front door and tipped his hat. "Ladies. What can I do for you this fine day?"

"Thee can sell us coffee at a fair price, Mr. Milikin."

"Mrs. Titus. You know I always sell at a fair price."

"We will be the judge of that," bellowed Virginia Wright. "We would see your ledgers."

"That's out of the question, Mrs. Wright."

"The key to the ledgers," she demanded.

He repeated "no," but the growls from the crowd of armed women brought a growing look of alarm to his face.

"Ladies, what do we say to that answer?"

A dozen women, led by Virginia, towering Mary Titus, and tough Phoebe Henshaw, lifted Mr. Milikin into the air and flung him onto his back in a small cart. "Tar and feathers!" cried several women.

Milikin's usually red face paled in panic and a shaky hand extended the key to his ledgers toward the women.

It took less than 10 minutes for the women to determine that Milikin was hoarding coffee and mocha (chocolate) to artificially raise their price. The women seized his entire stock and distributed it equally to Patriot households all across town. Patriot families refused to shop in Milikin's store. Within a month he had scampered away to Canada and was never seen in Groton again. Prices in other stores mysteriously dropped to pre-war levels.

At the knitting bee the following week the Groton Daughters of Liberty were still flushed with their victories—except for Virginia Wright, who held a letter she had received from her husband. "Ladies, we must still do more!"

"More? We're already guarding the bridge. Why us?"

"Because we are here and liberty needs us. My husband's letter says new wagons are needed and the Groton town cannons must be repaired and made ready to ship to the army. We need a blacksmith."

All eyes turned to stocky Betsy Hager, whose husband had run the town blacksmith shop until he left with the militia. "But the forge has been closed since my husband left."

Susan Parsons said, "But, Betsy, I have seen you shoe a horse before. Can't you run the forge?"

"What of my children and house work? What of my gardens?"

Virginia announced, "We will cover those chores if you become our blacksmith." There was a great cheer as Betsy shrugged and softly nodded. "I can try . . ."

The sound of hammers pounding on metal rang again in Groton. The bridges were guarded and safe. Fields were tended. Crops were weeded and gathered. Breads were baked. Laundry was washed. Children were fed. The pungent scent of salt water filled the town, as did the sound of buoy bells, screeching gulls, and clanging ropes against masts. But in Groton, Massachusetts, as in a hundred other American towns, the Daughters of Liberty had forged a new kind of citizen—the kind a new country would need as it spread, grew, and struggled.

Aftermath

Daughters of Liberty groups were organized throughout the Colonies. Some raised money; some collected food. Virtually all made clothes and blankets. Many sent volunteers to work in army camps, cooking and cleaning for the soldiers. Many acted as spies and messengers. Washington's army could not have survived, liberty would not have taken root so firmly, and the war could not have been won, without the steadfast and vital efforts of these women.

Follow-up Questions and Activities

1. **What Do You Know?**

   - What did women do during the war? With a few exceptions, they didn't fight, yet they made essential contributions to the war effort. What were they?

   - What were message riders? What did they do? Did both sides use messengers to carry news and plans back and forth?

   - Why do prices often go up during a war? Why were the Groton women worried about retailers raising prices? What is price gouging?

   - Why did the Groton women spend so much time knitting and sewing? Who were they sewing for? Typically, what were they sewing and knitting? Why was clothing for the army a concern of wives and women at home?

2. **Finding Out More.** Following are three important topics from this story for you to research in the library and on the Internet. The reference sources at the back of this book will help you get started.

   - This story covers some, but not all, of the responsibilities women commonly assumed during the Revolutionary War. Research women's responsibilities during the war. Were women's efforts more or less important than those of soldiers? Compare the list of women's chores to what you have to do today. Did women in 1777 have more responsibilities than you do? Why, or why not?

   - How did armies communicate and keep in touch with different units and posts with no telephones or radios? Research eighteenth-century communications. How did notes, reports, and orders get from post to post and from unit to unit?

   - What dangers did a message rider face? Why were patrols on both sides out searching for messengers? What did the messengers have that each army wanted? What protection did a messenger have if stopped by the enemy?

3. **Make It Real**

   • Try to determine the importance of "women's work" to an army. First make a list of all the services women provided for an army in the field. Now compare that eighteenth-century army to your school. Make a chart showing how cleaning, washing, grass trimming, food preparation, and supplying classrooms get done at your school. Chart how books, school supplies, school schedules, and plans are created and get to your classroom. Chart how facilities, trained teachers, and necessary equipment are made available when you need them. Who provides each of these services? What would happen if they weren't done?

   • Women's groups often acted as local activist groups to advance their cause. Research activist groups in your area. What have they formed to accomplish? How successful have they been? What tactics have they used?

4. **Points to Ponder**

   • Why do you think we don't usually hear about or read about the critical roles that women played during the Revolution? When we hear about women, it is usually only about those few who played a man's role—that is, actually fought in battles. Do you think the women who fought did more than those who didn't? Find as many reasons as possible to support your answer.

   • Do you think the roles of women in the home, the economy, the government, and the military have changed since the Revolutionary War? How or how not? Why or why not?

I'm an American, Too

Staying Neutral, 1777

Famous Patriot slogan and threat

At a Glance

War is always divisive. A civil war is the most divisive of all. The American Revolutionary War didn't pit regions of the country against each other, but rather pitted neighbor against neighbor in virtually every region and community of the country. Everyone grew suspicious of everyone else because few declared their politics openly. Loyalties and militia units were formed in secret. The very person you pleasantly did business with during the day might be part of the group that attacked and burned your farm at night.

Rampant suspicion made it very hard to *not* choose a side. Many thought "if you aren't for us, you're against us." A few groups, like the Quakers and Shakers, maintained official neutrality. But even many Quakers actively supported the Revolution and participated in it.

Many people felt that everyone *had* to choose a side, that it was impossible not to have a strong emotional bond with one side or the other. To these people, anyone who refused to admit loyalties was probably a spy for the other side.

The Revolutionary War was perhaps the hardest time in the history of this country to remain neutral. Yet there were some, like Gregory McDowell, who insisted on maintaining their neutrality. Gregory McDowell's story, like that of many neutrals, shows how heavy a price neutrality could carry.

Meet Gregory McDowell

Gregory McDowell, age 26 in 1778, was a hard-working craftsman with a wife and two children. McDowell was a devout Presbyterian, mostly apolitical but with a slight leaning toward being a Loyalist because that's the way he had always leaned. His people were Scottish but had been in America for three generations. He was the first in his family to live in a city (Annapolis), the first to leave the farm, and the first to have a trade. He was taught to read and write at home and finished his apprenticeship as a printer in 1775. He opened his own printing shop that same year. McDowell's fondest wish was to be left alone to do his work and live his life in peace with his family.

I'm an American, Too

Whispers.

Gregory didn't hear them as much as feel them, as if each whispered rumor was a dart thrown at him from the shadows. There had been a time—say, a year ago—when he would have turned and proudly confronted the rumors, the raised eyebrows, the slowly shaking heads as he passed. But now, in the fall of 1777, the British army sat in Philadelphia and the British fleet roamed freely through Chesapeake Bay, as the last few stubborn leaves still clung to the trees. Now it was harder to face the accusing looks of his neighbors. Gregory McDowell kept his hat squashed low over his face and flame-red hair as if to hide from the looks and whispers.

Gregory McDowell owned a small print shop on Gloucester Street near the corner of Market Street in the seaport of Annapolis, Maryland. In 1774 McDowell declared that he and his family were and would remain neutral. He could not take sides between his country and his motherland. In 1774 that had been easy to say and easy to uphold. But in late 1777, every new day seemed to bring new pressures to declare one way or the other.

So these days McDowell scurried—almost ran—home at the end of his work day up Randall and King George Streets to his house on Hanover. Stepping into his house and the smell of roasting apples, George pried his hat off his head and straightened his flattened hair.

"You look worried," said his wife, Mary, wiping her hands on her apron. "What happened today?"

"Nothing . . . and everything," blurted Gregory. He plopped into a chair, wringing his hands. "Every customer these days doesn't care if I do good work, if I know my trade. They just want to know who I work for. I say 'for my customers.' They reply '*Whig* customers or *Tory* customers?' I answer 'my customers don't have to sign oaths of allegiance. They just have to appreciate quality printing.' Then, no matter who they are, people sneer at me like I have just admitted to being a traitor. I'm losing business—all because I won't pick a side in this ugly family squabble."

Mary sighed. "Peace and tolerance have little place in today's world."

Their two children burst into the house. Nine-year-old Robert was tall, skinny as a rail. Melody was stocky and six. Both had carrot-top, red-orange hair inherited from their father. A galaxy of freckles tumbled across Melody's cheeks and nose. Robert was a student at a prominent Annapolis day school. Melody was scheduled to begin finishing school in another two years.

Robert was bold and brave, even though he lacked the muscle to back it up. "Father, two of the older boys called me a Tory today and shoved me." His fists were defiantly jammed against his hips. "I threatened to pound them if they ever called me that again!"

"Very brave of you, Robert, to stand up to two older boys. And certainly you are right. We are not Tories."

Melody's face reddened and her eyes lowered to the floor. "Oh. . . . Does that mean we're Whigs then, father? I kicked a boy in the shin today because he called me a Whig. Should I apologize?"

"Kicking is never good behavior, Melody. So, yes, you should apologize. But no, we are not Whigs either."

"Then what are we?" wailed both children.

"We are Americans."

"But which *kind* of Americans? Patriot or Loyalist?"

"Whig or Tory?" added Melody.

"We are neither of those things," insisted Gregory. "We are loyal to Maryland (our colony), to America (our country), and to Britain (our motherland)."

Both children scowled in confusion.

"There! See?" said Gregory, pointing at his children's faces. "*That's* the look I get from customers in the shop!"

Mary patted her husband's shoulder. "Maybe it is because this is a time when everyone *must* choose."

"No!" he exploded. "I will not be goaded into taking sides. If your own beloved parents were squabbling, would you pick one over the other? No. You would love and support them both. You would *have* to."

Mary rose, sniffing the air. "I think dinner's ready. Wash up, children."

Robert asked, "Are we pacifists, then, like the Quakers?"

"Certainly not," laughed Mr. McDowell. "We'll fight for what we believe in. I would fight for either England or America, but I won't fight *against* either."

The children looked more confused than ever as they shuffled toward the table.

The next morning, Gregory McDowell was cleaning his printing press while a misty rain dampened the cobblestone street outside. The shop bell rang as a plump, red-faced man, stuffed into a heavy cloak, stepped in.

Secretly Gregory groaned even as he tried to sound cheery. "Good morning, Mr. Simpton. How is your bank faring this fine day?"

"Ahh, exactly why I have stopped by, Mr. McDowell," replied the banker, with a smile too broad and forced to be anything but a warning. "I'm worried about your future, Gregory, and therefore about my bank's loan which allowed you to open this shop." All the while he spoke, Simpton leisurely ran a finger along the trays of type, the presses, and the counters, as if inspecting for dust.

Gregory stoically ground his teeth. "Worried? About *me*, Mr. Simpton?"

Simpton finally turned his gaze on Gregory. "I've noticed you haven't signed a Loyalty Oath or joined a local Loyalist militia. I also have heard that you have done printing for known rebels. One might suspect you of being a rebel, yourself."

"I am no rebel, Mr. Simpton, and I work for whoever wants quality printing. But neither will I take up arms against my fellow countrymen."

"Ahh, there, you see, is the rub. Once the rebellion is crushed, the army, I fear, will say that anyone who didn't actively support His Majesty was *against* His Majesty and treat you as if you had been a rebel. That would put you, your shop—and thus our loan—in jeopardy." Again a phony, thick-lipped smile spread across his face.

Gregory began to tremble, both with fear and anger. "Are you saying that if I don't become an active Loyalist, you will foreclose my bank loan and drive me out of business?"

"I'm only trying to protect the bank's position, Gregory." Simpton adjusted his cloak and hat and turned for the door. "Think hard about it, Gregory McDowell. The future is with mother England. If *you* do not care about your future, why should I?"

The bell clanged behind him as he slammed the door.

Gregory was still trembling with indignation when, less than two hours later, his shop bell clanged again as a squat, tough man muscled his way into the shop. This man stomped to the counter and came straight to the point. "Give me one good reason why I shouldn't treat you as a Tory, McDowell."

"And good morning also to you, Mr. Kantor . . . "

"That's *Colonel* Kantor," interrupted the bull of a man, who had long owned a sail-making and rope-making shop down at the foot of Shipwright Street.

Gregory was taken aback. "I knew you were a member of the local Committee of Safety, but a colonel? Of what?"

"I was elected to head the local Patriot militia last week—as you would know if you attended any Patriot meetings."

Gregory protested, "I am not a member of any militia unit or support committee for the revolt."

"And *that's* why I'm here," snapped Colonel Kantor. "You haven't pledged your support to the Revolution. You refuse to join the militia or to aid the cause. You still work for known Tories and Loyalists." His voice lowered to a threatening growl. "That sounds like the definition of a Tory to me, McDowell."

"I have told you a dozen times, Joseph Kantor, I and my family are neutral. *Neutral!* Do you hear?"

"What I hear sounds like a pack of Tory lies. How can you stay neutral when the whole country's at war? Either you're for us, or you're against us. Which will it be, McDowell?"

Colonel Kantor paused to turn at the door. "You don't have long to decide, McDowell—Patriot or Tory scum."

"I'm neutral!" whined Gregory to the closed door as the bell still clanged.

It was young Robert McDowell who, two days later, brought home a copy of the poster and an ugly-looking black eye. "They beat me up for being a Tory, father."

"Who did?" demanded Gregory.

"Four of them. It was because of this." And he handed his father the copy of the Patriot poster announcing the names of eight suspected local Tory spies.

Gregory McDowell's name was on it.

The poster challenged each person on the list to prove his innocence by openly declaring support for the Revolution or be prepared for the consequences. Gregory stared blankly at the page before saying offhandedly, "Not a very good printing job. Look at how the letter margins . . . "

"Gregory!" snapped his wife. "This is serious! They might destroy your shop and burn this house if they believe we're spies."

Gregory's head dropped into his hands, his face drained of all its color. "What can I do that I haven't already done?"

"Decide."

"I have. I am *for* both and *against* neither."

"You can't be. Not any more."

"But I am. I was educated in England. You were born there. Yet we both have lived almost all our lives in America. How, in good faith, can we turn our backs on either?"

Mary saw the fear and anguish in his face. "What will you do?"

With a small, helpless shrug he answered, "Try to explain again."

"Do you honestly think anyone will listen?"

Sensing her parents' fear, Melody began to cry. "I'm frightened."

Gregory wrapped her tight in his arms. "There, there. Don't cry. It will be all right . . . somehow."

At the public meeting held in Fish Market Square, two others on the list openly declared themselves in support of the Revolution, joined Patriot militia units, and received rousing applause. Colonel Kantor announced that four of the named spies had scurried out of town. Again the crowd cheered.

All faces now turned to Gregory McDowell as he climbed onto the platform made from several fish tables shoved together. "Most of you know me. I've done printing jobs for many of you. You know that I am fair and honest. You ask me to choose sides as if this were a game. You ask me to declare—Whig or Tory. But I tell you, in my heart I have no grievance with either party. I am a good citizen of this community and of this colony, but I will take no political stand. I cannot choose one deep loyalty over the other. I cannot."

Through a long moment of silence many eyes lowered to the ground; many feet nervously shuffled over the wood planks of the wharf that was home to the fish market; many hearts felt the same impossible tug-of-war that tormented Gregory McDowell.

Then Colonel Kantor barked out, "It is impossible not to have a side. If he isn't with us, he's against us! If he won't declare, he probably *is* a spy!"

The crowd cheered and shook fists at Gregory. "Get out of our meeting, spy!" shouted the colonel.

To chants of "Spy! Spy!" Gregory stumbled back to his shop. Inside, he locked the door, tears streaming down his face.

By first light the next morning, the wagon was loaded with their most prized possessions and with the equipment from Gregory's shop.

"Why must we leave, father? I like this house and I like my school."

"We aren't welcome in this town any longer, Robert."

Mary added, "We'll go somewhere better, where we can be safe."

"But *where*?" whined Melody.

"Up into Pennsylvania, I think, Melody," answered her father. "To the Amish communities west of Philadelphia. I think they will understand and accept us."

With a light snap of the reins, the two horses pulling the McDowells' wagon clopped slowly up Hanover Street. Mary turned in her seat, gazing ashen-faced at the house she had loved. Gregory's hat was pulled low over his flame-red hair. His face, set like a stone, stared cold and hard at the road ahead. He did not even once glance behind.

Aftermath

Gregory McDowell actually wound up in Hagerstown, Maryland, and lived peacefully there for the rest of his life. He also stayed neutral, although it cost him dearly in friends, home, and financial stability. He never returned to Annapolis.

Others who insisted on maintaining neutrality also suffered. During the war, many neutrals were treated like the enemy by both sides. After the war, neutrals were looked upon as being unworthy and undeserving of the benefits of hard-won American freedom. In many cases, neutrals were held in lower regard than were former Tories, who had chosen the wrong side but at least had stood up and fought for their convictions. Few people ever accepted that neutrals had had to fight just as hard, if not harder, to maintain their convictions.

Follow-up Questions and Activities

1. **What Do You Know?**

   - Is staying neutral (neutrality) the same as being a pacifist? How are these positions different? How do they both differ from not caring about an issue?

   - Why were both Patriots and Tories distrustful of someone who claimed to be neutral? Why did they often treat neutrals like the enemy? What were they afraid would happen?

- Why is it hard for people during any war to remain neutral? Why is it easier to choose a side?

- In this story, a Patriot mob drove Gregory McDowell out of town. What threats could they use to force someone to do such a drastic thing? Why didn't the police protect Gregory?

2. **Finding Out More**. Following are four important topics from this story for you to research in the library and on the Internet. The reference sources at the back of this book will help you get started.

   - Annapolis was a bustling colonial shipping center and is now the capital of Maryland and the site of the U.S. Naval Academy. There are more preserved colonial houses in Annapolis than in any other city. Research the history of this key colonial town. When was it founded? What happened there? How did it develop? What is it like now?

   - Research the idea of neutrality. Have ordinary people been able to successfully claim neutrality during other wars? Search for historical examples of declared neutrality, both by individuals and by countries. Have these people and countries managed to remain neutral? Have others respected that neutrality?

   - Printing was one of the active trades in the Colonies at the time of the Revolution. Research the trades active in America at the time of the Revolutionary War. What were they? How many people practiced each trade? Did each of the trades offer apprenticeships?

   - Research the political organization of Patriots and Loyalists during the war. What "committees" did each community and colony have? What militia organizations? Did they tend to remain secret? Why?

3. **Make It Real**

   - Make a list of controversial issues facing your community, city, state, and nation today. Are there some you feel strongly about? Are there some students, or family members of students, who feel just as strongly about the opposite viewpoint? Are there any issues you don't have an opinion about? Are you indifferent about these issues (don't care how they turn out), or is it that you care deeply but can understand both sides in the argument and can't completely support either side? (The latter is being neutral.)

   - Imagine that you are your own age living during the Revolutionary War and that your parents have declared that they will remain neutral. Your personal feelings and loyalties may lean in either direction. Write a journal entry describing how you feel about your parents' decision and how your friends at school and around your community have reacted to it. Also describe how other adults act and treat you because of your parents' decision.

4. **Points to Ponder**

   - Do you think it was acceptable for someone to *not* take sides during the Revolutionary War? Search for arguments both for and against the right of staying neutral.

- Do you think it made sense for an American colonist to love both America and England while they were at war? Try to make a list of reasons for Colonists to feel affection for each of the two countries. Why do you think neutral people didn't feel outraged by English injustice as did those who led the revolt?

- Can staying neutral (refusing to choose a side) ever make sense when it also makes sense for others to feel so strongly about something that they are willing to give their lives in support of their choice? How can both positions make sense?

Citizen Soldiers Meet British Regulars

The Battle of Freeman's Farm,
September 19, 1777

Battle of Saratoga

At a Glance

Through most of 1777, Washington successfully bobbed and weaved, hiding and surviving with his main army in New Jersey and Pennsylvania. General Howe seemed unable to pin him down and crush his army. So General Burgoyne devised a brilliant plan to split the Colonies, or "cut off the colonists' head."

Burgoyne proposed to use three forces to cut New England away from rest of the Colonies and stop the flow of supplies and men from that region. Washington would soon be dried up and easy as dust to blow away. General Clinton (under Howe) would sail up from New York along the Hudson River to meet Burgoyne, who would march south from Canada along Lake Champlain and the upper Hudson River, while Colonel St. Leger, with a smaller force, would march east along the Mohawk Valley from Lake Ontario and would meet the combined Burgoyne-Clinton force along the Hudson.

Burgoyne's plan was approved by the English War Department. The three forces were ordered to meet at Albany, New York, sometime in the late fall of 1777. If Burgoyne's plan worked, the rebellion would be crushed.

Washington, tied up playing cat and mouse, fox and hounds, with Howe around Philadelphia, was unable to move troops north to stop Burgoyne. That burden fell on a few thousand Continentals scraped together from across New England and New York and on local militia units. Would such untested, piecemeal forces be any match for "Gentleman Johnny" Burgoyne's seasoned British regulars, hired Hessians, and brutal Mohawk Indians?

The very Revolution seemed to hang in the balance.

The French were withholding overt support until they could be shown that there was a real chance for the Colonists to win against their long-time enemy. Spain waited in the wings, ready to pounce on England if it appeared that they had a serious fight on their hands. Without outside help, the Revolution was doomed.

All eyes turned toward upstate New York to see what untrained citizen soldiers could do against British regulars. How these citizen soldiers fared against Burgoyne's seasoned troops was sure to be one of the most important factors in the war.

Meet William Slater

William Slater was born near Manchester, Vermont, in November 1748, on his family's farm. As a 14-year-old, he was apprenticed to the owner of a candle factory and textile store in town. He worked there for a decade until the owner died in 1773 and left the store to William.

William married his childhood sweetheart in 1768 and bought a comfortable house in town. He lived in Manchester and ran that same shop all his life, dying in early 1830 at the age of 71, survived by three children, fourteen grandchildren, and seven great-grandchildren. His wife lived only three years after William died.

Citizen Soldiers Meet British Regulars

I never pictured myself marching in a military unit. But there I was, in a long rambling line of the 8th Hampshire Grants (New Hampshire) volunteers, tramping through the first blush of fall colors across the upper Hudson River Valley.

Maybe "marched" is the wrong word. We were all just walking in the same direction. We wore no uniforms. Those were saved for Continentals. Our muskets and rifles were our own, not government issue. Likewise, our cookpots and bedding came from home rather than from government stores.

Still, there I was, in a solemn line of almost 200 that made up our Militia Regiment. Before me walked Thomas Kent, a butcher from Bennington. Behind me walked—more correctly limped, for he was not in the practice of long romps across the countryside—young Jeffery Post, like me, from Manchester. Jeffery, still 19, was the apprentice at the grist mill on the west side of Manchester where I used to buy my grain.

My name is William Slater. I'm the owner of a small candle factory and textile shop in Manchester, a loving husband, and father of three children—boys age seven and four, and a daughter just past her first birthday. At 29, I am called the "old man" of the outfit. At first I protested because Jason Church, from just above Bennington, is 31. But the name stuck during our three weeks of training and now I wear it proudly.

How did I, an avowed pacifist who refused to carry arms in the French and Indian War a decade ago, come to be in this line of citizen soldiers marching to meet British General Burgoyne and his hosts of butcher lobster-backs? Jeffery Post is a hothead, quick to anger and slow to think, and has been begging to enlist in the Continentals for almost a year. One insult from a British soldier would be enough to make his blood boil for revenge.

But I had vowed to stay out of this frightful, bloody affair. Then Burgoyne stomped south from Canada, stripping farms, stealing all their grain and corn, turning decent farmers into destitute paupers. He sips champagne and changes shirts twice a day while the lives of local Patriot and Tory alike are destroyed in his wake. Then the Indians—pure savages—he brought south with him began their slaughter. When I heard what they did in the Mohawk Valley to the west, and then when they killed and scalped poor Jane McCrea, and when Burgoyne's rampaging Hessians slaughtered cattle for their cowbells and shot horses just for the joy of it, I had had enough.

If Burgoyne isn't stopped, it could be my wife and children who are next tortured and scalped. Stocks of wax and finished candles are both low. The bolts of linen I ordered three months ago haven't arrived yet. The store is left with just my wife to run it, and there's a leak in the store roof I ought to fix before winter sets in. But it no longer matters. Burgoyne must be crushed. And, since Washington and most of the Continental Army aren't within 500 miles of here, I guess it's ordinary citizens like me who are going to have to do it.

So here I am. And God help Gentleman Johnny Burgoyne if he gets in the sights of my long rifle. I may be slow to anger, but I am far slower to forgive.

We dragged into the Continentals' camp on the evening of September 13 just as great washes of red and gold spread across the western sky. The jovial lightness of our march was instantly shattered by the grim and serious expression on every face I saw. We were here for a battle—a real battle—with cannons, formal lines of battle, and death. Suddenly the sky's red looked like a premonition instead of an inviting fall landscape.

Colonel Talbert, our commander, marched us to General Gage's central headquarters to get our assignment. More generals and colonels than I could count milled around the headquarters, saluting each other, covered with braid and flounce, puffed up with self-importance while marching back and forth as if the Almighty himself had personally sent them on their errand.

We marched another half mile through the woods in the growing dark to reach the camp fires of Daniel Morgan's riflemen, the regiment we would support. The regular Continental troops looked just like us—lean and rangy, no fat paunches like you find on citified folk—and they grumbled and joked and laughed just like we had during our four-day march. These were country boys like ourselves. Half were under 20, half in their twenties. I was still the "old man" of the group. Morgan's regiment included free blacks, some black slaves serving for their masters (they were supposedly guaranteed their freedom at war's end), and a few Indians (mostly Onondagas from the Iroquois Nation).

Everyone was treated the same and got the same supplies and rations, too: $5.00 per month standard pay ($6.67 if you brought your own musket), but it seemed they never got it, or got it in worthless Continentals (paper money issued by Congress) instead of metal coin or British sovereigns. We each got a shirt, blanket, and straw for bedding. Well, some of the time we did. We each got the same daily ration: one pound of beef or three-quarter pound of pork or one pound of salted fish, one pint of milk, three pints of beans or peas, one-half pint of rice, one quart of spruce beer, and an occasional pull of rum. Many had signed up just for six months, feeling they couldn't stay away from home and farm any longer than that; some were in for three years or for the duration of the war.

The regulars welcomed us cordially enough and helped us get fires started to push back the chill and the dark and get our tents up and in an acceptably straight line. They also shared a double ration of rumors. There seemed to be no limit to the number of rumors each soldier was allowed to hear, enlarge upon, and pass on.

Burgoyne was marching steadily toward us with 7,000 regulars (some claimed as high as 20,000); 2,000 Hessian barbarians who never took prisoners, preferring to settle the issue with their bayonets on the spot; and 138 cannons, enough to flatten whole forests and any fool who dared stand in them. He even had lumbering 24-pounders whose great cannon balls could tear down any stone wall humans could build. They said he also had turned loose 1,000 bloodthirsty Mohawks pledged to scalp every captive while still alive!

Jeffery Post, Thomas Kent, and I shivered like we would after a good ghost story and inched closer to the safety of the fire. My heart raced and I began to wonder whether I could stand against this fierce enemy—if any of us could.

Every day companies of snipers eagerly marched out to hide in the trees and bushes to harass British pickets and outposts and slow the advance of Burgoyne and his ponderous train of supply wagons and cannons. Every night they returned with reports of how much closer the British were coming and stories of the Red-coats they had killed that day. My spirits were greatly lifted by the success and casual confidence of these groups of scout riflemen.

During the days, as September edged toward the glories of a radiant fall, we were free to explore the area—a heavily wooded place with few roads and trails and a few open fields—mostly those of an abandoned farm with a weed-masked cabin owned by one Mr. Freeman. And we were free to wait, to grow increasingly nervous . . . and to wait some more.

Three of the Continentals in the next camp were excellent singers and sere-naded us each evening. Their voices floated over camp like glowing sparks from our fire drifting peacefully off into the clear night sky. I could feel a toughness about these Continentals that can only be forged by months of deprivation and toil and hundreds of miles of forced marches. Still I could feel the growing ten-sion. Doom was drawing near. This would be no small skirmish or strutting and posturing show in a field; this would be war. I worried that the Redcoat regulars would be even tougher than Continentals after their years of training and that we humble farmers would be no match for their practiced ferocity.

In the blue-gray light before dawn on September 19 we heard the ghostly patter of distant drums sounding like squirrels' feet racing over a shingled roof. The crisp smell of fall lay across the Hudson River Valley that morning, a smell that always makes me want to stroll around my farm, kicking at the first crop of fallen colored leaves, peaceful and content with my crops grown and my family safe for another year. This day that smell reminded me only of my absence and made me angrier than ever.

We rifled militia were deployed early with Morgan's rifle brigade, gliding between and behind trees like half-seen men with fur caps, fringed shirts, and long, deadly rifles, not in neat lines like the British, but hiding behind, in, or on top of anything that would give us cover. Morgan's officers used an unearthly turkey gobbling for signaling. Rifle clutched tight, heart pounding, crouched down behind bush and tree, I could barely see into the open fields of Freeman's farm.

First we heard the approaching drum and fife, their noise washing over us like a heavy blanket to suck away our spirit and will. Then I could feel the trembling of the earth from the rhythmic marching of thousands of stiff British boots. The first lines of red took shape through the last mists of morning, which lay like thin gray fingers on the field.

These lines were not the precision terror we had imagined. Shirt cuffs were ripped or missing, coats faded, torn, and patched, white breeches stained the tan of light mud. Months of muck, mud, and sweat were ground into every fiber. There was a look of deep exhaustion to these bedraggled men, as if their three-month march from Canada had been almost more than they could bear. I almost felt sorry for the men who had had to endure so much toil—almost.

We cut loose with our first volley. Every officer and many enlisted men in this advance line fell. The rest ran. Sharpshooters high in the trees took out the officers and gunners of every cannon Burgoyne wheeled into the field. The sharp reports of their rifles sounding like popcorn exploded through the woods.

Back and forth across that field the battle raged for four hours. They attacked. We fired with deadly effect from the protection of the trees. Redcoated regimental lines closed up as the falling dead left holes in the line. Companies shrank to platoons; platoons to squads. Every time they advanced, another 50 or so of Morgan's boys scampered into the trees like squirrels for better aim, firing down from on high, picking off all officers who dared lift their heads above protective walls in the rear.

Their advance collapsed and they retreated. Then we advanced—blue-coated Continentals and leather-shirted militia. I let out all my fury in great lion roars as we advanced—fury because I was here instead of at home, fury because of what Burgoyne had done to this land, fury at the senseless killing of this war. We yelled and galloped past fallen bodies and weeds to the trees at the far side of the field where the British had halted their retreat.

I had never had a bayonet or been trained in how to use one. But suddenly I longed for a sword or gleaming bayonet of steel to slash through the crimson ranks hiding in the tree line, to slash my revenge, to hack out all my anger.

Now the British lines opened fire. Smoke and whining musket balls filled the air. Good men around me began to drop. British reinforcements arrived. We were pushed back just as they had been.

They advanced again, and we mowed down their precise ranks from our protected spots behind the trees, littering the ground with a new crop of crimson coats and crimson blood. By sunset, most of our ammo was spent, our cartouche boxes (powder and musket ball boxes) were empty. Both sides staggered back and called it quits for the day. Twice I'm sure I had Burgoyne himself in my sights. Once I know I put a fat hole in his fancy, feathered hat. But, dang it, I didn't bring that devil down.

That night we sat around our same campfires—just as we had for the past six nights. On the surface, everything looked the same, as if we hadn't fought at all. Was that the battle? Would it continue tomorrow? Did we win? What now?

Questions swirled thick as stew through my mind. We hadn't taken the field. We hadn't crushed the British. And yet generals strutted left and right through the camps, congratulating everyone and saying that we had won a great victory. Were British officers doing the same in their camp? Only the mournful howls from a pack of wolves rushing in to feed on the dead made the horror of war seem real to my addled mind.

For two weeks camp life returned to its former pattern. Companies of snipers marched out each morning and returned at night with empty cartouche boxes but a full packet of stories of their exploits during the day.

On October 8, Continentals attacked the British and their hastily dug fortifications on Bemis Heights. We were held in reserve and could only listen to the din of musket, cannon, yells of the advancing men, and cries of the fallen. Rumors said that General Benedict Arnold had fought like a rampaging bull, like a madman, and had won the day for America when he smashed into Burgoyne's small redoubts, toppling all resistance. All I know for certain is that we spent the day squatting in a small clearing near camp, collecting splinters instead of battle stories.

That night, Burgoyne made a dash in a pouring, cold rain for Ft. Ticonderoga in the north. I guess that means we had won and that he, being defeated, was scampering for a safe haven for the winter. He didn't get far, however, before Hampshire Grant boys under General Schuyler cut off his retreat.

Nine days later, it was over. Burgoyne surrendered near the village of Saratoga. He surrendered an entire British army to Continental rabble no one thought stood a chance against British regulars. We stood in formation watching the gaunt, tattered Redcoats march sullenly past.

I was filled with a sense of relief and of overwhelming pride. What a great country! Such power—not in the government and army, but in the people—in Jeffery Post, in Thomas Kent, in me—and no force on Earth can defeat such power. Content, I waved farewell the next morning and, along with the other Hampshire Grant boys, headed home to my shop and family.

Aftermath

The destruction of Burgoyne's army was the turning point of the war. Based on this one Continental victory, France openly declared support for the Colonies and declared war on England. Spain, also wanting to settle old scores, soon followed suit. A minor colonial revolution had suddenly transformed into a world war for England.

Supplies flowed openly into colonial ports on swift blockade runners from France and Spain. British General Clinton was afraid to venture out of New York City for fear his army would meet a fate similar to Burgoyne's. American hopes soared, everywhere except in Washington's headquarters, where his still pitifully small band of Continentals struggled to hold out against Howe, who threatened to take Philadelphia and seemed to be unstoppable.

Burgoyne's surrender at Saratoga meant help would arrive and the American Revolution would survive, but victory was still tantalizingly far away. Washington also had to survive and, even if he didn't win any battles, he knew he must never lose a decisive engagement. Cat and mouse, fox and hounds must continue. But now pressure would quickly mount on the British generals to finish the game quickly or lose the entire effort.

Follow-up Questions and Activities

1. **What Do You Know?**

   • The Battles at Freeman's Farm and at Bemis Heights were called the "turning point" of the war. Why? What "turned," or changed, because of those battles?

   • Two other British forces were supposed to join General Burgoyne when he reached Albany, New York. Who were they? Where were they supposed to come from, and what happened to them?

   • What were the accepted rules of conduct for European armies at the time of Revolution? Now armies follow the rules of the Geneva Convention. What does that convention tell all armies and soldiers to do and not do?

2. **Finding Out More**. Following are six important topics from this story for you to research in the library and on the Internet. The reference sources at the back of this book will help you get started.

   • "Gentleman" Johnny Burgoyne was a most fascinating British general. Research his life and military career. What had he accomplished before he designed the British campaign of 1777 that ended with his disastrous defeat? What happened to him when he surrendered? What did he do after the war?

   • It took many months for Burgoyne to force his way south to the Hudson River. Why did it take so long? What made the trip so difficult? Research Burgoyne's struggle to force his way south from Canada and discover the factors that so drastically slowed him down.

   • Benedict Arnold is most famous as a traitor, but before that he was the most successful and one of the best-loved of all Continental generals. Research this amazing fighter and his early career as an American general and trusted leader. Why did he switch to the British side? What happened to him after that?

   • During the several months before the Battle at Freeman's Farm, Burgoyne sent Hessian soldiers and Mohawk Indians into the countryside to seize supplies and fresh horses and to force the local population to support the British army. How did these raids affect the local population? Did his strategy work?

   • A murder happened about a month before the Battle of Freeman's Farm that outraged the New England citizens and made them terrified of the Mohawks and of Burgoyne—and also grimly determined to keep him from conquering New England. A Loyalist woman named Jane McCrea was captured, scalped, and killed by Mohawks. Research that infamous event and its effect on the New England citizenry.

   • General Howe never showed up with his army from New York to close the British trap. Why not? Where did he go instead? Why didn't he try to get word to Burgoyne? What happened to Colonel St. Leger's force? Why didn't they ever arrive to support Burgoyne?

3. **Make It Real**

   • Note the standard daily ration for the Continental soldiers described in the story. That ration was usually split between two main meals. Have a group of students measure out these portions of these foods for one of the two daily meals and see what it looks like. Does it look like a lot of food? Would it become boring to have the same thing every day?

   • Imagine that you are a British soldier in Burgoyne's army and write a letter home describing how you feel after the surrender of your army. After struggling through mosquito- and swamp-infested forests and through months of backbreaking toil, you have just been defeated by an untrained collection of volunteer citizen soldiers. Not only were you defeated, you were forced to surrender. Write down how you think you would feel about this and why. As best you can, describe what happened to the army after they surrendered.

4. **Points to Ponder**

   • Existing European "rules of warfare" in the 1700s required that (1) armies face each other in open fields and (2) officers be respected and not be shot at intentionally. The American army at Freeman's Farm (plus snipers before and after) violated both rules. Was it fair for them to do so? Why or why not? When is it all right to violate agreed-upon international codes of military conduct?

   Modern armies fight under what is called the Geneva Convention for military conduct. All armies, ours included, have pledged to fight according to the rules of this convention. Would it be acceptable for some other army to break the Geneva Convention in a battle against us? Would we protest their brutal and inhumane tactics? The British protested how we fought at Freeman's Farm. Should we have listened to their protests?

   • The last time the three British commanders involved in Burgoyne's grand plan to split the Colonies had any direct contact with each other was in May 1777. Does it seem foolhardy or bold to create a plan that calls for three forces to meet after five months of campaigning with no significant contact during all that time? Why do you think the British agreed to the plan?

Kill Them with Kindness

British Occupation of Philadelphia, September 1777 to June 1778

Dressed for a Philadelphia ball

At a Glance

In mid-summer 1777, the military situation looked bleak for the Revolution in every direction. Burgoyne advanced south from Canada, seemingly unstoppable. British forces were moving east from Lake Ontario. Terrible news continued to pour in from the mid-Atlantic states. General Howe, able to consistently outmaneuver and defeat—but not crush—Washington's army, believed that Washington would have to defend the capital of Philadelphia. He sailed his army of 30,000 men down the coast from New York, up the Chesapeake, and landed in northern Maryland, planning to march on Philadelphia and force Washington into a decisive battle.

At almost the same time, Burgoyne was defeated and Washington lost a long series of battles trying to save Philadelphia. To save his army, Washington had to retreat and allow Howe to march unimpeded into the capital of the American Colonies. Philadelphia patriots were shocked and dismayed. How could the army abandon their own capital? Congress had to scramble to move to safer quarters before the Redcoats arrived.

Philadelphia Loyalists, still reeling from the news of Burgoyne's defeat, took full advantage of Howe's arrival as an opportunity to cheer. Patriot supporters had to find ways to support Washington without attracting any attention and getting themselves arrested. Tension and friction ran high in Philadelphia. Sparks could fly at the smallest provocation. Still, the Loyalist and Patriot citizens in Philadelphia had to live together day after day no matter which army was in control of the city. While Philadelphia Loyalists happily rubbed elbows with British generals, local Patriots—like Lydia Darragh—had to be more subtle and clever in how they supported their army and their Revolution.

Meet Lydia Darragh

Lydia Maestrop was born in Philadelphia of Quaker parents in 1746. Both her parents were of German descent and had been born on American farms. After marrying, they moved into the city to open an upholstery and sewing shop. Lydia grew up in the bustle of the shops and under the stern, firm, but gentle hand of her father. From the age of eight on, she worked as a seamstress in the family shop.

In 1761 she met William Darragh when he stopped in the shop. He had just moved to Philadelphia to apprentice under a local lawyer after completing law school in England. His office was less than a block from Lydia's parents' shop.

Lydia and William were married in 1763 when he was 32 and she was only 17. The marriage caused a great uproar in the family because he was not one of the Circle of Friends (a Quaker). Lydia's father threatened to disown her, but he relented at the last minute.

Lydia and William lived in Philadelphia in the same house for the rest of their lives: she, a quiet but powerful guiding force; he, a big and boisterous voice for justice and equality. He lived to the age of 77, dying in 1808. Lydia lived quietly for another 19 years, dying in 1827.

Kill Them with Kindness

As he marched the cobblestone streets of Philadelphia, 46-year-old Henry Drinker's buckled shoes splashed through shallow puddles that were the lingering remnants of a heavy morning squall on the 22nd day of September 1777. He clutched the morning newspaper tight in his fist. A triumphant gleam blazed from his pale blue eyes and radiated across his face, making him unaware that his shoes and stockings were soaked from the shins down.

The power of this joyful glow almost—almost—hid Drinker's comical appearance. Thin as a rail, with bird-like legs but with a full, round belly, Drinker looked as if someone had stuffed a fat pillow in the front of an underfed scarecrow. A round, bulbous nose stuck out from his sunken face and nearly bald head.

Drinker threw open a door marked "William Darragh, Attorney at Law," loudly clanging the door-mounted bell. Storming past the startled secretary like a righteous missionary, Drinker slammed the paper onto William Darragh's desk and jabbed his finger at the two-inch headline. "Did you see *this*, William?"

Darragh pretended to be too busy to stop and notice the paper or his intruder. "Go away, Henry. I'm busy."

"Washington was crushed at Chad's Ford! Howe and Cornwallis crumpled his lines like a flimsy piece of paper. What do you say about your glorious revolt *now*, William?"

A fierce glare on his face, Darragh unfolded from his squat chair and rose to tower over Henry Drinker. At six foot two, William Darragh's shoulders were level with Drinker's eyes. He leaned far across his desk so his nose almost touched Drinker's. "The revolution *will* succeed. America *will* be free."

Drinker laughed. "Noble words, William. But how will you do it if your army can't win a single fight?"

"I'll take up a musket myself to defeat the British if I have to."

Again Drinker laughed. "I'm sure General Howe is trembling in his boots for fear of facing *you*."

Darragh's finger jabbed into Drinker's chest. "But my first bullets will be reserved for Tory traitors like you."

Henry Drinker wrinkled his nose as if smelling a foul sewer. "I am not an armed Tory, but rather a loyal citizen of the country and King who founded these Colonies, who protects and supports them, and who is the rightful ruler. And you should be, too. When Howe occupies Philadelphia—as he certainly will—fools who support the revolt will be in big trouble—*big* trouble."

"Maybe you'd like to step into the alley and see who's in *big* trouble, Henry."

"Threaten me all you like, William. It's just one more thing for me to report to General Howe when he arrives!"

William Darragh grabbed Drinker by the collar with one hand and the seat of his breeches with the other, half lifted him of his feet, and dragged him toward the door. "And now I'll show you how General Howe will be welcomed when he arrives!"

Halfway to the front door William stopped, halted by a gentle hand laid upon his arm. "Caution, William," said his wife in a soft, commanding voice. "It will not pay to mistreat a fellow citizen just before the British arrive."

Still seething, William stammered, "But . . . but he . . . "

A single, slender finger raised to quiet him. "Kindness is a more powerful weapon than the sword, William. Kindness is how the Revolution will be won in Philadelphia."

"But he. . . . " With a final growl, Darragh roughly released his neighbor and stormed back to his desk.

His wife, Lydia, followed. "You will see, William. Kindness will win where pride and threats will fail."

"How?"

"Somehow."

On the street outside two young women, both maidens in Philadelphia's top society circle, giggled in anticipation of the change of political winds. "I hear there will be over 100 British officers in Philadelphia—all in glorious red uniforms with sabers and sashes!" cooed Peggy Shipper.

"And I hear they are allowed to hold dances and parties every night," replied Rebecca Franks. Both women were 18, beautiful, and picture-perfect, fairy-tale princesses who tried to dress, look, and act the part. As fashionable society women, balls, teas, and parties were the events that defined a season, a year, and a life for them.

"*Finally* there will be some fun around here," giggled Peggy.

"Better the British than those stuffy Congressmen. We haven't had a decent ball in months," added Rebecca.

Three days later, hundreds of drums rattled windows for blocks. A vast procession of fluttering flags and banners seemed to fill the road for miles. Columns of heavy artillery rumbled past. Finally an army of fifes guided the endless close-packed ranks of red coats, like a moving red carpet, marching into Philadelphia on September 25. Congress had fled to York a week earlier. Patriots had hauled the famed Liberty Bell to Allentown on the 24th, fearing the British would melt it down for musket balls. Philadelphians lined the streets to watch the grim and endless columns take control of their city, some with shouts of joy, some in silent horror.

The first ball honoring the British officers was held the next night. Peggy and Rebecca were thrilled and spent the day preparing to make a lasting first impression on this crop of dashing—and eligible—dance partners that would be the talk of all Philadelphia. They vowed to fill every dance card for a year to overflowing and never repeat a partner in the same evening.

Henry Drinker beamed as he strode into the ballroom in the spacious home of the mayor. He lavished greetings on every British officer he met, bowing and scraping as low as his belly would allow. He quivered with delight at shaking the hand of any of the dozen generals in the room.

William seethed, refusing to attend a party honoring the British. His wife Lydia sweetly but firmly said, "We must go, William. We must be gracious."

"I know, 'Kill them with kindness'," he sneered.

"Exactly," answered Lydia.

"I'd rather just kill them," muttered William.

William cringed when Howe established his headquarters across the street from their house on 2nd St. Lydia smiled, said, "Perfect," and invited the general and his staff for tea, during which she offered them the use of her house any time they needed it. William was outraged that his wife had brought the hated British into his home.

"We will have a party here, I think," she announced. "The British like parties. Every one of the Patriot families in town will host parties."

"Are you crazy?" he bellowed. "Have you turned Tory?"

"If the town makes the British welcome enough, they may not want to leave."

"My point exactly," he said.

Lydia smiled and held up one slender finger to calm her husband. "If they don't leave Philadelphia, they will never venture out to attack General Washington. Then he can rebuild his army in peace over the long winter and we will have helped to ensure our nation's liberty."

William's eyes widened. His mouth unclenched and sagged open. "*Now* I see the genius behind your plan." His voice filled with awe and admiration for the quiet mastermind he had married. Then his face clouded "Can the British be foolish enough to fall for it?"

"They *are* British. They put pomp and pageantry above common sense. We must let our gracious kindness *make* it work."

October passed in a whirlwind round of nightly parties as fall colors gave way to first swirling snows. Officers rarely staggered off to bed before dawn. Peggy and Rebecca were in heaven. Each averaged three proposals a night. Each glowed as officers in gleaming uniforms thronged around when they entered a ballroom, begging for their names to be written on a dance card.

Lydia beamed with quiet pleasure at the progress of her plan—until one night in early December when General Howe's adjutant asked to use her dining room for an important meeting. Lydia was ordered to ensure that her entire family was in bed and asleep before the meeting began.

She herself lay awake, fretting while her family slept and while the voices of a dozen high-ranking officers murmured up from her dining room below. Consumed with fear and curiosity over what was being planned in her house, Lydia crept from her bed, tiptoed down the stairs, and pressed an ear to the closed dining room door. The booming of her heart almost overpowered the soft voices from inside. She jammed her ear harder against the door. The hinges creaked under the pressure.

The voices stopped. Lydia froze, afraid to breath. In the silence, seconds seemed like days. Then the voices began again. Lydia sighed, but her legs trembled too hard to stand and she sank slowly to her knees while she listened.

In 10 minutes she had heard enough to make her sick with apprehension. A 5,000-man British force would march out on December 11 for a sneak attack on Washington's position at Whitemarsh, 11 miles away.

Parties alone hadn't worked. The British were going to attack anyway. Lydia felt physically ill. She couldn't tell William what she had heard. He would sneer that he had told her so all along. There were few in town she could trust not to leak word back to the British. Yet she couldn't do nothing. There was only one thing left to do: warn Washington herself.

But leaving the city would be no easy task with martial law in effect and guards and patrols on all the exit roads. Claiming she needed flour, Lydia obtained a pass from General Howe himself, slung two burlap sacks over her shoulder, and headed for a mill she knew in Frankfurt, just beyond the guards and patrols.

Once in Frankfurt she left her sacks at the mill and started to walk the six additional miles to Whitemarsh and Washington's lines. To be caught during this two-hour walk would be to be exposed as a spy and shot.

Lydia lost time by trying to walk on the stones and bare spots so as to not leave a trail of footprints in the snow. Every distant clomping of a horse sent Lydia diving into bushes and thick shrubs for cover. Every hint of a human voice on the afternoon wind made her cringe and freeze.

Twice she lay motionless in deep snow banks while patrols trotted past, lost in idle conversation. Once she missed a turn and started on a looping road that would lead her back to Philadelphia.

It took her over three hours to make contact with an American patrol and be led to a captain who took her report and, without a word of thanks, raced back to the main lines with it.

Lydia was left alone to make the dangerous return trip, feeling that her trip was somehow incomplete. She had not seen Washington as she thought she would. She had not even seen the American fortifications, as she thought she would. She had not been praised and called a Patriot hero by ranks of cheering soldiers, as she thought she would. She stood alone on the snowy road wondering almost if it had even happened.

The return trip as the sun sank below the western hills was faster, but even scarier because she had been out so long. She gathered her two sacks of flour and, feeling emotionally drained and bitterly cold, trudged back home, now wondering if her trip had been worthwhile and if she had saved anyone or anything with her brash and risky venture.

Three days later the British Adjutant General, Colonel Ashton, pounded on Lydia's front door and entered with a threatening scowl. "A week ago we met in your dining room."

"I remember, Colonel."

"Are you sure everyone in this house was in bed and asleep?"

"Yes, I tucked everyone in myself. Why?"

The colonel paced as he spoke, periodically pausing to glare at Lydia. "Someone heard of our plans—plans created in this very room and not spoken of again—and passed word to Washington."

"Really?" interrupted Lydia with mock shock. "Whoever would do such a thing?"

"His army was well entrenched and waiting for our attack. We had to cancel the whole affair and return with nothing to show for our effort."

"I am sorry to hear that your efforts went for naught," cooed Lydia, patting the colonel's arm. "By the way, would you and your officers care to drop by for a party and dance tomorrow evening?"

"A party," he beamed. "You're so kind. We'd love to."

And Lydia secretly smiled with smug satisfaction. "You will always be welcome in my house, Colonel Ashton. Tea?"

Aftermath

A continual round of parties and dances lasted through the winter and spring in Philadelphia. Howe's British army ground to a lethargic and contented halt. Washington was given the time he needed to focus on mere survival at Valley Forge and to allow Baron von Steuben to train and discipline his troops. Washington entered Valley Forge with a listless, defeated mob of fighters; he left it in June with a trained army.

Because of his failure to win a decisive victory during the Philadelphia campaign, General Howe resigned. General Clinton took over as British commander-in-chief. Fearing Rebel uprisings in New York, he withdrew all British troops from Philadelphia in June 1778, and moodily consolidated his strength in New York. After a quiet year (1778) with little action by either major army, Clinton devised his "Southern Strategy," a plan to reconquer the South and then move north from this solid base. Having been defeated in the North and stalemated in the mid-Atlantic states, Britain moved the war south beginning in 1779.

Follow-up Questions and Activities

1. **What Do You Know?**

   • Philadelphia patriots had no weapons to use against the occupying British army. They didn't dare stage protest rallies for fear of being arrested. Still they fought against the British. How?

- In the story the phrase "kill them with kindness" is used several times to describe the Philadelphia Patriot strategy. What does this phrase mean? Can you find examples in modern times of other populations that have tried to "kill an occupying army with kindness?"
- Why did armies have to go into winter quarters? Why not continue to fight during winter? Why don't modern armies have to stop fighting each winter? What has changed to make warfare possible all year long?

2. **Finding Out More**. Following are four important topics from this story for you to research in the library and on the Internet. The reference sources at the back of this book will help you get started.

   - During the fall of 1777 a series of battles occurred in an ever-tightening circle around Philadelphia between British General Howe and American General Washington. Research that series of battles. Who won each one? Did Washington do as well as he was expected to do? What was Washington's one great accomplishment during that campaign?
   - Lydia Darragh was one of many well-documented Patriot women who risked their lives for the Revolution. Research these Patriot women. How many can you find? What did they do? Were any caught and imprisoned by the British?
   - Every year both British and American armies drifted into "winter quarters." For each year, 1776 through 1781, locate and research the winter quarters for both armies. What did winter camps typically look like for the British? For the Americans? Did the armies sometimes split into more than one winter camp? Why would they do that?
   - Philadelphia was only one of the American cities occupied by British forces during the war. Research the other occupied American cities: Boston (1773–1776), New York (1776–1783), Savannah (1778–1781), and Charleston (1779–1781). Did the citizens of these cities resist British occupation? How? What was the experience of each occupied city?

3. **Make It Real**

   - How did the Treaty of Friendship between France and America affect the war? Did America really need France's help to beat the British? What arguments can you find to support your answer? Hold a class debate, with one group arguing that we did need France and another arguing that we didn't.
   - Lydia Darragh risked her life and freedom to pass information to General Washington. What would it feel like to try to sneak information through enemy lines? Try a fun classroom game to see:

     Divide the class in half. The teacher will designate a receiver on each team. Everyone should know who the two receivers are. Each team meets and secretly picks a messenger for the team. The messenger's job is to get a message to the other team's receiver before the end of the school day without being caught by any of the other team members. The teacher will create and write a secret message for each team's messenger to pass to the other team's receiver. Only the team's messenger is allowed to know the message. The first messenger to successfully pass the message to the opposing team's receiver and "escape" back to his or her seat without being caught by the other team members is the winner. Teams may try to guard the receiver during lunch and recess to make it harder for the opposing messenger to reach that person.

Were the messengers nervous about being caught? Was it hard to figure out who the messengers were? Was either messenger able to successfully deliver the message? Imagine how nervewracking this would be if your life were on the line.

4. **Points to Ponder**

• Do you think Lydia's "kill them with kindness" qualifies as a legitimate defensive strategy for an occupied civilian population? Isn't it more courageous to actively fight against an occupying enemy? Why or why not?

• Why did the British plan to capture American cities (Boston, New York, Philadelphia, Charleston, Savannah)? Would this strategy have worked in Europe? Why didn't it work here, except for the attack on Charleston in 1780?

Red Snow, Leather Stew

Winter at Valley Forge, December 1777 to April 1778

Valley Forge

At a Glance

The defeat and capture of Burgoyne's army in upstate New York was a great victory for America. It sang of American military power and of foreign aid and hope. But at the same time, each and every one of a long series of smaller battles around Philadelphia was lost by Washington to British General Howe.

Howe occupied Philadelphia. Washington and his ragtag army were left out in the proverbial cold. Washington didn't dare move too far away from Philadelphia because that would allow Howe to forage freely across a greater portion of Pennsylvania. On the other hand, Washington couldn't get too close to Philadelphia for fear of inciting a British attack. Washington was still stuck in the mouse's role in a cat and mouse game, being constantly batted and battered by Howe the cat. And the best Washington could say was that he was still alive—if only barely.

This should have been a high point for America (later, Burgoyne's surrender would be called the turning point of the war), but it felt like a low point for the main Continental Army and for Washington. Many historians have agreed that the winter of 1777–1778 was the low point of America's struggle to meld into a free and united nation.

It was a confusing time. There seemed to be every reason both for optimism and despair. Washington's army was again collapsing, but Burgoyne's had been defeated. Citizens hoped for freedom and yet grew greedy and stingy and tended to horde. Merchants who had cheered Patriot victories refused to honor either Continental or state paper money, demanding to be paid in British sovereigns. Merchants rooted for Washington but often preferred to sell hay, food, and other supplies to the British because they had hard cash.

Washington's army was starving at Valley Forge in the midst of a land of plenty, in the midst of a region of the country where many granaries were stuffed full and the civilian population lived a life of comfort and plenty, where some helped (usually helping only their own state's or county's units) but where many didn't, turning a blind eye to the suffering of their own army and a deaf ear to the pleas of Washington and Congress.

The winter at Valley Forge should not have been a tortuous test of the faith and character of the Continental Army. It became so only because there was no nation or real national government to support the army and because there was much doubt in the country as to whether Washington's fledgling force stood a chance even if it could last until spring.

Valley Forge gave the Patriots every opportunity and excuse to quit, every reason to cave in and surrender. The path to victory lay not in glorious charges and deafening cannon volleys, but in grim and endlessly torturous survival amid an indifferent population and the capricious and brutal vagaries of Mother Nature.

Meet Abigail Trenton

Born in July 1759 in St. Mary's County, Maryland, Abby McDade was described as a bright, outgoing, lively girl. Her parents were second-generation immigrants of Scottish descent and ran a large farm with some tobacco and rice for export and livestock for local sale.

Abigail met her husband, Seth Trenton, through her community church. His family owned a farm less than two miles from the McDade farm. Seth had visions of buying the land between the two family holdings and creating one giant farm that might have qualified as a plantation. They married in 1775 when Abby was barely 16. In early 1777, after Washington's victories at Trenton and Princeton, Seth volunteered for service. Abby decided to travel with him. Partly, she didn't want to leave her husband. Partly, she knew she would be needed to cook, clean, and sew around the camp. Partly, she wanted to see places outside the small corner of the country in which she had been raised.

Seth was badly wounded at the Battle of Monmouth and left the service. Because of those wounds, Seth was unable to farm. The couple moved to Baltimore, where Seth took work as a clerk. They lived near the harbor and raised four children. Abby died in 1828 at the age of 69.

Red Snow, Leather Stew

It snowed again on Tuesday, January 20, 1778, light flurries that swirled with a bitter wind so that the cold crept under and through any clothes a person could find to put on. It had snowed every day for over a week, with only the wind to fill the cold gaps between snows, and with no stars or moon at night. The roads, which had thawed to slick mud during the chill rains of mid-January, were again frozen solid and looked like mounds of frosting with hints of chocolate poking through. Morning sun rose over some distant land, but only a dull gray light filtered through the unending leaden clouds that seemed permanently parked over the small plateau that rose above the meeting of Valley Creek and the Schuylkill River in Pennsylvania.

"A blanket. I'd give anything for a blanket this cold won't seep through," complained 18-year-old Abigail Trenton as she huddled on her wood plank bed. Her breath puffed into the early morning air and instantly froze to tiny clouds of ice.

"Ha! You'd have to stand in line for *that* blanket," moaned Susan Hollings through chattering teeth.

This winter of 1777–1778 was as cold as any that could be remembered. The area called Valley Forge (centered around an old forge that had been destroyed by British forces in September) seemed to be the very heart of this frozen invasion. These two women, and a hundred like them, huddled in the "wives' camp," a quarter mile down from the main winter camp of General Washington's Continental Army since the army had moved here in late December. The army depended on wives coming to the winter camp to cook, clean, sew, and tend to sick and wounded soldiers.

Susan shivered. "I swear, this winter and this dismal camp make me think the Revolution isn't worth it. British rule and my warm Providence (Rhode Island) house seem a bargain compared to liberty if it comes with this cold!"

"Hush with such talk," rebuked Abby. Her brown eyes flashed under thick eyebrows. Her dark hair, piled onto her head in summer, now flowed loose down over her ears and shoulders for warmth, framing a pale but pretty face. "Nothing is more important than liberty."

"Food and warmth," replied Susan. "I think today I'd rank both ahead of anything else in the world."

The eight wives sharing this makeshift cabin stiffly rose from their pallets and stretched aching muscles, sore from hauling and endless shivering. "Any wood for a fire?" called one. "I'm freezing."

Abby pawed through their wood basket with mittened hands. "A few sticks. But Dr. Waldo told me that one of the Connecticut regiments tore down an entire pasture fence for fire wood yesterday. We'll surely get some."

Susan snorted. "Ha! I'll believe that when I feel the warmth cheering this dump."

Abby frowned, "Our cabin is better than some . . . "

"*Hut*," interrupted Susan. "Not cabin. And it's barely a hut. It's not even fit to be called a dungeon."

The meager flames of their carefully tended fire absorbed each woman's attention as they crowded close to soak in any heat it provided. But the tongues of fire were no match for a thick Arctic cold that settled in like it owned the whole of Pennsylvania.

"Any food supplies make it in yesterday?" asked one of the older women in as hopeful a voice as she could muster. Susan grunted. Two others groaned.

Abby sighed and stamped her foot. "So many families and farms within a day's walk have plenty. Why won't they share with their army?"

Susan rubbed her hands over the fire. "It's a long winter and there may not be an American army come spring, they're deserting and dying so fast. Anyone who gives supplies to Washington may find themselves on a British gallows, or at least will run short of food and supplies, themselves, come summer."

"Washington pays," protested Abby.

"With Continental dollars," replied one of the other women. "They're worthless. You can't use them in any store from Savannah to Boston. Their paper is so poor, they aren't even good for kindling."

Abby continued, undaunted. "Several women are hiking out today—and one is riding—to forage at local neighbors."

"You mean *beg*," sneered Susan. "I hate the superior way they look when they offer us a few crumbs."

"Maybe supply wagons can get through now that the roads are re-frozen."

"Maybe," answered Susan, "*if* Washington and Congress can find anyone who'll sell."

Carolyn Minks, a lifelong friend of Abby's, said, "The British are using real metal coins—sovereigns—to buy food. They have their bellies full in Philadelphia."

"And their rooms nicely heated and cleaned!" scoffed another.

"While we starve out here on firecakes and water," concluded Susan, beginning to mix the thick flour paste they cooked on hot rock slabs near the fire as the staple of their diet. "All for the sake of a bunch of misfits Washington calls an army and that couldn't win a fight against school boys."

"Washington won at Trenton and Princeton," insisted Abby.

"And he lost everywhere else," Carolyn shot back. "He's lost Long Island, New York, White Plains, New Jersey, Baltimore, Philadelphia, and most of Pennsylvania. The rest he hasn't lost just because his army hasn't had a chance to lose it yet."

"I heard a joke from one of the soldiers in the hospital yesterday," offered Abby, trying to cheer the deep gloom in their hut. "A soldier in the 7th Connecticut said to one of his friends, 'I hear the New York boys are making their dinner stew out of smelly socks and cracked shoe leather.' And his friend replied, 'Those New Yorkers always get the best food.' " Then Abby stomped. "Well, laugh! It's a joke."

"Some joke," scoffed Susan as she fried their meager ration of flavorless firecake.

Abby scrunched up her face trying to remember, and then brightened. "Here's another one that really is humorous—I heard it from a Rhode Island boy whose frostbitten foot was amputated last week. 'What do you call a hand-sized piece of meat so thin you can see through it'?"

The other women groaned.

"You call it 'dinner for twelve'!" continued Abby. "Come on. Laugh a little. Things will get better."

"They can't get any worse," Susan muttered.

Only the column of replacements for the night guards had stirred from the meager protection of their beds when the women emerged into the whistling wind to begin their day's duties. They wrapped coats and scarves around their heads and bodies and shuffled through the blowing snow. Most of the women turned toward the Potter house, where Mrs. Washington led groups in knitting, darning, and patching soldiers' uniforms and socks.

Many of the guards they passed were barefoot and stood on their hats to protect their feet from the snow. All wore threadbare coats, scarred with rips and holes from months of marching and campaigning and now a patchwork of patches sewn on top of patches. Most were wrapped in thin blankets to block the worst of the wind. None seemed the kind of vigorous soldiers who won battles that Abby thought she would find when she joined her husband for this year's winter camp.

Susan and Abby first trudged to Washington's headquarters building, where they would turn in a request for food and fire wood for the wives' camp. The woods around the camp had been reduced to a stubble of stumps. Trees had been felled for crude cabins to replace the tents soldiers had used during the summer. The plateau looked like an orderly slum city of almost 1,000 ramshackle huts struggling to withstand the onslaught of wind and cold.

Abby refused to use any of the direct trails used by soldiers. More than one-third of the army was now barefoot. Most of the others' shoes were cracked and broken. Cracked and bleeding feet left trails of red in the snow wherever they walked. Abby couldn't stand to walk on these trails of red snow. Frostbite-related amputations were the most common operation in the hospital where she volunteered as a nurse.

Standing at the adjutant's desk at headquarters, Abby could see through an open doorway into the officer's meeting room. Washington and three other senior officers sat sternly at a long table. A man in handcuffs stood before them.

Armed guards lined the room. Another terrified prisoner was being roughly hauled away by two tough-looking sergeants.

The adjutant jerked a thumb toward the man. "Caught trying to desert. He'll hang this afternoon." Abby clenched her teeth and squeezed her eyes shut. She hated the almost-daily hangings. How could an army hang its own soldiers? Didn't Washington need all these men to fight the British?

"That man's not even a soldier," whispered Susan, nodding toward the handcuffed man in the courtroom.

"Caught him selling beef to the British," said the adjutant, a young captain. "He lied to our commissary officer, saying he didn't have any, and then sold to the British when they offered a better price. But he's a civilian, so he'll probably only get a couple hundred lashes."

"A whipping!" exclaimed Abby. "I thought they only whipped slaves."

The adjutant chuckled. "Happens every day in this camp, ma'am."

Abby looked troubled as the two women huddled under the protection of the adjutant's porch before parting. "What's wrong?" asked Susan. "He promised to have food and wood delivered this afternoon."

"Don't you see? We're part of a great struggle for liberty—us, right here at this camp. And yet all I see is hangings and whippings, misery and starvation. The army can't keep its horses alive. It can barely keep us alive. It makes men stand guard all night barefoot in the snow and almost naked. How can this be what the struggle for liberty is supposed to look like? Can this possibly be the road to liberty?"

Susan patted her cabin-mate's arm. "Don't think so much Abby. Thinkin' in a place like this will just make you depressed."

"But will any of these men be fit to attack the British come summer?"

"Ah, summer," sighed Susan. "Such a lovely word." And she turned west toward the Potter house across the plateau. Abby retraced their steps along the river road, past the prosperous Stewart and DeWees farms, to the one-room schoolhouse the army had commandeered as a hospital.

She found Dr. Waldo feverishly preparing for the day's surgeries. "I'll need more towels and hot tar, Abigail. We have five amputations today and smallpox cases are way up. I'll need you to scout out another building where we can house them all."

No matter how often she was part of these operations, Abby never got used to the screams of the men when the surgeon's saws began to tear through flesh and bone, and she flinched every time. There was nothing to give the men, not even a guzzle of rum to dull the pain.

It was after sunset when, feet and hands both numb with cold, mind numbed by the misery of this camp, Abby reached her hut and was greeted by an almost-cheery fire inside. "Wood and meat, as promised!" announced Susan.

The green wood burned slowly and billowed smoke that stung the lungs. But no one complained. It was far better than gnawing cold. Still, Abby's sense of foreboding was not lifted. "It's as if liberty, itself, drifts farther away each day as the army shrinks and suffers. What can we do?"

Susan grunted in the flickering firelight. "Survive."

"Just surviving isn't enough. We're supposed to be fighting for liberty."

"In a place like this, survive is all there is to do. And sometimes to survive is to fight. Sometimes, to survive is to win."

Aftermath

Washington's army survived the winter, although almost 3,000 died during the long months of bleak cold (almost one in six of the men who entered camp). Far more were lost to desertions and executions. Washington also survived the challenges to his command from other generals—Charles Lee, Benedict Arnold, Gates, and especially Conway—and emerged as a stronger leader.

Thanks to the training of Baron von Steuben, the army shrugged off their winter coats looking like and acting like a real army. The Continental Army emerged from winter famine with 10,000 trained, tough men—still in rags, still underfed, still unpaid, but still burning with a revolutionary spirit that kept them in the field and gave the revolution a chance to succeed.

Follow-up Questions and Activities

1. **What Do You Know?**

   - Why didn't local Pennsylvania farmers share their crops and their grain with Washington's army?

   - Why did Washington need to stay close to Philadelphia that winter of 1776–1777?

   - Why couldn't Washington buy the supplies he and his army needed? Why didn't Congress give him money he could spend on food?

   - Why did the army allow men to bring their wives to winter camp to live at the wives' camp? Why did the army need the wives in camp? Do armies still allow their soldiers to bring spouses to the camps where they are stationed during wartime?

2. **Finding Out More.** Following are six important topics from this story for you to research in the library and on the Internet. The reference sources at the back of this book will help you get started.

   - Soldiers stood guard barefoot in the snow on bitter-cold winter days and nights at Valley Forge. How could they do that and not freeze, or at least get severe frostbite on their toes and feet? Research this question and see if you can create an explanation. How many soldiers *did* suffer from frostbite that winter? How many had feet and legs amputated because of it?

- This story mentions the problems the army had with, and the harsh punishment for, desertion. Research military discipline for desertion through the ages. What punishments have different societies and armies meted out to those who try to run away?

- Two Continental Army generals, Charles Lee and Conroy, mounted challenges to Washington's authority and leadership during the Valley Forge winter camp. Research the careers and fortunes of these two generals. Lee, in particular, had a checkered and fascinating career as a general and Washington's second in command.

- Why couldn't Congress supply the army during the winter? They were the national legislature, and this was their national army. Why was it so poorly supplied by the national government?

- There were three Continental armies: Washington's and a northern and a southern army. What did these other two armies do during the winter? Where did they go? Why don't we hear about their winter hardships?

- Valley Forge wasn't rated by Washington's soldiers as their worst winter. The worst happened at Morristown, New Jersey, in the winter of 1778–1779. Research the two winters Washington spent at Morristown. How bad were conditions there? Why did Washington go back to Morristown the following winter?

3. **Make It Real**

- Make a Continental Army dinner of firecakes and weak vegetable stew, made by throwing all the available food into the squad's one cooking pot with water and hanging it over a small fire. There was no official recipe for firecakes; they were made with whatever was available. Primarily, firecakes were a mix of flour (corn or wheat) and water mixed into a thick dough. Pinches of salt and baking soda (if available) were added, as was sugar (generally available only for the officers' meals). Some kind of fat (lard, drippings from yesterday's meat, or butter) was cut and kneaded into the dough so that the cakes would sizzle on the hot stove rocks. Firecakes were formed into pancake-like shapes and fried until crisp on the outside.

    Compare firecakes to the following version of the Journeycake that was popular as a food to pre-cook to take on journeys. Note that this recipe gives modern measurements. Cups, tablespoons, and teaspoons did not exist until the late 1800s as cooking measures. In 1777 the recipe would have called for a pinch, a smidgen, or a bit of dry spices, for a "little" butter, and for a fist-sized lump of cornmeal. Ovens were wood heated and had no thermometers. The recipe would have said to "bake until done."

Journeycakes

1 cup yellow cornmeal
1/4 cup sugar
1/2 teaspoon baking soda
1 teaspoon cream of tartar
1/4 teaspoon salt
1 cup buttermilk
1 well-beaten egg
1 tablespoon molasses (or maple syrup)
1 tablespoon melted, unsalted butter

Directions:
Preheat oven to 425 degrees.
Lightly grease an 8-inch square baking pan.
Sift all the dry ingredients together in a bowl.
Add the milk, egg, molasses, and butter. Mix until smooth.
Bake for 30 minutes. Remove from pan and let cool. To
provide an entire class with a taste, double this recipe.

- What did soldiers *do* in winter camp? Sure, they were cold and hungry. But what did they typically do every day? What jobs had to be regularly performed? Who did them? What did the soldiers do for fun? Research what it was like to be a private in Washington's army in winter camp at Valley Forge and write a letter home describing your activities and feelings during a typical day.

4. **Points to Ponder**

- Why did our nation's army suffer from lack of food and clothing every winter? Especially, why did they nearly starve at Valley Forge, which was surrounded by the most productive agricultural land in the country? Local civilians didn't suffer and starve. People in nearby Philadelphia didn't starve. The British army didn't starve. Why did Washington's Continental Army suffer? How did Congress, the individual states, and local people contribute to its suffering? How did the army bring on its own problems?

- Many of the soldiers that winter had no shoes and walked barefoot across the snow to stand watches and conduct their army training. Few had enough food. Why did they stay? Why didn't the whole army quit and go home? *Did* any soldiers try to quit and go home? Why didn't more try?

1778
at a
Glance

The Armies Are Stalemated While the Frontier Burns

At the beginning of 1778 both sides in the conflict were wary and cautious. The Continental Army was locked in its struggle for survival at Valley Forge, Pennsylvania, and would not emerge until June. The British had just lost an entire army with Burgoyne's surrender and dared not risk another. Howe sat in Philadelphia and refused to venture out. He claimed he either wanted 5,000 new troops or to be relieved of his command. The British government was cautiously eyeing France to see how that age-old rival would react to recent events in the American war.

In February, France signed a treaty with America. Everything changed for England. It was now a world war against their most hated enemy instead of a pesky colonial uprising. The War Department decided to let Howe go and turned the American mess over to General Clinton, telling him to come up with a new plan for winning the war—quickly and without any additional help because the rest of the army would be tied up combating France at various spots around the world.

Clinton's first plan was to abandon Philadelphia and return to New York, but thousands of Loyalists had flocked to Philadelphia and now demanded to go with him if he left. It took months to organize the massive caravan. They could not leave Philadelphia until June 18.

Washington was again under tremendous pressure for a victory. He left camp on June 20 and decided to chase Clinton's stretched-out column and strike a blow at his rear guard, forcing a battle Washington could win—his whole army against Clinton's rear guard. But Washington got a late start. He had to send part of his army sprinting forward to catch even Clinton's rear guard.

The battle at Monmouth should have been an easy Patriot victory. But the Continental Army command (this time General Lee) muffed it again and the battle ended in a draw. Clinton escaped to New York to plan his southern strategy, and the major armies of the war never met in battle again although the fighting would continue for another three years.

By year's end Clinton had begun sailing his forces south to attack the major port cities of Savannah and Charleston. Because the British had lost in the North (Burgoyne's surrender) and had failed to trap and defeat Washington in the middle, they would try to secure the Carolinas and move north from a solid Southern base.

While all east coast eyes watched the dance of armies between Washington and Clinton, the British in Canada turned forces of Tories and Seneca Indians loose to pillage and burn the Patriot frontier areas that were supplying much of the food and grain for the war effort. The brutal fighting of 1778 occurred in western New York, Ohio, and northern Pennsylvania—vicious fighting without the gentlemanly rules that civilized armies followed. Civilians were slaughtered. Whole valleys and all the homes, fields, barns, and livestock in them were burned. It was a time of scalp collecting and sneak attacks, of mass murder more than warfare.

Key Events in 1778

Date	Event
February 6	Franco-American treaty signed. France enters the war.
June 18	Clinton evacuates his army from Philadelphia.
June 20	Washington leaves Valley Forge.
June 28	Battle of Monmouth, New Jersey.
July 4	Wyoming Valley, Pennsylvania, massacre.
August 20	French forces arrive in Rhode Island to join the war.
November 11	Cherry Valley, New York, massacre.
December 29	Savannah falls to the British.

Red, White, and Betsy
Women in Business During the War, 1778

Betsy Ross presenting her flag

We have all heard the story that Elizabeth (Betsy) Ross sewed the first American flag. Interestingly, it is virtually impossible to prove that the story is true, although it is plausible—it *could* have happened just that way. It is true, however, that Betsy Ross was a determined, successful businesswoman who owned, managed, and expanded a thriving upholstery shop from 1773 until her retirement in 1827, through two wars and three husbands. It is also true that Betsy Ross was a staunch Patriot and sewed many American flags once the design was approved by the Continental Congress. She was an interesting, skilled, and successful American businesswoman and is worthy of our attention, whether she sewed the first flag or not. This is her story of how the first flag was made.

Meet Elizabeth Griscom Ross

Elizabeth Griscom was born the eighth of 17 children of Quaker parents in 1754. She was named Elizabeth, but was always called Betsy. She attended a Quaker school eight hours a day, where she learned to read and write and received instruction in a "practical trade," sewing. At age 18, she talked her parents into allowing her to leave home while still a single girl (rare for any family in the mid-1700s and especially rare for a Quaker family) to apprentice in an upholstery shop in Philadelphia. It was also rare for girls to be allowed to apprentice in any trade.

Betsy had sparkling eyes, a keen intellect, good business sense, and a powerful (her parents said uncontrollable) will. She met John Ross at the upholstery shop. He was another apprentice and the son of an Episcopal minister.

In 1773 John and Betsy eloped, even though it meant Betsy would be cut off from all family, church, and Quaker community ties. Typical of Betsy, she did what she wanted to do. She and John established the upholstery shop she would own and operate for 54 years.

Red, White, and Betsy

A crackling fire radiated cozy warmth throughout the long living room of this spacious brick house in Philadelphia. Six young children drew, played, and wrestled on the floor. Six women sewed, talked, and laughed at the long eating table back by the kitchen.

A 75-year-old, white-haired woman eased herself into the comfortable rocker that had been "her chair" for almost 50 years. Slowly she surveyed this happy, noisy home with a deep sense of pleasure and pride. This was a house filled with life and love. Surely this was the old woman's greatest achievement.

She began to rock as she loved to do, and looked down at her hands. Gnarled and arthritic now, they had once been so quick and nimble. Once they had been champion sewers, these old hands. But that didn't matter now. Her eyes were going bad, and she couldn't see to sew anyway.

Even that didn't matter tonight. Tonight two of her three daughters, four of her granddaughters, and six great-grandchildren had gathered for a celebration. Tomorrow was Betsy Ross's last day working at the family upholstery shop she had owned, nurtured, and expanded for 54 years. This was her retirement party.

Seven-year-old Melissa stopped her drawing and flopped across her great-grandmother's lap. Her chin rested on the long skirt covering Betsy's knees. Her glowing face shone up at her great-grandmother, filled with wonder and excitement. That face reminded Betsy very much of her own seven-year-old face. The thought made her smile as she reached out to stroke the child's hair, yellow as golden wheat waving in the field.

"Tell us a story, Granny Betsy," Melissa asked.

"That's *great*-granny to you, Melissa," teased Betsy.

"Great-Grandmother Betsy's too long," complained six-year-old Joshua. "Granny Betsy is bad enough."

"*Please* tell us a story," Melissa begged.

In a flash all six great-grandchildren crowded eagerly at their great grandmother's feet, chanting, "Story, story, story!"

"All right," Betsy laughed. "A story it shall be."

"Yea!" cheered six young voices.

One of Betsy's granddaughters at the table leaned back and called, "Joshua. Back up and give Granny Betsy some room."

"Yes, mother."

One of Betsy's daughters, Clarissa, chuckled, "Here she goes. I've got a feeling *all* the old stories will come out tonight."

Betsy contentedly rocked. "Let me see. A story. . . . Ah, here's a good one. Did you know that I was a real rebel when I was young?"

"You mean in the Revolutionary War?" asked Melissa.

"Oh, way before that," said Betsy with a wave of her hand. "I drove my father crazy."

The children giggled. This sounded like a good story.

"When I was 16 I hounded my parents to let me work outside our home. My parents were fit to be tied! 'It isn't proper for a Quaker girl,' they said. I told them I didn't care a hoot for proper.

"My father crossed his arms and said, 'Industry itself is enough reward, whether the job be new or old.'

"I said that if it didn't matter if the job was new or old, I'd pick new, and somewhere new besides. Father would throw his hands into the air and mutter, 'Auch! That girl!' "

The children all laughed at Betsy's imitation of her stern Quaker father.

"When I turned 18 they finally let me get a job as an apprentice in a Philadelphia upholstery shop, since everyone knew I was a champion seamstress."

"Graaanny, when's the good part?" whined Joshua.

"I'll have you know it was exciting for a girl to get a professional job at all in those days," answered Betsy. "I was the only female apprentice in any of the shops for four blocks in any direction! And that shop is where I met John Ross, your great-grandfather. He worked beside me, and was only three years older than I was. John was kind, bright, funny, and he loved America with all his heart and soul. Of course, he wasn't nearly as precise and neat at his work as I was. But he was faster and stronger.

"In 1773 we wanted to marry. My parents wouldn't even discuss it because John wasn't Quaker. Quakers aren't allowed to marry outside the faith. But remember, I told you I was a rebel. John and I eloped!

"Father was furious when I told them I was married and that John and I were going to open our own upholstery shop in Philadelphia. Father exploded! He jammed his fists on his hips and said slowly enough to emphasize each separate syllable, 'Thee should not have done this thing!' "

One of the boys laughed, "That's not even angry, Granny Betsy."

"You never met my father. 'Thee should not have done this thing,' was *furious* for him."

The children howled at Betsy's exaggerated impersonation of her father. Several tried to imitate her with little fists wedged on hip bones. Then they laughed all the harder.

"Life in the city was so exciting for a sheltered country girl like me. Everywhere was something new and different to see and do. Business was brisk in our shop, and we soon established a reputation for fast and exceptionally good work. It felt wonderful to walk out our front door and see the sign, 'Ross Upholstery Shop,' and know it was *my* shop!

"Then in 1775 John joined the Continental Army. There were secret meetings, sudden drills, and John's hidden musket under a wide bolt of cloth in our shop. I thought it all very exciting—but a bit silly . . . "

"The war was silly, Granny?" asked Joshua.

"Until early 1776 when John was killed when an explosion destroyed a secret ammunitions warehouse he was guarding. I was devastated. But there was the shop to manage every day, my three girls (your grandmothers) to care for, and at night I secretly forged musket balls for the army."

"You made muskets, Granny?" exclaimed Joshua.

"Musket *balls*," corrected Betsy. "The army had no money and had to rely on local citizen groups to supply its needs. Besides, times were hard. Material to sew with was hard to come by with the British embargo in effect. Business was slow—especially when customers found out I owned the shop."

"Why Granny?"

"Because, Melissa, I was a woman. Folks didn't mind if I did the work. But most felt it wasn't right for a woman to own a business."

"Why not, Granny?"

"Because banks wouldn't loan money to a woman. A woman couldn't own property and equipment. So it wasn't considered proper for a woman to try to own a business."

One of the women leaned back from the table. "But you did, Mom."

"Folks gave me extra leeway after the war because I had two husbands die during the war."

"Two?" asked Melissa. "Who was the second one?"

"He was a smuggler . . . "

"A pirate?" interrupted Joshua.

"No, a privateer. He mostly smuggled material and dry goods to sell. He provided most of the material I had to work with." Betsy chuckled quietly. "The material he smuggled in for me to sew with got me in big trouble during the British occupation of Philadelphia in 1777. The British knew I was a Patriot supporter. But they never closed me down because they hoped to trap my husband when he came for a visit.

"They raided my shop six times that awful winter. Always in the dead of night. Pounding on the door with the butts of their muskets. I'd be forced to stand in a corner while they tore the shop apart, searching for Alfred—my husband—and for illegal weapons. Twice they made the girls get up, too. Lined them up in front of the fireplace. They wailed and sobbed, thinking they were going to be shot."

Betsy stopped and chuckled again.

"Getting shot's not funny, Granny Betsy," wailed Melissa.

A wrinkled hand patted the girl's head. "I was laughing, dear, at how funny it was that they never found any of the thousands of musket balls I made and hid around the shop. Clarissa was two that winter. On one raid she wailed so loud, the soldiers made her go sit on a bench in the far corner. They searched every-where—except under Clarissa's bench. And that's where a captain in the army was hiding who had come to pick up my stock of musket balls and bring me news of Alfred."

Then her face sobered. "But that winter was a bleak and frightful time. We never heard from my husband because he couldn't get through the British lines to visit us. I was constantly threatened with arrest. Three times the British confiscated every scrap of material in the shop because I didn't have proper British import papers."

"Weren't you scared?" asked six-year-old Joshua.

Betsy cocked her head and thought for a moment. "Some. But mostly I was too busy supporting the Revolution, trying to keep the shop open and support my girls to have time to think about it. By March of 1778, business was so bad I had to let two of my three workers go. I hated to do it, but we barely had enough food to live on ourselves."

Betsy sighed. "I'll never forget the March afternoon when a British major pounded on the door and sneered with obvious glee when I opened it. It was such a beautiful early spring afternoon, I couldn't help smiling at him. Then he told me that my husband's privateer ship had been captured. Alfred had been wounded and was in chains in a British dungeon. He died a year later in that prison without ever feeling the sunshine again."

The room was silent while Betsy slowly rocked. The women had stopped their work to listen. Melissa's faced was scrunched into a look of horror. "He *died?*"

"But Grannnnnny," whined Joshua. "When are you going to get to how you made the flag?"

"Oh, *that*," beamed Betsy with false modesty at being asked to tell her favorite story. "I suppose, if you insist."

"Yea!" cheered the children.

"Time for bed, children," called one of Betsy's granddaughters, leaning back to stretch from her quilting.

"Not just yet," said Betsy. "They can stay up for one more story. After all, it's a celebration night."

"YEA!" cheered the children.

"Now where was I . . . "

"The flag, Granny Betsy," huffed Melissa.

"Oh, yes. The flag. But first, don't you want to hear the rest about how through two wars and three husbands I, a woman, owned and ran a thriving business for 54 years right here in downtown Philadelphia? And all that time women weren't supposed to be able to do it. Hogwash! There was no reason why a woman couldn't do it then. And there's no reason a woman can't do it now. You remember that, each one of you, as you grow."

Her finger wagged in mock seriousness at them as she spoke. The children erupted in giggles at hearing their great-grandmother exclaim something like "hogwash."

She settled back in her rocker and surveyed the beaming faces before her. "Now where was I?"

"The *flag*, Granny!"

"Oh, yes, the flag. I remember the visit as clear as yesterday. It was just at dusk, the sky still glowed pink and orange. It was less than a month after John had been killed—early June of 1776. June the tenth if I recall correctly."

One of the women leaned back, smiling. "You always told me it happened on the twelfth, mother."

The children giggled.

Betsy's eyebrows shot up and her hands thudded into her lap. "I'm afraid your memory is starting to slip, Clarissa. If I can remember the whole visit clear as yesterday, I can surely remember the date."

Betsy turned back to the children as the women laughed among themselves. "Now, where was I? Ah, yes. I was just beginning to fix supper for my three girls—your grandmothers—when I heard an urgent knocking on my door—on that very front door behind you.

"I thought to myself, 'now who is it comes a calling, pounding so hard on my door at *this* time of day?'

"I opened the door to three gentlemen huddled in the shadows. The first was Colonel George Ross, your great-grandfather John's uncle. He often came to see me. Just behind him stood Robert Morris, a close friend of his. And behind him, gold-fringed epaulettes glowing in the twilight, stood General George Washington, himself!

"My mouth dropped open. I didn't know what to do. I felt like I should curtsy, or bow, or some such. *The* general of the whole Continental Army standing at my door!

"Colonel Ross asked, 'May we come in?'

"I remember I turned beet red with embarrassment, making three such important gentlemen stand waiting. They stepped into this very room. General Washington started to sit on that bench by the book case. I grabbed his arm, saying, 'Oh, no. Sit here, General. The rocker's more comfortable.'

"He said that the bench would be fine, and sat right there in that very spot."

As Betsy spoke she pointed at the middle of a bench across the room. All the children turned to gaze, half expecting to see the general materialize before their eyes.

"The General's face looked kind, but tired, as he spoke. He told me that each colony had its own flag. Most generals had their own flag, or pennant. Many army units had their own. But if this was going to be a nation, we needed one single flag everyone could follow. It had to be a flag that symbolized this new country, a flag that included everyone, a flag that would excite every soldier, and stir the heart of every citizen.

"As I recall, I said that was a pretty tall order for one piece of cloth. But he pulled a paper from an inside coat pocket and said that he had made some sketches of what he thought would do the trick, and would I be willing to make the first one so he could take it to Congress and get their approval?

"He unfolded a piece of paper and smoothed it over his knees. On it was a sketch for a square flag with 13 alternating red and white stripes. Across the top was a blue field with a circle of 13 white stars in the middle.

" 'Do you see?' asked Colonel Ross. 'One star and one stripe for every state, all equal, and the stars in a circle, a perfect union. It's perfect!'

"But General Washington was watching my face, and could tell I didn't think the idea was perfect at all.

" 'Do *you* have any ideas for improving the design?' he asked.

"I'm sure I blushed again, and got very nervous. After all, who was I to tell General Washington what was wrong with his very own design? But you know what my father taught me: If you have an idea, say it. So I said, 'It's a fine flag, and all, General. But if you moved the field of blue over to just one corner, then you could make the circle of stars bigger and you wouldn't have these empty blue patches on both sides.'

"My heart was pounding, half expecting General Washington to gruffly tell me to mind my own business. But he didn't. The general nodded, stroked his chin and thoughtfully said, 'Hmmmmm.' "

The children at Betsy's feet giggled as she imitated the famous founder of the country.

"General Washington asked me if I had any other ideas. I answered, 'As long as you've asked, General, I think five-pointed stars would look better in the circle than six-pointed ones.' Besides, I knew a neat trick for making perfect five pointed stars.

"By this time General Washington was getting a bit annoyed with all my changes to his carefully thought-out flag design. He crossed his arms and asked, 'Any *more* changes, Mistress Ross?'

" 'Just one more,' I answered trying to smile and blush at the same time. 'A square flag doesn't flutter as well in the wind as one that's wider than it is tall.'

"Mr. Morris tried to hide a smile behind a polite cough. Colonel Ross shrugged. 'I told you she was the best, General.' Now mind you those were his exact words. 'I told you she was the best.'

"General Washington just grunted and stared at his flag sketch. Finally he rose, letting his sketch flutter to the floor. 'So be it, Mistress Ross. We use your design. One final question. Can you make the flag?'

" 'I've never made one, General,' I said. 'But it's a good thing and I know I can if I try.'—That's something my father often said.

"And that, children, is how the American flag came to be the way it is today."

Clarissa said, "Mother, you always told me you were afraid to mention changing the flag's shape to General Washington, that you secretly made it a rectangle, and that he liked it when he saw it."

Betsy's eyebrows arched. "Fiddle-dee-dee, Clarissa. I worry about how poor your memory has become. If I made the flag, you'd think I'd remember what the General and I agreed to." She turned back to the children, "Now off to bed, all of you."

Betsy Ross loved to tell the story of making the first American flag, and told it many times. Additional bits of family evidence support her claim. General Washington, Colonel Ross, and Robert Morris were all in Philadelphia and not otherwise accounted for on the night Betsy claimed they visited her shop. But we'll probably never know for sure. There is no absolute proof that Betsy Ross sewed that first American flag.

Aftermath

Congress adopted the design of the American flag on June 14, 1777. That date each year is still celebrated as Flag Day. Whether or not she sewed the *first* flag, Betsy later sewed many American flags and, more important, managed a steady, successful business for over half a century at a time when very few women were able to run one at all.

Follow-up Questions and Activities

1. **What Do You Know?**

    • What did the army use for a flag before Congress approved Betsy's flag?

    • Why was Betsy Ross's flag laid out and designed as it was? What did the stripes and circle of stars mean? Can you think of a well-known English story when a king used a circle for the same symbolic purpose?

    • Betsy Ross's family were Quakers. Did any Quakers fight in the Revolutionary War? Did they support the Revolution? How?

    • Why was it not common for a woman to own a business in colonial America? What laws and policies made it difficult for women to own businesses?

2. **Finding Out More.** Following are five important topics from this story for you to research in the library and on the Internet. The reference sources at the back of this book will help you get started.

    • Research Betsy Ross. Discover her history and her accomplishments.

    • Research the origins and history of the American flag. What flags were used before Congress approved Betsy's? How did the flag change over the years?

- Betsy Ross has become a symbol of the American Revolution. What do we mean when we call something a symbol? What other symbols of the revolutionary period can you find? Of colonial America? Of American history in general? Symbols could be places, things, or people. How many symbols can your class identify? There are hundreds you could find.

- Where did the Quakers live in America? Where did they come from? Why did they come here? What did they believe? What is the difference between Quakers, Amish, and Mennonites? Research the Quakers' history in America. How have they fared in recent times? Have they been able to hold onto their unique beliefs without being persecuted? Have they been able to stay out of the military? How do they support themselves?

- Betsy Ross claimed to know a simple, quick trick for making perfect five-point stars. Search library sources and the Internet to see if you can find this same, simple trick. Practice making five-point stars until you are as good as Betsy was.

3. **Make It Real**

- Design your own flag for a new country being forged from 13 separate colonies. What shape would you use? What colors and design? How would you represent both the 13 separate units and the unity of the new, single country? Draw your design on paper and write an explanation of why you chose the elements and design you did.

- Design a flag for your school. What images and symbols will you put on this flag? What impression and information will you try to convey? What look, color scheme, and shape will you use? Why?

4. **Points to Ponder**

- Imagine owning an upholstery shop in Philadelphia in 1777 when the British seize the town, or a small wheel manufacturing plant in Front Royal, Virginia, during the Civil War when opposing sides seized and lost the town on a regular basis. How would you try to stay open? How would you ensure enough business to support your family and employees? What would you fear? What would you hope for?

- What is the point of having a flag? What is a national, state, city, or school flag supposed to do?

Home-Fire Heroes

Life Away from the War, Summer 1778

Typical 1770s farm girl dress

At a Glance

All along the coast of America—in Boston, New York, Charleston, and Philadelphia—and throughout New Jersey and upstate New York, the war was real and present in 1776, 1777, and 1778. Elsewhere it was marked only by the absence of some of the men who had marched off to join the army and by the occasional presence and drilling of a militia unit.

In rural outback areas, weather, crops, and livestock were of greater and more immediate concern than some distant war. On the rural frontier, every year was a test of survival on self-sufficient homesteads. There was little extra time to consider the philosophical or moral implications of breaking the Colonies' bonds with England.

Life on a rural farm was all-consuming and all-important to the Revolution. Without a steady flow of food, the Revolution could not survive. This story looks at farms and their role in the war.

Meet Emily Maitens

Sixteen-year-old Emily Maitens was born in Philadelphia less than six months after her parents arrived from England in 1761. Her father was American born, but lived in London for four years to study to become a doctor and surgeon. Her mother was English, but was adventurous and had longed for sea travel and colonial life.

Dr. Maitens quickly became a prominent Philadelphia doctor. He also became an ardent Patriot. Mrs. Maitens held no deep feelings about the war one way or the other. The doctor volunteered to serve with Washington and traveled with the army during each summer's campaign. The family stayed in Philadelphia during these tours because Mrs. Maitens was active in social circles.

Emily grew up as a smart, quick, city girl. She was part of the top social circles and was exposed to the arts and culture available in a major city. Emily returned to Philadelphia after the occupation of 1777 and lived there until she married the owner of a shipping company. She was able to sail around the world with her husband several times before settling in New York City, where she lived the rest of her life.

Home-Fire Heroes

"War. War. War. I am sick of hearing about nothing but the silly old war from you!" Twelve-year-old Josephine Wooten flung herself dramatically across her bed. The move looked comically out of place in her patched and faded farm work dress and the rugged wilderness of the Wootens' western Maryland farmstead.

Her sixteen-year-old cousin, Emily Maitens, sat primly erect in a stiff-backed chair in a fashionable "city dress." "Don't be silly, Jossie. How could anyone be sick of the war? Saying you are tired of the war is like saying you are tired of air."

Josephine lifted her head. "Those two are nothing alike, Emily."

Emily raised herself taller in her chair. Her eyebrows arched and an icy edge crept into her tone. "I am four years older and have seen Philadelphia and everything in between. I have even been to New Jersey! So I *know* what is and isn't the same!"

Jossie lowered her eyes, duly intimidated by the worldly wisdom of her cousin. "Sorry, Emily."

"What I was saying before I was so rudely interrupted is that air is the most important of the gasses because air sustains life. War is the most important of all events because it will determine how you'll live your life. Saying you don't care about the war is like saying you don't care about the air that gives you life."

Josephine stubbornly crossed her arms. "There's no war here in Hagerstown. We haven't seen even one soldier since the war started."

"Of course not *here*," scoffed Emily. "But *here* doesn't matter."

"Yes, it does," Josephine snapped. "This farm is all that matters." And she turned away to end the conversation. Under her breath Jossie muttered, "I still don't think war and air are any more alike than horse carriages and applesauce."

Emily Maitens had been raised in the bustling excitement of Philadelphia and, because of her father, she had seen Washington's army form and grow. It thrilled Emily to visit her father and see ranks of marching soldiers and to see the glitter of officers' uniforms around the headquarters.

But thrill turned to danger when the British occupied Philadelphia in September 1777. Emily's mother had been born in England and would be safe from English persecution, but Emily was the daughter of a known member of Washington's staff and she was a headstrong Patriot. "Spirited" is what the neighbors politely called her.

Dr. Maitens feared that, if the British moved into Philadelphia on Monday, Emily would get herself arrested by Tuesday. He ordered Emily to evacuate safely to the country in western Maryland with his distant cousin, Herman Wooten, until Philadelphia was again safe.

Lifting her skirts in both hands, Emily tiptoed her way out to the Wooten's barn the next morning. She was supposed to feed the cows and chickens. It was how Mr. Wooten said she could "earn her keep" while she lived there. But Emily knew that 18-year-old Jeb Wooten would always do her work if she asked sweetly.

Halfway to the barn the grass moved in front of her. A long, hideous blackness slithered into the dirt path. Emily screamed and sprang onto a nearby fence, clinging to the wobbly rails and screaming, "Kill it! Kill it!"

Jeb poked his head out of the small barn and laughed. "It's just a black snake. We want them around."

The snake wiggled back into the tall grass near the first in the line of apple trees. "You *want* to have snakes?"

"They kill rats and mice that eat hay and grain."

"Use traps," snapped Emily, cautiously climbing down. "They don't terrify passers by." She shook her head and added, "Farms are disgusting!"

Jeb dragged his left leg behind him as they stepped into the tidy barn with space for two cows, a hay stack, and racks for axes and scythes. "I want to leave the farm, too," he said. "I want to join the army and fight!"

"Why don't you? Washington is so desperate for soldiers he'll take anybody."

Jeb slapped his thigh and shrugged. "With this crushed leg I can barely walk. How can I march all over with an army?"

"Be a horse soldier," suggested Emily, smoothing her dress as she settled into the soft hay stack.

"They really have soldiers who ride on horses?"

"The British do," Emily answered. "I saw them and they all had swords and sashes and plumes in their hats, and their horses pranced down the street five across."

Jeb rubbed his dirty hands eagerly together. "Does *Washington* have horse soldiers?"

"Why even ask?" laughed Emily. "You don't have a horse . . . or a sword . . . or a plume."

"But we've got a hunting rifle and I'm a good shot."

Emily smiled her most charming city smile. "Jeb," she cooed. "Do my chores this morning and I'll watch you shoot this afternoon."

"Can't," he answered. "We all have to weed the fields this afternoon. So do you."

"Oh, fiddle-dee-dee. I hate weeding!" Emily stamped her foot on the dirt floor. Both cows moo-ed and shifted uneasily in their stalls. "I'm no good at weeding. Last time Aunt Mary yelled at me for pulling out the beans."

Jeb's hands modeled how the cornfield was planted. "The corn grows straight up from the top of each mound. Bean plants grow alongside and wind around the corn for support, and the squash grows along the ground at the base of the mound. Everything else is a weed."

Emily stormed out of the barn. "How can I care about silly old weeds when I want to be back in the city discussing politics and the war?"

After breakfast, Emily accompanied her aunt and uncle on the jarring three-mile, one-hour wagon ride into Hagerstown. Holding her hat with one hand and the metal wagon rail with her other to keep from being flung out as the wagon rolled through deep ruts, Emily said, "Philadelphia has paved streets and lights and music and row after row of fancy stores. That's the *real* America!"

Thirty-eight-year-old Herman Wooten had thick arms, a thick middle, and loved to laugh. "You lived in that stuffy city too long, Emily. *This* is the real America. Most Americans live on farms like ours, and grow food like we do, and go into town once in a while for supplies like we are."

"No! The real America is exciting, with theaters and music and dances with flowing gowns."

Trim, plain Mary Wooten answered, "That's the kind of exciting that could get a girl into trouble. Better a quiet life on the farm."

Mr. Wooten added, "Your cities couldn't survive without this America out here."

"But *that's* where the war is," insisted Emily. "Don't you care what happens in the war? Don't you want to be part of it and fight for freedom?!"

"The war will have to get by without us," chuckled Herman, adjusting his wide-brimmed straw hat and clicking his tongue at the horses. "We have all we can handle making this farm work. Got no time left over to take on other fights."

Emily stammered, "But . . . but the war is the most important thing!"

"Why? No matter what happens on the battlefield my cow still needs to be milked, the chickens need to be fed. The corn, beans, and squash need to be weeded, the hay cut down and gathered. The goats need tending to. We'll still sell apples, cheese, eggs, and extra hay at the Hagerstown market. What difference does the war make?"

Emily was almost too taken aback to answer. In the city everyone knew how important the war was and she didn't have to argue about it. "What difference? . . . Why all the difference. If we win, we'll have our liberty!"

Mr. Wooten rocked back and laughed. "Liberty, eh? I gave up my liberty to the farm animals a long time ago. No one's going to get it back for me by shooting at each other with guns."

"But . . . but . . . but . . . " Emily felt dizzy, her mind spun so hard. How could her father have banished her out here with these . . . these people who didn't even understand the most basic concepts of life?

That evening Emily collapsed on the living room floor. She stared vacantly at her hands soaking in a large bowl of warm water to ease the raw ache after an afternoon of weeding. "They're ruined. I'll have to wear gloves for the rest of my life."

"You'll get used to it," offered Jeb, sharpening an ax blade. "Harvest time is soon. Then it gets a bit lighter over winter."

Mr. Wooten helped his wife prepare beans for drying at the table. "Check on the cow when you're finished with that ax, Jeb. She may be ready to throw her calf tonight. Oh, and make sure the barn doors are latched good. Feels like a storm is brewing."

Emily muttered "Oh, I wish I could go home where it's exciting and where people care about the war!"

Thundering cannons rumbled through Emily's dreams that night. Each black muzzle exploded in great clouds of smoke and fire as they shot white-hot streaks across a battlefield. She awoke with a start in the pitch black, hearing Mrs. Wooten scream, "Emily! Wake up, child! We need you!"

Wind howled outside and rain pounded down so hard each drop bounced off the dirt. Lightning flashed, jagged and close. Thunder roared like cannon fire across the farm. Mary Wooten's face was drawn and tense. "There's trouble with the calf and we need everyone's help."

"I don't know anything about birthing cows," Emily protested, drawing her covers tight around her.

"No, but you know how to hold a lantern. So hurry!"

Inside the crowded barn, thunder rattled the scythes so that the metal blades clanged. Rain drummed on the roof so that everyone had to shout to be heard.

The family's youngest cow lay on her side, back legs pawing at the air. The new calf's front hooves and face were already out, smeared with blood and sticky fluid. Mr. Wooten lay on the dirt floor, one hand trying to feel around the calf and discover why it was stuck. Jossie held one dim lantern. Jeb used a board to protect his father from being brutally kicked by the cow.

Mr. Wooten called, "I think the back legs are bent up underneath. I can't get in to straighten then out." His arms were covered in blood and a big puddle of red soaked into the straw.

Emily paled and backed away.

"Get more light down here!" Mr. Wooten screamed. Mrs. Wooten shoved Emily and her lantern forward.

The barn doors rattled. One shutter on the house had come loose and slapped against the siding. Lightning bolts exploded around the barn, almost blinding everyone inside with their brilliance.

One crackling bolt struck a maple tree just behind the barn. A curving branch cracked off and thudded into the side of barn just as the thunder bolt exploded. Emily screamed and dropped her lantern. Hay caught on fire. The flames quickly ate into a billowing hay mound.

Jossie and Jeb grabbed blankets and pounded on the growing flames. Jossie's caught on fire. Jeb's seemed to fan the flames more than extinguish them. "Get that fire out!" screamed Herman. "I gotta save this cow."

Emily raced to the wide barn door and threw it open. Then she flung open the back door. Rain in torrents swept through the barn on the screeching wind. The flames flickered and helplessly succumbed to the downpour. All three youngsters had to strain to force the doors closed again, trapping the smell of smoke and smoldering hay inside the barn.

Rain still dripped off each person's face and slicked-down hair back at the kitchen table. The calf—a young bull—seemed fine. The mother and the barn had survived. "She'll live to give milk again," said Mr. Wooten as he sipped fermented apple cider from a mug.

Emily still shivered from the wet and their close call with disaster. "I'm sorry, uncle. I almost killed us all. The lightning bolt was just so startling."

He smiled and patted her trembling hand. "It's all right, child. You're still new out here. The battles on a farm take some getting used to." He took a long sip from his mug before continuing. "You see, Emily, *this* is our part of the war. Out there tonight we saved a barn and birthed a new calf. That makes America just a little stronger and richer. Soldiers help out their way. We help out our way. It may not match a fancy theater play or a big battle, but helping a new life come safely into being is pretty exciting in my book."

Emily's heart pounded from the excitement of the battle against the storm, the fire, and death. And for just a moment there in the dark, with torrents swirling outside, she understood how her uncle and his family felt.

Aftermath

Many small communities in America never felt the sting of war other than in the lists of local boys killed in battle or from disease while serving in the army. But many towns and farms were burned to the ground by Indian and Tory raids. Many fields were trampled and many more stripped by hungry armies on the march. Many peaceful families were left destitute by the passing war. Others made fortunes during and because of the war. There were few who were not touched by the war in a very personal way.

Follow-up Questions and Activities

1. **What Do You Know?**

   - What percentage of the American population during the Revolution lived on farms? What size were these farms? How do they compare to farms today, in size and methods of operation?

   - In the last paragraph of this story Emily "knew how they felt." How do you think the Wootens felt, and why?

   - Why did people living in the major cities think more about armies and fighting than did the rural farmers?

   - Were there differences between city folk and country folk? If so, what were they?

2. **Finding Out More**. Following are four important topics from this story for you to research in the library and on the Internet. The reference sources at the back of this book will help you get started.

   - We now think of the Midwest states of Indiana through Iowa as the "bread basket" for the nation, the area where most of our grains and crops are grown. Where was the "bread basket" for the nation during the Revolutionary War? Where were the farming areas that produced most of the grain and livestock for the colonies?

   - What crops did mid-eighteenth-century American farmers grow? Were different crops grown in different regions of the country? How much of each major crop did eighteenth-century farmers produce?

   - Eighteenth-century farmers didn't have tractors, threshers, and bailers. Research farm technology in that century. What equipment did farmers use? What inventions in the eighteenth century helped farmers increase their production?

   - Fire has always been a major threat and danger. Now we have fire trucks, high-pressure water lines, pumps, and hoses to fight fires. How did people fight fires in the eighteenth century? The danger of fire was greater then because people used candles and torches for light and open fires for warmth and cooking. Open flames and fires were an ever-present part of their daily lives. Research both how they fought a fire and what precautions they routinely took to prevent fires from starting.

3. **Make It Real**

   - Pick a distant city and try to learn as much as you can about it and its most recent election. What technology did you use to acquire this information? What would you do if you couldn't use modern technology (telephones, computers, fax machines) to obtain information? What else could you rely on? How else could you gather news? Try gathering the same information using only those means of communication available to someone in the eighteenth century.

   - What percentage of the American population actually fought during the Revolutionary War? The total colonial population in 1775 was about 2.7 million. The Continental army, navy, and militia forces that actually participated in battles, plus Tory militia units that fought with the British, plus estimates of the number of privateer seamen who saw combat only amount to between 70,000 and 80,000. What percent of the total population was that? What did the rest of the population do? If they didn't fight, does that mean that they didn't care about the war?

4. **Points to Ponder**

- How do *you* learn about the events of a distant war? How many of those methods of news gathering were available to eighteenth-century American rural farmers? How did *they* learn about the war and other distant events? How long did it take news to reach isolated settlements in the eighteenth century? How long did it take for news to come from overseas? Did the difficulty of gathering distant news affect what settlers knew and cared about?

- Do you think that the Revolutionary War was constantly on people's minds? It lasted for seven years and involved fewer than 20 major battles. What do you think people talked about and worried about when not thinking about the war?

- It is often mentioned by historians that the Revolutionary War was a war of ideas more than of armies. What do you think that means? What were those ideas?

Water and Fire!

The Battle of Monmouth, New Jersey, June 28, 1778

Mary Hays at the Battle of Monmouth

At a Glance

The American alliance with France changed everything for England. Suddenly they had to contend not with an upstart colonial rabble, but with their old rival, France, and especially with the French navy. General Clinton arrived to replace General Howe in early 1778 with orders to withdraw to New York (and if necessary to Canada) and to send 5,000 men to attack French positions in the Caribbean.

Clinton's first act was to pull the British army back from Howe's winter quarters at Philadelphia to New York. He departed Philadelphia on June 18 with 15,000 soldiers, 1,500 wagons of supplies, and thousands of Loyalists who had gathered in Philadelphia for Redcoat protection and the tinsel-gaudy days of occupation. The endless procession included bakeries on wheels, laundries, blacksmith shops, hospital tents and stores, and 12 miles of Loyalist civilians and camp followers.

Washington's army emerged from Valley Forge stronger, with a new sense of order and discipline, and ready to test their mettle in a scrap. Washington had become hungry to show the world he could win a battle with the British army. (It had been 18 months since he had shown any sign of victory—and those were only minor victories at Trenton and Princeton.) Even the battle of Germantown, which he was supposed to win, he had bungled so that it ended in a draw.

Clinton was in no mood for a fight. He just wanted to reach New York and re-group. Washington had to race to catch the British and force a battle before they were safely encamped on Manhattan. In the heat of late June, the armies sped across New Jersey, the roles of cat and mouse reversed from previous years. The stage was set for a major battle in the middle of New Jersey and for Mary Hays, the wife of a Pennsylvania artillery man, to become an American heroine.

Meet Mary Ludwig Hays

Mary Ludwig was born in 1755. She always preferred being called Molly. She had dark hair, brown eyes under thick eyebrows, and a pale but pretty face. Molly was raised on a farm in southern New Jersey and was always a "doer" with a restless itch for adventure. She never felt content with the quiet routine of farm life.

At 19 she married John Hays, a barber from Carlisle, Pennsylvania. When he enlisted in the Continental Army, Molly volunteered to travel with him. She was in wives' camp at Valley Forge. A wildly enthusiastic Patriot supporter, Molly was a bubble of bright enthusiasm in that winter of gloom.

Molly became the first real American heroine of the struggle for independence, but not because of the tireless, day-to-day support she gave to the cause. Thousands of women did that and more. Molly became a heroine on one day in late June when she crossed the line that was forbidden to women and joined a battle. This is the story of that day.

Water and Fire!

B y June 20, 1778, word had spread along the farm roads south and east of Trenton, New Jersey, that armies were on the move nearby. A British army under General Clinton was scurrying from Philadelphia for the safety of New York. General Lee, one of Washington's deputies, was in hot pursuit with 6,000 of Washington's finest. Locals said they could smell a big fight coming like you can smell a coming rain.

In the late afternoon heat of June 25 the first blue-coated units, scouts and lead guards, marched past the Ludwig farm 20 miles east of Trenton. The soldiers' grim faces remained hidden in the thick dust cloud they raised from the parched road.

On June 26, General Washington's main army marched by. Almost 12,000 bluecoats, with long French muskets, horses, sabers, wagons, and 500 French under General Lafayette, all rushed through the choking dust to catch General Clinton.

Twenty-three-year-old Molly Ludwig Hays trembled with excitement and ran back and forth between front porch shade and the scorching road to watch and wave as each new unit quick-timed past, hoping for a glimpse of her husband, John Hays. Her parents remained in the shade on the front porch, dabbing the backs of their necks with cool wash cloths.

Molly raced back to the porch. "Oh, isn't it exciting? John's bound to come by soon!"

"Awful hot to be marching that hard all day," said her father.

"They're liable to drop of heat stroke 'fore noon," said her mother.

In her eager excitement Molly hadn't noticed. It *was* hot, brutally hot. The thermometer was fast pushing past 100 degrees. A thick, muggy haze made the very land seem to suffer, and made breathing itself a draining chore.

"Oh, dear," sighed Molly. "I hope John's all right in this heat. He's never worked outside, you know. He was a barber until he joined the army."

With a clatter of horses and the creaking of wagons the 1st Pennsylvania Artillery rumbled by, cannons rolling backward up the road, tied on behind caissons and wagons.

"John! John!" Molly cried as her husband stood waving on his buckboard seat. He leapt to the ground and ran to his wife.

"Back on your mount, Private Hays," yelled a captain. "We're racing to catch the British, and got no time for family visits."

"I'll follow and see you in camp tonight," called Molly.

"No. There'll be a fight tomorrow or the next day for sure. As much as I'd love to see you, you shouldn't," he answered.

Molly stood gazing down the road as the billows of dust slowly settled back to earth. "Why not?" she called after her husband. Long after the columns of soldiers had marched over the rise and faded into shimmering heat she still stood, waiting for an answer.

Then she turned and dashed to the porch, her eyes burning with excitement. "They'll be exhausted when they catch the Redcoats. And the heat's just getting worse. If they have to fight in this awful weather, John will collapse. I know it. I'm going after them."

"But what for?" asked her mother.

"Women can't be around during a fight," said her father.

"Maybe I can carry water to the men, when they're dying of thirst."

Her father chuckled. "They won't let a woman onto a battlefield. You'd just be in the way."

"This is my country, too. I have to do *something*."

"You could get yourself *killed* is what you could do," said her father.

"I know it's dangerous, " she answered, "but I *know* I can help."

In late afternoon Molly rode hard to the north through the oppressive heat still shimmering up off field and road. Two large pewter water pitchers swung from the saddle of her father's horse. "Drat this weather," she muttered to herself. "It always seems to fight against us harder than the British do."

By sunset on the 27th, General Lee's forces had caught the British at Freehold, New Jersey, and forced them to turn for a fight. Molly and all other civilians traveling with the army were ordered back behind the Tennent Church meeting house well west of Monmouth Court House.

Just past 9:00 A.M. the next morning, Molly slung her pitchers over her shoulder on a thin rope and crept past the scattered guards protecting the civilians and supply wagons and through the crackling-dry fields toward the army's position. By 10:00 the steady boom! boom! of cannon fire guided her to a wide open field of parched grass and thick, scattered bushes. A thick smoke cloud hugging the ground across the field told her the battle had started.

It was already over 90 degrees. Heat waves shimmering above the grass made it hard to see whether the units she watched were American or British. Eight American six-pound cannons lined the crest of a low hill on the south side of the field.

British and American cannons roared with a steady, "Boom! Boom! Boom!" The sound rumbled like the pulse beat of the earth. "Boom! Boom! Boom!" Each cannon ball whined as it raced overhead.

Long, steady ranks of British Redcoats emerged from a thin line of trees at the east end of the field. "Boom! Boom! Boom!" Mounted couriers raced back and forth between each Patriot unit and General Lee's command post overlooking the field.

The stifling, humid day was edging toward 100 degrees by the time Molly found a small spring and a wooden bucket with rough rope handles just across the dirt Englishtown Road from the battlefield. She filled the bucket and poured precious water into both pitchers. At the edge of the field she crouched, waiting, as the cannon shells smashed into trees, just in front of a line of advancing Redcoats. Sweat pouring down her own face, Molly ducked and ran—looking much like a scurrying fiddler crab—across the field with her supply of water.

Now several American units broke from the lines and ran to the right to counter a British regiment trying to break around the American flank. Now American units ran back to their left to mass for a charge at the British right side. "Boom! Boom! Boom!"

By 11:00 heat had accomplished what the British could not. Continental soldiers began to drop to the parched grass, pale and feverish with heat stroke. Their lines grew too thin to defend.

Molly Hays raced onto the battlefield with her precious cargo of water. Many of the fallen men were too weak to lift their heads. She propped them up while they gulped long drinks. Always she said, "If you need more, just call for Molly."

Her pitchers soon ran dry. Molly dashed to the spring across the road on the north edge of the field.

The rough rope handle bit into Molly's raw hands as she hauled up the full bucket and refilled her pitchers. Watching men in heavy wool uniform coats crumple, she started back into the smoky battlefield. Caught between an urgent need to race as fast as her legs could run and a prudent desire not to splash any of her precious water out onto the ground, she half jogged, half waddled into the field.

Mounted on horseback on a hill just behind the American lines, the general staff watched in curious fascination as this one white-capped woman zigzagged across the field as if connecting fallen blue dots.

"Who is *she*?" demanded General Lee of an aide. "What's she doing down there?"

"The only name I've heard, sir, is, 'Molly.' She's carrying water to the men."

Lee angrily pointed toward Molly. "That foolish woman could get herself killed. And I won't change my battle tactics just to save her! I have called for all units to withdraw."

"Foolish?" scoffed General Anthony Wayne next to him. "I'd call her brave . . . *very* brave."

Soon the cry, "Molly. Molly. Pitcher. Pitcher!" could be heard from fallen voices along the length of the American line. Volleys of musket balls whined thick through the air and thudded into the earth. Cannon balls, like high-speed bowling balls, mowed down entire sections of the brave soldiers dashing back and forth. Smoke from muskets and cannons drifted across the field to sting the eye and burn the throat.

And the heat grew even worse. Just sitting was a torment on that broiling day. The field felt like an oven. The air of Hades could be no hotter than the air was around Freehold, New Jersey, that day.

Through it all one lone woman ran zigzag from fallen blue coat to blue coat.

"Molly! Pitcher! Molly! Pitcher!"

Others picked up the chant, thinking Molly Pitcher was the name of this invincible woman. "Molly Pitcher! Molly Pitcher!"

The American cannon fire faltered and slowed: "Boom! . . . Boom! . . . Boom!"

Molly dropped her pitchers and climbed the hill on the south side of the battlefield to find three of the eight cannons destroyed by British cannon fire. Many American cannoneers lay wounded or dead. Many more had dropped from the withering heat and the fiery exhaust of red hot cannons whose barrels glowed red.

"John! John Hays!" cried Molly over the roar of battle as she ran down the line of cannon. She found her husband's cannon fallen silent. Two of its four-man crew were down and wounded. John had collapsed from the heat and could not be revived. The fourth gunner slumped, panting, against a cannon wheel.

A messenger galloped up from General Wayne. "Why has this cannon ceased fire?" he demanded. "All cannons must fire. General's orders!"

"But sir," mumbled the wobbly gunner, "I'm all alone."

"No, you're not," cried Molly. "I watched you practice at Valley Forge. I'll be the scrubber and rammer."

Both weary gunner and mounted messenger warily eyed Molly and then shrugged. It seemed the only option at the time.

Molly lifted the long ramrod from where it had fallen next to her husband. She grunted in surprise, finding the iron rod much heavier than she expected. "Swabbing the bore," she called as she ran the ramrod's padded end down the cannon barrel to clear it before firing.

Her one remaining cannon mate loaded the powder charge.

"Ramming home!" called Molly as she jammed that charge to the bottom of the barrel with her ramrod. He loaded the cannon ball and wadding. She rammed it down. He primed, aimed, and, "Fire!" The cannon erupted, belching a fireball flash and smoke. Molly jumped and screamed at the deafening explosion. The cannon bucked in recoil.

"Swab!" commanded her cannon mate.

Molly shook her head to ease the painful ringing in her ears, and ran the ramrod down the barrel. "Swabbing the bore!"

Ram home the powder. Ball and wadding. Ram it down. Prime. Aim. Fire! Their cannonball streaked through the afternoon heat and crashed into the British line of cannons, collapsing one into the dirt. Four Redcoats fell inert to the ground with it.

"Swabbing the bore! . . . Ramming the powder home!" Ball and wadding. Prime. Aim. Fire! Swab. Ram. Fire! Swab, ram, fire!

A British cannonball screeched out of the sky and scorched right between Molly's legs, tearing away a great hunk of her dress and petticoats. Molly stood frozen in shock until her cannon mate yelled, "Swab!" Molly looked down in surprise to see that she was unhurt, except for a painful burn on one calf from the sizzling heat of the cannonball. Her legs were still there, attached to her body.

"Swab!" yelled her cannon mate.

"Right," answered Molly, shaking her head to recover. "Swabbing the bore. . . . Ram the powder home." Ball and wadding. Prime. Aim. Fire!

Redcoat units pressed forward. General Washington arrived with reinforcements, riding cool and regal on a great, white horse. Up and down the line he rode, cape fluttering, as the soldiers cheered. Relief units poured into holes in the American line. Then Washington paused and turned to stare at the woman gunner on Comb's Hill. He waved his hat and cheered before galloping off to organize a charge against the British right flank.

The Battle of Monmouth raged back and forth across the field all afternoon until darkness forced the weary armies apart. All that time Molly Pitcher worked her husband's cannon, the first woman to fire an American cannon in battle, the first dress on an American battlefield. By twilight almost 500 Americans lay dead or wounded. Nearly 1,000 had dropped from the heat. Of those, 150 had died. The British had lost almost as many men.

Molly's face, hands, and dress were black from the thick smudgy smoke. As the "cease fire!" order was yelled and repeated down the line, Molly sank down next to her husband to hold his hand until a stretcher came to carry him to the field hospital at the Tennent Church where Molly had started her day. Too tired to eat, she slept in the grass next to her cannon.

By first light on the 29th, the British were gone. They had fled, defeated, during the night.

A messenger rode up and stopped in front of Molly. "Are you Molly Pitcher?"

"Molly who?" she answered, trying to stretch and rub the grimy sleep out of her eyes.

"Come with me. General Washington wants to see you."

"Now? Me? I can't. I must look dreadful . . . "

General Washington said Molly had been a pillar of strength and courage for his whole army. He called her an angel of mercy to his suffering men. He said she was one of the best gunners he had ever seen. He said she had saved hundreds of men with her water, and had done as much or more than any man in the army to defeat the British. He awarded Molly the rank of Sergeant of Artillery and said she could tell her grandchildren that she had won this battle along the road to freedom.

Molly blushed as French and American soldiers cheered and saluted, but her heart swelled with a pride she would never forget.

Aftermath

Nothing was decided at Monmouth. Because of General Lee's bungling, the Americans did not gain their coveted victory. Lee was later court-martialed for his mishandling of this battle and drummed out of the army.

The British settled down in New York to devise their "Southern Strategy." Washington was free to roam through New Jersey and Pennsylvania, but was afraid to venture far until he knew what Clinton and his 30,000 British soldiers concentrated in New York and Long Island were going to do. Washington wasn't strong enough to attack and couldn't afford to leave Clinton free to retake New Jersey and Philadelphia.

The two armies sat down for a two-year stalemate. The major American and British armies would never meet again for the remaining three years of war—just smaller units on a number of southern battlefields.

The legend of Molly Pitcher quickly spread through the entire Continental Army after the Battle of Monmouth. "Sergeant Molly," the heroine of the Battle of Monmouth, became an inspiration for soldiers from the Carolinas to Vermont. No one knew her real name was Mary Hays, or that she was just a barber's wife from Carlisle, Pennsylvania. But everyone knew that a remarkable woman had sped tirelessly across the battlefield to save American soldiers with her water and had then beaten back the British with her cannon fire.

After the war, Molly and John returned to Pennsylvania. When she retired from her job working as a cleaning woman for the Pennsylvania Legislature in 1824, Molly was granted an annual pension for her bravery during the war of $40 per year, the only woman from the Revolutionary War era to receive a military pension. She died at 77 and was given full military burial—the first woman so honored.

Follow-up Questions and Activities

1. **What Do You Know?**

    • Why did the Battle of Monmouth take place? Why did Washington need to engage the British? Why wasn't General Clinton interested in a fight? What made that battle significant?

    • Beginning with 1773, name the British generals placed in charge of the war in America.

    • Why couldn't the British continue to send additional troops and supplies to fight the war in America? What else was going on in the world that involved the British military?

    • Why was Clinton moving his army to New York? Why not stay in Philadelphia?

    • Before the modern era of high-explosive artillery shells, what did the artillery try to do in battle? What were artillery shells like during the Revolution? What did the artillery primarily shoot at? Why? What usually happened?

2. **Finding Out More.** Following are six important topics from this story for you to research in the library and on the Internet. The reference sources at the back of this book will help you get started.

- Mary Hays (Molly Pitcher) became an American heroine of the war. But she was not the only woman who fought in battle during the Revolution. Research the lives and accomplishments of Mary Hays and the other women fighters of the Revolution.

- Was serving on an eighteenth-century artillery crew a good assignment or a bad one? Was it easy, exciting, dangerous? Research the dangers and benefits of serving in the Revolutionary War artillery.

- Use the library and the Internet to research the meaning of each of the basic Revolutionary War era artillery commands and what they were meant to accomplish. How is that system different from firing modern army artillery?

- Research Revolutionary War uniforms. What did the soldiers have to wear and carry when they went into battle? What materials were their uniforms made out of? How heavy were they? How hot were they?

- General Clinton is the British officer who created and directed the British plan for the last four years of the war. Research the career and history of this British general. Where did he come from? What was his plan for winning the war? What happened to Clinton after the war?

- General Lee, Washington's second in command, was in charge of the American forces at the Battle of Monmouth. Because of his blunders, the Americans missed a chance to win a major victory. What happened to General Lee?

3. **Make It Real**

- Write an essay about or hold a class debate on the pros and cons of women fighting in battle. Historically, how have most cultures felt about this issue? How do women's roles compare to men's roles in the U.S. military today? Should the roles be changed? Why or why not?

- Choose cannoneer fire teams from your class and learn the cannon drill for firing a Revolutionary War six-pound field cannon. (Six-pound refers to the weight of the cannon ball.) Use a log for your cannon (the diameter of a telephone pole is about right) and pretend to load and fire.

   Revolutionary War Cannon Commands:
   - Attention.
   - Tend the vent.
   - Advance the worm and worm out the piece.
   - Advance the sponge and sponge out the piece.
   - Retrieve the powder and charge the piece.
   - Ram down the charge.
   - Charge ammunition.
   - Ram the piece.
   - Take aim.
   - Prime.
   - Make ready . . .
   - Fire!

See if you can find a soldier or ex-soldier among the school parents who knows modern artillery drill to help you compare modern methods to eighteenth-century drill. How is aiming different? How far will modern artillery shoot, and how does that affect the way it is aimed?

- Imagine that you are a soldier on the battlefield at Monmouth and are writing a letter home about your experience of that battle. Describe how you would feel watching your friends drop from heat exhaustion. Desperately thirsty in the terrible heat, what would make you fight on even though you felt frightfully tired, weak, and sick? Would it frighten you to see more of your comrades drop from heat than from British bullets? What would you think of one lone woman in a full skirt and high-collar dress who dashed across the field carrying heavy pitchers of water to give dying men a much-needed drink? How would watching her make you feel? Include these reactions in your letter.

4. **Points to Ponder**

- Why didn't men want women on the battlefield? Did they not want the competition for their jobs and positions? Did they feel a need to protect women and so thought that any women in the area meant more risk and danger for them? Did men believe that women were more important to society because they could bear children and so shouldn't be risked in battle? Did men believe that women were weaker and so couldn't withstand the rigors and stress of battle? Which reasons do you believe were the real ones?

- Do men and women have separate roles during war? Do we still have gender-specific military roles? *Should* there be such gender-specific differences? Do you think it is a good idea to have women in battle? Why or why not?

War Paint

Indian Fighting on the Western Frontier, 1778–1779

War and Pestilence!

HORRIBLE AND UNPARALELLED
MASSACRE!

Women and Children
FALLING VICTIMS TO THE
INDIAN'S TOMAHAWK.

Broadside decrying Indian attacks

At a Glance

General Burgoyne's 1777 campaign from Canada included Colonel Legre's failed attack on Fort Stanwick in western New York by a combined British, Tory, and Mohawk force. The Mohawks suffered extensive losses during the battle and burned for revenge against the American Patriots. Their zeal drew the entire Iroquois Nation into the war on the side of the British.

The fertile valleys of the Finger Lakes region of New York and of northern Pennsylvania were an important food source for the Continental Army. British commanders, huddling in the safety of Canada, realized that if they could destroy that agricultural base, they could cripple Washington's army without having to trap and defeat him directly. The British didn't have enough troops in the frontier region to do the job, so they turned the vicious task over to Tory units and Iroquois Indians.

The ensuing frontier campaign included some of the most brutal and destructive fighting of the entire war. Battles ranged from Illinois to New York and from New York down to South Carolina. Nowhere was the fighting more violent and destructive than in Wyoming Valley, Pennsylvania (where 1,000 Patriot houses were burned and all their fields and livestock were destroyed) and in Cherry Valley, New York. Both valleys were attacked and burned in the firestorm summer and fall of 1778, as were a dozen smaller settlements in northeastern Pennsylvania and southern New York. This story covers the events of the attack on Cherry Valley.

Meet Red Jacket

Red Jacket had a rocky start to his adult life in the powerful Seneca tribe of the Iroquois Nation. Never brave, often timid, Red Jacket was consistently described as a coward in battle. Still, he rose to become a leader of his people as a famous orator—as a spokesperson for the beliefs, needs, and values of the Iroquois. He also learned to write, and wrote extensively of his experiences and of life in the Iroquois Nation during the last half of the eighteenth century. Red Jacket married late in life and fathered six children. In contrast to the anguish of his early life of shame, Red Jacket lived out his later life as a revered elder.

Meet Jane Young

Jane Young came from hardy Irish stock and lived most of her 97-year life in the rustic and rugged rural lands of the Mohawk Valley in New York State. She grew up surrounded by cherry trees and wheat fields and thinking it was normal to have milk delivered fresh each morning, squirted from their cow into a bucket at the back door. After surviving the Cherry Valley massacre, Jane lived with relatives in Schenectady for a time before marrying Richard Ferguson (also of Cherry Valley), the only survivor of the massacre in his family. They returned to Cherry Valley and raised five children along with their annual crops of wheat and corn.

War Paint

Thick smoke curled from the chimney of the long house of the Seneca chief nestled against the trees at the edge of a clearing in Canandaigua and within sight of the shore of the long lake in New York by the same name. On this late October afternoon in 1778, the great long house was filled with important chiefs and warriors and crammed with excited onlookers.

The six nations of the Iroquois were holding another war council, something that had become common in the past year as the Iroquois had been steadily drawn into the American Revolutionary War. Many of the great warriors sat in a wide circle on the hard-packed floor of the long house, over 80 feet in length.

Joseph Brant, leader of the Iroquois, was there. Fish Carrier and Corn Planter of the Cayuga were there. Twenty Canoes and Blacksnake of the Mohawk were there. Hiadagoo of the Onondaga sat tall and proud in the circle. Little Beard, Farmer's Brother, and Red Jacket of the mighty Seneca, most powerful of all the six nations, sat representing their tribe. Only lesser Oneidas and Tuscaroras were invited. Both of these tribes were suspect, having maintained relations with the Americans and more neutral positions on the war.

Blacksnake of the Mohawk was speaking. "We have not yet avenged our lost brothers from one year ago. We demand revenge!"

All present knew that the Mohawk had joined with the British one year earlier for a failed attack on Fort Stanwick in the Mohawk Valley of New York. Many Mohawk had been killed. These losses sealed the alliance between the Iroquois Nations and the British, an alliance first formed by Sir Guy Johnson in 1773 even though many of the Iroquois (and especially the Mohawk) had fought against the British during the French and Indian War a decade earlier.

"Are not our great victories in Wyoming Valley and other settlements enough to satisfy your vengeance?" asked one of the Oneidas.

"No," Blacksnake continued. "We must attack closer to the site of our losses. And we must attack our way, not the British way."

Joseph Brant glared at Blacksnake. "The British and their American allies, the Tories, are our allies." He held up a great chain belt of 21 strands of beads. "By this wampum belt we have agreed to uphold our alliance with the British."

Twenty Canoes shouted, "I say all whites are the enemy. They steal our lands, destroy our foods, kill our people with their diseases and rifles. I say there is no treaty with the whites and we should kill them all."

Many whooped in agreement.

"There are too many," replied Brant. "We would be destroyed."

"Joseph Brant is right," said Red Jacket of the Seneca. "We must concentrate on the most dangerous of the whites. The Redcoats live far away and do not care about taking the land. The Americans live close by and do want our lands. The Americans are our worst enemy."

Hiadagoo, one of the fiercest of all warriors, said, "But the Tory allies of the British are also Americans and also want our lands. They, too, should be our enemies."

Joseph Brant said, "We must conquer them one at a time. First the Americans with British help. Then when the British leave, we will attack the Tories."

Murmurs of agreement drifted around the circle. It was a visionary plan worthy of a great leader.

Blacksnake sprang to his feet. "But we must be avenged before another snow falls to push us into our winter camps."

Again there were general murmurs of agreement.

Red Jacket said, "There is a large settlement of Americans in Cherry Valley. Would an attack there satisfy our Mohawk brothers?"

Blacksnake and Twenty Canoes both nodded.

Joseph Brant now rose. "Then it is agreed. I will lead a party to attack the . . . "

"To *destroy*!" interrupted Blacksnake.

"We will destroy the American settlement in Cherry Valley," Joseph Brant concurred.

"And we will attack our way, not by the British rules," continued Blacksnake.

"No!" commanded Brant, again glaring at Blacksnake. "We will abide by our treaty and follow British rules. The Council is finished. We will leave from this camp in eight days."

Blinking as they stepped into the bright fall sunlight from the dim interior of the longhouse, Blacksnake leaned close to Twenty Canoes. "Brant may do what he likes. But we will attack our way to attain proper revenge."

Twenty Canoes grimly nodded. Red Jacket, walking close behind, whispered, "Many of the Seneca are with you and believe the British rules do not allow for great victories."

The three solemnly shook hands before departing for their own camps to prepare.

Cherry Valley was not a town, but rather a wide, unspoiled valley with 80 homesteads scattered along its length. A tributary of the Susquehanna River ran through the valley, and on this waterway wheat, the most important product of the region, was floated toward coastal markets. Life for the largely Patriot settlers was self-sustained. Few products made the long trip into the area. If something was needed, it had to be made there in the valley.

Jane Young was 13 years old in 1778 and had lived in the north end of Cherry Valley, called Springfield, since her parents moved from Philadelphia when she was four. The Youngs' house, with its orchards and wheat fields, stood near John Kelly's and William Campbell's homes and about a mile from the river where Robert Wells's house (the Patriot headquarters) stood and where Colonel Alden's regiment of 200 Continental soldiers had built Fort Alden.

The years 1777 and 1778 were filled with foreboding and tension for Cherry Valley residents. Tory, British, and Iroquois units were on the loose. Substantial American reinforcements were too far away. The threat of attack hung like a gloomy cloud over every valley activity. Even Jane, a care-free teenager, suddenly felt cautious and timid, hesitating to walk trails she had previously frolicked along for days.

Jane hid in a side room of Robert Wells's house to listen to the frantic meeting in August after word of the Wyoming Valley massacre reached Cherry Valley.

"One thousand homes and barns were burned!' exclaimed Jane's father.

"And thousands of cattle and miles of fields!" yelled another.

Colonel Alden raised his hands to keep order. "But the towns and garrisons were allowed to surrender. Outside of direct battle losses, only 13 were killed."

"Because British and Tory units were in charge of the attack," countered Robert Wells. "What if the Iroquois had been in charge?"

"But they weren't," insisted Alden.

"What will *we* do if attacked?" asked John Kelly. "Fort Stanwick is too far for reinforcements."

Colonel Alden tried to smile reassuringly. "We have Fort Alden and we have a network of scouts blanketing the area. Don't worry yourselves. Grow wheat for the country and rest assured. You will have plenty of warning if an attack should ever come."

The Colonel's assurances sent a chill shiver through Jane. They reminded her of when her parents told her not to worry about snakes in the wheat field and that she was safe to do her chores. A week later she had been bitten.

After the meeting Colonel Alden took Captain Warren aside and whispered, "Take a detachment of 12 men and ride to General Wade at Fort Stanwick to request immediate reinforcement up here. I fear the worst with Joseph Brant on the war path."

Throughout August, a warm September, and a mild October, the valley remained quiet but tense. Rumors and stories of towns burned and men murdered by Joseph Brant's Iroquois seemed to arrive each week with the post rider.

On the cold afternoon of November 8, with leaden clouds scurrying across the sky and the last fall leaves crinkled brown on the ground, scouts rushed into Cherry Valley with word that the enemy was near.

Panic rippled across the valley.

Joseph Young grabbed his family by the hand and made them run the mile to the fort. Other families, wide-eyed with terror, had already gathered, pounding on the gate to be let in.

Colonel Alden arrived from Robert Wells's house, where he had been enjoying lunch. "There is no need for panic!"

"The Indians are here!" shouted the mob.

"There is only a report of enemy sitings in the region. I have ordered scouts out to investigate. You are all safer sleeping in your own beds at home. The scouts will sound the alarm in plenty of time—should that be necessary."

The settlers reluctantly wandered away from the fort, clustering in small knots to nervously talk among themselves. Colonel Alden ordered Captain Warren to ride back toward Fort Stanwick and see why his reinforcements hadn't arrived yet.

In the pre-dawn dark of November 10, Red Jacket, Twenty Canoes, and a small band of 50 Iroquois discovered one of the scout camps. They had orders to wait until Captain Butler's 200-strong Tory regiment and Captain Colvile's 50-man British detachment arrived to command and coordinate all actions. Red Jacket volunteered to stay back as a guide for the others. Twenty Canoes and his Mohawks refused to wait and slithered like ghosts into the Americans' camp. All five scouts were killed in their sleep and scalped before Joseph Brant with his 650 Iroquois, Butler, and Colvile could arrive.

Blacksnake hissed, "Why were the whites allowed to come?"

"It is written in our pact," answered Joseph Brant. "Besides, this is their war."

"No. *This* is our war." And Blacksnake stormed off to huddle with his fellow Mohawks.

The attacking force of 900 camped that night in an eerie silence in a thickly forested area near the river, every warrior's heart pounding with anticipation at the chance for battle and glory. The plan was simple. Butler with his Tory rangers, the 50 British, Joseph Brant, and half the Indians would attack the fort. Corn Planter and Blacksnake would lead the others in surrounding the Wells house, where many of the officers were meeting, and cut them off from their fort. Women, children, and noncombatants were to be spared. Butler and the British never noticed that Blacksnake, Twenty Canoes, Red Jacket, and others remained silent and never actually agreed to these terms.

Around dawn a hard snow began to fall. By mid-morning it had changed to rain, so that a thick slush covered the ground. Butler's men found the fort closed and well guarded. The attackers surrounded the fort but were reluctant to begin a direct assault.

Officers poured out of the Wells house at the first sound of alarm. Colonel Alden was tomahawked, and scalped almost before his body could hit the ground. Four captains, five lieutenants, and six sergeants were cut down before they could reach the front gate.

At this point, the Indians were supposed to join the Tories in their attack on the fort.

But they didn't.

Blacksnake and a dozen Mohawks massacred the Wells family—three servants, two women, and six children. They spread out across the valley to plunder, burn, and kill. Pastor Dunlap raced home upon hearing the alarms only to find his house in flames and the crumpled bodies of his family strewn about the yard. An arrow and two tomahawks cut him down before he could cry in grief.

Twenty Canoes and Red Jacket led a dozen warriors against the Mitchell house. Three shots were fired at them through first-floor windows. Red Jacket dove behind a tree, trembling, and curled up into a frightened ball. The other warriors laughed at his cowardice and left him shivering and shamed behind the tree while they butchered the family and burned the house and barn. Red Jacket spent the rest of the day hiding alone in the woods and would forever live with the brand of coward, even after he became a famous orator and civic leader.

John Kelly was behind his barn chopping wood when he heard screams from the house. He raced around the barn, ax in hand, in time to see his seven-year-old son die, but not in time to utter a word before he himself was cut down.

Jane Young was out back by the wood pile when the Senecas descended on her house. She crawled into a swampy part of the woods and lay there shivering, listening to the screams of her family and the crackle of burning wood as she watched the bright orange glow and billowing smoke that had been her house. She lay there, still clutching the dolls she had been playing with, afraid to move, for almost two days before a patrol of Continentals found her and led her to the safety of the fort.

Joseph Brant and Captain Butler were dismayed as they saw plumes of smoke begin to rise above the trees around the valley and realized that they had lost control of the Senecas and Mohawks. Detachments were diverted from the fort attack to fan out across the valley and stop the carnage.

By nightfall the valley was in flames. Every Patriot (and a number of Loyalist) houses had been destroyed. Fields, barns, and livestock were in ashes. Blacksnake had jammed eight scalps onto the pole he carried. Twenty Canoes had six. In all, 15 soldiers and 52 local inhabitants—mostly women and children—had been slaughtered.

Bonfires were lit in the open area in front of the fort and the Iroquois celebrated most of the night. In the morning they withdrew, leaving the fort and its soldiers intact but the valley destroyed.

"It is done. Revenge is ours!" Blacksnake cried, shaking his scalp pole.

Fierce pride smoldered in the Indians' hearts, matching the smoldering ruins of Cherry Valley as they marched back home to celebrate.

Aftermath

All America was outraged by the brutal killings in Cherry Valley. As so often happens, the Mohawks' revenge became not an ending, but a beginning. Cries for revenge rippled through the Colonies. Congress created new Ranger Units especially to hunt down and destroy Iroquois forces. The western frontier would continue to burn for another two very bloody years. But now it was mostly Tory and Indian settlements that burned and Rangers and patriot militia that did the burning.

The hatred between Tories and Patriots intensified in upstate New York. Their bitter civil war would continue for another two years until it became clear that the British were going to abandon the war effort. Then most Tories fled the country, settling in Canada, England, or the Caribbean.

Follow-up Questions and Activities

1. **What Do You Know?**

   - What were the six tribes of the Iroquois Nation? Why were they important to the Revolutionary War?

   - Research the six individual tribes of the Iroquois. Which are best known? Why? Which were most important during the era of the Revolution? Why? Do these tribes exist today?

   - What was the Iroquois experience with European armies? Which side were the Indians on during the French and Indian War?

   - How many frontier settlements were there? When new people moved there, how did they get land to live on and farm?

   - Why were frontier settlements so important to the Revolution? What did they provide that the Continental Army, in particular, needed?

2. **Finding Out More.** Following are five important topics from this story for you to research in the library and on the Internet. The reference sources at the back of this book will help you get started.

   - The relationships between European armies and settlers and the Iroquois were primarily defined by events during the French and Indian War. Research that war. When and where did it take place? Who sided with whom? What happened? What was the outcome of the war? What were the Iroquois feeling at the end of the war?

   - Research the history of scalping. When and why was the practice started?

   - How did scalping affect the loyalties of the settlers along the frontier?

   - Why did the Iroquois decide to join in the Revolutionary War fighting? It wasn't their war. They weren't fighting to be free. What did the Iroquois hope to gain by fighting on the British side?

   - Research how settlers got land in frontier areas. How did they stake and file a claim for land? How could they be sure the land was available? Who sold it to them?

3. **Make It Real**

   • Pretend to be an Iroquois tribe member. Do you think you would be confused by all these different groups of whites who looked alike to you but who seemed to feel so differently about each other? Would you fear whites in general? Would you trust any of them? Why or why not? Which ones would you fear and hate the most? Why? Write a page on how you would feel about the British, the French, and the Americans in general and the Tories, Loyalists, and Patriots in particular.

   • Pretend that at your present age you are living in Cherry Valley at the beginning of the Revolutionary War. What would your life be like? Was there a school? What would you do? How many other people would you see on a regular basis? Whom would you play with? Where would your family get supplies? Research life on the frontier and then write an essay describing a typical day in your life there.

   • Find all the frontier settlements that existed during the Revolutionary War and mark them on a map. Shade in the frontier areas controlled by the British and Tories and those controlled by Patriots and the Continental Army. List the major items each frontier area produced and shipped back to the coastal cities.

4. **Points to Ponder**

   • What did the Indians teach American fighters that helped them win many battles against the British? How did Indian tactics differ from traditional European army tactics? Did the American Colonists use Indian tactics at Lexington and Concord? Did American guerrilla fighters like Francis Marion use Indian tactics? Where else during the Revolution did American fighters use Indian tactics to good advantage?

   • By modern standards, slaughtering women and children is brutal and unacceptable behavior. But did the Iroquois agree, or did they think it was legally and morally acceptable behavior? If they did think so, did that make it any less wrong?

1779
at a
Glance

The Land War Stagnates;
the Seas Catch Fire

The year 1779 saw small strikes by army units on both sides and continued brutal fighting in the West. The Continental Army created new Ranger Units to combat the Indian terrorism along the frontier. The British slowly, leisurely consolidated their hold on Savannah and seemed in no rush to move up the coast to attack Charleston.

For most of the year, General Clinton sat scheming and brooding in New York. Meanwhile, Washington sat in New Jersey wondering what Clinton had up his sleeve; his army was not strong enough to attack the British New York stronghold and he was afraid to take it elsewhere for fear of what the British general might do.

The Continentals did have several minor victories to celebrate. Anthony Wayne took Stony Point, New York, and seized control of most of the lower Hudson River. Henry Lee captured several minor British posts along the Jersey coast.

All in all, 1779 was a rather uneventful year—on land. At sea it was a different story. The American privateer naval force was in full swing by 1779. Attacks on British merchant shipping were beginning to take a toll on the British army's supplies. America had also put to sea a few ships as an American navy. Most were small, old, undergunned sloops. They stood no chance in one-on-one combat against modern British frigates and ships-of-the-line, but like pesky mosquitoes they disrupted England's mastery of the sea and carried a nasty sting—which English shipping regularly felt.

Key Events in 1779

Date	Event
June 16	Spain declares war on England.
July 16	Anthony Wayne captures Stony Point, New York, and control of the lower Hudson River.
August 14	Naval battle at Penobscot Bay, Maine, is greatest American naval disaster of the war.
August 18	Henry Lee captures Paulus Point (Sandy Hook, New Jersey).
September 23	Naval battle between *Serapis* and *Bonhomme Richard*.
October 9	American attempt to recapture Savannah ends in bloody failure.
October 20	British abandon Rhode Island.

Patriotic Plunder

The American Privateer Navy and the Battle of Penobscot Bay, September 1779

Privateer schooner

At a Glance

England owned the seas. Her navy boasted a fleet of 60 ships of war on duty along the American coast plus almost 200 merchant ships supplying British needs and ferrying British troops. Because there were few good roads in America, virtually all goods had to be transported by ship. If England controlled the seas, she also controlled the movement of goods and supplies.

America had no navy when war erupted—only fishing boats and a few small merchant cargo vessels. Neither was there a national treasury or budget to build ships. Still, the war could not be won without somehow challenging England's dominion on the open seas. So Congress authorized individuals, cities, and states to build and arm their own ships to attack British interests. These ships acted like pirates but, because they were sanctioned by Congress, they were officially called "privateers."

The goal of each privateer captain, crew, and owner was to capture British merchant ships, steal their cargo, and sell it at the nearest port. The ship's owner and crew split the proceeds.

Privateering was very profitable. Hundreds of ships, hastily slapped together, were thrown into the fray with visions of treasure dancing in their owners' heads.

None of these flimsy ships could stand up to British navy ships. Some were little more than long rowboats with one mounted cannon. Most were of the schooner class—two mast, small, sleek, fast, built for speed and maneuverability, cheap to build

201

and quick to be scrapped. None possessed much fire power. Cannons were expensive and heavy and required the ship to be more stable. But these privateers could hold their own against merchant ships and, more often than not, they won the day.

Many privateer ships were sunk or captured, but many garnered huge profits for their crew. All of them harassed British shipping and diminished Britain's ability to supply the army fighting on foreign American soil. The story of Israel Trask illustratess the typical life of privateers and also describes the greatest American naval disaster of the war.

Meet Israel Trask

Israel Trask was born in Gloucester, Massachusetts, in 1767, and was raised by his father, after his mother died giving birth to his sister when Israel was two. The sister died three days later of complications. Israel's father was a clerk in a local general store, so Israel spent most of his days at a neighbor's house. His father joined the army in 1776. Israel went with him and became regimental assistant cook as a nine-year-old boy.

In April 1779, Israel's father became severely ill and left the service. Israel left with him. By late June, Israel's father was still sick in bed and they were penniless. Israel signed on as cabin boy for the *Black Prince*, a privateer ship, to support the family.

As a cabin boy, Israel received one-half of one share of the ship's take. The owner got five shares, the captain three, the mate two, and most of the crew either one or one and one-half. Israel sailed on two privateer ships after the *Black Prince*. After the war, he returned to Gloucester with a fortune of well over $20,000 in gold and goods and lived comfortably until he died at age 82.

Patriotic Plunder

"Israel Trask, you worthless lubber! Get up here!"

Twelve-year-old Israel scrambled up the narrow, creaking staircase to the main deck. The ship's cook, Jonathan Bollard, who always wore a stained and graying apron—even in battle—caught Israel by the arm. "Where have you been hiding when the mate's callin' you?"

"Down cleaning the crew's room, sir," Israel stammered, blinking in the bright afternoon sun this day in May 1779.

The cook ground his teeth together. "That's *quarters*, not room. You're on a . . ."

"I know. I'm on a boat now."

"Not a boat you scurvy lubber! This is a *ship*. You savvy?"

"Sorry, sir."

"There's only two men you call 'sir'," spat out the cook. "The captain and the mate. And it's the mate what wants you." Half-lifting Israel off the ground by the arm, the cook turned and shouted toward the quarter deck. "Mr. Bryce, I found yer cabin boy!"

"Why don't *you* have to call the mate 'sir'?" whispered Israel.

"I'm the cook. Now prance yerself up there to see One-Eye Bill."

"One eye?" repeated Israel.

"He took a pistol shot at close range on a British frigate we plundered almost a year back. . . . Now, get goin', lad. He's waitin' on the quarter deck."

A blank look crossed Israel's face. His sky-blue eyes clouded.

"The poop deck at the *stern*, lad," Cookie hissed.

Still a blank look.

"That way," he growled, pointing to the rear of the ship. Israel scrambled aft as best he could on the pitching deck as the schooner slammed through five-foot swells with a stiff breeze. Cookie threw up his hands as Israel slipped and sprawled across the deck. "The lad's useless. Why'd we ever sign him on?"

Bill Bryce stood rock solid on the rolling deck, hands clasped behind his back and three peacock feathers rising like antlers from his broad-brimmed hat. Deep scars, like cracks in a piece of glass, knifed out beyond the edges of the purple patch and black ribbon tied across his left eye. A stained blue coat reached almost to his knees. Bryce had been first mate of the American privateer *Black Prince* since she had been launched two years back in Machias, Massachusetts. (The area is now part of Maine.) "The Cap'n gave you a job when you signed on with this ship's company in Providence yesterday, didn't he, lad?"

"Yes sir, sir. He made me the cabin boy and cook's helper, sir."

"Cabin boy, eh?" repeated Bryce, rocking heel to toe.

"Yes, sir, sir."

"Well, if you're the cabin boy," Bryce bellowed, twisting his face into a frightful rage, and jabbing his nose right against Israel's, "Why wasn't the ward room cleaned after breakfast, I would like to know!"

"I . . . I . . . I . . . don't . . . ah . . . the *what* room?" stammered Israel, eyes growing both wide with fright and cross-eyed from staring at the wrathful countenance only four inches from his own.

"Cookie!" Bryce screamed. "Get this bilge rat out of my sight and make sure he learns his duties."

"Aye, Mr. Bryce," the cook's voice answered from below. "I'll beat it into him if I have to."

Cookie hustled Israel one deck below to the galley area and wagged an angry finger at him. "You signed on thinkin' it'd be easy to become a rich man, didn't you?"

"No sir. I signed on to fight for American liberty."

"One of them idealists, eh? Well, first you have to act like part of this crew. And that means learning yer way about and yer duties. Then you can claim a share of the plunder and also strike a blow fer America."

Israel Trask had signed onto a privateer ship (some called them pirate ships) because his father—Israel's only living relative—lay sick and near death in a hospital and told Israel that earning a share of the pirate's plunder was the only way to support the two of them. Israel never thought about what life onboard a pirate schooner would be like. He just knew he needed to earn the money to support his father. Yesterday, boarding the schooner *Black Prince*, was the first time young Israel had ever set foot on any boat larger than a row boat.

"First," continued Cookie, "You got to know yer way around a ship." He stepped back from the cooking hearth and pointed up through the forward hatch at the intertwining ropes that climbed like spider webs up to the masts and spars. "What are they?"

"Rope ladders?"

"They're called *ratlines,* and they're part of the *rigging*, boy, the ropes." He pointed at the billowing sails. "And them?"

"Sails. Even I know that one."

"The *sheets*, lad. The sheets. The wood crossbars the sails hang from are called *spars*. You'll see them up close afore long."

Israel gulped. "I will? How close?"

"And by the by, the sheets are now rigged fore and aft of each mast to give us more speed since the seas are so calm."

"This is calm?" asked Israel, still having to hold onto posts and rails to keep from falling over.

Cookie laughed. "Aye, this is very calm for the North Atlantic. Now point to port." Israel hesitated then pointed with his left hand. "Aye, lad. And now starboard. . . . Good. And fore . . . and now aft. Good." Cookie nodded, smiled, and then bellowed, "And don't forget it again! You savvy?"

"No, sir!" Israel barked. "I mean, yes sir . . . "

The cook sighed and threw up his hands. "I told you not to call me 'sir'."

"Sorry, si . . . er, I mean, just sorry."

"And remember, the *Black Prince* is a schooner—only two masts and only 65 feet long. Boasts a crew of 24—well, 25 counting you. It's fast, maneuverable, and can outrun most British navy ships-of-the-line. But its only got four cannon on board."

"But I saw eight cannon ports on each side, Cookie," interrupted Israel.

Cookie laughed and reached out to muss the boy's curly brown hair. "Very good for sayin' port instead of window. But what gives you the right to be callin' me Cookie yet like the mate does? You have to earn usin' that name. I think you can call me Mr. Cook for now."

"But why only four, Mr. Cook?"

"Cannon cost thousands of dollars each and they're heavy—slow down the ship. Four's a lot for a privateer ship."

A bell on the quarter deck gonged. Clang, clang . . . clang, clang . . . clang, clang.

"And what does that mean, lad?"

Israel squeezed his eyes shut, struggling to remember. "Six bells means that the first six 30-minute segments of this watch are over."

"And . . . "

"And that there are . . . two more before the watch changes."

"*And* . . . how many watches a day?"

"Six of four hours each."

"Very good, lad. We'll get some sea legs on you yet."

Israel beamed. Cookie said, "Now, yer duties. . . . " He paused, fingering one of his long carving knives. Then he bellowed. "Get yer fanny aft and clean the ward room—the officers eat there; you clean there. Savvy? Then you have a date with this knife and that choppin' block to chop the dried potatoes and pork so I can cook supper. Then you'll serve food to the ward room and clean up again before you go on night watch. After yer watch ends, you get four hours to do whatever you like before yer face had better be smilin' and back in this kitchen to start all over again tomorrow! You savvy?! Then get a move on!"

While Israel toiled, cleaned, and chopped, the *Black Prince* roared out of Long Island Sound and into the violent North Atlantic, heading for the rich shipping lanes in search of an unescorted, loaded English merchant ship.

The stars were covered by heavy clouds and the wind had whipped the waves into towering whitecaps when the bell rang for the night watch to come on deck. Waves crashed across the bow. Deck and masts groaned. Sheets snapped in the gale-force winds. Spray lashed at exposed skin and stung the eyes. It looked like a world gone mad to young Israel, who clutched at railings to keep from being flung into the swirling sea as the deck pitched like a bucking horse.

First mate Bill Bryce stood calm as if on a Sunday picnic, next to the wheel in a knit cap and rain slicker. "Storm's comin'," he hollered above the moaning wind. "Prepare to furl top and main sheets! Man the clew lines! All watch hands up the ratlines. Secure the sails!"

Feet scurried across the slick and bucking deck. Experienced hands grabbed ropes hooked to the lower corner of the main and top sails and hauled them in to raise the corners of each sail and reduce the wind's tight hold on the stretched canvas.

Frozen in awe and terror at the monstrous waves surrounding the ship, Israel crouched motionless as, like ants scaling a spider web, the rest of the watch crew climbed the rigging. Jeremiah Douglas, a lean black man—a free black who didn't care at all about the war, but who had signed on for the money—seized Israel by the arm. "That's you, too, boy. Mate said 'all hands'."

"Up *there*?" squeaked Israel.

The slippery ropes of the ratlines vibrated in Israel's hands with the violent wind. They snapped in and out as the ship pitched over wave crests and into three-story-tall troughs. Breath coming in ragged gasps, heart pounding in his throat, feeling smaller and in greater danger than he had imagined possible in his worst nightmare, Israel followed Jeremiah rung by rung up the rigging with wind shrieking in his ears and tearing at his clothes, trying to rip him loose from the ratlines and fling him into the angry sea.

The sails flapped and snapped like thunder as the clew lines (ropes tied to the bottom corners of each sail) were lowered and the main sail lost wind. Israel wanted to scream. If he had thought the *deck* pitched, 30 feet up along the mast the whole world seemed to sway like a monstrous earthquake. One second the deck was below him. The next, the mast had swayed out over the boiling sea. "Keep both feet on the foot rope as you slide out the spar and help haul in the sheet," yelled Jeremiah right into Israel's ear so as to be heard. "Use the rope gaskets to secure the sail."

"Out *there*?" cried Israel as a lightning bolt crackled nearby, announcing the approach of drenching rain. "We have to climb out *there*?"

Step by terrified step, Israel followed Jeremiah out the long spar with nothing between him and empty, heaving space, supported only by one thin rope his feet balanced on as it rocked and swayed and by the round and rain-slickened spar his hands clutched. Israel inched his way out the rope and spar as the great canvas sheet flapped wildly in his face.

Three bells had rung before the main and top sails were furled and the watch crew collapsed on the deck, looping ropes around arms and legs to keep from being washed away by crashing waves in the dark.

A cold downpour mixed with the spray, foam, howling wind, and crushing waves to create a watery world of terror for young Israel.

"First storm, boy?" asked Jeremiah Douglas.

Israel nodded and held out one hand to shake. "My name is Israel."

"Your name's 'boy' until I say different," snarled Jeremiah. "And you're lucky to have such a light storm as your first."

"*Light* storm," spluttered Israel. "This is a *light* storm?"

Next morning, as the clouds broke and the sea settled into long rows of six-foot swells, Israel had a chance to glance at the ship's log after delivering breakfast to the ward room. "Main and top masts furled during mild storm. Watch uneventful."

"*Uneventful?*" stammered Israel over and over. "That was uneventful?"

After one week at sea, Israel could not remember what walking on solid ground felt like. He could barely remember the smell and feel of land. It was as if he had been a cabin boy on the *Black Prince* all his life. It seemed that he had never tasted food other than hardtack and the mush-like stew of beef or pork, dried potatoes, and dried peas served twice a day. Israel's movements picked up the rhythm of the waves and he could easily step through hatchways and dodge around coils of ropes without breaking stride as he lugged food and supplies fore and aft.

Israel was chopping stringy beef for dinner when the ship's bell gonged incessantly. The captain's whistle blew, shrill and hard. "All hands on deck. Prepare for battle! Cannons to port. Quakers to starboard!"

Now Israel noted an ominous, deadly earnest tone to the crew's scurrying rush across the decks as the 25 men scrambled to prepare for battle.

The captain stood on the quarter deck staring through a three-foot glass (a small telescope) at a tiny dot far off the port quarter. "Rifles to the fighting top!" yelled Bryce. "Roll the cannon into place!"

"Boy!" called Jeremiah Douglas. "Roll the Quakers starboard and lash them down!"

"What . . . what's a Quaker?" asked Israel.

"Haven't yer learned anything, lad?" cried Cookie, apron tied tight around him as he helped to secure one cannon with ropes to a port-side gun mount. "The black logs, the fake cannons. Those are called Quakers 'cause no matter how many times you ask, they won't fire. But from a distance they *look* real and make merchant ships think we have more guns. Now get them all to starboard to make room for the real cannons here on the port side. You savvy?"

"Come 10 degrees into the wind," called the captain. "We'll take her to leeward. Run up the American flag and let them know who's conquering their ship." A tattered American flag was hoisted up a pole at the back of the quarter deck.

"Grappling hooks at the ready!" bellowed the mate.

Six men with rifles climbed to the wide platform two-thirds of the way up the forward mast. From there they could fire down onto the deck of an enemy ship. Cannon balls and kegs of powder were rolled onto the deck and lashed tight between the cannons. The assistant mate lugged a chest with sabers and pistols on deck for the crew to use during boarding.

"She's tacking to port to make a run for it," called the captain. "Come about—30 degrees. We'll cut her off."

"Coming about. 30 degrees port. Aye," called One-Eye Bryce, swinging the great ship's wheel and watching the compass mounted beside it.

Israel's hands trembled with excitement. His mouth grew desert-dry. His first sea battle for liberty! Then he noticed that most of the crew's eyes gleamed with greed instead of national pride. They were not out to strike a blow for liberty, but for their own fortunes.

"I guess that's why they call us pirates," he muttered as he lashed the painted Quakers to the starboard rail.

The distance between ships closed with agonizing slowness. Finally the captain called," Give 'em a broadside! Fire high into the rigging. I don't want that hull damaged until I can strip her of her cargo."

One-Eye Bryce hopped down to the gun deck to command the cannons. "Roll out yer pieces!" The cannons were rolled forward so that their muzzles extended through the ports. "Aim and prime! . . . Fire!"

The four-cannon blast knocked Israel to the deck. His ears rang and ached. A great cloud of acid fumes billowed over the deck. The boat rocked violently.

"Retract and reload yer piece!" cried the mate.

"Run up the flags," commanded the captain.

"But our flag is already up, Mr. Cook," called Israel, still rubbing his ringing ears.

"Nay, lad. These flags call on them to surrender or die."

Israel's heart pounded. He gulped for breath. This was it! Hand-to-hand fighting to the death. Would he have to kill some helpless English sailor? Would he be able to kill? Would he be killed? Would an English pistol explode in his face and tear out an eye? Israel clenched his teeth and crawled to the arms chest for a cutlass.

Then the crew began to cheer. "She's striked colors, Cap'n."

"She's heavin' to."

"Mr. Bryce," called the captain. "Take a boarding party of eight, all armed, to secure the ship. Release all unwilling crew in long boats. And sing a round of 'Yankee Doodle' once yer over there."

"Aye, Cap'n!"

Israel blinked and looked up, his face filled with confusion.

"We won, lad," said Cookie.

"But . . . but, there wasn't any fighting."

"They didn't stand a chance, lad. Only one gun, probably only 12 in the crew. They knew they had to surrender."

"What happens now, Mr. Cook?" asked Israel as grappling hooks were flung across to hold the two ships side by side while Mr. Bryce led his boarding party in climbing across the gap.

Cookie shrugged. "England loses a ship and cargo, and we gets 'em. The sailors who pledge loyalty to America will help Mr. Bryce sail her to port. The rest of the crew will be turned loose in a long boat to row to shore."

"But we're in the middle of the ocean!"

"Nay lad," laughed Cookie. "We're less than 12 miles from the coast. Can't be more than 80 down to Boston."

By dawn the next morning the *Black Prince* and her prize, the *Breeman*, dropped anchor at Portsmouth, New Hampshire.

"What will happen to the *Breeman* now, Mr. Cook?" asked Israel.

Cookie said, "First, you can drop the 'Mr.' and call me Cookie. Second, don't stop yer choppin to watch, lad. We still have a breakfast to serve. You savvy? This afternoon there will be an auction to sell the cargo. If we're lucky, Cap'n will find a buyer for the *Breeman*, herself. Then he'll announce what each crewman's share is, we take on supplies for a day or two, and head back out on the next tide."

"We each get some of the cargo?"

"The plunder, lad. Aye. That's the way a privateer ship works. Last cabin boy earned a share of $5,800."

"$5,800! I didn't know there was that much money in the world!"

"Aye, and plenty more than that. Plus the lad got 75 gallons of rum and a half-ton each of sugar and cotton in six months. Then, of course, he was killed on shore leave when he started braggin' 'bout it."

"I'm taking my share straight to my father in Gloucester!"

"Best find a swift horse, lad. You don't want to be late gettin' back. Crew members get hung fer missing a sailing."

With $530 in his pocket, a fortune in Revolutionary War times, and a paper saying he owned one-half ton of molasses and two barrels of sugar that were locked in a local warehouse, Israel bought the best horse he could find, sped south, and was four hours early on his return to the ship the next day.

Israel Trask was the only member of the crew to ever take a share of the *Breeman* plunder off the *Black Prince*. All other crew members stored their shares in the ship's chests.

Cookie looked worried as the *Black Prince* slipped out of Portsmouth harbor. "What's wrong, Cookie?" asked Israel.

"Owner signed us on to attack a British fort."

"Just us?" gulped Israel.

"Nay, lad. We're joinin' a flotilla. Owner signed an agreement with Congress to have us join with 18 privateers, 3 navy ships, and over 20 transports to attack a fort the British are building on the high bluffs overlooking the mouth of the Penobscot River [along the southern coast of what is now Maine]. You mark my words, lad. This voyage will be all trouble and no money."

In two days they joined the flotilla just as it rounded a rocky point in high winds and choppy seas and came within sight of the fort—barely two walls built, but already a row of cannons mounted and ready to fire. Six British navy frigates lay at anchor in the harbor.

The ship's bell clanged. The Captain's whistle blew. "All hands on deck! Battle stations!"

Two American navy warships led the attack: the *Warren* and the *Hazard*. Cannons roared from 14 of the attacking ships. Answering cannons belched fire and smoke from the fort and the British ships. Sea water exploded around the *Black Prince*. One mast on the *Warren* was hit and toppled to the deck. Cannon balls shrieked through the air thick as hail.

Israel was terrified and fascinated at the same time. He wanted to hide but couldn't tear himself away from the rail, needing to watch every shot of this mighty battle. Clouds of stinging gray smoke covered the bay.

One of the British ships exploded when a cannon ball struck a row of powder kegs. Flames and black smoke billowed into the sky. Gunners on the *Black Prince* cheered, claiming credit for the shot.

But five of the American ships had also been badly damaged. The attack was called off. The ships retreated just out of range of the fort's deadly cannons.

"Will we attack again at night?" asked Israel, back down in the galley chopping dried potatoes and stringy beef for dinner.

"This is as ugly as a situation can get," sighed Cookie. "We can't attack the fort until those ships are driven off or sunk, and we can't attack the ships until the fort is silenced."

"What will happen?"

"No good, I can tell you that. Other British ships—warships with 50 guns each, and maybe more—have got to be on their way here. If we don't strike fast or leave, I fear disaster."

The first inklings of dread and panic settled into the pit of Israel's stomach.

For three days the stalemate continued. Continental ships fired at the fort. The fort fired at any Continental ship that floated within range. No damage was done on either side. Through those nerve-wracking days, Israel chopped, hauled, and cleaned, all the while sensing the mounting shipwide tension.

While preparing each meal, Cookie grumbled that they should weigh anchor and skedaddle while they still had a ship. Israel asked why they didn't leave. Cook rolled his eyes toward the ceiling. "The owner wants to be a good American."

"So do I," protested Israel.

"Aye, lad. And so do I. But I don't want to be a dead one."

No sooner had the words left his mouth than the ship's bell began to clang urgently.

"All hands on deck! Battle stations!"

Israel's heart sank as he scrambled up the narrow stairs. Eight mammoth British warships were churning through the choppy waters of the outer bay. Three rows of giant cannon barrels bristled from each side of each ship.

"We're in for it now, lad. There are no Quakers on them ships. Those are 18-pounders—or even bigger. Over twice the size and range of our guns."

"All hands hoist the sails! Mains and tops! Rig fore and aft!"

"Aren't we going to man the cannons and fight?" asked Israel.

"Against them?" snorted Cookie. "We'd be blown apart afore we got off one broadside. No, we're running."

Crawling out the main spar 40 feet above the deck, Israel saw the first puffs of smoke from the new British fleet. Giant geysers of water sprayed across the decks of the poor American ship farthest from shore. Several cannon balls crashed through the deck. Several more must have torn giant holes below the water line. The flimsy schooner began to list and settle lower into the water. Fire broke out near the quarter deck. Sailors leapt overboard into the chilly waters of the bay.

"Can we race past them out to sea?" called Israel.

"Not a chance," answered Jeremiah Douglas, next to Israel working to release the sheets. "They got the sea lanes blocked. We'll have to run up the river and hope they can't follow."

The American fleet raced for the curving Penobscot River as the fort's cannons opened fire from above. Fire from the British ships and fort rained down on the fleeing American fleet. Nine ships sank before they could enter the relative safety of the river. Eight more were badly damaged and had to be intentionally beached for fear of blocking the channel for the ships still behind them. All eight were set on fire to prevent the British from seizing and using them.

The *Hazard*, biggest of the American warships and lead vessel in the flotilla, grounded in mid-channel. The schooner *Curran* tried to pass to starboard and also grounded. Other ships had to heave to and cast out anchors to keep from ramming into the stuck ships. British cannon balls from the mouth of the river could easily pick off the American ships as they sat at anchor.

The order was passed to burn the fleet to prevent the British from using any of the ships or their supplies. Black columns of smoke curled into the afternoon sky as the constant rumble of British cannons and the screeching of British cannon balls filled the air.

A cannon ball smashed into the side of the *Black Prince*, splintered the hull and deck timbers, and struck the store of powder kegs in the hold. The entire ship was lifted out of the water by the explosion of those kegs. It settled back into the river in a giant fireball with the hiss of steam as water poured through gaping holes in the hull.

Israel staggered back to his feet in the galley as water swirled around his knees. Cookie was dead, killed in the explosion. Smoke, fire, gurgling black water, and the screams of burning and wounded men were everywhere.

The stairs had been torn away by the blast. Israel was trapped as the ship rolled heavily to port and settled lower in the river. He sucked in three deep breaths and dove under the rising water, kicking and feeling his way toward the hull. The dim light of day filtered through the river water and guided him to a monstrous hole in the belly of his dying ship. Israel kicked through and broke back into daylight as burning timbers dropped like confetti all around him.

He swam to shore and struggled up onto the bank next to three other shivering sailors from different ships. Then they turned and sprinted into the woods, seeing long lines of Redcoats marching up both shores of the river to capture any survivors.

Israel walked almost 200 miles to reach home. The last hundred he managed barefoot after his shoes wore out. Yet with each step Israel Trask was dreaming of his next ship and of their next haul of plunder.

Aftermath

The fiasco in the Penobscot River was the biggest single disaster, and worst defeat, for the American navy during the Revolutionary War. Five hundred men died and 38 ships were lost. The British lost 1 ship and fewer than 20 men. Only eight of the *Black Prince's* crew survived the blast. Four were captured. Only Israel and three others escaped to fight again. But even after this a hundred privateer ships still sailed the coastal waters, disrupting British shipping, and a growing Continental Navy began to challenge the British for supremacy of the seas.

Follow-up Questions and Activities

1. **What Do You Know?**

   • What was the difference between privateers and pirates? Did the British consider American privateers to be pirates?

   • Many privateer ships carried only a few, relatively small cannons. Most were small ships. Why wouldn't a privateer want a big ship with lots of cannons? Think about the price of the ships and the cannons. Also think about speed and maneuverability. Which characteristics would you choose if you were going to launch a privateer ship?

   • What is scurvy? Why did sailors so often suffer from this disease? How is scurvy prevented? Why couldn't sailors easily keep themselves from getting scurvy?

   • Why did so many sailors volunteer to serve on privateer ships? What was their motive?

2. **Finding Out More**. Following are three important topics from this story for you to research in the library and on the Internet. The reference sources at the back of this book will help you get started.

- How did sailors at sea know where they were and what direction they were going? How could they measure the ship's speed? Use the Internet and the library to learn about sailing ship navigation in the centuries before satellites and electronic navigation systems. Build or find a simple sextant or quadrant and learn how to use it.

- Research the motives for and dangers of privateering. What happened if a privateer was caught by the British? How many privateer ships operated during the Revolution? How badly did they hamper British war efforts? What did the British do to try to keep privateers from attacking merchant ships? How effective were their efforts?

- What was a "fortune" in Revolutionary times? To be considered "rich," would you need to have $1,000? $10,000? $100,000? $1,000,000?

3. **Make It Real**

- Pretend your classroom is a sailing ship. What names would you have to use for things and people: doors, windows, the floor, the room, the front and back of the room, your teacher, other students, etc.? How would you enter and leave the room? What do sailors do when boarding a ship? Find as many terms related to life onboard a ship as you can and apply them to your classroom. Print these terms on signs and hang them around the classroom in appropriate places.

- Make a typical sea meal of beef stew and hard tack for your school lunch one day, using the following recipes.

Beef Stew

All measurements are approximate. On board ship, cooks threw in what they had and scrimped on the items that were in short supply.

Salted beef, 1/3 lb per person. Soak strips of beef in saltwater for several months. If this isn't possible, landlubbers can use corned beef and slice it into thin strips.

Dried peas, 1/2 cup per person.

Dried potatoes, 1 cup per peson. Use the sliced potatoes from scalloped or au gratin mixes or backpacking potatoes.

Just cover the beef, peas, and potatoes with water and soak for several hours. Then bring the mixture to a boil, adding more water if necessary to keep all ingredients covered. Cook until the mixture becomes a thick, stew-like mush. When the potatoes begin to fall apart, the stew is ready. Serve in bowls.

Hardtack

1 teaspoon salt
1 pound flour
enough water to make a very stiff dough

Combine all ingredients, then cut the dough into four-inch sections and punch tiny holes in each piece. Then bake on a greased cookie sheet at 250 degrees for two or three hours, until light brown.

Each sailor also got one-quarter pint of rice and a one-quarter pint mug of grog, which was watered-down rum (90 percent water and 10 percent rum, to kill some of the germs and the terrible taste of the stale water).

4. **Points to Ponder**

- Debate the morality of privateering. Is a privateer different than a pirate? Did privateers take the law into their own hands as did vigilante committees a hundred years later?

- Do privateer ships operate anywhere in the world today? If so, what do they look like? What do they do? How does the world react to their activities?

Patriot Son, Tory Traitor
Patriot Versus Tory Battles in Upstate New York, 1779

Militia skirmish

Although battlefield action between the British army and Washington's Continentals cooled after the Battle of Monmouth (June 1778), the friction between community-based Tory and Patriot militia units continued to smolder. By 1779 it had risen to searing flames, becoming especially violent in upstate New York, where small British attachments enlisted Tories and Indians (mostly Mohawk and Seneca tribes of the Iroquois Nation) to break American control of the key upper Hudson River Valley. The final outcome of the war was decided as much by these clashes between neighbors as it was between uniformed armies marching across fields farther south. This story of young Hugh McDonald embodies the conflicts, contradictions, confusions, and difficulties of this neighbor-versus-neighbor war.

Meet Hugh McDonald

Hugh McDonald was a second-generation Scot immigrant born in Tarrytown, New York, in August 1764. Hugh's father and grandfather were fiercely loyal members of the McGregor clan. In Scotland, the leader of the clan received substantial gifts of land and title from the king and pledged the support of his entire clan to the king. In America, Hugh and his family's leanings were strongly Patriot and Whig—until the McGregor clan decision.

Hugh was a bright boy and promising student. At age nine he could read, do all basic math, and had studied astronomy. His father was a farmer and operated a small tannery, but always held visions of much grander accomplishments for his son.

Patriot Son, Tory Traitor

Hugh McDonald had only been 14 for three weeks when, on May 11, 1779, he skipped along Connel Road on the edge of Tarrytown, New York, toward home, too excited to merely walk or run. Mrs. Sarah McCall, a neighbor of the McDonalds, was out hanging wash in the bright afternoon sunshine. "Well now, Hugh McDonald. What's got you bubbling over on this fine day? A girl?"

Hugh stopped and blushed. "*No*, Mrs. McCall. It's a secret." His toe scratched at the soft dirt next to the McCalls' picket fence. He *wanted* to tell her. He was pretty sure he knew where she stood and that she would approve. But still he didn't dare.

She put down her wash and wiped her hands. "And what sort of a secret could turn you into the very picture of springtime happiness?"

"I can't tell, Mrs. McCall. That's why it's a secret."

She laughed and waved him off with both hands before turning back to her work. "Ah, be off with you, Hugh. And say 'Hello' to your folks for me."

Hugh turned and sprinted for his house another 200 yards along the road.

"Father! Father!" Hugh raced through the house and found his father sitting quietly on the bench under a shade tree far behind the house, which he used for his "serious thinking." Hugh was too excited to consider what brought Mr. McDonald to this bench. "Father! Jason Rogers is a captain of the Tarrytown Patriot militia. Elias just told me. He let Elias join the militia and he's a whole month younger than I am." (Elias Drew had been Hugh's best friend for four years.)

Mr. Fergus McDonald still sat, stony faced and silent, barely acknowledging his son's presence.

"You know Jason Rogers, father. He helped build our new barn. He'd be our . . . captain." Still there was no reaction from Mr. McDonald. "What's wrong, father?"

"We will not join the Patriot militia."

Mr. McDonald's words crashed into Hugh like heavy boulders. "But father, just last week we agreed that we'd both join the militia and help stop the brutal Indian and Tory raids."

Under the shoulder-length brown hair and the wild hedges that were Fergus McDonald's eyebrows, his eyes seemed sad, almost heartbroken. His shoulders sagged as if carrying a heavy burden. "We will *not* join the militia. We will *not* stop the raids. This morning I met with Colonel James Skyles and enlisted us both in the *Tory* militia." There was no enthusiasm in his voice, only final certainty.

Hugh staggered back, clutching his stomach as if his father's words had mortally stabbed him. "But . . . but, father. How can we? We have always supported American independence. You taught me to hate the Tories and their vicious raids."

"I have also taught you to honor your clan, have I not?" bellowed Fergus, now shaking the letter he clutched in his left hand.

Hugh simply nodded, wide-eyed with foreboding.

"We are part of the McGregor clan, are we not?"

Again Hugh dumbly nodded.

Now Fergus tapped at the letter with his right hand. "This is a letter from Fergus McGregor, himself, head of the clan and the man for whom I am named. It is written in his own hand. He says that all McGregors *must* support the King. And so that is what we shall do."

Hugh's legs could no longer support his weight. He sank into the grass near the edge of the family corn field. His mind whirred drunkenly. His stomach churned. His voice was barely a gurgled whisper. "But . . . but father. The McGregor clan is in *Scotland*. How can they know what's best for *us* here in America?"

"No!" shouted Fergus, slamming his hand down upon the bench. "Don't argue with me. Above all we are loyal McGregors and we do what the clan leader says."

All Hugh could stammer was, "How can this be?"

Mr. McDonald sighed and shrugged. "Personally, I think the King gave Fergus McGregor new titles and lands to buy the clan's loyalty. But none of that matters. We are now loyal Tory militia soldiers. And until Fergus McGregor's own hand tells me different, that is what we shall remain."

There was a long silence broken only by the constant buzz of insects and the occasional cry of a large bird circling high above. Suddenly one of his father's statements registered in Hugh's mind. "We're going to serve under James Skyles?! You, yourself, said that only the Devil could like so sour and heartless a . . . "

"No more!" interrupted Mr. McDonald. "He is now your colonel and your leader. Speak no ill of him." Mr. McDonald tried to smile, but had little success. "I understand Alfred Biterly will be in our company. He's a friend of yours, isn't he?"

"That weasel?" sneered Hugh. All of his shock and resentment erupted in a bitter torrent. "I'd rather shoot Al Biterly than serve with him. And the same for that weasel Mr. Skyles!"

Hugh turned toward the house, sick at heart, wondering how he could ever face his mother and 11-year-old sister, Jessica, as a Tory soldier. But in two fast strides, Mr. McDonald, a thick and powerful man, caught his son, lifted him off the ground by his shoulders, and shook him hard. His gray eyes glared hard as stone and hot as fire. "James Skyles is now your colonel and you will not speak ill of him again. Do you understand?"

Hugh felt that he couldn't breathe in this new Tory house and stumbled out onto Connel Road. In the winter, when leaves were off the trees, you could glimpse the Hudson River from this part of the road and you could see most of Tarrytown as it spread down the rolling slopes to the eastern shore of the river below. Thirty miles south lay New York City. Tarrytown was part of upstate New York, which had erupted in bitter and bloody civil strife between Tory and Patriot militia while the official armies tramped across fields farther south and farther north.

Hugh plopped onto a flat boulder at roadside, trying to absorb the terrible enormity of his fate.

"Why all of a sudden so glum, Hugh?" asked Mrs. McCall, who had finished hanging wash and had begun to weed her newly planted vegetable garden. "Your moods seem to change faster than the weather."

How could he tell a faithful Patriot supporter that he was now the hated enemy instead of a trusted fighter for liberty—just because someone he had never met who lived thousands of miles away had made a secret deal with a king he had never seen or cared about? How could he tell a neighbor that his own father had betrayed everything that Hugh believed in?

No. He couldn't say any of that. It was too awful and evil. Hugh simply shook his head and stared at the distant horizon.

"You'll get over it soon enough, Hugh," she chuckled. "You're only 14. At that age, wounds heal quickly."

"I don't think this *can* heal," thought Hugh.

Hugh sought comfort from friends and, as the sun sank toward the western hills, found Elias Drew helping Frederick McCord finish his afternoon cleaning chores at his father's grain mill. Elias held his broom as if it were a musket and he were marching in a parade. "Isn't it exciting? We'll all be in the same militia company together."

"Frederick has joined too?" asked Hugh.

Elias shouldered his broom as if ready to fire. "Maybe they'll let us be part of a Ranger Unit and we'll tramp all over chasing Mohawks and Redcoats!"

Frederick looked up from cleaning the grist stones. "Why so glum, Hugh? We've all wanted to join the militia for *years*."

"Sure, the *Patriot* militia," Hugh muttered.

"What does *that* mean?" demanded Elias. "Of course the Patriot militia."

Hugh realized he faced a new dilemma: If he was now a Tory, he shouldn't talk with known Patriot soldiers, and certainly not confide in them. But neither could he abandon his best friends. He felt trapped between worlds in a frozen no-man's-land.

"What's wrong, Hugh? You're supposed to be happy."

"I can't . . . " Hugh stammered. "Fergus McGregor, our clan leader in Scotland supports the King. And my father . . . "

"This is America," interrupted Elias. "Those old-world clans don't matter here. Here everyone answers only to themselves and their own conscience."

"Not if you're a McGregor."

"But you're name's McDonald."

Hugh explained. "McDonalds are part of the McGregor clan."

"Not in America," said Frederick. "Here we don't have clans and castes and social stations. Here we have liberty!"

Hugh slumped onto one of the flour sacks along the mill's wall. "Tell that to my father."

Elias said, "Cheer up, Hugh. We'll talk to Jason Rogers. He'll know what to do."

Hugh snapped, "You don't understand. My father enlisted us in the *Tory* militia because Fergus McGregor told him to. I can't talk to a Patriot captain."

"You're a good American and so is he. Besides, he's older and will know what to do."

Reluctantly, Hugh allowed his two comrades to drag him to the Blue Swallow Inn, a favorite tavern of Captain Rogers. In a dimly lit private back room, around a small dinner table, Hugh spilled out his story to the quiet, dependable carpenter, Jason Rogers, while he listened, "hmmmm-ed," and nodded.

"That's quite a dilemma, Hugh: how to be loyal to both your father and your own beliefs." Rogers paced while he spoke, hands clasped behind his back. "Your father is loyal to his clan—am I right so far?" Hugh nodded. "But not specifically to the King or to England—isn't that true?"

"We both hate the King . . . " Hugh began.

But Rogers continued, "I know he really wants to be loyal to America. I've talked to him about it." Another nod from Hugh. "Now, *you* want to be loyal to your father and to America—isn't that it?"

"Yes, exactly," began Hugh.

But Jason Rogers talked over him. "And you *can* by being loyal to that part of your father that wants to be loyal to America and fight England, the real enemy." Rogers smiled as if he had just solved a particularly difficult problem.

"But I don't understand," said Hugh. "Should I be a Tory militiaman or not?"

Rogers clapped Hugh on the back. "Of course you should, Hugh. It's the perfect solution."

"What is?"

"Be a Tory militiaman to honor the wishes of your clan. Be a patriot spy to honor your *own* loyalties."

The word cut through Hugh like a knife. "A *spy*? I can't! We've always hated spies. They lie and deceive people. "

"But it's the best way to serve your country. You *are* a Patriot, aren't you?"

"Yes. But . . . "

"Then prove it. We need to know what the Tory militia is planning."

Hugh squirmed on his chair. "You won't tell anyone?"

"Never."

"My father will never know?"

"Never. I promise."

"No one will get killed because of me?"

"Only Tories you would have been willing to kill as a Patriot volunteer soldier."

"But now *I'm* one of those Tories, and so is my father!"

Hugh felt gut-punched. Four hours ago he had been a proud, eager, and patriotic citizen soldier, wanting to shout it to the world. Now he was everything he despised—a Tory and a spy who would have to slink through a web of lies, deceit, and mortal danger.

Over the next three weeks the Tarrytown Tory militia regiment (really only 75 local citizens under the supervision of Colonel James Skyles, who owned a fleet of river barges and had bought the rank and position from the British) conducted a series of secret drills. At first many in the company resented the presence of Fergus McDonald and his son, claiming they were self-proclaimed Whigs.

Colonel Skyles, a short, tough man sour as lemons and hard as iron, dragged Fergus and Hugh out in front of the company. "This man has pledged himself and his family to the Loyalist cause. He signed a loyalty oath. I trust him, and so will each of you."

"But what if he's a *spy*?" called one man with sergeant's stripes pinned to his collar.

Hugh cringed and blushed deep red. His knees began to wobble.

Colonel Skyles said, "I have known the McDonalds for years. None of them are liars. If they say they are loyal, then they are."

The company nodded and murmured acceptance. Hugh felt sick and was sure each one of them could tell he was a spy.

For three weeks the Tory militia met in the vast fields of Frederick Campbell, one of the richest farmers in the Hudson Valley, where they could practice in secret. They practiced assembling in firing formations. They practiced using bird calls to coordinate an attack by two groups of soldiers coming into a field from opposite directions. And they practiced the firing commands until Hugh's arms ached from holding up his musket.

All the while Hugh felt he was drowning in a pool of guilt and doubt. How could he disobey his father's command? How could he participate in a Tory raid and *not* tell the Patriot cause he loved about it ahead of time?

For weeks he avoided Elias and Frederick, not knowing what he would say when they met. He also avoided his father's eyes, always looking down and away at meals and during drills, fearing one glance would give away his thoughts.

At the end of the June 3 drill session, Colonel Skyles announced that the regiment was ready to conduct the raid he had been planning on the Patriot store of supplies in a warehouse across the Hudson River in Nyack. They would assemble at 3:00 A.M. on June 6 and strike a blow for King and country that would be heard from New York to Canada.

The regiment cheered.

Hugh thought he would be violently ill. There was no more time to linger in indecision. This very day he would have to tell, or decide never to tell. He would either have to become a spy or a willing Tory. In either case, by nightfall he would be something he hated.

Late that afternoon Hugh wandered aimlessly along Connel Road, struggling to sort out his loyalties, his duty, and his desires.

"You look like you're carrying the weight of the world on your slender shoulders, young Hugh," called Mrs. McCall from her garden. "I've never seen a 14-year-old boy walk so heavy."

Hugh halfheartedly waved and tried to smile.

"You must have a big problem to fret so hard."

"I sure do, Mrs. McCall."

She stood and leaned on her picket fence. "I find that big problems often seem big because we make them complicated. Find the simplest truth, Hugh, down deep in your heart and you'll be steered right every time."

"My heart?" he repeated.

"Your heart, boy. What does your heart tell you to do?"

Images of the new American flag and of Hugh and Elias as dashing Rangers racing after fleeing Tories and Mohawks flashed across his mind's eye. "My heart . . . " Then Hugh saw an image of his father standing proud in their wide corn field.

And he knew.

Hugh ran to Elias's house and told him to fetch Jason Rogers so he could report without being seen meeting in public with a Patriot captain. Hugh paced behind Elias's house waiting for his friend to return, always fearing that either Colonel Skyles or his father would step from the shadows to confront him.

Before sunset had faded into dark of night, Hugh had unloaded his burden of the Tory attack plan to Captain Rogers. "Nothing bad will happen? Right?" asked Hugh.

"With this warning, we'll simply move the supplies so that the raid will find nothing."

"You're sure?"

Captain Rogers nodded and extended his hand. "Thank you, Hugh. Timely information is what will win this war. You have done a valuable service to your country."

Hugh still felt like a cheat and a traitor as he slinked back home, wondering what story he would tell his parents if they asked where he had been.

At 3:00 A.M. on June 6, 70 members of the Tarrytown Loyalist militia regiment gathered with hushed whispers and marched a mile upriver to North Tarrytown where a dozen boats had been hidden. The shuffling column disturbed only a few local dogs who barked in protest at their passing. As silently as they could, the men clambered into longboats and dipped their oars into the flowing waters of the Hudson.

Hugh could see that his father was deeply troubled and lacked his usual enthusiasm and energy as he halfheartedly pulled on his oar. Hugh rowed happily, knowing they would find only an empty and deserted warehouse.

The raiding party landed just north of Nyack, beached their boats, scrambled up the western bluffs of the river, and marched toward Nyack as first light crept toward dawn.

"Be careful, son," whispered Mr. McDonald. "If shooting starts, duck low and stay under cover."

"Don't worry, father. Everything will be fine. You'll see," Hugh answered.

The Tory force split into two groups as they had practiced. The main body approached the sleeping town of Nyack along the river bluffs. A smaller detachment circled inland to attack along the main road and cut off any Patriots who tried to escape.

Just at dawn, Hugh heard the bird-call signals that called for final attack. Hugh and 45 other Tories rushed into town to overwhelm the Patriot supply warehouse . . . and walked into a wall of Patriot musket fire.

Eight Tories crumpled to the ground on the first volley. The rest scattered, looking for cover. Colonel Skyles yelled for his regiment to assemble in line and prepare to return fire. Six more were slain before a single Tory shot could be fired. Patriot snipers on the roofs began to pick off Tory officers. Frederick Campbell went down. James Skyles was hit but stayed on his feet.

"It's a trap!" yelled the colonel. "Retreat to the bluff and reform!"

By this time the second group of Tories had stumbled into the crossfire. Bodies were piling up in the road deep enough for others to hide behind.

Twenty-five of the raiding party were down. The remaining 45 reformed behind a barricade along the waterfront. Fergus McDonald bled from a bullet wound in his upper arm.

"Someone leaked information!" growled the colonel. "Gentlemen, we have a spy and a traitor in our midst."

Tears streamed down Hugh's face as he tried to stem the flow of blood in his father's arm. "I'm sorry, father. This wasn't supposed to happen! They promised!"

Mr. McDonald glared at his son, then ground his teeth and turned his back. With a deep sigh, he leaned back toward Hugh. "Don't say another word. And dry your tears this instant!" he hissed. "These men kill spies and burn their houses and fields."

It was a slow, dismal row back across the Hudson for Hugh, feeling both betrayed and betrayer. The men were surly and angry now that immediate danger had passed. Accusing glances and whispers drifted between boats. Hugh stared at his hands and pulled on his oar, terrified every moment that he would be snatched up by his collar and shot.

On June 7, Fergus McDonald sent his son to live with a cousin who had settled in southern New Jersey. They told the neighbors Hugh was making the journey to help out on the farm while the cousin lay sick in bed. Hugh's mother and sister never learned what he had done.

Hugh never saw Elias, Frederick, or Jason Rogers again. By early July, Hugh had joined the Continental Army. He served faithfully for 15 months, and was killed in the fall of 1780 in a small skirmish in Virginia, dying for the cause he had already risked so much to help.

Aftermath

Families and communities all across America were ripped apart by Tory-Patriot battles and loyalties. The bitterness and conflict were worst in upstate New York and in South Carolina, where families were slaughtered and houses and farms burned on the strength of a rumor or to avenge past slaughters. The Tory-Patriot civil war became a blood bath where no one was safe and no one was beyond the reach of the opposing militia. Fighting along the Hudson River continued in an endless series of small, meaningless skirmishes between opposing militia until mid-1782, when it became clear that the British were going to abandon the fight. Then most Tories fled to Canada in the mass exodus of 1782 and 1783.

Follow-up Questions and Activities

1. **What Do You Know?**

   - Why was Hugh McDonald torn between the two sides in the conflict when the Tarrytown Tory militia attacked the Nyack Patriot store house? What drew him to each side?

   - Hugh McDonald passed information to the enemy. What is that action called? What is the usual penalty for getting caught?

   - At the story's end, Hugh's father sent him away. Why? What might have happened if he hadn't?

   - Was Hugh being loyal? How? To whom? What does loyalty mean?

2. **Finding Out More**. Following are five important topics from this story for you to research in the library and on the Internet. The reference sources at the back of this book will help you get started.

   - Throughout history, what has happened to spies when they were caught? What happens to spies in modern times? Are spies viewed as heroes by their own country? Why or why not? Search for historical examples. Why would anyone become a spy?

- Research famous spies throughout history. Are there any famous American spies? What do they all have in common?

- Research the Tory-Patriot fights in upstate New York during the years 1778 through 1781. Where else besides Tarrytown did fighting take place? What kinds of units were involved in the fighting? What was the outcome of the different fights in different places? Which side finally gained control of the area? How? When?

- This story describes neighbor-versus-neighbor disagreement and fighting. Have other American conflicts created this type of bitter, personal fighting? What about nonmilitary movements (labor movements, the Civil Rights movement, etc.)? What about other countries, for example in Africa and Eastern Europe?

- The American Revolutionary war pitted neighbor against neighbor, brother against brother. This resulted in a cruel and vicious civil war. Use the Internet and the library to study recent wars and search for events that seem similar to our Revolutionary War in the way they tore communities apart.

3. **Make It Real**

- Hugh McDonald had to sort out his conflicting loyalties. What does *loyalty* mean? Hugh felt conflicting loyalties to his family clan, his parent, his beliefs, and his country. Make a list of all the things and people to whom you feel some loyalty—family, friends, school, clubs, church, scouts, sports, community, country, humanity, etc. What would you do if some of these entities to whom you feel loyal opposed each other and each demanded your support?

- Find out about an issue in your community that creates strong feelings and significant opposition (an environmental issue, a water use issue, a growth issue, a transportation measure, etc.). Write an essay describing the position of the side you believe in. Now imagine that the issue heats up to the point where riots happen and fights break out on the streets. Supporters on both sides take up arms like vigilante gangs and roam the town searching for a fight with the opposition. Also imagine that your family declares itself in support of the side you *don't* believe in. How would you feel? What would you do? Write a journal entry or a letter to a sympathetic friend describing how you feel about what is happening, what you plan to do, and why.

4. **Points to Ponder**

- What is the difference between a revolution and a civil war? How did the American Revolution differ from the American Civil War? How did both of these wars differ from recent wars (e.g., in Chechnya and Kosovo)?

- In this story, Hugh McDonald had to choose between obeying his father's command and his own beliefs. How and what did he decide? How would you have decided if you were in his place?

- Do you think spying is a morally acceptable activity? Are there times when spying is not acceptable? Do you think it would be acceptable for the boys in your class to spy on the girls, or vice versa? Is it all right for reporters to spy on movie stars? Is that different from one country spying on another? Why or why not?

"I Have Not Yet Begun to Fight!"

Naval Battle Between the *Bonhomme Richard* and the *Serapis*, September 23, 1779

Battle between the *Bonhomme Richard* and the *Serapis*

At a Glance

England owned the seas. She boasted the biggest, best-trained fleet in the world: 270 warships in 1775. Eighty were ships-of-the-line, often with over 100 guns, including mammoth 24-pounders as well as a full complement of 18- and 12-pounders. These giant battleships were cumbersome, lumbering, but almost indestructible because of their immense firepower and the great range of their guns. England had 150 frigates—lighter, faster, more maneuverable, but with only 40–50 guns. Most of those were 12- and 18-pounders.

America authorized three frigates in 1775. Two were purchased by Benjamin Franklin and were worm-eaten, French surplus ships. All other American warships had to be privately financed and built. The Continental Navy hit its peak at 23 warships in 1778. After that date, battle losses and storm damage removed ships faster than they could be replaced. By 1780 the Continental Navy was virtually nonexistent.

Still, the fledgling American navy logged many small victories over merchant vessels and small frigates. During the entire war, there was only one great naval victory for the Continental Navy. That victory didn't decide the war, but it did buy respect and support for colonial efforts from countries around the globe and established that America really did have a navy. America's first naval hero, John Paul Jones, emerged from that brutal fight. So did the war's most famous quote: "I have not yet begun to fight!" This is the story of that bloody naval battle.

Meet Jeremiah Cottles

Jeremiah Cottles, called Jessie, was born in February 1756, in New York City and was orphaned at nine when both parents died of disease. The city dumped him into an orphanage, but he ran away at 10 and took a job as cabin boy on a British merchant ship. He lived on that ship for three years, then spent six months on a navy frigate and two years on a whaling ship out of Groton, Massachusetts. Finally, he served as mate on an American (Quaker-owned) merchant ship—mostly smuggling non-English goods—before joining the crew of a privateer schooner in 1775.

By 1775 Jessie had grown to hate the British because he had seen them force captured American seamen—many still young boys—to do the hardest and dirtiest of their navy's work and whip many he believed to be innocent, just for the sake of maintaining harsh discipline on board.

After two years of privateering along the New England coast (and building up a considerable nest egg for his retirement), Jessie joined the Continental Navy. He was assigned to the *Ranger* under John Paul Jones, and had just turned 23 in 1779 when Jones landed the *Ranger* in France and shifted his crew to the *Bonhomme Richard*.

Jessie stayed in the navy after the war until he retired at age 52 (in 1808). He died in Groton, Massachusetts, at 61. He never married, but was a popular, growly-voiced spinner of sea yarns in pubs and with local children, many of whom believed he was really a pirate. Jessie, apparently, encouraged that belief.

"I Have Not Yet Begun to Fight!"

"I don't trust these Frenchies."

American seaman gunner Jessie Cottles lay propped on one elbow on his cot and gazed through the open window of their small, rented room toward the harbor below.

"*Which* Frenchies don't you trust?" laughed Bill Skeeterman, his 21-year-old roommate and fellow cannoneer. "*All* of them or just a chosen few?" Skeeterman (Skeet) focused his attention on the small piece of whalebone scrimshaw he was carving.

Jessie flopped onto his back, hands laced under his head while he thought. "Can't say as I trust any of them. But especially I mean the French seamen we're supposed to sail with. Oh, they bow and smile politely enough. But I think they'd each ram a knife into your back the first chance they got."

Skeet and Arthur Targus, the last of the trio sharing this small, third-floor room, nodded and chuckled.

Jessie Cottles, Skeet, and Art Targus, who called himself Pete, were three of the 24 men Captain John Paul Jones had kept in France when he sent his first warship, *Ranger*, back to America in April 1779. For the first three months of the year, *Ranger* had cruised up and down the English and Irish coasts like a hungry shark, plundering British merchant ships and coastal towns, making England feel the bite of the colonial Revolutionary War. Then Jones landed his crew in France to repair and restock his ship. There Jones decided he needed a more powerful ship and sent the *Ranger* home.

Jessie said, "Look at us! Stuck here in this French city with nothing to do. What a lousy way to fight a war!"

Skeet paused in his carving. "I say lounging at our leisure in the city of L'Orient on the coast of France with nary a care in the world is a mighty *fine* way to fight a war. I could get used to fighting my wars like this."

Targus laughed.

Jessie pounded his fist against the wall. "Why didn't we all sail back to America where the fighting is? Where we could do some good?"

Skeet blew dust and wood shavings away from his carving. "I still say this is the best way I ever heard to fight a war."

Pete explained, "Jones was assigned to disrupt shipping around England. If he can force the British to pull three or four ships-of-the-line and half a dozen frigates back from America to patrol English waters, he will have done more than he ever could in American waters."

Jessie growled and turned back to the window. "I still don't like just *sitting* here."

The crew lounged in the port city of L'Orient for a month before the French king gave Jones a new ship, *Duc du Duras*, and assigned four other small navy frigates and sloops to sail with him when he returned to English waters to disrupt English shipping. A three-month refit of the *Duc du Duras* was nearing completion. The fleet was due to set sails in mid-August.

"Why not use a solid American ship?" asked Jessie, rising to stare through the lone window at their new ship, gently tugging at its mooring lines as the tide ebbed. The third-floor walk-up room they had been given stood above a first-floor bakery and about halfway up the steep hill that rose from the harbor. Jessie was convinced he had put on 10 pounds just from the wafting smell of fresh baked breads and cakes.

Pete Targus looked up from the French novel he was trying to read. "America doesn't have the money to build a solid warship or a decent shipyard to build it in."

Jessie began to pace as he pressed, "Why not stay with the *Ranger*? She did just fine."

Skeet shook his head. "*Ranger* was small and slow. That's all right for conquering a lone merchant vessel or two, but no match for a British ship-of-the-line."

Pete added, "Captain Jones was right to send it back to America. If we're going to take on the British, in British waters, we need a better ship. Besides, he gave the new ship an American name, *Bonhomme Richard*."

"What kind of a name is that?" Jessie demanded. "That's not American."

"It means 'Poor Richard.' Benjamin Franklin helped Jones get the ship, so he named it after Franklin's almanac."

Jessie shook his fists, seemingly at the ship, the harbor, and also the entire country of France. "Well, I don't trust that French ship. It's a worm-eaten dog built for hauling. You'll see. It'll be no good in a fight."

The *Duc du Duras* had been built as a 900-ton merchant ship and plowed the East India trade for years before being sold to the French navy as an outdated surplus ship.

"You don't trust much, do you, Jessie my boy?" Pete Targus, the oldest of the trio at 28, often called Jessie "my boy."

Jessie still hung under his dark and gloomy cloud. "And I don't trust French guns, either. Those 18-pounders we mounted in the lower gun room are ancient. You'll see. They're no good."

Pete and Skeet both laughed again. Skeet asked, "Is there anything you *do* trust?"

"Captain Jones. I'd follow him anywhere."

"Ha!" snorted Pete. "He doesn't even use his real name. Did you know that, Jessie my boy? He was a Scottish merchant captain wanted for murder by the British. He fled to America and just added the Jones to throw off British naval authorities. His real name is just John Paul."

"I don't care. I still I trust him and I always will."

A fleet of six ships sailed from L'Orient on August 19, 1779, accompanied only by the screeching of gulls and the groan of ropes and old timbers under the strain of a brisk morning wind. Within 24 hours of entering the Irish Sea, Captain Pierre Landars of the *Alliance* refused to follow the orders of John Paul Jones, the fleet commodore, and sailed off on his own to seek British merchant ships to plunder. On the third day out, the two smaller French sloops had a bitter disagreement and both turned back to France.

The French captain on *Vengeance* was sullen, moody, always objecting to attacks, often refusing to participate unless he got first claim on the plunder and the easiest, safest duty during the attack. Only the smaller, 32-gun American Frigate *Pallas* hung like a faithful lap dog in line with the *Bonhomme Richard*, following every order.

Jessie, Skeet, and Pete were assigned to 12-pound cannons on the main deck. Their days were spent cleaning, first their cannon and then the deck. Their nights dragged by stacked four high in tiny hammocks in the stuffy, overcrowded crew's quarters. "I don't trust the English deserters on this crew," Jessie grumbled.

"You better," answered Pete. "They make up over half the crew including most of the petty officers."

"They're better than the Norwegians, Portuguese, Arabs, and Poles," grunted Skeet. "At least you can talk to the Brits."

"But they're *English*," continued Jessie. "And we're fighting the English in English waters. What's to keep them from turning back?"

"They'd be hung as deserters. That's what, Jessie, my boy."

"There are over 200 in this crew," said Skeet. "Including the 14 American officers, only 75 Americans could be found to man her. The rest had to come from somewhere."

Up the west side of England and around Scotland the tiny fleet sailed, plundering ships and small towns and harbors as they went. Heading down the east side of England, on September 23, just off Flamborough Head, lookouts spotted a 40-ship convoy. Two new navy frigates escorted the line of full, fat merchant vessels.

The British warships detached and turned to face Jones's flotilla as soon as they were sighted in late afternoon. Bells and the mate's shrill whistle called the *Bonhomme Richard* to general quarters. Sailors scrambled grim-faced across the decks and up and down passageways. There was an urgent rush to roll out powder kegs and hoist cannon balls, double-enders (two cannon balls connected with a four-foot chain), and grape shot (metal cans filled with metal scrap) up onto the firing line.

The *Alliance* veered off, away from battle. The *Vengeance* followed. Captain Jones was left with only two ships to oppose the British—his own and the *Pallas,* which he ordered to take on the small (20-gun) *Countess of Scarborough.* Turning to port to run with the wind, the *Bonhomme Richard* drove through the light ocean chop to engage the new, top-of-the-line frigate, *Serapis,* bristling with 50 guns, including four 24-pound giants, ten 18-pound brutes, and thirty 12-pounders and smaller quarter deck and fo'c'sle guns.

Jessie could feel that this would not be another of the easy victories they had enjoyed against merchant ships. The *Serapis* was faster, newer, more maneuverable, and far more powerful than the *Bonhomme Richard.* She was crewed by skilled British navy seamen. This would not be an easy victory at all. Jessie gripped the ropes that ran out his 12-pound cannon and glanced at Pete and Skeet, both readying the next cannon over. Even though a chill wind had begun to blow, Skeet's face was covered in sweat.

This time the enemy ship had a strong bite. This time blood would flow and men would loose their lives. John Paul Jones had had the main deck and gun deck painted red back in France. Now Jessie saw why. Red paint would conceal the blood that washed across the weathered deck boards.

The winds had been slack all afternoon. Now they ripened, brisk and cold out of the northwest as the sun set. Waves began to kick up about the bow. In the deepening twilight, the sails of the *Serapis* stood out like luminous, white ghosts floating above the dark ocean.

Jessie's mouth grew painfully dry. His heart pounded and his hands trembled slightly as he crouched below the deck rail waiting, wanting to pop up and look, listening to the dreadful silence broken only by the ever-present creak of wood and the gentle snap of flags and sails.

A voice shouted through a megaphone, floating over the waves. "What ship are you?"

Captain Jones cupped a hand to his ear, pretending not to hear.

"What ship are you? Answer immediately or I shall . . . "

"Fire!" shouted Jones.

Jessie touched fire to fuse and his cannon, along with 20 others on the *Bonhomme Richard,* roared and flashed fire into the growing darkness. Almost at the same moment 24 guns from the *Serapis* answered with their own thunder. For a brief instant there was silence while the speeding balls of iron hurtled through the air.

And then the decks exploded in a shower of splinters and flying wood. Men screamed as red-hot cannon balls tore through them. The *Richard* seemed to rise slightly out of the water as a great explosion rocked her belly.

"Was that the powder room?" called the captain.

All deck hands stared at the hatchway, waiting for an answer to be shouted up from below.

"Reload!" yelled the deck officer.

"Not the powder room, sir!" called a bloodied petty officer, staggering to the top of the stairs. "Two of the 18-pounders exploded on firing."

"Any casualties?" called Jones.

"Every man save six in the lower gun room. We dare not fire the other 18s again for fear they will also explode."

"Damn!" cried Jones, stomping his foot. "Now I've only got 12-pounders to go against 18s and 24s!"

Pulling the ropes to run out his 12-pound cannon, Jessie growled. "I told you not to trust those French 18s."

"We'll have to withdraw now," said Skeet. "Can't fight 18- and 24-pounders with just 12s."

"Prepare for broadside!" cried the deck officer.

"Fire!"

Again the *Richard's* 12-pound cannons erupted deadly fire and billows of acid smoke. Before the guns could be retracted for reloading the answering salvo arrived from the *Serapis*. Great holes were torn in the hull and decks. One sail took four great tears and began to flop in the breeze. Bodies piled upon bodies, making it difficult to haul powder and cannon balls across the deck.

"Rifles to the fighting top!" called Captain Jones.

Jessie watched 30 seamen with long rifles scamper like spiders up the ratlines to the wide platforms two-thirds of the way up each mast. Whenever the ships drew within rifle range, they poured a wall of fire into the fighting tops of the *Serapis* and onto her decks to add a new hazard to serving on one of her cannon crews.

For two hours the battle raged on, with the *Serapis* steadily gaining the upper hand. Her 18- and 24-pound shot often crashed straight through the *Richard* and out the other side. The *Richard's* decks were smashed and difficult to walk upon. One fierce salvo tore into *Richard's* main deck, forever silencing six of her 12-pounders. One cannon ball crashed through the railing and blasted into the cannon next to Jessie's, killing both Pete and Skeet. Jessie was too numb with terror and shock to notice. Mechanically, he reloaded his cannon and hauled on the ropes to run it back out for the next round. Only ten of the *Richard's* 42 guns were able to respond to the next call for firing.

Several small fires smoldered on the listing, crippled ship. Water sloshed in through a dozen gaping rents in the hull. Prisoners and crew were diverted to man the pumps. Smoke mixed with flickering lantern light and night-time shadows to make the *Bonhomme Richard* look like a scene from Hell.

"It has to end soon," mumbled Jessie, his face and hands blackened by the soot of exploding gunpowder, his arms spattered with blood from fallen comrades. "It has to end."

Jones maneuvered the *Richard* right behind the *Serapis*, the battered bow of the *Richard* actually touching the stern of the other ship. Neither ship had a cannon in a position that could fire upon the foe. "Do you surrender?" called the *Serapis's* captain.

Jessie's heart sank as he realized that his mangled ship and crew could not possibly fight any further. The few remaining crew members stumbled like walking zombies across the bloody, torn deck. The answer would have to be "yes" and he would spend his days in a British dungeon.

But John Paul Jones cried, "I have not yet *begun* to fight!"

The words seemed to instill new energy and confidence in the soul of each sailor struggling to stand on the bloody deck. They seemed to rumble like fresh reinforcements across the water to strike fear and caution in the heart of each British sailor.

"Has he gone mad?" Jessie thought.

"Come on, lads!" cried the captain, leaping from the quarter deck to the main. "We'll have *them* surrendering before we're through!"

Maybe it was the calm certainty of his voice. Maybe it was the fierce gleam of his eyes. But with a growing cheer, the weary crew responded, redoubling their deadly efforts. Soon the ships were on a parallel course. Cannon fire from the *Serapis* poured into the crippled *Richard*. The six remaining guns on the *Richard* bravely responded to the onslaught.

The *Richard* pulled ahead and Jones turned his ship hard across the bow of the *Serapis*. "Fire!" yelled the deck officer. The five functioning 12-pounders of the *Richard* tore away a huge chunk of the *Serapis*'s forward deck and splintered her forward mast.

The ships were too close to avoid collision. The *Serapis* rammed into the *Richard* near her aft mast. Jessie was thrown across the deck by the force of the impact. The *Serapis*'s bow tangled in *Richard*'s rigging. "Use grappling hooks to lock the ships together!" called Captain Jones.

The wind slowly pushed *Serapis*'s stern around so that the two ships lay locked together, side by side. Cannons fired at point-blank range. Sailors reached through cavernous holes in the hull and rails with pikes and cutlass to tear at the enemy.

The riflemen in *Richard*'s tops managed to kill all those firing from the *Serapis*'s tops and now directed their fire toward the *Serapis* deck crew. But the *Serapis*'s big guns in the lower decks still blasted into *Richard*'s hull, tearing monstrous holes in the weakened wood.

Fire erupted in one of the *Serapis*'s sails and raced through the rigging to *Richard*'s top sails. Both ships burned like torches in the night. All fighting ceased until each crew successfully fought to bring the fires under control.

American riflemen crawled across the tangled rigging lines to take possession of *Serapis*'s fighting tops, firing straight down onto her decks.

Jessie sat in a shell-shocked stupor on his now useless cannon with a bad shoulder wound, streaming blood down his arm.

"You, there," bellowed Captain Jones, pointing at Jessie. "To the quarter-deck!"

"What for?" Jessie mumbled.

"Man the 9-pound cannon, man!" cried the captain. "By God, we have them now!"

"We're winning?" Jessie stammered as he gazed around at the ruin and death that filled the *Richard*. "This is winning?"

"Quickly man! We need that cannon!"

Jessie hesitated, watching the fevered gleam shine in his captain's eyes, as the flickering light of small deck fires and lanterns danced shadows across his face. Part of him said "go." Part of him said "this is crazy. Don't do it. Just sit here and give up."

"Trust me, man! We can win!"

Summoning a strength Jessie thought he had lost hours ago, he ran up the stairs to the quarter-deck, fueled by blind trust alone. "Load double-enders in that 9-pounder and take out their center mast. I'll use grape shot in this one to clear *Serapis*'s decks!"

In 30 seconds the last two working guns on *Richard* fired as shots from *Serapis*'s big guns on the lower gun deck continued to pound *Richard*'s battered hull into something resembling swiss cheese. Jessie's shot cracked the center mast so that its rigging creaked and snapped. Captain Jones's shot killed the only four sailors who dared to show themselves on *Serapis*'s main deck.

At the same time American riflemen began to drop exploding hand grenades, which had been carried through the rigging to *Serapis*'s fighting top. Several exploded on deck. One bounced through a hatchway and down a set of stairs. It landed in the midst of 20 powder kegs.

The deafening explosion ripped apart *Serapis*'s innards. Fifty British sailors were instantly killed. Others were burned and maimed.

The will of the British to continue the dreadful fight seemed to collapse. Their resistance and cannon fire ceased. The British captain crawled to the back of the quarter-deck and lowered his colors, signaling surrender.

The three-hour battle was over. Both ships were battered beyond recognition. John Paul Jones moved his command to the *Serapis* because it was clear that *Bonhomme Richard* would soon sink. Only 66 of Jones's original crew of over 200 were alive to make the transfer with him. Only 18 were free of any wounds. Jessie Cottles was one of only 43 who were fit for duty. Losses on the *Serapis* had been almost as bad. Almost three-quarters of the sailors who had begun the fight at sunset died before dawn's light had shown the extent of the carnage.

Escorted by the trusty *Pallas*, John Paul Jones and the *Serapis*—with Jessie Cottles in the rigging manning the sails—limped back to France and into history.

Aftermath

The battle between the *Serapis* and the *Bonhomme Richard* meant nothing strategically, yet it meant everything. Over 350 died—three-quarters of each crew. Jones limped back to France in a captured—but badly damaged—ship.

Still, this insignificant battle rocked the world. An American "pirate" with an undergunned, worm-eaten, sluggish ship had beaten the best and the newest that the British navy could put to sea. It was a moral victory of incalculable magnitude.

The American navy accomplished little, if anything, during the rest of the war, becoming almost nonexistent by 1781 due to heavy losses. Still, the combined efforts of hundreds of privateer and navy ships had hampered British merchant shipping and military resupply efforts and stolen thousands of tons of British goods.

Almost as many men were involved in the sea war as in the land war. American seamen didn't win the war, but they certainly made an important contribution by hindering British forces in America and by greatly increasing the cost of the war to England.

Follow-up Questions and Activities

1. **What Do You Know?**

   - Fire was a major fear on wooden sailing ships. What were other common fears of sailors? Did you include drowning in your list? Did you know that few sailors could swim? Why do you think they never learned?

   - Why did the *Serapis* surrender to John Paul Jones when it was the *Bonhomme Richard* that had been most damaged and was sinking?

   - What happened to John Paul Jones and his *Bonhomme Richard* crew after the battle with the *Serapis*? Where did they go? How long did they stay there? What did they do with their captured ship? What else did they do during the war?

   - Why did John Paul Jones, whose ship was badly damaged, on the verge of sinking, and badly outgunned, cry his famous line, "I have not yet begun to fight!"? He had been fighting for hours by that time. Most of his guns had been smashed. His ship had more holes than he could count. Most of his crew had been killed or wounded. Why didn't he surrender to save the lives of the rest of his crew?

   - Why were naval battles so bloody and dangerous for the sailors? Were all naval battles as deadly as that between the *Serapis* and the *Bonhomme Richard*?

2. **Finding Out More**. Following are five important topics from this story for you to research in the library and on the Internet. The reference sources at the back of this book will help you get started.

   - John Paul Jones was America's first naval hero. Research this naval captain. Where did he come from? What had he done before taking command of the *Richard*? What did he do after the war?

   - The *Serapis* was a new British ship and the pride of the British navy. Research the brief history of this ship and of other British sailing frigates. What was a frigate? How was a frigate different from a ship-of-the-line? What were the strengths of a frigate?

- Naval vessels of the eighteenth century were armed with "24-pounders, 18-pounders, 12-pounders, and 6-pounders." These numbers refer to the weight of the cannon balls they fired. Research these various cannons. How big were they? How far could they fire? What sort of damage could they do?

- This story describes only one naval battle. Research the actions, battles, and accomplishments of the fledgling American navy during the Revolutionary War.

- What was the significance of John Paul Jones's victory on the *Bonhomme Richard*? Was any land or territory captured? Did it force England to withdraw any ships or troops from America? Did it hasten the end of the war? How did this victory help the American cause during the war?

3. **Make It Real**

- Pretend you are a sailor on a navy ship in the eighteenth century. Write a letter home describing life onboard ship. Do you mind the lack of privacy? The cramped quarters? The long days of boredom with nothing fun to do? The monotony of your routine? The bad food? What parts of being a sailor do you like?

- Imagine yourself a sailor during a naval battle in the eighteenth century. Giant cannons erupt at point-blank range, belching fire and thunderous roars, tearing great holes in the other ships. Sulfur smoke stings your eyes and obscures your vision. Fires rage through your ship. You know that at any moment an enemy broadside could tear away your part of the ship—and you. And there is nothing you can do about it.

- Research the kinds of jobs, or positions, sailors had on a fighting ship and choose one for you to be. What would you be doing during the battle? What would you be thinking and feeling? What would you be worried about? If your ship sinks in the middle of the ocean, what will likely happen to you? What if your ship is captured? Write a journal entry or letter describing your imagined battle experience and what happened to you during it.

4. **Points to Ponder**

- Why did this battle between just two ships become so famous? What was the point? Was anything decided? What did this victory do for America? Was it really a victory when the American ship was sunk? Why or why not?

- How did the American navy contribute to the war? Was the navy a significant part of the total war effort? Why or why not?

- John Paul Jones's actions are said to have been "symbolic" rather than strategically important to the war effort. What does that mean? He was said to be an irritating mosquito in the British naval machinery. Find other symbolic acts in American history. Nathan Hale's brave line as he was about to be hung as a spy, "I regret that I have but one life to give for my country," is one. General Doolittle's long-distance bombing raids on Tokyo from aircraft carriers during World War II is another. How many others can you find? Make a chart that shows where, when, and why each symbolic act happened. What is the value of such symbolic acts?

1780
at a
Glance

Southern Blood Must Flow

In 1780 the war exploded across South Carolina. General Clinton successfully conquered Charleston, capturing the entire American southern army. Then lightning strikes by Tarleton and Cornwallis destroyed the relief forces marching south from Virginia and North Carolina.

Rebel resistance in South Carolina seemed to dissolve. Most South Carolina Whigs accepted defeat and pledged to be good British citizens once again. Georgia had been under solid British control for over a year. The deep South appeared to have lined up behind the British, as planned. Cornwallis prepared to move his army north into North Carolina and Virginia.

But Clinton went too far. He ordered that every South Carolinian had to not only accept British rule, but actively support the British war effort. If they didn't, their property could be confiscated or destroyed. Former Patriots and neutrals howled in protest. Worse, Cornwallis placed Tories in charge of most local government functions so that he would have to leave only a minimal force behind and have a larger army available to meet Washington as he moved north.

Tories had lived for the first four years of the war under the thumb of harsh Patriot leaders. This was their chance for revenge. Killings, burnings, and lootings were rampant. Resistance swelled, first as guerrilla units that harassed British supply lines, then as newly formed volunteer armies like the Overmountain Boys, who met and crushed Cornwallis's left wing at Kings Mountain in October.

Suddenly South Carolina was anything but secure. Cornwallis had to halt his advance and scurry back to South Carolina for winter camp. Virginia and the North breathed a sigh of relief.

Key Events in 1780

Date	Event
May 12	British capture Charleston and the American southern army.
May 29	Tarleton slaughters Buford's American force at Wexaws, South Carolina, refusing "quarter" (mercy), and is labeled" Butcher Tarleton."
June 8	Massachusetts adopts a state constitution, becoming the second independent state.
August 16	Cornwallis defeats the new American southern army at Camden, South Carolina.
September	General Benedict Arnold defects to the British.
October 7	British slaughtered at Kings Mountain, South Carolina.
October 29	Cornwallis falls back to Winsboro, South Carolina, for winter camp.
December 8	General Nathanial Greene takes command of the American southern army.

Which Road to Freedom?
The Dilemma of Southern Slaves, 1780–1781

"Butcher" Tarleton's slaughter of Buford's Continentals

At a Glance

By the middle of the eighteenth century, slavery existed in all 13 colonies. In the South, the number of black slaves already approached or outnumbered the number of whites. Ghettos of free blacks were hidden on the fringes of most towns.

Blacks wanted freedom as much as, or more than, American whites did. These feelings gushed to the surface during the Revolutionary War, which was being fought for liberty and freedom.

Black slaves wanted their share of liberty and freedom, and they were willing to fight to earn it. But which side should they support? Which side represented the road to *their* freedom? Support for the British and Tories seemed to mean supporting the status quo. Support for the Revolution sounded good, but most of the signers of the Declaration were slave owners.

So who should black slaves support?

The British claimed to support black freedom because they wanted the manpower of black servants and workers. But they couldn't advertise their support openly for fear of alienating Loyalists and Tories who owned slaves. The Continental Army offered freedom to all blacks who joined the army. But, again, many Patriots owned slaves and didn't want to abolish slavery.

239

Both sides talked about freeing slaves who helped their cause, but both sides really seemed inclined to continue slavery without change once the war was over. So what should slaves do to further their own aspirations, surrounded by a Revolution to promote white folks' freedom? What *could* they do? Different groups of slaves devised a variety of schemes and plans to work toward their own freedom. This story tells of the experiences of the slaves on the Montclair plantation in South Carolina.

Meet Darcy Montclair

Darcy Montclair's mother was born in South Carolina near Charleston in 1736 and sold to the Montclairs as a young girl. As with most slaves of the period, she was given the last name of her owner. She worked as a house slave until she died in 1758. Darcy's father was bought off the boat as a 13-year-old boy who survived the ocean voyage chained in the hold of a slave ship in 1745.

Darcy was born in the winter of 1752 when his mother was 16. His father was killed while trying to escape in 1756 when Darcy was four. Darcy began working in the fields as a six-year-old. By age 27, he already felt old and stooped from a life of hard field work. Uneducated, but viewed as a wise, smart man by other slaves, Darcy tended to be quiet and reserved when any whites were near. Still, he burned with the same desire for freedom that sent his father running to his death.

Which Road to Freedom?

Jefferson Frederick Montclair flicked the reins of the pair of horses pulling his loaded wagon and squinted out into the fields through the late afternoon steam-bath haze. It was still May 1780, but it felt more like late July. Out on the open road he sang to the horses as they plodded along the dirt roads of northeastern South Carolina. But he always stopped singing as he neared the plantation where he had been a slave all his life so as not to offend any of the white folks with his off-key warbling.

"Hmmmm-ummm!" he muttered, dabbing the sweat from his aged and wrinkled face. "This is surely one lousy day to be workin' in the fields. It surely is!" Jefferson Frederick was a house slave for the Montclairs, tending the horses and gardens near the main plantation house, and was often sent on supply runs in the wagon. It gave him the important position of "news gatherer" for the ramshackle community of Montclair slaves.

The late afternoon sun filtered through a tall line of cottonwood trees on the west side of the indigo fields, casting long, much-appreciated shadows across the workers toiling through the endless rows of plants.

Squinting into the sun, Jefferson Frederick whistled and clicked and gazed into the fields until several of the field hands turned to look in his direction. Then he stood on his buckboard seat and stretched both hands high above his curly white hair. It looked to any whites like a simple stretch at the end of a long ride. To the field hands it was a signal meaning there was news to share.

"See that?" whispered Darcy Montclair to Sampson and Clara, working near him. "Jefferson Frederick's got news."

"See *what*?" replied Sampson. "All I see is blisters and sweat."

"I seen the *signal*. There's news tonight."

"I didn't see no signal," said Clara, a fierce cement block of a woman.

"Quiet!" yelled Bufford Clayton from his horse. Bufford's eyes were always hidden in the deep shadow under his wide-brimmed hat. "Quit yammering and get back to work!"

"Don't you shush me, Bufford Clayton," snapped Clara, rising from her weeding crouch. "I was just checkin' on how they'se holdin' up in the heat."

Clara was the only slave who could get away with talking back to the plantation's harsh overseer. Twice they had had run-ins. Twice she had clawed his face, leaving deep scars. On both occasions Mr. Montclair had laughed at his overseer, saying that, if he couldn't handle a mere female slave, maybe he should find a new job. But he had also refused to allow Bufford to lay a hand on Clara in retribution.

With a final "Back to work!" Bufford spurred his horse and trotted down the row.

"I'm tellin' you. It's *big* news tonight. I seen the signal," repeated Darcy with a knowing nod. Darcy was considered a wise "thinker" by the Montclair community of 26 slaves. Aunt Bea, the cook, was the final authority, but everyone listened closely when Darcy spoke.

As final chores were finished and darkness settled over the line of huts that bordered the swamp defining the northern edge of the Montclair plantation, the Montclair slaves eagerly gathered for news. Jefferson Frederick sat as tall and important on a tree stump as his withered old body would allow, soaking in every moment of his time on center stage. "As you may know, I rode all the way over to Camden . . . "

"Shhh!" hissed Aunt Bea. "Wait for Mary to go back to the big house."

"But Mary's a sweet chile," said Sampson. "I like Mary."

"But she's a *white* child. That's fine for playin' with Clover and Sunflower. But what she hears, she'll tell her daddy. And don't you know, he probably sends her—on purpose—out here to spy on us."

With Mary skipping back to the main house at her mother's call, Jefferson Frederick resumed. "I rode clear over to Camden for supplies today, and that town is surely abuzz today. It surely is! See, I was pickin' up a load of . . . "

"The *news*," interrupted Darcy. "Tell us the *news*."

Jefferson Frederick dramatically cleared his throat. "As I was sayin', Camden is surely abuzz! Word was being whispered and shouted all over. The British have captured Charleston. They surely have."

"Well, I'll be!" exclaimed Darcy and several others in the tight circle.

"I heared the British was *losing* the war," said Cleevis, the thick-armed blacksmith. "Does this mean they's all-of-a-sudden winnin'?"

All eyes turned back to Jefferson Frederick for interpretation. He squirmed on his stump. "It just means the British have captured Charleston. That's what it means."

"It means," said Darcy, "that the war has stepped into South Carolina."

Many of the adults nodded in the near darkness. "But what does *that* mean?" pressed Sampson. "I don't want no trouble *here*."

"It means a chance for freedom is hangin' so close in the air you can smell it," continued Darcy.

"You be careful with your wild ideas, Darcy Montclair," cautioned Aunt Bea, arms folded over her ample chest. "You lived your whole life in these same fields and you don't know the whole world."

"I know this war is about freedom," said Darcy. "And I know that when the war comes near, the chance for freedom comes right along with it, waitin' for someone to snatch it up."

"War this. War that," huffed Clara. "I heared *talk* of war and British Redcoats, but I never seen any of it. The only war I *seen* is with Bufford Clayton. Whites is whites an' blacks is blacks. *That's* the war."

"I heared somethin' else," announced Jefferson Frederick. All eyes turned back. All mouths hushed. "Two slaves on the Clifford Plantation ran away to the Redcoats and the British let them join the army and made them free."

"I *told* you freedom was ridin' close enough to grab it!" squealed Darcy.

"If the British win will they set all slaves free?" asked Sampson.

"I guess," answered Cleevis. "Anyway, I heared some white men worryin' 'bout that exact thing."

"Ain't true. Ain't true!" snapped Aunt Bea. "Here's the way I heared it in the big house. The British and some Americans are fightin' to keep things the way they was."

"We surely don't want that," interrupted Jefferson Frederick.

Aunt Bea continued, "And other Americans is fightin' to make things different."

"You mean, 'free'," said Darcy.

"No. I only said 'different.' But lots of them folks got slaves, theirselves. So I figure they don't mean any different when it comes to us."

"Then what does the war mean?" asked Sampson. "It sounds the same either way."

Darcy insisted, "I'm tellin' you. Helpin' the British is the road to freedom, an' bein' free is all that matters."

Cleevis shook his head. "That's true only if your master fights *against* the British." Everyone stared questioningly at Cleevis. "Hey, I heared plenty of things at the blacksmith forge when white folks stops in to fix a wagon wheel or horseshoe."

Sampson asked, "Which is Master Montclair—fightin' for the British or against the British?"

A moment of silence followed before Sally, a 16-year-old house servant, answered. "I know." Sally was shy and silent, as if afraid of the whole world, her eyes always cast down toward floor or ground. But she heard more of their master's conversations than anyone because she served in the big house. "He's called a Whig and he's in the Patriot militia. He's *against* the British."

Darcy's eyes gleamed in the dark. "There it is, then. Help the British and we're free."

"*If* they win the war," cautioned Aunt Bea.

"They already took Charleston," argued Darcy. "What else is there to take? They must be close to winning already. If we help fast, we'll be free fast."

"But how do we help?" demanded Clara. "Kill Bufford and the Montclairs?"

"Naw!" answered Aunt Bea. "If we did that, white folks 'round here would surely kill us all."

Darcy rubbed his chin, deep in thought. "We's good as free if we can jus' do . . . do something . . . "

"But what?"

Seven-year-old Clover had wandered into the circle after Mary had gone back to the big house. "What's 'free'?"

Aunt Bea laughed. " 'Free,' chile, is when you can do whatever you want and no one can order you or beat you or whip you or sell you."

"Am I free?"

"No, chile, we's all slaves. We's owned by the Montclairs."

Clover thought for a second. "Can I *be* free, then, if I want?"

Darcy answered, "Maybe tomorrow you can, Clover. I's workin' on it. Maybe tomorrow."

The next night Jefferson Frederick returned from delivering a load of flour and tobacco to the small river town of Wexaws with even bigger news. "The Continentals is all confused and discombobulated. They surely is! These soldiers come down from Virginia and North Carolina and four days ago they marched through Camden headin' south. Now word is that they got theirselves turned right around and tomorrow will march right back through Wexaws headin' north."

"What's it mean?" asked Sampson.

"It jus' mean that they is heading north. That's all it means!"

Darcy said, "It means the war is almost over. The British is winnin' and the Continentals is runnin' away. We got to help the British fast or we'll miss our chance to makes ourselves free."

"Maybe we can run away in the confusion," Sampson suggested.

Darcy shook his head. "My Daddy tried to run. He only got 20 miles 'fore they caught him. I think he was already dead from the beatin' 'fore they dragged him back here to be hanged. He was so broken an' bloody. . . . No. We ain't runnin'. We're helpin' the British so they'll set us free."

"Help *how*?" demanded Clara.

The gleam of an idea sparkled in Darcy's eyes. "Jefferson Frederick, did you hear where the Continentals was goin'?"

"Word was, they was surely goin' to camp for a day or so in the wide fields on the north side of Wexaws and then skedaddle on north."

"When will they get there?"

"They gets there tomorrow night."

"That's it!" declared Darcy. "I'll lead the British to where the Continentals is, an' they'll be so grateful to me for helpin' end the war, they'll set us all free."

"How you gonna find the British?" Sampson asked.

"Simple. I head south and looks for a bunch of white folks wearin' red coats."

"How you gonna lead them anywhere?" asked Cleevis. "You never been off this plantation. Jefferson Frederick is the only one who's seen the roads and places."

"Jefferson Frederick is too old to go. 'Sides, I've heard all his stories, so I got pictures of every place out there locked tight in my mind. I'll find it."

Aunt Bea folded her arms across her chest. "And how is you gonna get off this plantation without bein' missed and hunted as a runaway?"

Darcy laughed. "I think I needs a day of bed rest."

Everyone glared skeptically at Darcy.

"You'll see. I got it all figured out in my mind."

Aunt Bea said, "You jus' be sure your mind isn't figuring out a mistake that's gonna get us all in a heap of trouble!"

There were many ways to get whipped and beaten as a slave: refuse to work, threaten a white, sabotage plantation operations, run away, steal even the tiniest item, show disrespect to any white, even work too slowly. Most of the Montclair slaves had been beaten and whipped, but none severely since Darcy's father's failed escape attempt almost 20 years before. A little beating was supposed to be good for slaves. It kept them in their place. It kept them in line. But what Darcy had in mind broke almost every known rule and could easily get him beaten to death.

All morning Darcy had rehearsed his plan in his mind. For hours he had tried to find the courage to put it into motion. In the early afternoon, with the heat waves shimmering up from the fields, Clara was weeding next to Darcy. "Where is your big plan, Darcy?" she hissed. "I don't see you prancin' out to be the hero and set us free."

"Patience, woman! These things take timing."

"Humph! Don't take no 'timing.' Jus' take courage, which I's afraid you ain't got."

Darcy's face contorted in anger. "Hush up, woman!" He raised his hoe with his right hand and slammed it down as hard as he could onto his left. The hoe blade whistled down, slicing into the back of his hand, splintering bones, cutting tendons, shredding skin.

Darcy gasped and screamed. His face paled. Blood poured out to stain the red South Carolina dirt.

Bufford Clayton reigned in his horse and galloped down the row, pushing his way through the cluster of slaves gathered around Darcy's crumpled figure lying on the ground. "Get up, you!" he growled, snatching his leather whip from his saddle horn.

"My hand, suh. I done broke my hand."

Crack! The whip lashed out, catching Darcy full across the back. His eyes bulged and he gasped in pain.

"That's for being a clumsy fool." Crack! The whip lashed out again, slicing through Darcy's shirt and raising an ugly red welt on his back. "That's for damaging Mr. Montclair's property. That hand belongs to him."

"One day's rest, suh. Jus' one day to mend it and I'll be back in the fields doin' my work, suh."

Bufford sneered, "You probably hurt your self on purpose to get a day off. I ought to . . . "

"No, suh! I wouldn't do such an awful thing, suh. You knows I'm a good worker, suh."

Clara stepped forward and planted herself between Darcy and Bufford. "Let me tend his wound afore he bleeds to death and the master takes after you for lettin' a perfectly good slave die!"

Bufford snarled, "Get him out o' my sight," and spurred his horse on down the row.

With his bloody hand wrapped in the remnants of his shirt, Darcy and Clara walked back to the slaves row of shacks. "Only two lashes," giggled Darcy. "I told you I'd do it! We're as good as free!"

At sunset Darcy scampered like a deer through the swamp, circling east and then south away from the plantation. He had a little food wrapped in a bandanna and his left hand wrapped thick in gauze. Through the quiet night he used the stars to guide him. After sunrise he used the sun.

Twice he asked for directions, once of a group of free blacks living in hand-made shacks along a swampy lake and once, while hiding in the bushes along the edge of a plantation, of some slaves trudging toward the fields to begin the day's work.

Before the sun had climbed above the trees, Darcy felt the road under him vibrate from the distant rumble of moving horses and men.

"An army's comin'. I *knowed* it'd work!" sang Darcy as he trotted down the road toward the growing din. Then he froze. Uniformed riders approached, a column of well over 100—wearing green coats, not red.

An apple-sized lump tightened in Darcy's throat. What if these were the Continentals instead of the British?

"Out of the way!" yelled a horseman as they approached Darcy, standing frozen with indecision in the road. His mind whirled, realizing that if he guessed wrong, he would die. How could he word his question to find out, without *being* found out?

" 'Scuse me, suh. But is you chasin' or bein' chased?"

"Get out of the road!" the rider yelled, reigning his horse to a stop—which stopped the whole column.

"I got information, suh."

A man on the next horse eyed Darcy, sizing him up. "We're chasing a regiment of Continentals. What kind of information could you have?"

Darcy's face spread into a beaming grin. "You's British, then, suh?"

A lone rider galloped along the stopped line of riders toward the front. "What's the reason for this delay?"

"Colonel Tarleton, sir," saluted the men in front as they pointed at Darcy.

This man, young, muscular, and "pretty" looking, wore tight white pants and an ornate red coat with a monstrous—almost comical—purple plume billowing out of the top of his hat.

Darcy sighed. A red coat. "I knows where the Continentals is, suh."

"Where?" sneered the Redcoat colonel with the plume.

"In the fields just past Wexaws, suh. Arrived there las' night and plannin' to stay for a day or so afore movin' on north."

"There, you see!" cried Colonel Tarleton, turning in his saddle to face his regiment of Tory riders. "The majority of Americans *want* British rule. I tell you, this *whole country* will rise up in loyal support of England once they see how fiercely we deal with rebels." He snapped his fingers at a lieutenant who had ridden up behind him. "Bring our new guide a horse and prepare for battle!"

To Darcy the column of Colonel Tarleton's Dragon Guards seemed to stretch for miles. Really, there were only 700 in this infamously savage New York and Pennsylvania Tory unit of cavalry, a small part of General Cornwallis's British army.

Bouncing clumsily on his mount, Darcy's eyes filled with wonder at every new sight he saw—a river, a town, endless miles of other plantations, each with a community of slaves that looked just like his own.

By that mid-afternoon, the 29th of May, 1780, Darcy stood in open-mouthed fascination as the lines of Dragon Guards—some on foot as tight-packed infantry, some mounted as cavalry—charged with blood-curdling cries and wails against Colonel Buford's 400-man Virginia militia. Clouds of smoke enveloped the lines. Volleys of musket fire roared like thunder. Men on both sides began to drop. The ground shook.

"Lord have mercy," whispered Darcy. "I didn't think a war could look like *this*!"

Surrounded and outnumbered, Colonel Buford sent out a messenger with a white flag of truce. Both sides momentarily ceased fire. The Continentals laid down their muskets.

"Now the fun begins," called Colonel Tarleton. "Come, Darcy, and see how the British treat rebels!"

Tarleton raced to the front on his horse, sword drawn. "Bayonets!" he yelled. "Charge!" The messenger with the flag of truce was hacked to death in three swift swings of the colonel's saber.

The Dragon Guard ripped into the Virginians like a tiger pouncing on a helpless squirrel. Now unarmed men with hands raised in surrender were sliced to ribbons. Cries of "Quarter! Quarter!" [an old English word for "mercy"] were answered with vicious jabs and hacks by flashing Dragon sabers and bayonets.

Not one of the surrendering Americans survived the butchery. Many were trampled and killed after sinking defenseless to their knees. Tarleton's Dragon Guard hacked the life out of every man on the field.

Darcy stood rooted in horror. "Lord have mercy. Lord have mercy," he mumbled. "Is *this* how the British treats folks? Americans don't even treat *slaves* like this. . . . What has I got ourselves into?"

"Will you join the British army and become a free man?" asked the colonel, casually wiping blood from his blade.

Wide-eyed with terror, Darcy stuttered, "Ahhh, n-n-no, suh. I got to get back."

Tarleton shrugged. "Very well. But tell everyone what you saw here, Darcy. Tell the whole South what Tarleton's Dragon Guard does to those who oppose us!"

"I will, suh. I will surely do that!"

Sick at heart, still tormented by the screams of a hundred dying men, Darcy stumbled and jogged back to familiar swamps and trails and to the Montclair plantation, arriving an hour after dark. His tortured mind was flooded with images of the nightmare butchery of the British. His hands refused to stop shaking.

In fits and starts, Darcy poured out the story of his adventure, struggling to find words to describe the savage cruelty of Tarleton's soldiers. The circle of blacks listened in open-mouthed, spellbound fascination through every moment of Darcy's brief taste of freedom. He ended by saying, "You don't *ever* want British freedom—you get hacked to death by British freedom. An' you don't ever want them British to come here. They kills men jus' for surrendering and dropping to their knees!"

"I tol' you I didn't want no trouble bein' stirred up," growled Sampson.

"An' I tol' *you* you didn't know everything in the world," said Aunt Bea.

"What we gonna do now?" asked Cleevis.

Aunt Bea answered. "I knows what I's gonna do. I's goin to bed. I got to work tomorrow."

Young Clover asked, "Will I be free tomorrow?"

"No, not tomorrow, chile," answered Darcy. "Not tomorrow. But I'm workin' on it."

Aftermath

Tarleton's victory over Buford at Wexaws on May 29, 1780, was little more than a skirmish. Still, Tarleton's brutality created bitter hatred of the British in many southerners and actually helped to rally the population *for* the Revolution. "Tarleton's quarters" became a Patriot slogan meaning "show no mercy." A surge in enlistment in Patriot militia through late 1780 could be partly traced to Tarleton's brutality.

Few slaves were freed as a direct result of the Revolutionary War, and those few were almost all males who served in various army units. Both Tories and Whigs in the South were terrified of a possible slave uprising. Many senior officials on both sides were reluctant to free even the slaves who actually fought in the war effort. It was embarrassingly clear that "Liberty" in the Revolutionary War sense was never meant for blacks.

Follow-up Questions and Activities

1. **What Do You Know?**

   - Darcy had to find his way over strange terrain with no maps, street signs, or directions and where he couldn't ask anyone for help. How did he do it even though he had never left the plantation? What information did he have?

   - Why did the British think that the slaves would side with them? Why was it important to the British to have the support and service of blacks?

   - Who was Tarleton chasing in this story, and why was this battle important?

   - How did Colonel Tarleton gain the title "Butcher" Tarleton?

   - What did the word *quarter* mean? Where did it come from?

2. **Finding Out More**. Following are four important topics from this story for you to research in the library and on the Internet. The reference sources at the back of this book will help you get started.

   - How could slaves in separate and isolated communities communicate and share news with no television, radio, satellites, phones, faxes, Internet, computers, newspapers, books, or letters? Research communication systems developed by American slaves. How did slave communications compare with non-slave communications?

   - Colonel Tarleton was one of the most colorful of all British commanders during the Revolutionary War. Research his life and career. What did he do after the war? What had he done before it?

   - Research the slave trade that brought African slaves to America. Why was it called the "triangle trade?" Who started that famous trade route? How many Africans were captured and enslaved? What parts of Africa were they from?

   - Research the role of slaves in the southern economy. What jobs did they perform? For which crops was abundant, cheap (slave) labor essential? Which of those crops developed first? When did cotton become the dominant crop?

3. **Make It Real**

   - How would you make a trip similar to the one Darcy had to make? What information would you want to know? Write down exactly what you would say if you had to tell someone how to get from school to your house. What kinds of information did you write down? Do you think that the words you wrote could really guide someone to your doorstep?

- Research slavery in the Colonies in the mid-eighteenth century: the origins, slaves' living arrangements, their jobs. Then imagine that you are a plantation slave in South Carolina and write a detailed essay describing a day in your life and in the life of your plantation. What job do you have on the plantation? How old are you? What do you typically eat? Who cooks it? Where do you live and sleep? How many other slaves are on the plantation with you? Are any of them directly from Africa, or were they all born in America? Where were you born? What are your hopes and fears? How is your health?

4. **Points to Ponder**

- Do you think it was acceptable for the Founding Fathers to fight a war for liberty and freedom while many of them owned slaves? Can you think of why they never considered the inconsistency of wanting to be free while not granting freedom themselves?

- The slave trade flourished in America partly because shipping slaves from Africa to America was part of an easy and profitable triangular route ships could follow. Make a list of the products that were carried along each leg of this shipping route. If the ocean current flowed the other way around the north Atlantic Ocean, do think African slaves would still have been brought to America?

Swamp Fox Hunt
Southern Patriot Guerrilla Fighters, 1780–1781

Swamp Fox's camp

At a Glance

In early 1780 the British army and navy captured the two major southern coastal cities, Savannah and Charleston. The main army moved freely up and down the roads. Tory bands of thugs had government power and rampaged unchecked across most of South Carolina and parts of Georgia and North Carolina. Patriot resistance in the South seemed to have totally collapsed.

But, like swarms of pesky mosquitoes, several Patriot militia units harassed the British supply line and continually nipped at the British heels. These small units never offered real battle, never faced the British in the open. They used hit-and-run guerrilla tactics and were monumentally successful. They slowed Cornwallis's movement north and created time for Patriot forces to gather and later win major victories at Kings Mountain and Cowpens.

These seemingly insignificant guerrilla units forced British General Cornwallis to abandon his original plan for conquering America from the South.

The best known of those Patriot militia guerrilla fighters were Colonel Thomas Sumpter and Colonel Francis Marion, called "the Swamp Fox" by Colonel Tarleton, whom Marion tormented through the important and precious months of late 1780 and early 1781. This story describes several of the Swamp Fox's early raids.

Meet Francis Marion

Francis Marion was descended from Huguenots (French Protestants) who fled to America at the beginning of the eighteenth century. Francis grew up on a small plantation in Bell Isle, South Carolina. He was a pale, frail, slight man with a swaying limp and an eagle nose. All who knew him said that Francis was a man of few words who hated military formalities and never wore a uniform.

Marion joined the army as a young man and was a veteran of the campaign against the Cherokee, where he was known as a cunning planner and fierce fighter. He served as a captain in the Continental Army under Colonel Lincoln, who defended Charleston. Lincoln's entire army was captured except for a few wounded sent from the city, including Francis Marion, whose broken ankle saved him, even though it never properly healed and created his lifelong limp.

Swamp Fox Hunt

fternoon rains had rumbled through the swamp region of northeast South Carolina, but shafts of the late afternoon's slanting light had broken through the clouds. The 25 horsemen racing down a narrow trail that wound into the swamp's interior hardly kicked up any dust as they sped by. The men on these horses didn't look like soldiers, but rather like country backwoodsmen. They passed in a swarm of buckskin coats and leather leggings and black caps.

These men raced with urgency, with necessity, but not with fear on this steamy afternoon in mid-August 1780. On the contrary, they laughed and whooped as they sped into the swamp. They were being chased in a deadly game of tag, but it was a game they knew they could win. The lead rider, wearing only an outdated helmet of the 2nd South Carolina Infantry to indicate that he was both in the army and an officer, raised his hand to stop the band.

Oak and pine trees shouldered close to the trail. Long beards of Spanish moss draped from tree limbs waving in the afternoon winds kicked up by growling thunderhead clouds.

"We'll split here," said the officer, Colonel Francis Marion. "Eight go with Captain Horry. Loop around past Lynch's Creek and enter the swamp from that side. The rest stay with me and swing up to ford the Pee Dee River into the swamp. Let's see if Colonel Tarleton's northern Tories can follow."

The buckskinned ruffians grinned and saluted, then spurred their horses and galloped down diverging paths. Anyone who saw Colonel Francis Marion would never have guessed him to be a tough, battle-hardened guerrilla fighter. He was short and frail and walked with a pronounced limp from a broken ankle that never healed. But Marion was not only a fighter. He was the one-man leader and genius behind the guerrilla movement that was systematically undercutting Cornwallis's iron grip on South Carolina.

The first distant sounds of Colonel Tarleton's 400-Tory cavalry rumbled in the distance. Tarleton had become the most hated man in the South for his repeated acts of butchery. He had personally sworn to bring down Marion's brigade and to bring back Marion's head on the end of his sword.

Marion waved his helmet over his head and sped off into the swamps.

A lone young man, stocky and freckle-faced, hiking along the same trail with bedroll over one shoulder and musket, canteen, and powder horn jangling over the other, waved both arms to stop the riders. "Are you boys with Marion's brigade?" he called.

"Who wants to know?" answered Marion.

"Joseph Hanley, sir. I've come to join up."

"That so?" answered the colonel. "Why should we show you where Marion's camp is?"

"Colonel," muttered one of the other riders. "We should go *now*. I can hear Tarleton's men gettin' closer."

Joseph Hanley answered, "Major Weymas, one of Tarleton's men, burned my house and my barn and run off my cattle. I never did nothin' to them. But I sure plan to now!"

Colonel Marion nodded to the rider behind him, who extended an arm and lifted young Joseph onto his horse.

They rode another half mile before the colonel stopped. "This is the perfect spot," chuckled Marion. Mists hung low over the swamp; muck and ooze stretched as far as the eye could see; the sluggish black waters teemed with alligators and would frighten anyone but a swamp native. Impenetrable nettles and brambles, rotting vegetation, twisting trees with ghost-like beards of Spanish moss, and arm-thick water snakes made it the most dismal, forbidding spot on Earth.

"We'll cross here where's it good and soft. Two stay with me to watch how the British take to our swamps. The rest back to camp."

The horses, used to the muck of the swamp, lightly eased into and through the sluggish black water. Colonel Marion's horse, as always, led. The other horses followed where the colonel's horse showed them it was safe to tread.

Colonel Marion dismounted on a raised patch of dry ground, well hidden behind thick brambles and a thick tangle of trees and vines. The remaining 13 riders galloped along well-known paths to Snow Island, a dry expanse of land in the middle of the swamp surrounded by the meeting of the Pee Dee River and Lynch's Creek. The horse carrying young Joseph Hanley stopped with Marion.

Even in the swamps, 400 horsemen rattle the ground. Marion felt Tarleton's approach before he heard it. Then the green uniform coats of the Tory cavalry unit appeared, skirting the twisting river channel.

"Duck down, boy," Marion whispered. "Don't move." He turned to the other two men. "Keep one hand on the horses' muzzles. They must stay quiet." The men nodded. Both they and the horses knew the drill well.

A lead Tory scout dismounted and peered at the ground and then saluted Colonel Tarleton (easily recognized by the monstrous plume on his hat). "Sir, I think some of them crossed about here. But there's been so much water on the trail the past half mile, it's hard to tell. They could have crossed anywhere."

Tarleton slapped his thigh with a riding crop in anger. "No! He will not slip away to hide in his swamp again! We're too close on his heels this time. I can smell it. One squad cross here. See if there is a trail on the far bank. The rest will follow with me along this bank."

"If there *is* a far bank in this cursed swamp," grumbled one of the riders.

Colonel Tarleton's riding crop lashed out to smack the soldier's shoulder. "Silence!"

"Sorry, sir."

Ten soldiers bravely slid and stumbled down the bank into the murky waters on their horses. Two horses stumbled into thick muck and began to sink. One bucked, its rider sailing like a flying trapeze artist into the black and stagnant stream. A thick water moccasin hissed as it swam away from where he splashed. One horse sank too deep in the mud to lift its feet and slowly sank out of sight and drowned. Its terrified rider thrashed through the water and scrambled onto shore.

Several horses and riders panicked at the sight of an alligator sliding below the water's black surface. The riders brutally spurred their horses back toward shore, afraid that they would feel the gator's jaws close around one of their submerged feet.

Horses on shore whinnied and nervously pranced. Riders struggled to control their mounts. Chaos reigned at the water's edge as riders struggling to get out of the water pulled others in.

Tarleton thwacked his riding crop against his thigh. "Enough! He's long gone by now. It's getting late. I want to be out of this . . . this dismal swamp by sunset. We'll head back." He turned to a captain. "I want guard posts at every known entrance to this swamp." He turned and screamed at the swamp. "You may be a swamp fox, but I will have you yet!"

As Tarleton's cavalry regiment trotted off, Marion rose. "Swamp fox . . . swamp fox. I like that."

Sliding out of the saddle in the middle of camp, Francis Marion said to young Joseph, "Welcome to the Snow Island home of the bushwhackers."

Joseph gazed around the clearing in the dense Snow Island trees and its ramshackle collection of lean-tos and tents. "Where are the rest of your men?"

Marion scanned the camp. "We're all here except for four sentries, all 75 of us." Then he called out. "Captain Horry, please show the new man around camp." He turned without another word and marched off to check on his men and review supply sheets and horse feed.

As they began the tour, Joseph asked, "Did I do something to make the colonel mad?"

"No," answered Captain Horry. "He's never been much of a talker. That's already the most he's said to one person in a week."

Joseph asked, "How can you battle Cornwallis's 3,000 regulars and 2,000 Tory militia with only 75?"

Horry stretched and smiled. "We only fight 25 at a time."

"But you were being chased by 400."

"Today our brigade of 75 raided a British supply detachment at Briton Neck. We killed 20 Brits and destroyed their supply depot—of course, we took enough powder and shot for ourselves. When we heard Tarleton was on our trail with 400, the colonel let a few riders be seen to draw a company of Tories down a trail into an ambush. We killed 20 more from our hidden spots in trees and behind bushes. Then we skedaddled back here as Tarleton's main body thundered after us."

"That's how we do it. We don't fight the army all at once, and we don't fight *like* an army. We attack the British supply line. Cornwallis and his 4,000-man army are running around well north of here, but can only function if supplies flow up from Charleston. We attack that supply line."

Marion met Joseph as the men gathered at the mess tent for dinner. "Tell me about Major Weymas."

Joseph spat in disgust before answering. "Major Weymas's Tory spies gave him a list of suspected Patriots in this part of South Carolina. On Tarleton's orders, Weymas burned the houses, barns, and fields of every person on this list. He's seized all our livestock, killed any of the men he found at home, and run off the women and children. I never helped either side. I'm no Patriot, just a farmer. But Weymas burned my house and fields anyway. Now I'll be on any side that kills British!"

"Then you've come to the right place," said Marion, extending his hand. "Join us for dinner."

Dinner at Marion's camp day after day consisted of boiled beef and sweet potatoes served on oak-bark plates—no bread, no butter. All sat on logs and ate from their laps. The only exceptions were after raids that brought in stocks of stolen British supplies.

Marion, as always, sipped water mixed with vinegar from his canteen. It was an old habit that protected him from drinking bad water. Many in his brigade had picked up the habit out of respect for their commander. "You'll get used to it," laughed several bushwhackers, seeing Joseph's face turn up like sour lemons at his first sip.

After dinner Marion and his other officers huddled together, squatting on the sandy soil. Marion drew maps and diagrams in the sand with a stick.

"What are they planning?" Joseph asked another man.

"The next raid, I suppose."

As the meeting ended, the officers rubbed out the diagrams with their feet.

"Scouts!" shouted Marion, who then huddled with four rugged-looking men while others cleaned up camp after the meal.

"What's the plan?" Joseph asked one of the officers.

"Scouts will ride out at first light to check two British supply camps, one at Tarcote and one at Shepherd's Ferry across the Black Mingo."

"That's near my farm," Joseph answered. "I know the Shepherd's Ferry Camp."

"Colonel," the officer shouted. "The new man lives near Shepherd's Ferry."

"Can you draw a map of the camp?" Marion asked, while other bushwhackers crowded around.

Joseph nodded and roughed out the small British camp with a stick.

"How many men?"

"About 25, commanded by a Captain Ball."

"Do they store powder and food?"

"Can't say, Colonel. They never let me see inside the storehouse."

Marion rubbed one fist into the other palm as he thought. "How long would it take us to get there?"

"I walked from there in just under two days. Probably three hours by horse once you clear the swamp."

Marion paced for a full minute, mulling over his plans. "Three scouts leave at first light to map Tarcote. Meet us at Shepherd's Ferry by mid-afternoon day after tomorrow. We'll rest here tomorrow and then see if we can hit two depots in one raid. That ought to steam Colonel Tarleton!"

"What about the guards Tarleton said he was going to post around the swamp?"

Marion just grunted. Captain Horry explained, "It would take 1,000 good men to block all the ways in and out of this swamp—and it would take *5,000* British and Tories!"

The men's chuckles died away as they heard the signal from a sentry that a rider was entering camp. By uniform he looked to be a Continental infantry captain. He asked for Colonel Marion, clicked his heels, and saluted.

"That's the most formal salute this camp ever saw," said Marion. The bushwhackers again chuckled.

The captain asked for a private meeting. He and Marion walked to the end of the camp and sat under a giant willow tree. Handing Marion a report, the captain said, "I'm afraid it's bad news."

The report described a battle at Camden, South Carolina, on August 16 between Cornwallis and General Gates's army of 3,000, the entire Continental Army for the South. The Continental Army had been crushed. No units of the army had escaped. All were either killed, captured, or scattered in tiny bands and squads trying to flee north. The report concluded by saying that Marion was the only Patriot resistance left in South Carolina and that the fate of the state, and maybe the entire Revolution, now depended on Marion's brigade alone.

"I'm Captain James, sir. I'd like to join your command," said the captain, saluting again.

"You may," Marion answered, "If you promise not to salute anymore."

Marion crumpled the report into a ball. "Tell no one of this."

"What will you do?" James asked.

Marion sighed and walked to the campfire so he could watch the wadded report burn. "We will do, Captain, what we do best. Fight and run. Fight and run. And survive until resistance can build a new army to oppose the British."

Just at first light on August 23, 1780, as the first birds were beginning to chatter in the trees, the Swamp Fox and his brigade rode out of camp.

Joseph Hanley rode next to Marion and acted as guide. By noon the brigade had crossed the Black Mingo and approached the east landing of Shepherd's Ferry.

"The ferry's too well guarded to cross there," Joseph reported. "But there's an old, unguarded bridge about a mile upstream."

Seventy wary horse soldiers clomped cross the bridge of loose wooden planks. Mid-span Marion stopped, listening to the horses' steps reverberating down the river. "Too loud," he hissed. "Walk your horses across."

But he feared that the enemy had already heard and been warned.

Marion split his tiny force into four groups. One group, as a decoy, would ride up to the front of the house that served as British headquarters and supply house. Two groups would dismount and circle through the woods, one approaching the British camp from each side. One group, with Marion, would remain in reserve and attack where needed.

Joseph Hanley rode with the decoys. Captain Horry led the group circling to the west. Captain Biltcher led the group circling east. All was quiet—too quiet—as the bushwhackers crept through the woods. The decoys reached the main house and found it deserted. Marion waited nervously on his horse. This was not going well. He was used to surprise attacks. He *depended* on quick surprise attacks. He couldn't afford pitched battles where the enemy had a chance to fire back. But this attack had the markings of being anything but a surprise.

Captain Horry's group reached a grassy field that led to the west side of the compound . . . and walked straight into an ambush. A volley of heavy fire poured into his men from British soldiers lying in the tall grass and crouching behind bushes.

"Everyone down!" Horry cried. "Return fire!" Before his group of bushwhackers dove to the grass, six fell, clutching mortal wounds. Captain Biltcher's men met no resistance sweeping in from the river side on the east and rushed across the open grass, yelling as they surged past the main house to assist Horry's stricken group. The decoys dismounted and joined Captain Biltcher's charge.

But the British did not surrender as hoped. They reformed and met the new attack with hot and heavy fire, refusing to buckle even though they were being attacked on two sides. Musket fire poured across the field at almost point-blank range. Sulfurous smoke billowed across the grass from the thick musket fire.

And now Marion's reserves attacked, screaming fierce battle cries as they thundered past the house and smashed into the rear of the British formation. The British resistance collapsed. Firing ceased. British muskets were flung down, British hands raised into the air. Captain Ball, their commander, lay dead on the field. So did 30 of his 40 men.

Captain James rushed up to Colonel Marion, waving his saber in elated joy. "What a glorious battle. We won!"

"No," answered Marion, sitting dejectedly on his horse. "We lost." Joseph Hanley sat on the grass near him, his coat stained red from an arm wound that would take a month to heal.

James was confused. "But the field is ours! They have surrendered. We won."

Marion sneered and shook his head. Captain Horry said, "The British have thousands and can easily afford to lose 40. We can't afford to lose even one. These open fights are not our way. This was a terrible loss."

Marion's three scouts galloped in, their horses' flanks covered in foamy sweat. The men were panting from their ride. "Tarleton has learned that you plan to attack this post and is riding hard to this camp, sir, with over 300. He's less than half an hour behind us."

Marion nodded. "Good."

"*Good*?" cried Captain James. "That's terrible. We have to leave."

"It's good because now I know where Tarleton is." Marion turned back to his scouts. "What of Tarcote?"

"The supply camp lies on a fork of the Black River, sir. It is very lightly guarded because Tarleton took most of the soldiers stationed there to ride here to trap you."

Marion smiled and nodded. "Perfect! Captain Biltcher, take five men and gather up all the horses at this station and all our extras from the fallen men. Ride south toward the swamps, leaving a heavy trail that even Colonel Tarleton can follow. At the edge of the swamps, release and scatter the horses. Then the five of you split up and singly work your way back to camp."

"Why release the horses?" asked Captain James.

Captain Biltcher leaned toward James and whispered, "Tarleton will pick up the trial of massed horses leaving this place and follow it to the swamp, where the trail will suddenly vanish, to his bitter frustration. Meanwhile you all will destroy his supply base at Tarcote."

Marion called to his men. "Wounded and prisoners ride with us. Ride softly from this place in small groups and reform just above the bridge. Take only the powder, shot, and food you can easily carry. Burn the rest."

"What will you do with the prisoners?" Joseph Hanley asked.

"Release them at Tarcote. I can't keep them and by then they will have no worthwhile information for Tarleton."

As silently as they arrived the bushwhackers melted back into the woods. Twenty minutes later, the ground shook as 300 Tory cavalry led by Colonel Tarleton arrived to see British dead sprawled across the field and the British supplies in flames.

One of his scouts picked up the trail of massed hoof prints heading south toward Marion's swamps. Tarleton didn't even wait to put out the fires. He raced his brigade south until, at the edge of the swamps, the trail of hoof prints mysteriously vanished into thin air.

Shortly thereafter, a messenger galloped up with the news that Marion had destroyed the supply base at Tarcote and stolen most of the food and ammunition. Shouting curses of rage, Tarleton raced his weary men and horses back toward Tarcote on the Black River near where it joins the upper Santee. But by the time he reached that destroyed base, the bushwhackers were resting comfortably on Snow Island, eating their fill of stolen British cuisine.

Aftermath

Marion's guerrilla war kept Cornwallis from pushing north into North Carolina and Virginia. The British had to regularly send more and more men back south to protect their supply lines. These delays gave the Patriots time to muster new forces, including the Overmountain Boys, who smashed British forces at Kings Mountain. Marion also gave Congress time to appoint Nathaniel Greene to take command of the southern army and for him to begin a year-long game of cat and mouse that depleted Cornwallis's forces and stamina and drove him to Yorktown hoping for the British fleet to resupply him with men and equipment.

Marion and his guerrilla tactics didn't win the war, but they kept the British from winning it in the South until forces could be gathered who could force final victory. Marion's brigade attacked and defeated British forces at over a dozen posts through late 1780 and 1781 and helped drive the British back to Charleston and free South Carolina. Marion is considered a South Carolina state hero and was elected to the state Senate, where he served until he died in 1795. One national forest, several lakes, and over 40 towns and counties are named in his honor.

Follow-up Questions and Activities

1. **What Do You Know?**

   - Was Colonel Marion the only guerrilla fighter trying to slow down the British advance through the Carolinas? What other Patriot units existed in South Carolina?

   - What did Marion's guerrilla fighting accomplish? Why was it important?

   - What did American guerrillas try to attack? Why?

   - The British could have easily defeated Marion's guerrillas in battle. Why weren't any British units able to force the American guerrilla units to stand and fight?

2. **Finding Out More**. Following are six important topics from this story for you to research in the library and on the Internet. The reference sources at the back of this book will help you get started.

- Marion was a French Huguenot. Research the history of this interesting group. Where did they come from? Why? When did they immigrate to America? Where did they settle? Did they immigrate to other countries as well?

- Francis Marion is one of America's most famous and successful guerrilla fighters. Research his life and accomplishments. Where did he come from? What did he do both before and after the war? How many towns, counties, and other places are named for him?

- Colonel Thomas Sumpter was another significant American guerrilla commander operating in South Carolina during 1780 and 1781. (Fort Sumpter, where the Civil War began, was named for this guerrilla commander.) Research his life and military career. Why did he decide to lead a guerrilla brigade instead of joining the main Continental Southern Army in North Carolina?

- Research guerrilla fighting and famous guerrilla fighters throughout history. Why is this approach called "guerrilla fighting?" How many guerrilla fighters have been successful? Why did they choose to conduct guerrilla campaigns? What causes did they support? How many of these fighters became heroes to the general population of their countries?

- Marion and other guerrillas typically attacked the supply lines and bases of their enemy. What supplies did an eighteenth-century British army regularly need? How much of each kind of supply did they need? How did they get it? What happened if they temporarily ran out of one of these supply items?

- British Generals Clinton and Cornwallis instituted a number of policies for the South during the summer of 1780. Many of these policies backfired and turned southerners against the British and greatly increased Patriot strength in the South. Research these failed British policies. What did the British hope that they would accomplish? What did they *really* accomplish? Why did they fail?

3. **Make It Real**

- Write an essay comparing Marion's guerrilla tactics against the British with the tactics used by the Viet Cong guerrillas against the American army during the Vietnam conflict. How are they the same? How are they different?

- Create a map of all the places attacked by Francis Marion's raiders. Now find Snow Island in the Pee Dee River swamp. How far from his base was Marion willing to venture on a raid? Why not travel farther? Can you figure out why the British were never able to find Marion's camp?

4. **Points to Ponder**

- What is the difference between guerrilla fighters and criminals, outlaws, or bandits? *Is* there a difference? Does it depend on who is making the decision or on which side wins?

- Should guerrilla fighters have to follow the same rules of conduct and constraints that regular armies do? What makes guerrilla fighters different than an army? Should there be a different ethical standard for guerrillas than for soldiers?

- Do you think Colonel Marion was more worried about British forces or about local Tories? Why?

Revolutionary Revenge
Brutal Southern Civil War, 1779–1782

Small citizen battle in South Carolina

At a Glance

In 1780 the military activity of the Revolutionary War headed south with attacks on the ports of Savannah and Charleston. But the civilian elements of the war had been smoldering there since 1776. Early Loyalist/Tory losses in 1775 and 1776 in the South meant that the Patriots controlled the South from the beginning of the war through early 1780.

Then the British took Savannah. In May Charleston fell. In June, General Gates's Southern Continental Army was destroyed at Camden. Dominance flip-flopped. Now Tories and Loyalists controlled South Carolina, and many of them wanted revenge.

Southern Patriots believed the war was lost and over. They just wanted to go back to the way things had been, live in peace, and try to make some money. En masse they were willing to abandon the Patriot cause and concede the war. All seemed to go smoothly for about two months. But by September, Britain had decided to promote a "join us or else" policy and revoked its policy of tolerance. The British military also placed Tories in positions of authority and power. The stage was set for a bloodbath of revenge—Southern style. This is a story of revenge piled on top of revenge.

Meet Isaiah McPhearson and Jake Dawkins

The grandparents of Isaiah McPhearson and Jake Dawkins immigrated from Ireland and settled in South Carolina (inland from Charleston) in 1720. Their daughter married a Dawkins (of Scottish descent) and moved inland to Greenwood, South Carolina, in 1731. These Dawkinses were uneducated, subsistence farmers. Jake was the fourth of eight children. Only four were still alive in 1780: Jake, two sisters who both lived in Spartanburg, and a brother who was with the Tory militia serving under Cornwallis.

Jake still lived on the original farm with his wife and two children. He also ran a small livery service for the Greenwood community. Jake usually wore a stained leather apron and smelled of horses and horse manure. His two oldest boys were already out on their own. One was reported to be a highwayman. The other, William, or Billie, squatted a farm near his father's. Both sons followed after their father and were strong Loyalists.

The McPhearson side of the family moved into Charleston and became merchants, slowly working their way up both the economic and social ladders of that bustling port city. Isaiah went to school in Charleston but never to college. In 1775 Isaiah moved to Greenwood to escape the violence he foresaw coming to major cities. A supporter of the principles of the Revolution, but not of violence, he owned the mercantile in Greenwood as well as a bake shop and was a prosperous man with a wife and four daughters. One daughter was grown and living in Greenwood with her new husband, a captain in the Patriot militia. The other three still lived at home with Isaiah and enjoyed a gracious southern life of ease.

Revolutionary Revenge

T he 14th of September, 1780, blossomed into a sultry-hot mid-summer day in western South Carolina. Still, the four men huddled together in the house of Isaiah McPhearson shivered and wiped a cold and chilling sweat from their faces as they talked in hushed whispers.

Isaiah McPhearson's house was a fashionable, two-story dwelling built of stone and mortar, with wide, well-maintained lawns, nestled at the edge of Greenwood, South Carolina. Six miles away sat Fort 96, one of the British garrisons established by Lord Cornwallis in June when British forces had swept all Patriot resistance from the colony.

Back in June each of these four men, all active Whigs and American Patriots, had admitted that the war seemed to be over and that Britain would continue to rule the Colonies. They each, as did hundreds of other Patriots in South Carolina and Georgia, made peace with the British and extended the hand of friendship. They each said they were glad the war was over and that they wanted nothing more than to get back to the way things had been before the war and make some money.

That was June.

The peace held through July and much of August. But by mid-August it was clear that there was still a guerrilla resistance movement alive in South Carolina. To root it out, England began to change the rules.

First, Cornwallis decreed that South Carolinian males must either actively support and fight for England or they would be considered enemy rebels and be dealt with accordingly. There were howls of protest. Former rebels had been quite willing to stop supporting the Revolution in any way. But to have to actively fight *against* it was another matter. Eloquent Whig voices told the British it was a bad policy because it might encourage more men to join the rebellion.

Instead of revising this policy, Cornwallis took it further. He wanted to gather his army for a push north through North Carolina into Virginia. Most of the military garrisons at each of the six forts he had established around South Carolina would be withdrawn. On September 7, he decided to put loyal local Tories in positions of authority to replace the military and to run the local governments.

And so, one week later, on September 14, local Patriot leaders trembled in fear.

Three other Whigs huddled with Isaiah McPhearson, a tall, almost noble-looking man of 49 with wavy salt and pepper hair and commanding gray eyes. Squat Cleetis Murphy was of Irish descent, as was Isaiah. Joseph Wilton's parents had shipped over from England. Although a prosperous tavern owner, Joseph always dressed like a commoner. Alfred Phernaugh was the son of French Huguenots. Here Alfred was a farmer. In France, his ancestors had owned a vast estate.

"I fear the worst," muttered Joseph. "This will be disastrous."

"The Tories around here are *sure* to abuse their power," said Cleetis.

"British Redcoats were able to keep the Tories in check," agreed Alfred. "But now . . . "

"The *British* are reasonable," added Isaiah. "They believe in order and fairness. But promoting *Tories* to posts of authority and setting up Tory Committees and Tory Militia to take the reins of local government. . . . Who knows *what* they'll do!"

"Certainly no good," muttered the others.

"A disaster . . . " repeated Joseph.

Isaiah stroked his chin. "The key is: Who did they appoint?"

Cleetis sadly shook his head. "We've *tried* to make peace."

"To let bygones be bygones," added Alfred.

"To get on with our lives and put war behind us," concluded Joseph.

Isaiah repeated, "We need to know who is being appointed, *whom* we have to deal with. It might not be so bad if the British appointed a reasonable fellow to head the Justice Committee—maybe someone from outside the community."

All three others turned toward Isaiah. "*You* find out and meet with him, Isaiah. You're good at bringing out the best side to things."

Isaiah thought for a moment and nodded. "All right. I will."

Joseph raised a cautioning finger. "You remember to tell 'em, these last three years we were just enforcing the law, just doing our duty."

Cleetis added. "And we're sorry if we had to burn a couple of folks out in order to do that. But it *was* the law . . . "

"You tell 'em we had nothing personal against Tories in these parts," said Alfred. "We never wrote those laws. And what could we do? We were *forced* to carry 'em out."

"Gentlemen," said Isaiah, rising to gather his hat. "I will do all I can to create an atmosphere of peace and understanding."

The other three sighed and nodded.

Isaiah McPhearson usually walked the broad streets of Greenwood with a confident, almost haughty air. Today he slinked like a frightened school child into the Red Pheasant, a cramped, dingy tavern and a known Tory gathering spot.

"Any . . . news?" Isaiah asked of the tavern owner.

"Look who's graced us lowly common folk with a visit," answered the heavyset man with small, beady eyes and a grizzled beard.

Isaiah ignored the insult. "Any . . . news today?" he repeated, eyebrows arching toward the low roof.

"So," sneered the owner. "The high and mighty merchants are gettin' a might nervous now that us Tories are in a bit o' control. Is that it? And so you thought you'd prance in here and find out what we've heard from the fort . . . "

Other men in stained back-country buckskin chuckled as the owner poked fun at this wealthy area merchant.

"I've always been more than fair with you, Amos," Isaiah started. "Who helped you rebuild this place after that storm last year?"

"There's some news," the owner finally admitted. He carefully wiped off several tables just to make Isaiah wait before answering. "The British commandant at the fort appointed a local Tory to be Assistant Commandant and Justice of the Peace."

"A powerful and important post," said Isaiah thoughtfully. "Who got it?"

"Certainly not one of you Whigs, you can count on that!" the owner answered. Most of the men in the place laughed.

"But *who*?" pressed Isaiah.

"Don't know. I guess you'll have to inconvenience yourself and hike down to the fort to see."

Again the men chortled and laughed. Isaiah gritted his teeth and marched out. "Very well," he muttered. "I *will* go find out."

Halfway down the three-block long main street of Greenwood, Isaiah found his 42-year-old cousin, Jake Dawkins, swaggering past Isaiah's mercantile store. Isaiah and Jake were cousins but lived worlds apart. Isaiah traveled in the fine society of South Carolina. Jake was the son of a poor dirt farmer and barely scratched out a living for his family with a few acres of rocky land and a small, smelly livery stable. Jake, an avowed Tory, had built up a lifetime of bitterness and resentment being snubbed instead of helped by his rich kin. Isaiah was embarrassed by his lowly cousin and seemed offended that they were related.

Jake was active in the local Tory militia. Maybe *he* would know the news. "Afternoon, Jake. You're lookin' mighty satisfied on this sweltering afternoon."

Jake grinned past his unwashed face and the gaps of his missing teeth. "Maybe you should add a 'sir' when talkin' to me, cousin."

"You?" snorted Isaiah. "Don't be ridiculous. I never call anyone 'sir' who smells more like horse manure than a person."

"I run a clean, fair stable!" Jake snapped. "In fact, ain't there two of your horses there right now?"

"I know you do," soothed Isaiah, trying to calm his cousin. "I meant no offense."

Jake's grin was too big for Isaiah's comfort as he lifted an arm and dramatically smelled his grimy sleeve. "But now I smells like the law."

"You?" exclaimed Isaiah.

"*Me*! I am the new Assistant Commandant and Justice of the Peace for this whole area. Now how's about that 'sir,' cousin?"

"*You*?!" Isaiah stammered

The two men circled each other in the street, like verbal gun fighters itching to draw.

"*You're* the one the British appointed?" sneered Isaiah in disbelief.

Jake unfolded a paper from his pocket and waved it triumphantly at Isaiah. "Lookie here. That's what it says."

Isaiah laughed. "You can't read."

"But I knows what it says! It says I am the law! Not you. Not your rebel friends. *Me*!"

Isaiah scanned the letter from Colonel Maxfield, the acting British post commandant. "Well, I'll be . . . "

"That's 'I'll be, *sir*'," Jake sneered.

Isaiah's finger jabbed at the air between them. "Now don't you get too high and mighty, Jake Dawkins. British soldiers are still the real authority."

"No! Me and my deputies are the authority. *We* decide who's breakin' the law, and *we* enforce the laws—especially the new ones!"

"What new laws," stammered Isaiah, his face turning pale.

"The new ones we decide to pass," grinned Jake. "So you best pay a little respect!"

Isaiah could see this was not going well, not well at all. "All right, now Jake. Remember, we're cousins, and I always liked you."

"Liar! You always treated me like dirt. Last couple of years—just 'cause I like the British—you treated me worse than dirt."

Isaiah was beginning to sweat. Maybe Joseph Wilton was right and it would be a disaster. "I'm just formal, that's all. And I have a social position and reputation in this area to maintain. I got no quarrel with you, Jake."

"You don't? Well maybe I got a quarrel to pick with you an' all them high falutin' rebel friends of yours."

"The war is over, Jake."

"Not here it ain't," hissed Jake. "And as the new Justice of the Peace, I believe there's some folks who need a little reminder of the error of their ways."

Isaiah's heart began to thump. A lump formed in his throat. "We were just enforcing the law, Jake . . . "

"And now *we're* enforcing the law."

Blood pounded behind Isaiah's ears. His face brightened to blotchy red. "We all have to live together. Don't do anything rash."

"Oh no, cousin, I won't do anything rash. I've been planning this for *years*." Jake laughed and strolled on down the street, leaving his cousin feeling the icy grip of fear for the first time in years.

Isaiah McPhearson couldn't stop trembling at home that night. Isaiah decided it was the ice-cold calm of his cousin that was most terrifying—as if he had gone insane with power.

"Trouble's coming," Isaiah muttered over and over again as he stared vacantly at the floor and slowly shook his head as if trying to relive his meeting of the afternoon and make it turn out differently.

"Some ugly old wounds are going to be reopened, I fear," he told the other Whig leaders.

"What do you think they'll do?" one man asked.

Isaiah sadly shook his head. "Mark my words. There will be no peace with Tories in control."

Another man said, "Jake is your cousin. He's a bit rough, but a decent man. He'll be just."

"You didn't see the twisted gleam in his eye," answered Isaiah. "I'm certain something terrible will happen."

"But what?" they demanded.

Isaiah could only tremble and shake his head. After the men departed he gripped his wife firmly by the shoulders. His gray eyes were filled with fear and foreboding. "I think you should take the three girls and visit relatives for a while. Your sister is in Savannah. Get down there where the British are still in charge and it is safe."

"Isaiah," she cooed. "I think you exaggerate the danger. There are still laws that must be followed."

"I fear the law of *revenge* is the only one that Jake will follow," he snapped. "I fear for your safety. Tomorrow, you must go!"

Every new day that inched past felt like torment to Isaiah. He felt that he was walking on tender egg shells. Jake swaggered through town with an exaggerated grin plastered on his face. He even began to "accidentally" bang shoulders with known ex-Patriots—a Patriot tactic started in Boston in the mid-1770s. Then he would make the other person apologize. A pack of Tory thugs followed him around town, armed as deputies and militia men.

On September 20, Cleetis Murphy was arrested by Jake and 20 armed deputies for failure to actively support the British, being accused of withholding supplies for use by rebels. His house, farm, and all his possessions were burned to the ground while he was made to watch. His wife and children were left with nothing but the clothes on their backs to fend for themselves. As he was dragged off in chains to the fort's prison, Cleetis called to his wife, "Go to Isaiah's house. Tell him what happened."

Isaiah raced to Fort 96 and arrived just before Jake's patrol arrived—carrying the dead body of Cleetis Murphy. He had been shot 10 times.

"He tried to escape," shrugged Jake. "We had no choice."

Isaiah trembled with rage. "The man was in chains! How could he escape?"

Jake just grinned and shrugged.

"And the supply of hay he was accused of withholding was winter feed for his two cows!"

Jake scratched his chin as he said, "If he'd given the cows to support the cause like a good citizen, then he wouldn't o' needed the hay."

Isaiah nosed his horse right next to Jake's, their faces only inches apart. Daggers of venom and hate seemed to flash between their eyes. "The man had a right to feed his family and to live. This was unjustified revenge!"

Jake shoved his hat back off his face and grinned. "That's not what you called it when you imprisoned my son, Billy Dawkins, and left his pregnant wife to starve!"

"First, she didn't starve. She went to live with relatives," answered Isaiah. "And, second, Bill set fire to a Patriot warehouse and tried to kill a major commanding the post! That's different."

"No," hissed Jake, "Just the same as I see it."

He turned and rode back to Greenwood, leaving Isaiah in front of the fort, suddenly fearing for his very life.

On September 27, Isaiah's daughter was burned out of her home and her husband (a gentle carpenter who had done nothing to support either side) was dragged out of the house and hanged as a rebel spy from a tree while he watched everything he had built burn to the ground.

Isaiah stormed through town searching, but didn't find his cousin until the next afternoon. Isaiah grabbed Jake by his lapels and almost lifted him off the street, his face twisted in rage. "I warn you, Jake . . . "

"No! I warn *you*," Jake interrupted, struggling out of Isaiah's grasp. Jake pretended to dust and adjust his coat before saying, "Four good Tories said he was a Patriot spy. You saying they're all liars? We could hold a trial and see who the Justice of the Peace believes—you, or them." And then he broke into the evil grin he had worn since taking office.

Isaiah hissed, "You burned my daughter's house and killed her husband and all their animals."

"They're no deader than were the animals and lives of my two best friends you burned out two years back."

Isaiah threw up his hands. "Those men were convicted spies!"

"Same here," grinned Jake. His Tory thugs nodded and chuckled.

Isaiah leaned close so that Jake could feel the hot breath of his voice. "You be careful, Jake Dawkins. You are making enemies!"

"I'm the law, Isaiah McPhearson! *You* be careful."

On October 3, Isaiah arrived at his mercantile to find the windows smashed, counters hacked into ruin, and all his merchandise destroyed. A crowd had gathered in the street to stare at the ruin. His bakery around the corner still smoldered from the night-time fire that had gutted it.

"The fire must have been an accident," said Jake. "Your bakers should be more careful." His militia men laughed.

"And my store?" demanded Isaiah.

"I received a report that rebel spies and messengers were hiding in the basement of your store."

"I don't have a basement!"

Jake shrugged. "The report must have been wrong. Sorry if we mussed up the merchandise a bit. But I had to check. Just enforcing the law."

Again the thugs laughed.

"I'll report you to the British, Jake. This has to stop!"

Jake grinned, "I ain't hardly begun!"

On October 9, news reached Greenwood of a great battle between Patriot and British forces at Kings Mountain, along the South Carolina-North Carolina border. The British had been routed. Most had been killed or captured. Cornwallis's main army was stuck way up in eastern North Carolina. Suddenly control of the western Carolinas seemed to have shifted back to Patriot hands.

Jake Dawkins slinked out of town in the middle of the night, abandoning his wife and three children in their beds. Next morning it was reported that he must have fallen off his horse and broken his neck before he got 20 miles from Greenwood.

That afternoon, no tears were shed by the wide circle of men who stood and watched the flames climbing up the sides of Jake Dawkins' cabin and livery stable to lick the sky.

Only Jake's wife and children cried. But what was one more chorus of weeping to men with a bitter score to settle? In South Carolina, the flames were far from over.

Aftermath

Tory excesses during their short reign helped spur many neutrals and non-committeds to support the Revolution and join Patriot militia units. Former Patriots who had pledged neutrality were outraged and poured back into Patriot commands. Patriot ranks swelled. With these greater masses of men and support, it became relatively easy to push the British out of their posts in South Carolina and retake the state, except for Charleston. It is one of the odd quirks of the war that the British plan to secure South Carolina for the Crown by placing Tories in positions of power had, in reality, the opposite effect. It greatly increased Patriot strength in the state and led to the ultimate collapse of Britain's "Southern Strategy."

Follow-up Questions and Activities

1. **What Do You Know?**

   - During the two years 1780 and 1781, war raged across the South. What was going on in the North and mid-Atlantic regions during these same two years? What were the British and American armies in those regions doing?

   - Why didn't Washington rush his entire army south to South Carolina in 1780 to oppose Cornwallis's advance north from Charleston into North Carolina?

   - General Cornwallis is most famous for his surrender at Yorktown in October 1781. Research this British general and his command of the British southern army. How and why did he wind up at Yorktown? What battles did he fight? How many did he lose? Why did he have to surrender? What did he do before and after the war?

   - Where did the British establish outposts in South Carolina during 1780 once Charleston fell? Why did they feel they had to create these posts?

2. **Finding Out More**. Following are five important topics from this story for you to research in the library and on the Internet. The reference sources at the back of this book will help you get started.

   - Research the civil unrest and fighting in South Carolina during 1780 and 1781. Many of these fights looked more like gang warfare than battles between military units. Much of the fighting was conducted as "secret" raids on the houses and property of known enemies. See how many incidents of this neighbor-versus-neighbor fighting you can identify. How many of them seemed to be revenge for some previous act of violence by the other side?

   - There were a half-dozen major battles in the South before Yorktown (Charleston, Camden, Kings Mountain, Cowpens, Guilford Court House, and Eutaw Springs). Research these battles. Where and when did they take place? Who fought? Who won? What was the importance and outcome of each battle?

   - The British tried to create new civilian governments of known Loyalists in every community in South Carolina when they took control of the region in the summer of 1780. Research the positions they created and the authority they gave to each. What gave these civilians the power to enforce their policies?

   - A force of Patriots called "The Overmountain Boys" swept into South Carolina and destroyed a British force at the Battle of Kings Mountain. Who were these backwoodsmen? Where did they come from? Why were they called "The Overmountain Boys?" What happened to them after the battle?

   - Research life in the port cities of Savannah and Charleston during British occupation, 1780 through 1783. Did life go on normally? What happened to most Patriots during those three years? What demands did the British place on citizens of those cities?

3. **Make It Real**

- Create a game to simulate the cycle of revenge. Pick two students to play the game in front of the class. Before any person can stop the game, that student must feel satisfied that he or she is even or ahead, not behind. The teacher or a third student is appointed as referee to ensure that neither player is allowed to hurt the other.

   To play the game one person taps the other person's shoulder with one finger. The other person then taps back. The only rule is that each tap you give has to be just a little bit harder than the last tap you received. How do you feel after four taps? After 12? How can you ever end the game? Did this game give you any insights about the civil war in South Carolina and how it turned so brutal and bloody?

- Create a timeline of the events in the south during 1780 and 1781. The fighting seemed to jump all over the place. See if you can make sense of the entire southern campaign and understand what each commander was trying to do and how he tried to go about doing it.

- Create a map of southern army movements, battles, and major forts for the years 1780 and 1781. Mark the British posts and army movements in red. Mark the American army posts and movements in blue. Was it difficult to track all of the frantic maneuvering across the Carolinas? Do you think it would have been confusing for local citizens to try to keep track of the various armies and their activities?

4. **Points to Ponder**

- What's the difference between justice and revenge? We believe deeply in ensuring justice. Do we believe in assuring revenge? Do you believe revenge is ever justified? Why or why not?

- Why do you think the Revolutionary War generated such strong feelings of resentment and such a desire for revenge? Does that always happen in a war? What was significant about the Revolutionary War that made so many want revenge?

- When attacking the South, the British first attacked the port cities of Savannah and Charleston, figuring that they would control the entire region if they controlled the major shipping ports. Why were port cities so important in the eighteenth century? Would they be that important in war today? Why or why not?

Pigtail Spy
Southern Spies, 1781

Betsy Drowdy escapes capture

At a Glance

We have all heard about the brave deeds of Paul Revere and often forget that he was just one member of an organization of spies and messengers (riders) in Boston. We also often forget that brave Americans were spying on the British forces from South Carolina to Maine and boldly riding out through the night to spread the word of impending British movements.

Surprisingly, many of these spies and riders were women. More surprisingly, many were young women, girls really. Some were actual spies; some rode messenger routes to warn local militia of British movements. A select few did both. One of this group of unheralded fighters for American liberty was Betsy Drowdy, who had just turned 15 in February 1781, when Cornwallis and his southern army lumbered into Hillsboro, North Carolina, to establish winter camp. This is the story of her bold efforts as both spy and message rider.

Meet Betsy Drowdy

Betsy was born on the family farm in late 1765. The farm, located between Hillsboro and Cedar Springs in North Carolina, certainly didn't qualify as a plantation, but it was prosperous. The Drowdys didn't own any slaves.

Betsy had always been a tomboy. She rode as well as her two older brothers and she carried her share of the farm workload from the time she was six. As a teenager, Betsy was stocky and her mousy brown hair was usually worn in pigtails. Although certainly not pretty and usually called "plain," she was bright, eager, and mentally quick.

One of her brothers was sickly and rarely left the farm. The oldest, Patrick (and Betsy's favorite), joined the Patriot militia and was killed in Colonel Tarleton's massacre at Wexaws in the summer of 1780.

Betsy was devastated and swore revenge against the British in general and Tarleton in particular. Two of her distant uncles joined the Tory militia. (One was killed in 1779; the other served in a unit in Maryland.) Betsy was able to talk (lie) her way into a housekeeping job at Cornwallis's winter camp by using their names as references and pretending that they were close relatives of hers and that she was a loyal Tory.

Pigtail Spy

etsy Drowdy's heart always skipped a beat when she passed through the guard post at General Cornwallis's winter camp and the grim-looking sentries with their muskets, bayonets, and sabers. Would this be the day she was caught? Would someone have leaked word to the British that she had lied to obtain her job in the camp? Would they somehow be able to tell today that she hated the British and wanted to spy?

Picturing herself standing weakly on the gallows with a rope around her neck, hoping that *she* would have the courage to yell out, "I regret that I have but one life to give for my country," Betsy squeezed her eyes shut, prayed for luck, and once again walked as quickly as possible through the gate. The British guards thought that Betsy was just a shy and meek Loyalist girl and no longer asked her any questions. This was the end of February 1781, and she had been passing through their post every day for over three weeks with a pass signed by Cornwallis's adjutant.

Throughout the last months of 1780, General Cornwallis had been unable to trap Nathaniel Greene's Continental Army and force a decisive battle for final victory in the South. So he had reluctantly settled into winter camp in Hillsboro, North Carolina. Local Loyalists were overjoyed at finally having British military in the area and had flocked to the Hillsboro camp to either join Cornwallis's militia ranks or find work in the camp and earn some money.

British and Tory agents had screened and questioned each applicant to make sure they allowed no rebel spies into camp. Each night, leaving the British camp and walking back toward home, Betsy smiled privately, quietly to herself, knowing that she, a 15-year-old North Carolina girl, had once again fooled the British and safely marched in and out of their headquarters.

The Drowdy family farm (several miles outside Hillsboro) had for several generations been a thriving farm—some tobacco for export, lots of corn, squash, hay, beef and chicken for local markets. They owned no slaves, but did have one free black who worked for them for room, board, and the equivalent of two dollars (in British coin) each month. In 1778 one of Betsy's two older brothers, Patrick, had joined the local Patriot militia. In 1780 his unit had marched south to aid the besieged city of Charleston. Along the road they met British Colonel Tarleton's fierce regiment. Many in the unit, including Patrick, were killed.

Betsy wept for a full week. Then she turned grief into anger and pledged to forever hate the British and especially Colonel Tarleton. While war raged through South Carolina during the rest of 1780, Betsy was frustrated that she could do no more than hate from afar and work out her anger by punishing a hay stack with her pitchfork. Then Cornwallis rode into Hillsboro for winter camp and Betsy saw her opportunity.

Her parents were against the idea. It was far too dangerous. She would surely be caught. They had already lost one child. They flatly refused to allow her to walk into Hillsboro each day to spy on the British.

But Betsy would not be talked out of her plan and said she would go even without their permission. Two of Betsy's distant uncles had been Tory soldiers. One, well-known to the British as an excellent militiaman and loyal soldier, had been killed in a raid by Francis Marion's guerrilla raiders in the fall of 1780. He had even been given a British medal. The other was stationed way up north in Maryland. Two Tory uncles seemed like perfect references, even though local Tories were not satisfied about her parents' political leanings.

Cornwallis's adjutant, Colonel Fitsgerald, liked Betsy—she reminded him of his own beloved daughter back in York, England. The colonel was a short, round man with a wide smile and a thick handlebar mustache. If it weren't for his uniform and the fierce gleam of his eyes, he would have been described as "jolly." He offered Betsy a job as his assistant orderly, to dust, sweep, and file around his headquarters office in the spacious house of a Mr. Alfred Billingsworth, which Cornwallis had taken as his headquarters. Betsy eagerly accepted the job.

On this day of February 20, Betsy had extra reason to fear being caught as she marched toward the guard post. As of last night she was not only a spy, but also a hated message rider. What if one of these guards had been on the patrol that chased her through the dark, and he now recognized her? Flashes of last night's ride exploded through her mind as she approached the guards.

Her parents had begged her to let someone else make the deadly-dangerous ride. "Haven't you done enough?" But who else could go? Her brother had a lame leg. Her parents were too old. It would waste precious hours to rouse a Patriot neighbor and explain the British plan. Over the last three days of careful listening and sneaking peeks at notes and scribbles on Colonel Fitsgerald's desk whenever he stepped out of the office, Betsy the spy had pieced together a British plan to raid a suspected Patriot militia supply depot in Roxboro the next day.

At first Betsy couldn't believe she had pieced together some real, valuable information. Then doubt was replaced by elation. She, plain little Betsy Drowdy, had outsmarted the whole British army! Then elation turned to terror. What if Colonel Fitsgerald knew she was a spy? What if he was watching right now? Would guards stomp in and drag her off to a dungeon?

Betsy's knees trembled so much they almost couldn't hold her up as she rushed home. The Patriot militia in Roxboro *had* to be warned and there was no one else to ride the 20 miles to Roxboro, and no other time than right now for that message rider to go.

"It will be dangerous," her parents said. "I know the way," she answered. "You could be shot." "If stopped, I'll say I'm on my way to an aunt's house."

She had to dodge British and Tory patrols that seemed to be thicker than mosquitoes in summer. For over a mile she had raced down the road, head bent forward like a horse-racing jockey, hearing galloping hooves behind her. Four times she fled off the road into swampy forests to hide deep in the trees from sounds that she feared were British, branches slapping hard into her as she rode, tearing her dress, scratching her face and neck. It felt to Betsy as if it took days instead of hours to reach Roxboro and to find and wake the three Patriot families whose names her father had given her.

Creeping back through the dark well past midnight, Betsy heard the clomp of horse hooves somewhere ahead in the blackness. Fearing that the riders could hear her horse just as well and would spring out upon her at any moment, she dared not ride another step. She slid from the saddle in the pitch black night and tore her petticoats into long strips to wrap around the horse's hooves before she dared continue toward home, her heart still pounding with terror.

Betsy emerged from her fearful memories as one of the guards said, "Good morning, Betsy."

"What do you mean?" she snapped, her mind still on her midnight trail of terror.

"Just that it is a mild and lovely day," he chuckled.

She blushed deeply and hurried past the guards, her face and eyes tilted down toward the road to hide her fear, as the guards shook their heads in confusion.

Exhausted and bleary-eyed from lack of sleep, Betsy shuffled into Colonel Fitsgerald's office and found him scowling from behind his desk in a dark and gloomy mood. Arms folded, he was leaning back in his chair, ignoring the mounds of paperwork on his desk.

"I'm glad *you're* here, Betsy. I need someone to cheer me up this dismal day."

"I brought you muffins," said Betsy, curtseying and gesturing to the basket looped over her left arm.

He faintly smiled. "You are such a dear child to have spent your evening thinking of me."

"I was definitely thinking of you last night," she agreed, setting the basket and its sweet, steamy smells on his desk. Betsy's mother, of course, had made the muffins to keep herself busy while she worried about Betsy out riding the dangerous trails.

Seeing that Colonel Fitsgerald didn't suspect her foul deed, Betsy grew braver and primly perched on one of the hard-back chairs in the office. "What's making you look so unhappy, colonel?"

"My raid failed this morning."

"Raid?" she asked, trying to sound innocent and confused. "What's a raid, Colonel Fitsgerald?"

"I found evidence of a rebel supply base in Roxboro and sent a force out just past midnight to capture it. I had five screening patrols out to guard the roads all last evening to snare any messengers . . . "

"Five?!" interrupted Betsy.

Colonel Fitsgerald shook his head in frustration. "But still somehow word leaked through and the rebels found out about the raid. A courier just returned with the news that my men found nothing—except evidence that the warehouse had *just* been emptied of supplies!"

"I'm sorry your raid failed, Colonel Fitsgerald," said Betsy, sounding as innocent as she could.

Again he smiled as he munched on one of Betsy's corn muffins. "It was just a raid of a Patriot supply depot, Betsy. The failure of the raid isn't important."

"It's not?" Betsy sounded noticeably deflated.

"What's important is that the rebels found out about it. I suspect a spy."

Betsy realized she was talking far too much and had best quietly go to work, cleaning and dusting, before she brought suspicion upon herself. "I'm just a girl and I don't understand these things."

"I know," answered the colonel soothingly. "And I don't mean to be harsh. I'm just frustrated because the rebels *somehow* sneaked an informant into this camp. But who?"

He missed the slight blush that spread across Betsy's face.

"Spies, Betsy," he continued, eyes narrowing. "Spies are everywhere in this awful country."

"Mercy!" she exclaimed, cringing behind a dust cloth so as not to look too guilty.

"There are malicious men out there and one of them learned of my plans and rode out last night to warn the rebels."

Betsy attacked a bookcase with her duster to keep from having to look at the colonel.

"Where did you get that nasty scrape on your cheek?" he asked.

Betsy was so startled she dropped the duster and knocked over four books. "My cheek?" she squealed. "I . . . I fell off my horse."

"You have your own horse at the farm?"

"Well, actually, it's my father's horse. Last ni . . . afternoon."

"You fell last afternoon?" he questioned.

Betsy blurted, "I probably shouldn't have been riding—I'm just a girl. But . . . but it's fun."

The colonel nodded and stuffed another muffin into his mouth. "What worries me," he said around the mouthful while he gazed up at the ceiling and rocked back in his chair, "is that I told no one of my plans for the raid—except, of course, the commanders involved."

Then he slammed the front legs of the chair back down. "The question is: Who is the dastardly spy and how do we catch him?"

Betsy gulped and tried to laugh. But no sound would come out. "*Will* you catch . . . him?" she stammered.

"Oh, we'll catch him, all right," Colonel Fitsgerald fiendishly chuckled.

Betsy returned to her frenzied dusting, hoping he couldn't hear the pounding of her heart.

February 21 was uneventful, as was the 22nd. But when Betsy arrived at Colonel Fitsgerald's office to begin her day's work on the 23rd, she found the colonel beaming behind his desk.

"My goodness, Colonel," she exclaimed. "You look like you have just won the whole war."

"Bring any of your delicious muffins today?"

"Sorry, not today, Colonel."

"No matter," he giggled. "I feel positively wonderful—even without your muffins."

Betsy felt prickling fingers of fear creep down her spine. Did he know?

"A Tory messenger reported to me last night that a South Carolina Loyalist cavalry unit is on the way to join us—over 300, scraped together from over half the colony."

Betsy sighed. She hadn't been caught—yet. "300 men. Golly, that's a lot!"

"A powerful addition to our cavalry that we desperately need," agreed the Colonel. "With those riders, we'll be able to sweep the Continental cavalry and army from the field very early in the spring."

"You will?" squeaked Betsy. She feared her voice betrayed her dismay at this terrible news.

But Colonel Fitsgerald seemed too self-satisfied to notice. "They're already on their way and should arrive within the week."

Betsy's heart dropped. Still she tried to smile. "That's . . . great news."

Colonel Fitsgerald folded his arms and leaned back, as if completely satisfied. "To make sure they arrive safely, I have written orders for Colonel Tarleton, himself, to ride out tomorrow to meet them along the trail and escort them in."

Betsy's heart felt like it skipped a beat or two. She could barely breathe. "Colonel Tarleton? He's here?"

"Been here over two weeks. His is the green-coated cavalry regiment you've seen during drills."

Betsy cheeks flushed bright red at the mention of her sworn enemy. Her hands trembled and began to sweat.

"Have you heard of Tarleton?"

"Yes," she managed to stammer. "I think my . . . my uncle mentioned the name."

"Ahhh, your uncle. Good militia man. Did you know I knew him? Too bad he was killed."

Betsy hardly heard. Her ears roared. "Colonel Tarleton will be in charge?" she pressed. "Will he ride out himself?"

"Oh, yes," chuckled the colonel. "That one is a real fighter. Colonel Tarleton never passes up a chance to get into the field with his regiment—fiercest and most effective unit in this army."

Betsy realized she had to change the subject before her hatred of Tarleton spewed out. "300 . . . do that many soldiers really need an escort to be safe? I'd think that many would be safe all on their own."

"It's just a precaution," he answered. "To *ensure* that nothing goes awry." He straightened a stack of forms and reports on his desk and smiled. "We can't be too careful these days, can we?"

"No. We certainly can't," Betsy answered, trying to hide a deep blush as blood thundered through her head. This was a huge war secret dumped into her lap. She tried to smile and look natural, but found that her hands trembled too hard to dust.

Betsy felt that she would burst before she made it home that evening. It felt as though the entire Revolution suddenly depended on her, alone. She had to concentrate to make her feet walk and then to break into a stumbling run. She had to clamp her mouth shut to keep it from screaming.

Then doubts crept in. This news was almost too good to be true. Did Colonel Fitsgerald tell her on purpose as a test? Were British soldiers secretly watching her every move? Maybe she should say nothing until she was sure . . .

No! This wasn't news of some small raid. This was BIG. This news could affect the whole war, and she was the only one who knew. Patriot units *had* to prevent those South Carolina Tories from joining Cornwallis!

Her parents again begged her not to go. Colonel "Light Horse" Harry Lee's Continental cavalry were off somewhere to the west. But no one in Hillsboro knew where. It could take days to find them and the roads teemed with British and Tory patrols. She had already done her part.

Betsy heard not a word. Nothing could keep her from going. This was Tarleton. This was for her brother, Patrick!

A light mist fell from a solid cover of clouds and a blustery winter wind rattled through the bare tree limbs as Betsy wrapped herself in her heavy cape and stepped from the warmth and light of the house into the dangerous dark of night. Silently she climbed into the saddle and leaned low as if to hide while her father's horse trotted into the night.

Betsy skirted south, wide around Hillsboro to avoid Tory patrols, before she turned west into unfamiliar territory. If she rode far enough west, she felt sure she would meet a Patriot patrol or guard post.

An hour into her trek, she heard a twig snap to her left . . . or maybe it was a branch. Or was it just the wind? No! There was another. Should she race forward or turn back? In a blink she was surrounded by four riders with pistols drawn and aimed at her.

The riders leered as they slowly circled, firing questions at her. Who was she? Why was she on this road at night? Why should they let her pass their road block? What was a girl doing out alone?

At first Betsy was so frightened she couldn't answer and stared back help-lessly, her mouth flopping open and closed.

The Tory soldiers made her dismount. They searched her horse, saddle bags, and saddle. They pried into her pockets and felt through the lining of her cape.

Finally, Betsy regained enough composure to say, "I work for Colonel Fits-gerald, General Cornwallis's adjutant. He has given me permission for this ride."

"Sorry," said the patrol leader, showing sudden respect for Betsy, "but *no one* is permitted to pass to the west of this post. You'll have to turn back."

Not knowing what else to do, Betsy turned her horse around and started back toward Hillsboro. But it never occurred to her to give up. After several hundred yards, she thought she could see a wide field through the deep gloom that stretched out to the south side of the road. She spurred her horse into a full gallop as she turned into the field.

"Get her!" cried a voice back in the dismal dark. A shot rang out. Then another.

Betsy jabbed her heels into her horse's flanks and sped through the black night across the field. Distant hoofbeats told her she was being chased by the patrol. Occasional thunder-clap shots and flashes of fire told her they were not very far behind.

Through the field. Across a low wall. Through a small pasture. Over a fence. Into a thick and tangled woods she rode. Branches and tree trunks forced her to slow to a fast trot to keep from being knocked off her horse. Even then she rode with one arm up to protect her face. Her cape was torn off. Her skirt was shredded by branches, vines, and brambles. The dense woods seemed to last forever as she blindly stumbled forward, terrified that at any moment one of the Tory riders would reach out from the dark and grab her.

Groping her way past trees and vines, Betsy veered her horse to the right around a thick cluster of trees and stumbled into a deep ravine. Dizzy and stunned, she stopped at the bottom and dismounted. Holding her horse's muzzle to keep it from snorting or braying, she tried to hold her own breath so she could listen for the Tory riders.

At first she only heard the pounding of her own heart. Then, faintly at first, she heard the snapping and crackling of breaking branches. They were coming, following her trail. "Through here," called a voice, growing ever closer.

Now Betsy could hear the heavy breathing of horses. She could hear branches scraping across leather leggings of the riders. She could hear the breathing of the men.

They had to be near the top of her ravine even though she could see nothing beyond her own fingers wiggling in front of her eyes.

"Spread out a little. Look for broken branches or bits of cloth," called one voice that seemed to come from right on top of her.

"I know what to do, and if'n you'd hush up, Billy, I'd see if'n I can hear her up ahead," whined another.

"We shouldn't leave our guard post this long," said a third, sounding like he had already passed Betsy's hiding spot. "What if the Captain comes by?"

Slowly the voices and stomping of hooves faded into the night. Betsy was alone again. For almost an hour she was too terrified to move. Had they stopped? Were they waiting for her?

But she had to push on and find Colonel Lee's Continental cavalry.

Except now she was lost. She had no idea of how far she had ridden or in what direction. She had no idea which way was west, or which was east.

She was as likely to ride right back into the Tory lines as to escape to find the Continentals.

Still, she had to try.

Betsy sucked in a deep, slow breath to calm herself and led her horse back to the top of the ravine. She mounted, wished for luck, and turned her horse in the direction that felt most like west.

The ground grew softer. Pools of standing water suddenly seemed to lie in every direction. She had stumbled into a swamp!

The horse balked and whinnied. Betsy patted its neck and urged it forward. Gingerly it eased through the muck and mud. Hanging tendrils of Spanish moss brushed across Betsy's face. It felt like snakes sliding down her skin.

There was a loud splash off to her left. The horse bucked and reared. Betsy was thrown off, splattering into knee-deep water, mud, and cat-tails. By the time she scrambled to her feet, the horse was gone.

The swamp and the night settled upon Betsy like a smothering blanket. She was lost, alone and on foot in a pitch-black swamp. She would have hidden if there had been anywhere to hide. She would have cried out if she thought anyone was there to hear.

Instead she did the only thing she could think of to do. She began to walk and wade through the ooze and slime of the swamp. At every step she was sure a snake was waiting to bite her or that an alligator was about to clamp onto her leg.

Still she walked—walked and sobbed from fright and frustration. She had failed in her attempt to reach the Continentals and would probably die in the swamp before morning.

As first light began to dull the grays of the eastern sky, Betsy scrambled onto raised ground and found a road that bordered the swamp. She looked worse than a half-drowned rat as she plopped onto the deep, dirt ruts to catch her breath and quiet her choking sobs.

Almost before she sat, a man stepped from the shadows with a gun.

The man knelt and asked if he could help. He introduced himself as a sergeant in the Continental cavalry.

Betsy's sobs turned to a flood of joyful tears as she poured out her story.

It was three days later, February 26, before Betsy was safely delivered home and could return to work.

"Where have you been?" asked Colonel Fitsgerald. "I've been worried about you."

"I've been sick," Betsy answered. "I'm better now."

The colonel nodded and smiled. "Skip the dusting this morning. Filing has piled up." He pointed at a stack of papers with his quill pen.

"I'll get right on it, Colonel Fitsgerald," Betsy answered, glad that he hadn't pressed for any details.

A courier arrived, still out of breath, obviously having ridden hard and long. He saluted and handed a dispatch to Colonel Fitsgerald. The colonel read the report, sank slowly into his chair, and muttered, "Damn!"

"Colonel, what could be the matter?" Betsy asked.

"Bad news," he answered vacantly, staring off into space.

"Please tell me," begged Betsy, who felt that she had walked on pins and needles since delivering her news, wondering if it did any good.

Colonel Fitsgerald sank his head into his hands. "The South Carolinians were slaughtered. The unit is destroyed."

"Slaughtered? . . . *Killed*? How?" Betsy pressed. She had never pictured her news causing the death of hundreds of men. She had vaguely thought that they would just be sent back to South Carolina.

"Somehow Colonel Lee knew not only that they were coming but that they were expecting to meet Colonel Tarleton. Lee's Continental cavalry pretended to be Tarleton's unit—both wear green uniform coats. The Continentals rode right up and massacred the Loyalist militia before they could shoulder arms."

Betsy was both horrified and thrilled. She had helped the Revolution. She had saved the Continental army from deadly spring attacks. She had also caused almost 300 deaths, had left almost 300 families without a father and husband.

Still she found that there was one thing she needed to know most. "What of Colonel Tarleton. Was he hurt?"

"He was still over a day's ride away when the attack occurred. He's fine, but very angry."

Betsy ground her teeth and turned away so the colonel wouldn't see her disappointment.

Colonel Fitsgerald smiled congenially. "But don't trouble your head anymore with such frightful matters."

"You're right" answered Betsy. "I'll just dust and get to that filing."

Aftermath

Cornwallis broke his Hillsboro camp in April both because the Continentals were on the move and because the area around Hillsboro was being depleted of food stocks. He spent the spring and summer chasing General Greene in a cat and mouse game before retiring to Yorktown, badly depleted of both men and supplies. The efforts of many spies and messengers (riders) helped to keep him from trapping and overwhelming the far weaker Patriot forces in the South.

Betsy Drowdy lived to be 73. She married and lived in rural North Carolina all her life. Until the letters she wrote to a granddaughter were published in the early twentieth century, no one knew that this 15-year-old girl had been such an instrumental spy for the American cause.

Follow-up Questions and Activities

1. **What Do You Know?**

   - How did the British army check on the background and loyalty of local citizens before hiring them to work in a winter camp?

   - Why was it often easier for women to spy than for men to do so?

   - What was the goal of the British southern campaign? How did they think occupying the Carolinas would help them win the war when they hadn't been able to win it in the North or mid-Atlantic regions?

   - How did opposing armies locate each other during the Revolutionary War?

   - What did the British look for in choosing a place for a winter camp? Make a list of what they needed while there.

2. **Finding Out More.** Following are five important topics from this story for you to research in the library and on the Internet. The reference sources at the back of this book will help you get started.

   - Nathaniel Greene took command of the Continental Southern Army in late 1780. His appointment was cheered by Congress and by almost all other generals. Why was he so popular? What had he done before 1780? How did he do as commander of the Southern Army in 1781? What happened to him after the war?

   - General Benedict Arnold defected to the British late in 1780. Why did he do it? How did his defection affect Washington and army morale in general? How did it affect Washington's position?

   - Betsy was one woman who successfully spied on the British. There were many other women spies. See how many you can discover. Research who they were, why they decided to risk their lives by spying, and the effect of their efforts. Were there women who spied *for* the British as well as *on* the British?

   - Research famous wartime spies throughout history. How many were caught? What made them famous? Did any of them have a significant impact on the outcome of a war?

- Do armies and countries still use spies, or do they rely on satellites, electronic eavesdropping devices, and modern technology to gather all the information they need?

3. **Make It Real**

- Play a spy game to see how difficult spying really is. Divide the class into two teams. Appoint a commander for each team. The teacher should secretly designate one student on each team to act as spy for the other team. Each team commander must choose a "Secret spot" on the school grounds to act as their team's hidden supply base. Each commander must tell enough team members where it is to be sure that it stays guarded. Commanders may also spread false information by telling some team members the wrong spot. Each spy has to discover the location of their team's supply base and pass that information to the other team without being caught as the spy, and must do it within a time limit designated by the teacher (such as an hour). A spy who is caught is always put to death. Each commander can, of course, also appoint fake spies to pass incorrect information to the other team and try to confuse them.

  When the time limit is up, have a class discussion about the results. Was it difficult for the spies to be sure they had the correct information and to then pass it to the other team without getting caught? Did the other team believe the correct information? How could each team's commander tell the correct information from the phony? How did the knowledge that a spy was in the group's midst affect the group? Did group members become suspicious of each other? Do you think this situation would be worse if something as important as a war were at stake?

- Pretend to be one of Betsy's parents. Write a letter to a close friend describing how you would feel if your only daughter daily risked her life to try to spy on the British, including all the things you would say and feel as Betsy's father or mother during the early months of 1781. Would you worry about writing this letter? What might happen to it and, then, to your daughter—and to you?

4. **Points to Ponder**

- Why do you think the British army hired so many local women to work in their winter camp? Do armies do the same thing today? What do modern armies hire civilians to do?

- Do you think spying is ethical? Should countries spy on each other? When is, and when isn't, spying acceptable? Is *any* action acceptable if it helps win a war?

Did We Win?

The South was still center stage for the action of the Revolutionary War as 1781 began, but not for all the drama. Washington's army had been sitting idle in New Jersey for over two years. Each winter seemed to be worse than the last. The soldiers never got paid. Food and clothing seemed skimpier and less satisfying with each passing season. During the winter of 1780–1781, many of the soldiers went past grumbling and grew downright angry. On New Year's Day several Pennsylvania regiments mutinied. New Jersey regiments followed suit three weeks later. Many of the senior officer corps tried to mutiny against Washington's leadership (the Morristown Mutiny) shortly thereafter.

Luckily, General Clinton never learned of Washington's woes and grave vulnerability and allowed his massive army to continue in peaceful stupor in New York. Washington spent the winter and spring struggling to bring order to the angry chaos that had become the main Continental Army and to patch his forces back together.

Even more fortunate was that General Greene, the new southern commander, was a shrewd, wily, and aggressive man and managed to survive against Cornwallis's greater strength without support from Washington.

In January, Greene managed to isolate one wing of Cornwallis's army under Colonel Tarleton and soundly defeated the Butcher at Cowpens, South Carolina. A cat and mouse game ensued for the rest of the year. Greene would strike. Cornwallis would race after him but would never be quite fast enough. The two did meet in several battles, including at Guilford Courthouse and Green Springs, while other commanders met in battle at Eutaw Springs. Cornwallis, like Howe before him, won the battles, but couldn't defeat General Greene, who always danced away with his army still intact.

By September, Cornwallis had been ordered to establish a port on a major river in Virginia. He gladly limped to Yorktown, badly in need of supplies and fresh troops. But the relief never came. A French fleet defeated the British fleet at the entrance to

Chesapeake Bay. Washington and the French army under General Lafayette raced to surround Yorktown, and, in October, Cornwallis was forced to surrender his 8,000-man army.

Yorktown was a great American victory. But at the time, it did not seem to end the war. The British still held Charleston and Savannah, the most important cities in the South. They still had a vast army in New York. They still had Canadian bases with forces ready to be thrown into a new offensive. Tory militia recruiting proceeded through the winter of 1781–1782 with great vigor and success. The American army raced to fortify West Point, New York, to defend the Hudson River from British attacks.

In hindsight, it is clear that, after Yorktown, the British people and government lost all interest in the war and wanted out. It took the Americans until the late spring of 1782 to realize this and see a shining light at the end of the tunnel. The war seemed to truly be over except for the negotiating, which took another year.

America faced three great challenges in 1782 and 1783: (1) what to do with a powerful and angry army full of soldiers that hadn't been paid in years and who had little to look forward to after the war; (2) how to organize a government with no money, no national constitution, and no national authority (It rested with the states.), terrible debt, and no credit; and (3) what to do with the hundreds of thousands of Loyalists and Tories who wanted to flee the country, and what to do to protect the ones that wanted to stay from Patriot reprisals and revenge.

The Treaty of Paris was signed on September 3, 1783, officially ending the war. But it was far from a happy, carefree time for Americans. The war seemed to have created more problems than it solved.

Key Events after 1780

Date	Event
1781, January 17	Battle of Cowpens, South Carolina.
1781, March 15	Battle of Guilford Courthouse.
1781, July 6	Cornwallis defeats Wayne at James River.
1781, September 7	The French defeat the British fleet at Chesapeake Bay.
1781, September 8	Battle of Eutaw Springs.
1781, September 15	Cornwallis arrives at Yorktown.
1781, September 28	Siege of Yorktown begins.
1781, October 19	Cornwallis surrenders.
1782, June	Defenses at West Point and iron chain across the Hudson are completed.
1782, July	British evacuate Savannah.
1782, December	British evacuate Charleston.
1783, September 3	Peace Treaty signed.
1783, November 25	British evacuate New York.
1783, December 4	Washington resigns from army and bids farewell to his officers.

Free and Equal
Northern Slavery, 1781

Colonial courtroom debate

At a Glance

There was never a law legalizing slavery in America. It started because no one forbade it to start. Although we think of slavery as a southern phenomenon, it actually existed in each of the original colonies. Most of New England had peacefully abandoned slavery by the beginning of the nineteenth century. The rest of the northern states soon followed. It took a bloody Civil War 50 years later to force the South to follow suit.

Not all the heroic struggles to end slavery happened in the South. One of the boldest confrontations with the institution of slavery happened in the state of Massachusetts, even before final victory in the Revolutionary War ensured that Massachusetts was truly a state instead of an English colony. This brave legal challenge to slavery was brought by a lone slave who also happened to be a woman. This is a story about her.

Meet Elizabeth Freeman

Elizabeth Freeman was born a slave in 1742. She was bought at the age of two by Colonel John Ashley and separated from her mother. (Her father had been sold off during the pregnancy.) Young Elizabeth was one of Ashley's "most prized possessions" and most trusted slaves. She performed the duties of a house servant and was described as intelligent with a "bright mind" and as an "independent thinker."

She married another of Ashley's slaves, John Freeman, a field worker, in 1778, six months before he was sent to join the army to take the place of Ashley's son, who had been drafted. John was killed in battle in the fall of 1779. Elizabeth's first daughter was born in early 1780.

Elizabeth Freeman was the first black to try to apply the words of the national Declaration of Independence and the state constitution (Massachusetts's constitution was drafted while war still raged in mid-1780) to a slave—or, for that matter, to a woman.

Free and Equal

It was a bitter winter day in the earliest days of 1781. It wasn't the coldest of winter days; far from it. It was one of those slushy days, with gloomy overcast skies holding in a wet and penetrating cold that stung the skin and drove straight through to the bone no matter what a person wore. It was a miserable day of old, crusty snow and heavy, black mud.

Still, on this day a lone black woman trudged the long four miles from Colonel John Ashley's estate to the town of Sheffield in the southwestern corner of Massachusetts. A heavy cloak wrapped around her, the 30-year-old woman held her one-year-old baby in her arms as she struggled to keep her balance through mud and over slippery snow.

Halfway to Sheffield a thin, freezing rain began to swirl in her face and mat down her jet-black hair where it stuck out around the edges of the bandanna wrapped tightly around her head. The woman hardly noticed. One thought kept circling through her mind and driving her feet: "I heard them write it into the state constitution. All are born free and equal—free and equal, free and equal. I'm gonna' get me some of that free and equal."

The Revolutionary War still raged across the country. American armies in the North under Ethan Allen and Nathaniel Greene had met with considerable success. However, Washington's army in the mid-Atlantic colonies struggled desperately, and the southern forces were all but crushed. While it was still far from decided if Massachusetts would become a state or remain an English colony, a group of Massachusetts leaders had already written a state Constitution based on the approved Federal Articles of Confederation. In it, they had written that all men are created free and equal.

At noon this black woman knocked on the trim front door of Theodore Sedgwick, a young, eager lawyer who had been part of the committee that drafted the Massachusetts State Constitution at John Ashley's estate the previous fall. As the door opened, she introduced herself.

"Good day, sir. I'm Elizabeth Freeman from Colonel Ashley's."

"Ah, yes. I remember," answered Theodore, ushering her into his home and office. "They call you, 'Bet,' as I recall. Well come in, come in. Take off your wet things. You must be soaked. I'll get towels for you and the baby."

Elizabeth's trim body and starched servant's uniform were soon perched on the edge of a chair before Mr. Sedgwick's long desk, a mug of hot tea steaming in her hand, her baby playing quietly on the floor.

Theodore settled into his high-backed chair and leaned forward. "For what important mission has John Ashley sent you out on such a miserable day? I hope every one's all right . . . "

"The Colonel didn't send me," answered Elizabeth. "I come on my own to get free." Her face was ordinary, even "plain," but very alert. Her eyes sparkled with excited energy.

Theodore's eyebrows raised as if he hadn't heard correctly. "Excuse me, Bet, what was that you said?"

"I want to be free *now*." The words flowed across his desk—simple, powerful, and sincere.

Theodore rocked back in his chair as if struck hard in the chest by some mighty force and clasped both hands behind his head. Weakly he stammered, "Well now, I'm sure you do. Yes, indeed. I don't know . . . "

Bet continued to gaze, unblinking, into his face. "What's not to know, Mr. Sedgwick? The Massachusetts Constitution says that everyone is born free and equal. You were part of the committee that wrote it. I was serving in Colonel Ashley's house that day and I heard everyone say those words, 'free and equal'."

Theodore's mind slowly regained its balance and raced through the enormity of her claim. "Yes, well certainly, that *is* in the Constitution. But, Bet, you're a . . . a slave."

Bet nodded. "I've been thinking hard 'bout that, too. Is a slave free?"

Theodore chuckled, "Of course not. Not being free's the definition of slavery."

"And you say I'm a slave," continued Bet, " 'cause Colonel Ashley says that he owns me; that he bought me when I was a baby."

"That's right," agreed the lawyer.

"Now, I *was* born, wasn't I?" she asked.

He laughed. "I presume so, Bet. How else would you be . . . "

She interrupted, "And I *am* a person, a human?"

"Yes," he agreed. "You're pretty safe on that one, too. But . . . "

Again she cut him off. "Now, does, or does not, the Massachusetts Constitution state that all men are *born* free and equal?" The lawyer thoughtfully tapped his finger tips together and started to answer when she added, "And I presume that when the Constitution says, 'men,' it really means 'people.' I mean, white women aren't 'men.' But they're free and equal. So it really says all *people* are born free and equal."

Theodore gazed at the ceiling and gestured vaguely, stirring the air with his hands. "Bet, this is really an intriguing—but very complicated—issue you raise."

"Why complicated?" she demanded, still gazing straight into his face. "It sounds simple to me. I am a person. I was born. I live in Massachusetts. So the state Constitution says I am free and equal. Or does the Constitution lie?"

"Oh, no," he reassured her. "The Constitution is the most sacred legal document of the state. It certainly does not lie. It's just that . . . well, no one thought of slaves when we wrote those words. You see, Bet, slaves are property."

Again she cut him off. "Slaves are *people*."

Theodore leaned forward and patted her hand as a parent might pat a child who asks an innocent, but foolish, question. "But slaves are also property. And state law says that a man's property cannot be taken away without compensation."

Elizabeth nodded thoughtfully. "You say *property* isn't free. So be it. But the Constitution says all *people* are free."

Sedgwick nodded, trying to follow Bet's logic.

"Now the only way I can make those two fit is if no people can be property. Since I'm 'people,' I must not be property, and no one needs to 'compensate' Colonel Ashley."

Theodore Sedgwick groped for a valid explanation, his mind whirling through volume and verse of Massachusetts law, his eyes slowly wandering along the walls. "But, Bet, why do you want to be free? Why upset the apple cart that takes such good care of you? You live better at Colonel Ashley's than most free working white people in this part of Massachusetts. Why jeopardize that?"

Instantly she answered, "Why do you want to be free from the good life provided by England?"

Theodore spluttered, "Oh, that's a different situation entirely."

"Is it?" she asked. "What law says it's right to own people without their consent?"

"Where did you get all these fancy words and ideas?" he asked, both astounded and impressed by the forceful way she argued her case.

"I do my job in the Ashley house, and I listen close, and I think hard," she answered.

Theodore sat upright, again tapping his finger tips together, and began to seriously consider her claim. "While it's true, Bet, that no specific law authorized, or created, slavery in Massachusetts, no law specifically forbade it, either. Moreover, since slavery has existed in Massachusetts for a hundred years, legal precedent and custom have both been set that acknowledge slaves as property, and laws have been written *about* slaves—many, I should remind you, to require humane treatment of slaves."

Still Elizabeth Freeman gazed straight at the young lawyer. Her voice was quiet, but filled with power and conviction. "Three years ago my husband, who was also a slave, was sent to join General Washington's army to fight this war for freedom for America. Just over one year ago he died fighting for America's freedom. His daughter there," she pointed back toward her daughter crawling across the hardwood floor, "will never know her daddy because he died fighting for freedom. The Declaration of Independence says all men have a right to freedom. The state Constitution says all are born free. My husband died to make me free. Now I want some of that freedom for me and for my daughter."

Theodore realized it had never occurred to him that black people might want to be free as much as whites did. He had always thought blacks struggled, and sacrificed, and toiled just because some white told them to. But in the determined face of this black woman before him, Theodore saw that blacks were suffering and struggling through a long, hard war—much longer and harder than the one white colonists fought against England—dreaming of their own rights to life, liberty, and the pursuit of happiness.

For the first time he gazed straight back into her strong black eyes. "I'll do what I can, Bet. I'll research it. But there are very complex legal issues here." His mind swirled with a thousand uncertainties. How would his neighbors react? What arguments could he use? What legal precedents could he rely on? What judge and court would hear him? How could he convince a judge and jury to free a slave when a number of them owned slaves of their own?

"Is that what lawyers do," Bet asked, "take a simple thing and make it complicated?"

He laughed and slowly shook his head. "Unfortunately, Bet, this is anything but simple. Still, I will do my utmost to . . . "

There was a fierce pounding on the Sedgwick front door that froze Theodore's sentence mid-stream. Before Theodore could rise from his chair the door burst open. Cold, wet wind gusted into the room. Colonel John Ashley strode in with it, eyes blazing.

He stood in the doorway, glaring at the two people huddled around Theodore Sedgwick's desk, fists and jaw tightly clenched, the wind moaning behind him. Slowly his gaze focused solely on Elizabeth. His words were measured and clipped, as if struggling to control his rage. "Come . . . home . . . with . . . me . . . now . . . Bet."

Her eyes turned pleadingly to the lawyer. "Make me free," she whispered.

Colonel Ashley strode forward and slammed his fist on the desk. "You have deeply embarrassed me and my family, Bet. Reverend Reeve saw you walk through town to Mr. Sedgwick's and rode all the way out to my house to see what was the matter. Can you imagine my awkward embarrassment at that moment?"

He began to pace as he spoke, his hand ripping at the air for emphasis. "I didn't even know one of my slaves had left my property. Can you imagine how foolish that made me look in front of one of the most esteemed members of our community? I don't know what foolishness has brought you here to waste good Mr. Sedgwick's time, but you come home now!"

Again he slammed his fist on the desk for emphasis.

Elizabeth Freeman rose out of her chair, standing as tall and proud as she dared. A long skirt hid her trembling knees and churning stomach. She forced her terrified eyes to look straight into John Ashley's. "No, sir. I will not go home a slave. I came here to be free."

That Bet was able to actually say such brave words to her powerful owner greatly surprised herself and shocked John Ashley.

"To be what?" he demanded, shaking his head to clear his hearing. "You came here to be *what*?"

"I came here to be free and equal, sir, like it says in the Massachusetts Constitution."

Ashley turned to the young lawyer. "What is this nonsense she's babbling about, Theodore?"

Sedgwick gulped and pulled at his collar. "She does have a case, John."

Ashley exploded. "A case! A case? She's my property. Could my chair suddenly decide not to be my chair any more and walk off? Could my trees decide they liked my neighbor better and move there?"

In frustration he ran both hands through his thick, graying hair. Then he let out a deep breath and turned to Bet. "Haven't we given you a good home?"

"Yes, sir," she answered.

"Good and sufficient food?"

"Yes, sir."

"Good clothing?"

"Very good, sir."

"Enough heat in the winter? Time to enjoy the cool afternoon breezes in summer?

"Yes, sir."

"Bet, we have worked very hard over the years to ensure you lived free from want, need, or care. You live far better than most of the free white laborers in this valley. Doesn't that make you happy?"

"Happy doesn't matter, sir. I want to be free."

Exasperated, John Ashley threw his hands into the air and slumped against a book case stuffed with thick law books. "This is ridiculous. There is no argument. There is no case. You are a slave, *my* slave."

Again he turned to Sedgwick. "For her own sake, talk her out of this foolishness, Theodore. Everyone knows blacks lack the capacity to support themselves. Where will she go? Where will she live? What will she do? Where will she ever find a home as good as ours?"

A faint smile crossed Theodore's lips as he thought, "He sounds just like King George talking about ignorant American Colonists."

Elizabeth answered, "Maybe I won't find a home at all, sir. Maybe I'll live in rags and starve. But I'll do it free and equal and happy."

Now Theodore struggled to hold in a chuckle as he thought, "Bet sounds just like us stout Colonists talking back to the good English King."

Ashley turned back to Elizabeth. "Gather up your child, Bet. I order you to come home *now*."

Elizabeth planted her feet. "The lawyer is going to make me free."

Sedgwick shrugged apologetically. "I can't do that, Bet. I'm only a lawyer, not a judge. You'll have to go with him, Bet. You're a slave until a court decides your case and passes a verdict."

Elizabeth Freeman felt empty and defeated on the long, silent walk back to the Ashley estate. It was as if the cruel joke was finally clear to her. Fancy words in laws, declarations, and constitutions only granted freedom to those who already had it, only helped those who didn't need the help. The future looked more bleak than the dismal sky.

Bet was forbidden to leave the main house, and mechanically trudged through her duties all that long winter.

In March the sheriff arrived with a summons and writ for both Elizabeth and John Ashley to appear at the Great Barrington Court for the trial of Elizabeth's petition for freedom on Tuesday, August 19, 1781. Elizabeth's heart soared. Her knees scarcely held her up. She felt like she floated three feet off the floor. Theodore Sedgwick had done it! He'd maneuvered her case onto the court docket.

As a steamy August sun spread orderly patterns of light across the courtroom floor, an eager crowd jammed into the viewing benches. Theodore Sedgwick nervously fidgeted with notes and his coat. Elizabeth sat next to him feeling a great calm. She whispered, "The words 'free and equal' are in the Constitution. There's no words about 'custom,' and precedent,' and 'subsequent laws,' in there. Just the free and equal words. You tell them that in fancy lawyer talk and everything will be all right."

Lawyers argued back and forth. The judge carefully listened and took notes. The jury eagerly leaned forward so that no word escaped them. The crowd excitedly murmured as each point was made, refuted, and then remade. The neat splotches of sunlight marched slowly across the floor and climbed the east wall. For three days Bet sat and watched the light march its way across the crowded room as lawyers argued and tempers flared.

A wave of soft contentment washed over her when she heard the final verdict. The legal community called it a great precedent for freedom. Newspapers claimed the case destroyed slavery forever in Massachusetts and other freedom-loving states. Elizabeth Freeman said simply that now everybody knew what she had known in her heart for some time: She was free and equal.

John Ashley was also ordered to pay back wages, damages, and court costs totaling five pounds, forty four shillings, and four pence.

Elizabeth stared at the money and whispered to Theodore, "All I wanted was my freedom. I never had money before. What do I do with it?"

"First," he answered, "pay your lawyer. Second, buy three new dresses. I am impressed with your keen mind and abilities. I want to hire you to run my household. You'll need something new to wear."

Bet had a natural gift for organization and efficiency, and brought both order and joy to the Sedgwick home. Both before and after her hard-won freedom, most called Elizabeth Freeman by the name, "Bet." Theodore Sedgwick's children often affectionately called her, "mother Bet," or "mum Bet." His grandchildren never called her anything but, "Mumbet."

When she died in 1829 Mumbet had faithfully run the Sedgwick household as a hired housekeeper for over 50 years. She brought order and joy to the house, and Theodore gave her much credit for his success as a lawyer. Her income supported her grandchildren and great-grandchildren.

Aftermath

Massachusetts was the first state to outlaw slavery in the late 1790s. The rest of New England followed suit in the early 1800s, and the rest of the northern states by the 1820s. It took a bloody Civil War in the 1860s to eliminate slavery in the rest of the nation.

Mumbet's struggle is often viewed as the first shining blow in the great fight against slavery in this country. She viewed herself simply as a lucky woman who lived at a time when a constitution was written and set her free. It was just that lots of people's memories needed a gentle nudge to make them remember to do what their words promised they would.

Follow-up Questions and Activities

1. **What Do You Know?**

   • What made slavery legal in the American Colonies? Why wasn't it challenged right away? Has slavery been legal in other countries? Which ones, and when? Can you list the eras and countries when and where slavery was legal and wasn't legal?

   • Were there slaves in all 13 original Colonies?

2. **Finding Out More**. Following are four important topics from this story for you to research in the library and on the Internet. The reference sources at the back of this book will help you get started.

   • Slavery existed in each of the northern states at the end of the Revolutionary War. Research northern slavery. When did it begin in each of the Colonies? How extensive was northern slavery? What jobs were slaves given in the North? How does that compare with the typical roles of slaves in the South? When and why was slavery abolished in the various northern states?

   • In 1780 Massachusetts became the second state to pass a state Constitution. There was no national Constitution yet, so that made the state a free and independent state. What did the Massachusetts Constitution look like? See if you can find a copy of the state Constitution. When did other colonies pass state constitutions? How did the Massachusetts Constitution compare to the constitutions of other states? What powers did it grant to the state? Did it grant any powers to a national government?

   • Elizabeth Freeman (Mumbet) became a symbol of the fight for freedom and equality. Research this important person in our national history. Where was she born? Where and how did she live her life? What was the importance of her fight for personal freedom and equality?

- Other blacks made important contributions to the early history of this country. One was Phyllis Wheatly. Research Phyllis and her work as well as other important blacks of the Revolutionary era and their accomplishments.

3. **Make It Real**

- Hold a court trial of your own to see if Elizabeth should have gone free without having to compensate Colonel Ashley. Search for all possible arguments on Colonel Ashley's side as well as those on Elizabeth's side. Appoint a judge, witnesses, and teams of lawyers to present the case before the rest of the class, which will act as jury.

- Make a class list of evidences of inequality and lack of freedom that you have seen in your own community. Decide as a class what "free and equal" is supposed to mean.

4. **Points to Ponder**

- Why do you think slavery started in the American Colonies? It didn't exist in England, so why did it start here in the English colonies? *How* did it start?

- When the creators of the Declaration of Independence wrote the words "free and equal," whom did they think should be free and equal? Should every human be free and equal? What about little children? Should first graders have the same rights as fifth graders at your school? Should students be equal with teachers? What about old and frail seniors? Should everyone be "equal to" police officers? "Free and equal" to do what? For what?

Surrendering to a Woman

Fighting along the Hudson River, 1782

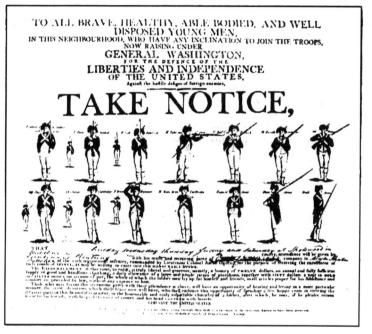

Revolutionary War recruitment poster

At a Glance

After Yorktown the war began to wind down. British politicians knew it; the British War Office seemed to know it. British citizens were disgusted with the war and were demanding an end. Congress desperately hoped that the British would tire of the war and give up. (Congress was flat broke and couldn't have funded another year's campaign even if they had had to. One more push by any British force would have toppled the fragile Continental government.) Washington might have suspected it; but no one else in America knew it.

Tory recruitment drives were still forming new Tory militia regiments to train over the winter of 1781–1782 to be ready to join the Redcoats and take up the fight in the spring of 1782. British generals in New York planned another push up the Hudson River to sever New England from the rest of the Colonies and try to win the war from the North down because their plan to win it from the South up had just failed.

Washington moved the bulk of his army into upstate New York to counter the expected Redcoat drive up the Hudson Valley. The key to the Hudson River became a spot 55 miles upriver where the Hudson made two sharp right-angle turns. Here ships had to slow to negotiate the tight turns—especially when sailing upstream against the current. Here the Continental Army built a sprawling fort and stuffed it with cannons that could pulverize any British ship trying to pass. Here also the Continental Army stretched several iron chains across the river to stop all ships. Each black-painted link weighed hundreds of pounds and was over three feet long.

If the Continentals could defend this stronghold at West Point, England's last chance to win the war through a second Hudson River offensive would fail. What the Continentals needed were soldiers to fill out the army to defend West Point from land attacks by the 30,000-man New York British army.

Precious few men volunteered to take up the uniform of the Continental Army. To the best of our knowledge, only one woman did. She not only sneaked her way into the army disguised as a man, she also qualified for one of the elite Ranger Units. She became a decorated hero of the unit. This is her story.

Meet Deborah Sampson

Deborah Sampson had what would be commonly called "a hard childhood." She was born in Plympton, Massachusetts, on December 16, 1760, one of six children. Her oldest brother (Robert Shurtleff Sampson) died when he was eight, the same year Deborah was born. When Deborah was five, her father died at sea. Her mother, sick and desperately poor, scattered her children to homes that could better care for them. Deborah was sent to live with her mother's elderly cousin, Miss Fuller, on a farm in Sheffield, Massachusetts.

Miss Fuller was kind, but frail and an invalid. Deborah had to do virtually all the work around the house and farm as well as care for Miss Fuller. Deborah worked like a slave from sun up to sun down. When Deborah was eight, Miss Fuller died and Deborah was sent to live with a distant aunt, 80-year-old Miss Thatcher. Deborah again had to do all the house work and farm work and care for (even feed) Miss Thatcher.

Two years later, Miss Thatcher died and Deborah was bound out as a servant to deacon Benjamin Thomas. Deborah was assigned lots of heavy farm work—plowing, milking, stacking hay, carpentry. Deborah grew up aware that she was different from other girls and that she was excluded from polite society. She was big boned, muscular, and tall. She also had sparkling blue eyes and long brown hair, which she cut off to join the army.

After the war, she married in 1784, lived in Sharon, Massachusetts, and raised three children. In the early 1800s she began to tour and lecture—one of America's first touring/lecturing women. Her son joined the army during the War of 1812. Neither daughter expressed any interest in the military.

Surrendering to a Woman

Although her brown hair was now streaked with gray, 42-year-old Deborah Sampson still stood tall and straight behind the lectern on March 24, 1802 at Federal Hall in Boston. Her blue eyes still sparkled. A "standing room only" crowd jammed into every nook and cranny to hear what she would say. On the stage beside her a French Charleville flintlock rifle with gleaming bayonet leaned against the lectern. It was smaller than American-made muskets, and was typical issue for the Continental Army's Light Infantry and Ranger Units.

Staring at this sea of eager faces, Deborah took in a slow, deep breath. "How odd," she thought. "I feared I'd be jailed, flogged, or shot if anyone found out. Now everyone knows. But instead of throwing eggs, they cheer. The sign out front says to come in and hear America's first fighting heroine. How very odd."

She thumbed through the stack of cards on which audience members had jotted down questions for her to answer. She stacked the five or six she felt most able to answer on top. She took in one more deep breath and began.

"Good evening, ladies and gentlemen. I must admit I am a trifle overwhelmed to see all of you here. The only thing that marked me as different from so many other soldiers was that I lied and cheated to gain the uniform. I always feared I would be prosecuted and despised if found out. Instead I am honored by having all of you come to hear me talk. I will now try to answer some of the questions you have asked."

She held up the top card on the stack and read, "Why did you want to join the Continental Army knowing you'd have to hide your true identity?"

A murmur blew through the crowd as heads nodded in agreement with the question. Deborah thought for a moment before answering. "Many of you here in Boston made great sacrifices to help create these United States. Many of you committed yourselves in whatever way you could to winning the war. So did I. It is far too simple to say that I impersonated a man and joined the army just to escape a complete dolt my mother picked out for me to marry, even though I was very glad to get away from him."

Deborah blushed before continuing. "I, of course, couldn't tell even my family that I had joined the army, only that I was safe and had left of my own accord. Two weeks after my unit arrived at West Point, the dolt passed through during his search for me. I actually bumped into him on the parade ground. He didn't recognize me in uniform."

Laughter rippled through the room.

"It is also too simple to say I joined because the delight, freedom, and sense of adventure I felt after shedding the limits imposed on womanhood outweighed my sadness at having to give up my beautiful long hair and my feminine identity, even though they did. I knew I would face great dangers every day—not from British musket balls.

"Rather I risked being found out by my fellow soldiers. I knew I would have to be ever-vigilant not to slip, always alert for danger of exposure, that I would have to carry this great secret all alone and never be able to relax or get close to the soldiers around me. I would have to be always alert—when I ate, when I bathed, when I laughed and gestured, even when I slept.

"We received orders to bathe in the river every day. I got around it by rising before dawn for a solitary morning swim. Some joked that I needed no razor. Luckily six other youths in my company did not yet shave either. Still, exposure seemed never more than one tiny slip away.

"But this is my country too. And I couldn't stand by and watch it struggle through a difficult birth without pitching in. I was tall (5 feet, 9 inches) and sturdy from years of farm work, and had a naturally deep voice. In 1781 Washington called for 30,000 new volunteers. Only 8,000 men signed on. I did whatever I had to do to join the army because my country needed me and because it is *my* country."

A great wave of applause thundered across Federal Hall as head after head nodded at the sentiment of Deborah's answer. This rousing response put a crimson flush on Deborah's cheeks, and confidence in her voice as she snatched up the next card. "Why did you pick the name, 'Robert Shurtleff' when you enlisted?"

Deborah smiled. "Those were my brother's first and middle names. He died at age eight in the same year I was born. I never met him. But my mother missed him dearly, so I know he was a good person and his name deserved to live again through me."

Again her answer fetched a generous round of applause. Deborah beamed. Speaking tours might be more enjoyable than she had thought. She read the third card. "What was your scariest moment with the army?"

"Two stand out in my memory. One was a moment not of fear for myself, but for the poor victims of the first Mohawk Indian raid I came across. Children had been scalped and left to slowly bleed to death in agony. Women's bodies butchered. Men hacked to pieces. I never forgave the Mohawks for that raid, and I was glad to volunteer for the 40-man . . . er, person . . . "

A roll of laughter skipped across the fascinated horror of the crowd.

" . . . Ranger Unit that captured over 500 of them during the winter of 1782–1783.

"The other moment was my first battle. I joined in May 1782. Things were going very much our way. Cornwallis had surrendered at Yorktown in October 1781. But the war was far from over. The British still held New York City with a strong force, and had a large army fighting its way south down the Hudson River from Canada. If those two forces met, the Colonies would be cut in half and the tide would turn back to the British. Complicating things, many thousands of fierce Tories, organized into cutthroat brigades, and bands of Mohawks, were raiding Patriot houses and posts throughout the lower Hudson River Valley.

"Our one stronghold was the narrows where the Hudson makes two abrupt turns around the bluffs called 'West Point.' That's where I was stationed. My Division of Rangers was first assigned to push back the Tories, and then to stop the Mohawks.

"I had been in camp three weeks, in the army only one month, when we marched out for our first extended patrol. Up to that moment my whole focus had been on getting through the normal daily routine of a soldier without being discovered: figuring how to sleep, eat, bathe, and use the facilities without being seen to be a woman.

"Now as part of a company of 50 Rangers I marched out with flintlock, stuffed haversack, and cartridge boxes to go to war. On our third day out, we crossed a field just north of Tarrytown, deep in territory controlled by vicious Tory brigades. Suddenly a volley of musket balls whizzed over our heads. We whirled around to see a large company of Tories on horseback led by two Redcoats who had been waiting in ambush at the top of a hill.

" 'Form your lines!' shouted our sergeant.

"A second volley screamed past us. One ball punched a hole in my hat and split my feather in two. Two of our lads dropped to the ground, blood flowing out across the grass.

" 'Prepare to fire!' yelled the sergeant, now waving his sword like a conductor's baton.

"The Tories charged down the hill with fierce yells as they tried to reload on horseback.

" 'FIRE!'

"Four of the Tories fell from the saddle. Two Tory horses went down.

" 'Reload and hold your line!'

"Feverishly I ripped open the paper around a cartridge and poured the powder into my pan. I wheeled over my musket and dropped powder and ball in.

"The Tories regrouped and fired. The man next to me cried out in surprise and pain, and crumpled to the ground. The earth trembled as the Tory horses charged again.

"I rammed the powder down hard and replaced my ramrod. It felt like I took hours to reload. But I was the third Ranger to re-shoulder my piece and wait for our sergeant's command.

" 'FIRE!'

"Our muskets exploded with a thunder clap roar and a cloud of choking, sulfurous smoke. Six more Tories fell dead. The others wavered and hesitated.

"We heard a loud commotion off to our left. Two long lines of infantry Loyalists under direction of a Redcoat sergeant broke from the woods ready to fire. There must have been 80 of them closing in on our flank. We had walked into a trap and were badly outnumbered.

" 'Volunteers to shield that flank,' yelled the sergeant.

"Instinctively I stepped forward.

" 'Good. You, Shurtleff, take 10 men and stall that infantry until we've regrouped in the woods,' the sergeant commanded. 'Then rejoin us as fast as you can.'

"With 10 uniformed Rangers behind me I sprinted to our left flank to face the lines of oncoming Tories. I wondered what these hardened Rangers would think if they knew a woman was leading them into battle.

" 'Line here!' I yelled, coming to a stop. 'On one knee. Prepare to fire!'

"We saw the smoke rise as a forest of Tory muskets exploded. Balls whined past my head like a gust of hissing wind. One man in my line collapsed backward, a gaping hole in his chest.

" 'FIRE!' I yelled. Our few muskets erupted in red flames, smoke, and thunder. Five Tories fell, but the rest continued to march down upon us.

" 'Reload!'

"Desperately we tore open the paper of our powder charges and rammed ball and powder home.

"The Redcoat sergeant yelled, 'Fire!' Two more of my line fell silent on the field.

" 'FIRE!' I screamed as soon as I saw all muskets up and shouldered. 'Retreat for the woods!' I called, and we scurried for the safety of the trees before the next Tory volley could rip into us. I turned to see four additional Tories lying crumpled on the field. The rest broke ranks and charged at a full run after us, bayonets gleaming.

"We rejoined our company amongst the first trees of the woods just as the mounted Tories charged in on top of us. All was a sea of confusion: smoke, shouts of pain, neighing horses, the roar of muskets, clashing of steel bayonets. And then my eyes saw the wondrous sight of Redcoats and Tories streaming back to the field in retreat.

"The ranks of our besieged company had suddenly swelled. Two volunteer Patriot units had rushed up from Tarrytown at the first sound of gunfire. Now nearly 200 Patriot muskets tore into the Tory ranks. And they fled.

" 'Fire at will and pursue with bayonet!' cried our sergeant. 'Charge!'

"It was my first bayonet charge. With shouts of triumph I raced out of the trees after the Tories, feeling very much like a gazelle as I bounded across the field. We poured a flood of musket balls into the fleeing Tories as we ran.

"Suddenly I stumbled straight into a small cluster of Tories who had formed in a protected pocket around a fallen friend. A Tory bayonet swung at my head, flashing in the afternoon sun. I had time neither to think nor even to scream. Instinctively, as we had been trained, I raised one arm to deflect the blow and lunged forward, low and straight, with my own bayonet.

"The eyes of the Tory before me winced in pain, then shot open in shocked surprise. He trembled for a moment and collapsed to the grass, blood spilling out of the ragged gash across his coat. The rest in the pocket threw down their arms and surrendered as other Rangers rushed in.

"My legs turned to rubber and my knees began to tremble. My breath came in rapid gasps. I couldn't stand, and collapsed to the grass next to my wounded enemy as the terrible emotion of the moment caught up with me. My only thought had been to stay alive. Now at its end, the horror of this battle and of striking my fellow man flooded over me. I began to weep. Then my sobs turned to laughter. A pocket of six fierce Tories had just surrendered to a woman."

The dead silence of Federal Hall was broken first by appreciative laughter, then by thunderous applause and a wave of relief, as if the listeners had held their breath throughout the tense story and finally were able to exhale and gulp in a fresh supply of air at its end.

Deborah raised the next card. "What are the most humorous and embarrassing moments you can recall?"

Deborah's face furrowed in thought, and then suddenly brightened. "The wrestling match," she answered.

"In October 1782, things were slow in camp and we all had time to kill. Some of the boys in our Ranger Company started a wrestling contest. As I walked past, unaware, two of the lads dragged me in. 'Shurtleff takes on the winner,' they cried, and everyone cheered.

"I tried to back out. I said I was in a rush, but then couldn't think of where to or what for. I complained of a sore back and said I had just eaten. Nothing worked. I was pushed forward into the ring. My only thought was, 'Oh, no. They'll find out I'm a woman for sure.'

"The man I was to wrestle was a thick, powerful brute from Kentfield. 'Ah,' he smiled. 'This should be a real match. Shurtleff's a fighter. I remember you from the battle at Tarrytown. I better take this match seriously.'

"Then to my horror he stripped off his shirt to fight bare chested. 'Come on, Shurtleff, strip off that shirt and wrestle man to man.'

"In the midst of my panicked protest he bolted forward, snatched me up, spun me high in the air, and slammed me to the ground on my back.

"The crowd roared at how he had tricked me. 'You're not as quick as I thought,' he said.

"Another challenger leapt in to try his luck. I lay on my back for a long moment, joints aching, eyes closed, lips smiling gleefully, silently whispering to the heavens, 'Thank you, thank you, thank you!' It had been close. But I had escaped and my secret was safe.

"My most embarrassing moment had to be when an important local couple wanted me to date their daughter. I tried politely to decline but they pleaded and offered me a lavish dowry just to date her. I couldn't think of any excuse not to and actually had three dates before my unit was transferred to Ft. Ticonderoga and I was saved."

Boston women blushed at this story. Men howled with laughter. All cheered and demanded another answer. Deborah lifted the next card. "What are you most proud of in your service as America's first woman soldier?"

"That's an easy one," said Deborah. "There are two things. First, that I successfully hid my feminine identity from every soldier and officer around me for over a year. I never slipped and never let anyone find out until the war was over. It was a greater and more demanding effort than any one can imagine.

"Second, that I proved myself to be a worthy and competent soldier and was selected over many others (all men, I might add) for assignment to our Ranger Division. I earned the respect of officers and fellow soldiers alike as a brave fighter and reliable worker. It is very gratifying for me to know that, even though women are not allowed to join the army, I proved that they are fully qualified to do so."

Having said this, Deborah Sampson stepped away from the lectern, snatched up her flintlock, and smartly ran through the manual of arms. She finished by loading and firing in less than 15 seconds.

The great thunderclap roar of her musket slowly faded from the hall. Ears rang. A surprised murmur of voices was slowly replaced by a standing ovation, as voice after voice acknowledged Deborah Sampson's place as a heroine of the Revolution.

Aftermath

The West Point stronghold prevented the British from trying one last, desperate push to split the Colonies in two and continue the war. West Point also acted as the base for the effort to quell Tory and Indian uprisings in upstate New York, more prevalent in that region than in any other part of the Colonies. The strength of the fort at West Point helped to ensure that the war would formally, finally, and completely end. Because of its importance during the later stages of the war, this site was chosen as the site for the nation's military academy, founded at West Point in 1802.

Deborah Sampson was the first American woman soldier. A street is named in her honor in Sharon, Massachusetts. A monument stands in her honor in Plympton, Massachusetts. Even more than for her military deeds and honors, however, Deborah Sampson should be remembered by us all as an early American example of that unshakable spirit that lets no obstacle, no matter how great, stand in the way of a worthwhile goal.

Follow-up Questions and Activities

1. **What Do You Know?**

   - How do you think it was possible for a woman to get away with pretending to be a man? Why didn't she get caught during her initial processing? Why not during her basic training? Could someone get away with it today? Why or why not?

   - Washington's call for new enlistments over the winter of 1780–1781 was mostly ignored. Why wasn't army service popular during the Revolution? Why didn't the army have a flood of eager volunteers?

- Why did the American army create special Ranger Units? Whom were they designed to fight?

- Why did the British Parliament give up on the Revolutionary War in 1782 and begin peace negotiations? The American army was bankrupt and couldn't continue to fight. The British still controlled most of the major port cities. Why didn't the British send in a new army and continue the war?

2. **Finding Out More**. Following are five important topics from this story for you to research in the library and on the Internet. The reference sources at the back of this book will help you get started.

- Have women always joined the military by pretending to be men? Has this happened during American wars other than the Revolution? Which armed forces throughout history have allowed women to join and fight alongside men? Search the library and Internet for examples. Does your research indicate that attitudes toward women serving in the military have changed and are changing? How? Why?

- Research Deborah Sampson. Find out about her entire life history and her many accomplishments after the war.

- Search the library and Internet for information about other women who fought during American wars. Why did they fight in battle? What happened to them?

- After Yorktown, Washington assumed that the war would continue. What did he think the British would try next? Why? How did that force him to re-deploy his shrinking army? What river did he think was the key to holding the country together? Why?

- The Hudson River Valley was a hotbed of fighting throughout the war. After Yorktown, Washington thought it was so important that he shifted his whole army there. Research the Hudson River Valley and the wartime events in that region from 1775 through 1783. What fighting took place there? Who controlled the valley?

3. **Make It Real**

- Imagine that you have a terrible secret that you can't share with anyone at school, a secret that you are terrified will be found out. How would that constant worry affect your daily school life? Imagine that you have such a dangerous secret and write a letter to a close friend describing how it has affected your life at school

- At the end of this story, Deborah Sampson loaded and fired her musket in less than 15 seconds. Research and learn the manual of arms for a flintlock rifle (what you do to load and fire it). Pretend to have a real flintlock, practice the moves, and put on a Revolutionary War demonstration of musket firing for other students.

4. **Points to Ponder**

- Is it a good idea for women to join the military and fight in wars? Why or why not? Do most countries now agree with your position? Have they always done so?

- Deborah Sampson lied to join the army. Should she have been praised or punished for that lie? Why?

- The British entered the Revolutionary War with the best-trained and most well-equipped army in the world, with the most powerful navy in the world, and with an enormous economic and financial machine behind them. They were opposed by an untrained, poorly led, ill-equipped army, by a virtually nonexistent navy, and by a government that was broke before the war began. It should have been the easiest victory in British history.

    But they lost. Why? How could they lose with such an overwhelming initial advantage? Research why and how the British lost something they should have so easily won and discuss your findings in class.

A Fearful Farewell
Loyalists Flee for Their Lives, 1782

New York street scene near war's end

At a Glance

Yorktown did not end the Revolutionary War. Raids, skirmishes, and local fights continued for over a year. But after Yorktown the major armies simply stopped fighting. The American Congress was broke and couldn't fund another campaign. The British army had lost all public and political support at home and so sat in their barracks awaiting new orders.

As peace negotiations dragged on through 1782 and early 1783, and as the British army and British colonial authorities slowly abandoned what control and influence they still had in America, life became increasingly difficult for Tories and Loyalists.

Victorious Patriots were in no mood to forgive and forget. Verbal abuse (and often physical abuse) was heaped upon those even suspected of being Loyalists, as were threats and taunts. Loyalist property was seized. Merchants refused to sell even necessities to Loyalists.

Many feared even worse treatment once the Redcoats finally left. Many fled; most of their property was seized by various self-appointed Patriot Committees at dockside and along the road. Many life-long American Loyalists were forced to flee America as penniless paupers.

Almost 200,000 Americans left during the two-year period 1782–1783—almost 10 percent of the total population. Streaming in fear to docks and borders, taking only what they could carry on their backs, they must have looked much like the floods of refugees who fled violence in their home countries during the twentieth century. This is the story of one loyalist woman.

Meet Vivian Vanderslice

Vivian Childers was born in New York City in 1724. Her parents owned a prosperous shipping company. At 18, she married a prominent New York Loyalist and merchant (Charles Vanderslice), who rose quickly in colonial New York political society. Mr. Vanderslice was held in such high regard by the colonial governor that in 1773 he received one of the four New York franchises to import and sell British East India Tea (before the Boston Tea Party destroyed British tea sales).

When Mrs. Vanderslice's husband died in 1775, she was well established as a pillar of Loyalist society in New York. She hosted regular parties for Generals Howe and Clinton and their top staffs in her spacious downtown home. However, her fortune began to dwindle as prices in New York skyrocketed in 1780 and 1781 because of war shortages. When Patriot-appointed Committees snatched up the power of local and state government in 1782, her economic and social world collapsed. She fled to Canada and lived along the lower St. Lawrence comfortably, but humbly, for another dozen years.

A Fearful Farewell

Mrs. Vivian Vanderslice, as was her custom, lay still for a long minute after she awoke, enjoying the feeling of being on top of the world. Then she rose from her postered bed and sucked in the morning air in a deep, satisfied breath through the second-floor windows of her elegant New York City home. The early morning sun peaked over the East River and Long Island Sound like a glowing orange ball. It promised to blossom into a glorious summer day—a trifle hot, but New York was always a trifle hot in summer. That's how it *should* be, she thought. The summer of 1782 should be no different. Summer heat was why she had fans and servants.

Fifty-eight-year-old Mrs. Vivian Vanderslice pulled the call-bell rope fastened next to her bed. Almost instantly she heard the satisfying sound of hurried steps on the marble staircase in response to her call. The bedroom door opened to a fashionably dressed man in his early fifties, tall and plump, who bowed his head respectfully as he spoke. "Yes, madam?"

"Good morning, Jensen," she gushed. She thrilled at the sense of power afforded each day by the simple act of having others jump at her beck and call. "I think eggs this morning, Jensen—3 eggs—poached. With muffins."

He bowed slightly in his laced shirt and waistcoat. "Muffins. Yes Madam."

"Muffins *and* eggs," she corrected. "Three. Poached, Jensen."

He paused, awkwardly uncertain of how to phrase his reply. "Sorry, Madam."

"Sorry?" she demanded. Mrs. Vanderslice was in the habit of rolling her "r's" with great relish as if it proclaimed her superior breeding and position in society.

"There are no eggs, Madam."

"Then get some prrrromptly, Jensen."

"Sorry, Madam," he said with great solemnity.

"Sorry?"

"Eggs are hard to find these days and cost over £5 a dozen when I can find them, Madam."

Her hand rose to the top of her sizable bosom in shock. Her voice rose an octave. "£5? For a dozen? Preposterous."

"Yes, Madam. Still, it is true, Mrs. Vanderslice." He spoke in the slow, steady voice an adult uses when instructing a young child.

Mrs. Vanderslice seemed to swell to a frightening size as she sucked in a great breath. "I am a pillar of New York society. My late husband was the commissioner of ports for this city and an assistant treasurer for the entire colony. I am a distant cousin of the colonial governor. I am close personal friends with Generals Howe, Clinton, and now Carleton! Don't tell me I can't have eggs!"

Jensen stood in the door, a tower of composure and calm. "30,000 British soldiers in New York City for five years have stripped the countryside of all edible commodities, Mrs. Vanderslice."

Her eyebrows arched. She stomped across the room. Her voice rang like thunder. "We are *thrilled* that the British troops are here!" she gushed, taking every opportunity to roll her "r's." "We relish the chance to have more regiments in our resplendent city!"

"Yes, Mrs. Vanderslice." Jensen's face was the perfect picture of compassion and understanding as he bowed and backed out of the room. "Still, there are no eggs, Mrs. Vanderslice."

"The governor and all his assistants shall hear of this!" she threatened to an empty room.

After a quiet breakfast of muffins and bruised melon, Mrs. Vanderslice glanced into the rooms of her 20-room house that had so often been crammed with gaiety and laughter over the years. "We must buy some flowers for the tables and living room."

"Yes, Mrs. Vanderslice," answered Jensen. "If I can find some, Madam."

"Of course you can find flowers. It *is* the city."

"I will try, Mrs. Vanderslice."

She gestured vaguely around the empty house. "And I believe we shall have beef pie for dinner. I will invite the staff of General Carleton for a rousing party."

"Sorry, Mrs. Vanderslice, but beef is too expensive any more in the city."

"Beef? Too expensive for *me*?"

"Yes, Mrs. Vanderslice."

"An outrage! The governor shall hear of this ridiculousness!"

"The replacement governor has disappeared and I suspect he has fled for England, Mrs. Vanderslice. The appointed governor was driven out of the country three months ago."

Life was so new and uncertain in the summer of 1782. Rumblings of uncertainty seemed to crack the fabric of ordered British life in every corner of the city.

"It is those damnable rebels!" muttered Mrs. Vanderslice, as though that one disclaimer explained all of the social ills befalling the city. "I shall order General Carleton to roust them out this very evening!"

Ten elegantly dressed ladies sat in a circle late that morning in the parlor of Mrs. Weemer's house, two blocks from Mrs. Vanderslice's. Servants scurried in and out with tea and small cakes as the ladies sewed. ("If those wretched Daughters of the American Revolution can do it, so shall the upstanding loyal women of these colonies!" Mrs. Vanderslice had said back in 1778 to start the Women's Sewing Committee of the Board of Associated Loyalists.)

Only 10 women showed up this summer day of 1782 instead of the 50 that sewing luncheons had drawn back in 1779 and 1780. The face of Gloria Skinner, sitting across from Mrs. Vanderslice, was bruised and swollen from a mob attack on the street. Her husband had been Treasurer of New Jersey and fled to Canada to escape the mobs in 1777. He had returned in May 1782, hoping to reestablish his business position. Last night he had been badly beaten by a mob calling themselves the New York Committee for Public Safety. Some of the blows found their way to his wife. They threatened him with execution if he ever set foot in New Jersey again.

"And he committed no crime," Gloria moaned through her sniffles. "He wasn't even *accused* of anything except carrying out the duties of his post!"

One woman in the circle was the cousin of Prosper Brown, a Connecticut Loyalist who had been held in chains for two years by privateers wanting a high ransom. With the war ending, he had been killed and the family threatened with the same if they didn't leave immediately. "I fear I will be next," she sighed while dabbing at the tears forming in the corners of her eyes.

"It's those awful committees," complained one woman as they stitched socks and uniforms for the Loyalist militia.

"They are thugs, a mindless rabble," thundered Mrs. Vanderslice. "I intend to complain to General Carleton about it this very evening."

Another woman paused in her work. "It's so confusing. Suddenly there are committees for everything—Equity, Justice, Appointment, Civil Order, Taxation."

"The taxes!" groaned several women. "Taxes are so high, it's not worth making money anymore."

"They tax you even if you don't," scoffed another.

Mrs. Vanderslice snorted in agreement, then paused to gaze around the circle. "Why are so many missing today?"

"I'm afraid they're gone."

"Gone? Gone where?"

"Nova Scotia, mostly."

Mrs. Vanderslice shuddered. "Such a wretched, unruly choice for a holiday—and so uncompromisingly cold."

"No, Vivian. Gone *permanently* to escape the rebel committees and mobs."

"Gone? Why ever go?" Mrs. Vanderslice demanded. "Those wretched rebels will never reach into New York City to disrupt *our* safety."

"Why do you say that?" asked the battered Mrs. Skinner.

"Why, indeed! New York is the headquarters for the might of the Royal British Army."

"A lot of good they do anymore against the Committees," grumbled one woman. "Besides, they're only here for a few more months"

"What?" bellowed Mrs. Vanderslice.

"The war is over, Vivian. Britain has been defeated."

"Preposterous! Britain can't *lose*."

"They've quit the war. We are being abandoned."

Prosper Brown's cousin said through growing tears and sniffles, "I leave tomorrow for Nova Scotia. But I'm trying to look on the bright side."

Mrs. Vanderslice insisted, "But the future is *here* in New York. Mother England will rise again. You'll see!"

The other women shook their heads and sadly, silently returned to their work.

Jensen arrived in mid-afternoon to escort Mrs. Vanderslice home. They had to walk because the New York Committee for Equity had confiscated her carriage and horses three days earlier, leaving a receipt that could be filed with the Committee on Public Finance for compensation in worthless Continental paper dollars.

"Preposterous!" snorted Mrs. Vanderslice. "I shall buy a dozen new horses."

"There are none to buy, Madam," said Jensen in his low, steady voice.

One block from Mrs. Vanderslice's home, they were stopped by a mob that had barricaded the street and was checking each passer's identification.

"These ridiculous mobs are ruining our city," Mrs. Vanderslice snorted. "Why isn't the army here to clear away such riff-raff?"

One of the ragged women guarding the barricade pointed at Mrs. Vanderslice. "Her! I know *her*. She's a rich Tory spy!"

Many in the crowd surged off the barricade toward the accused spy. They yelled and shook fists. A few shoved against Jensen, who was bravely trying to shield Mrs. Vanderslice from the mob. A brick was thrown. It whistled past her head and crashed into the building behind her.

A volley of eggs sailed out of the crowd. Several splattered on target. The crowd laughed as yoke dribbled down Mrs. Vanderslice's face.

"Eggs," she muttered, eyes wide in befuddlement. "At £5 a dozen, how can they waste eggs?"

"They steal them, Madam," Jensen whispered as he hustled her back up the street and as he tried to wipe the worst of the assault off her face and dress.

"Where were the police?" she later demanded over and over. "Where was the army? Where is civil order?"

Only five officers from General Carleton's staff arrived for a dinner of vegetable and chicken pot pie with sweet plum sauce that evening. "The rest at another party?" inquired Mrs. Vanderslice.

"No, ma'am," answered a thin, mustached colonel. "General Carleton is in Charleston completing the evacuation of that city. Many other officers have already departed for England. The rest are busy closing facilities around New York and preparing to leave ourselves."

"Leave? How can that be?" she demanded.

"The war is over, Mrs. Vanderslice."

"The war is ours to win!" she bellowed, grasping and squeezing a dramatic fistful of air. "The King's American Dragoons were just formed. Recruitment is brisk. The Board of Associated Loyalists is strong and active. The wretched rebels are crumbling in chaos."

The colonel shifted uncomfortably in his chair. "You should consider leaving New York, Mrs. Vanderslice."

She laughed. "Leave New York? Oh, dear me, no, Colonel. Who ever would want to leave the most perfect residence in the Colonies?"

He cast his eyes sheepishly down to the rich Persian carpet. "We cannot protect you from the mobs . . . "

"Rubbish! Of course you can. Two companies of dragoons could easily do the job."

"We have orders not to engage in *any* confrontation. The war is over. We will be leaving soon."

The edges of panic swirled across Mrs. Vanderslice's face. Her voice turned small and frightened, "Mother England can't *leave* me unprotected . . . "

By morning Mrs. Vanderslice had regained her composure and decided to stop this foolish nonsense about British forces leaving New York. She stormed to the colonial governor's office. It was abandoned. He had fled to England three months before. His replacement had never settled in before deciding it was better to leave.

Undaunted, she pushed on to the lord high mayor's office. The rooms were in a shambles, having been demolished by a mob. The mayor had sailed for Canada 10 days before. In General Carleton's headquarters she could find only a clerk-orderly. All officers were busy planning the evacuation of troops from various British posts to Canada and England.

Still determined, Mrs. Vanderslice marched to the police chief constable's office. His title, painted on the door to his set of offices, had been smashed and replaced by a poster that read "Committee for Civil Order."

"Good morning, Mrs. Vanderslice," a man in ordinary worker's clothing sneered. "What can the New York State Committee for Civil Order do for one of the city's most loathsome Loyalists?"

"A rebel . . . " she mumbled. "Wretched rebel committees have taken over the police." Fear grew like a burning lump in her stomach as she glanced around the ring of leering faces staring back at her. "They are all rebels . . . .."

Mrs. Vanderslice turned and stumbled out of the central police station. "Rebels are everywhere." Her hands trembled. She gasped for breath. "I am . . . alone. . . . What shall I do? How shall I manage all alone?"

Mrs. Vanderslice sat alone through the afternoon in her vast living room that had so often held over a hundred at merry gatherings of shining uniforms and swishing, full gowns. Bare spaces marked where gilded furniture and precious artwork had been taken from the walls and floor by the Committee of Taxation and the Committee of Public Equity. She felt shrunken, confused, and adrift.

"How could the greatest civilization on Earth lose a war to a revolting, uncouth, disorganized, ragged rabble? How can Mother England have . . . lost?"

The faint echo of her own voice in the mostly empty room was the only answer she heard.

Her country estate on Long Island had been seized. So had her bank accounts and land holdings. Her friends had been driven off. More and more of her household possessions disappeared to the mobs each day. Now she could not even freely walk the streets of the city she had always felt that she personally owned.

Jensen stood quietly in the shadows by the pantry door.

"What can we do, Jensen?"

"I suggest we leave, Mrs. Vanderslice."

"Leave? But New York is our home."

"It is not our New York any longer, Madam. We should go to Canada."

"Canada? Good gracious, never!" she snapped. "If we go at all, we will go to London to be close to the royal court whom, I am sure, will welcome us."

"I have tried, Mrs. Vanderslice. But I can't book passage to London until October."

Mrs. Vanderslice smiled wistfully. "October. . . . Fall is a lovely time to travel. We'll leave in October."

Jensen fidgeted slightly. "I suggest we leave *now*, Madam, to Canada. I managed to secure most of your funds in cash before the accounts were seized."

"No, Jensen. I have decided. We leave in October."

"New York is not safe for you anymore, Mrs. Vanderslice."

"London. In October, Jensen."

Jensen sighed and softly shrugged, as if unable to find a way to conceal the truth any longer. He seemed stooped and less vigorous as he stepped forward holding a scrolled piece of paper. "You *must* leave now, Madam. This Committee of Justice summons for Public Court arrived today."

"Summons? For me?"

"Yes, Madam."

"To testify against some rebel scoundrel?"

There was deep sadness in Jensen's voice when he spoke. "No, Madam. To stand trial, yourself, as a Tory spy during the war."

"Preposterous! I will not stand trial!" her eyes blazed as she spoke. "I am a loyal English citizen! I'm protected by the King and his army. They can't try me."

"I'm afraid they both can and will, Mrs. Vanderslice, unless we leave."

The very room seemed to vibrate with the fury of her thunderous voice. "They can't run me out on a rail like some commoner! I am related to the governor . . . "

"Who was run out three months ago, Madam."

"My husband was . . . "

"He is dead, Madam, and his commission and post have been dissolved."

"I am a close friend of General . . . "

"Who is preparing to evacuate the entire British army, Madam."

Her fire slowly faded to a fragile, needful ember. She took on the look of a frightened, trapped animal. "*You'll* stop them, won't you, Jensen?"

"It's called the Bill of Attainder, Mrs. Vanderslice. The Committee claims that it gives them the right to haul you away to jail in chains. I can only stall them off for another day—two at most. And there is a ship leaving . . . "

"To Canada?" she asked.

"Quebec City is quite tolerable in summer, I understand, Madam."

Her hands kneaded the air as if trying to wring out a better solution. "I can't run away from my beautiful city. My husband and parents are buried here. My accomplishments are here. My memories are here."

"It's not our city any longer, Mrs. Vanderslice."

She shook her head, desperately trying to understand how her seemingly perfect world could have so quickly and totally dissolved. "It is a world gone mad, Jensen. Totally mad."

"These American rabble," he answered, "have learned a dangerous truth: All power is derived from the common people. Now they seem determined to wield that power themselves."

She gazed far off at a terrifying future. "I will be nothing more than a common refugee, a meaningless, unconnected lump in the frozen north . . . "

During breakfast the next morning, a brick crashed through one of the front bay windows. Shards of glass exploded across the room, slicing through fabrics, gouging furniture and floor. The rumbling voices of an angry crowd poured through the gaping hole. Window glass, lamps, and chairs disintegrated as a second barrage of bricks smashed into the room.

"I'm afraid, Jensen," Mrs. Vanderslice whimpered, crouching in the breakfast room. Fear was a sensation she had not known in her privileged life.

"We must leave, Madam."

"I'll begin packing," she said in a wooden voice.

"No, Madam. We must leave *now*."

Fists pounded on the door. Voices yelled for the traitor to come out.

"Quickly, Madam. Out the back! Now!"

"But my jewels . . . my precious art . . . my husband's collections of artifacts . . ."

"Leave them, Mrs. Vanderslice. You must run!"

She stared, uncomprehendingly. "But. . . . But these things, this city, this place . . . these *are* my life."

"Not any more, Madam." Jensen grabbed her arm and jerked her out the back door and through a service entrance into an alley. It was the first time he had physically touched her in over 20 years of service.

Late that afternoon, two figures huddled on the deck of a merchant schooner. The land surrounding the Verazanno Narrows slid past, gray and lifeless as a rain squall rolled in to obscure their final glimpse of New York City. The land disappeared into gray, swirling mist. They shivered in the dismal rain, hair plastered to their cheeks, clothes hanging limp and matted, eyes straining to see home through the formless gray.

In that moment these two refugees seemed the perfect symbol of the crumbled English colonial empire in America—a heavyset older woman still clinging to just a shadow of her former splendor, now looking frail and pale, who trembled and sniffed back the tears that secretly trickled down her face. A man—tall, plump, and stiffly formal, who patiently held a cloak around her to fight off the worst of the afternoon storm and who dreamed of a safer life in the frozen wilds of the north.

Aftermath

Almost 100,000 loyalist refugees fled from America in 1782. Another 100,000 left in 1783. Ex-British and Hessian soldiers who deserted the British army and settled in America were often welcomed more openly and favorably than were Tories and Loyalists who had lived their whole lives as faithful citizens.

Virtually all was taken from those who fled. Most were forced into lives of poverty in other places held by the British: Nova Scotia, Quebec, the Upper and Lower St. Lawrence River region, Lake Ontario, British posts at Niagara and Detroit, Florida, the Bahamas, Caribbean Islands, and of course, England. Living out their lives as unwanted beggars in unfamiliar countries that neither cared for nor pitied them was the cruel, final chapter to a long, bitter, and cruel war.

Follow-up Questions and Activities

1. **What Do You Know?**

   • Why did the Loyalists feel they had to leave America? Why weren't they protected by the laws? What did they fear?

- How many Loyalists left, and where did they go? What percentage of the total population did that represent?
- Why weren't the Loyalists allowed to take all their possessions with them?
- Why were so many Loyalists concentrated in New York City by 1782?

2. **Finding Out More.** Following are six important topics from this story for you to research in the library and on the Internet. The reference sources at the back of this book will help you get started.

   - What happened to the Loyalists who fled? See if you can create a profile of their fate in Nova Scotia, the Caribbean, along the St. Lawrence River, in Florida, and in England. How many settled in each of these areas? Did they stick together in separate communities or did they integrate into the local population? How many built new, successful lives? How many struggled to support themselves and to fit in? Did most remain poor? Did some become rich?

   - The diplomatic effort to arrange a peace that would officially end the war began in early 1782 and lasted for a year and a half. Why did it take so long? Who handled the negotiations for the "United States?" What were the most difficult issues to resolve? Research this important final phase of the Revolutionary War.

   - Research British army life in New York in 1782 and 1783. The troops had nothing to do but sit in their barracks for almost two years. What did they do? What activities were they allowed to take part in?

   - What happened to the Tory militia units at the end of the war? When did they stop recruiting new members? When did they stop meeting? When did they disband? How did they keep from being arrested?

   - Long before the war was officially over cities like New York were ruled by Patriot citizen committees. Several are mentioned in this story. Who formed and authorized these committees? How did they get their power? What happened to them after the war?

   - How long did it take after the war to form a national government? What form did it take? How did the country function until then?

3. **Make It Real**

   - Make a list of what you would take if forced to flee from your life-long home and country. If you could only take what you could carry, what would that be? What would you take if you had to run to save your life? Make a list of what you would *want* to carry and what you would *need* to carry. What would you leave behind? How would you feel about leaving everything else behind forever?

   - Make a map showing the location and date of significant Revolutionary War events *other than battles*. What kinds of events did you find? Where did these events take place? Why and how were they significant to the war?

4. **Points to Ponder**

- Do you think Congress should have done something to protect Tories and Loyalists after the war? *Could* Congress have done anything? Why didn't they?

- Was the fate of Loyalists after the Revolutionary War unique, or have such mass exoduses often happened at the end of a war? Has this happened in the past century? Where? Why? What happened to the refugees? How disruptive do you think it is to have 10 to 20 percent of a community's population leave? How does the influx of refugees affect the countries they go to?

Alone, Broke, and Forgotten
A Soldier's Farewell to the Army, April 1782

Bidding farewell to comrades

Yorktown had been won; Cornwallis had surrendered. But the British still held New York in strength, as well as major southern ports. British armies were still a threat up and down the Hudson River. Viewed through American eyes, the war seemed far from over.

However, England had lost the taste for a nasty and endless colonial entanglement. War with France and Spain had escalated into global conflict. England had no more resources to pour down the drain fighting the Americans.

Tentative peace overtures and then preliminary peace talks began in 1782. They would lead to formal peace negotiations and to a treaty in late 1783.

With the threat of war beginning to diminish, Congress could breathe a momentary sigh of relief and begin to assess the devastation of the war. America was broke. Congressional (national) coffers had never been full. Now they were mired deep in red ink. Expenses needed to be cut—immediately.

One way to trim national expenses was to disband as much of the army as possible. The problem was that Congress owed the officers and soldiers a fortune they could not pay. Congress initially promised to pay officers the equivalent of six years at half salary when they left the army. Officers couldn't be discharged because there was no

321

way to pay them such a huge final sum. Worse, many enlisted men hadn't been paid at all in years. If they were mustered out, all back pay would have to be handed over. But there was no cash to hand over, whether Congress wanted to or not.

Congress couldn't afford to keep the army. And it couldn't afford to let the army go. It seemed an insoluble dilemma that could easily end with an army revolt.

Then a brilliant congressman thought up the concept of furloughs. Soldiers would still be in the army (so there was no need to settle back pay) but would not be part of the *active* army while on furlough. Officers wouldn't have to be given discharge bonuses because they weren't exactly being discharged. Soldiers wouldn't have to be paid any more because they were on furlough, not on active duty. Soldiers were free to go wherever they wished until called back from furlough to active duty.

Send the army home on indefinite furlough and *never* call them back, never have to pay old debts to those who had fought bravely for American freedom but who were now a burden on the public coffers: It seemed the perfect solution to Congress. Most enlisted soldiers never realized that they were being cheated and trudged off, waving furlough papers, to pick up the broken pieces of their civilian life with nothing but worthless promises. This is the story of three such soldiers.

Meet Marcus Raymond Stanton and Oliver Cromwell

Marcus Raymond Stanton was born a South Carolina slave in 1757. His mother also had been born on the Stanton plantation northwest of Charleston. His father had been purchased as a teenager. Marcus, a field worker, had never set foot outside the boundaries of the modest Stanton plantation when he was shoved into a recruiter's wagon and hustled 1,500 miles north to join the army, taking the place of Mr. Stanton's son, who didn't want to serve.

Marcus didn't know what an army was, that there was a war in progress, or even that there were other countries and colonies when he climbed out of that wagon and found himself thrown into the chaos surrounding Washington's retreat up Manhattan just after the battle of White Plains. Marcus survived the war and then drifted west, settling first in Kentucky and then in Ohio. He never returned to South Carolina for fear of again being made a slave.

Oliver Cromwell was born as a free black in a ghetto on the south side of Philadelphia in 1752. His father died of disease when Oliver was a young boy. His mother and her three surviving children worked their way to New York and then to Boston, arriving when Oliver was 12. His mother died when he was 14. His older brother and younger sister moved west to start a farm. Farming held no attraction for Oliver, who stayed in the city to scrounge whatever work he could. Over the years, he always found enough work to survive but never enough to climb far ahead of starvation.

Oliver jumped at the chance to join the army, thinking it meant a steady source of food, clothes, and income. He held no ideological leanings one way or the other during the war, seeing it only as a practical way to survive. After the war he headed west, planning to meet up with his brother and sister. However, there is no record of him after his split with Marcus Stanton.

Alone, Broke, and Forgotten

Evening camp fires had just been lit as the crystal blue sky of day faded to deep royal blues in the east and to gold and crimson over the hills to the west. It was early April 1782, as the Continental Army garrison at West Point, New York, dropped their shovels and pickaxes for the day, stopped their forced and fevered labor of building an impenetrable ring of forts, and settled in for the night.

After Yorktown and four days of celebrating the sweetness of triumph, most of the army had been marched double-quick up here to the Hudson River north of New York. But it felt more like a victory parade than the usual dusty summer march of an army on the move. People in the towns they marched through had lined the streets to cheer. Folks had turned out by the hundreds to wave and shake their hands, to pass out pies and tell them what heroes they were. By the eighth or ninth town, a lot of the men began to believe it. They began to strut instead of march. They began to think that others should salute and call them "sir" just like the officers.

Then they reached West Point, a lonely spot 55 miles north of New York, where the Hudson River makes two tight, right-angled turns as it worms its way through high bluffs. Every ship had to slow to a crawl to negotiate those turns, which gave cannons mounted on the bluffs above an easy chance to pound ships into kindling. West Point was the key to controlling the Hudson River.

After Yorktown, Washington feared that the British army would need a quick victory to regain favor in Parliament and would strike north from New York to seize West Point. The Continental Army spent the fall and winter of 1781–1782 building forts and redoubts to defend West Point from a land attack. Many of the soldiers hadn't picked up a musket or served guard duty in months. Each morning they formed in ranks, did right-shoulder-arms with a shovel and pickax, and marched off to toil like slave laborers instead of fierce fighters and national heroes.

In the evenings, back at camp on the great, grassy plain overlooking the river and the thickly wooded, rolling hills of the Hudson River valley, the soldiers lit fires, sang songs, rubbed aching muscles, and told stories of more glorious days. Many of the young soldiers around those fires were recent recruits, training to serve in the new Ranger Units of the army. These eager recruits sat spellbound, listening to the tales of seasoned veterans.

At one of these neatly aligned fires, two black sergeants slouched against log supports with a confident—almost arrogant—ease that only came through the forging of years of hardship and danger. Sergeant Oliver Cromwell, his cap mashed low across his face, paused to confirm the awe in his rapt circle of listeners. The dancing firelight flickered light and shadow across his beaming face.

"An' that brings us to October 18 of las' year." The crowd of recruits nodded and murmured in acknowledgment of the importance of the day. Oliver's big hands and long, slender fingers seemed to re-create the scene in the air as he spoke. "October 18, 1781, dawned clear at Yorktown, Virginia, after a violent downpour during the night. We was dressed in new, French-made uniforms of blue and brown. American artillery units shattered the dawn stillness with the thunder of a hundred cannons."

The other black sergeant, Marcus Stanton, began to laugh as he rocked back into the deepening evening shadows. "Where'd you learn them big words? 'Shattered the stillness . . . ' Lawd, that ain't what you said 'dat mornin'. *Then* you was grumblin 'cause we had to get up so early."

The recruits chuckled. Oliver waved his hands as if to dismiss his friend and glared around the circle to regain his listeners' respect. "You hush up, Marcus, an' let me tell this da' way I worked it out."

Marcus said, "Is that what you been doin' in da' afternoons on that 'special detail' while I grow a new crop of blisters building redoubts on redoubts? 'Workin' out' a story? Lookin' up fancy words in the adjudent's office?"

"I said for you to hush up!"

Marcus Stanton rolled his eyes and threw up his hands with a deep sigh. "All right, 'den, Oliver. Let's hear what you been sneakin' off duty to work up."

Oliver grumbled, "Now, if there's no mo' interruptions . . . " And he glared around the circle again, especially at Marcus. "The ground rumbled from the barrage of American artillery . . . "

" 'Barrage!" Now *dat* was one *real* fancy word, Oliver," Marcus laughed.

"Hush up, Oliver and let me tell it!" He cleared his throat to help find his place in the story again. "An occasional weak shot fired back from the British redoubts. But I could tell they were startin' to crumble. Through the drifting smoke, a lone drummer boy emerged from the British lines, marching fearfully down the slope toward the Americans and French. Behind him walked a lone British officer waving a white flag.

"Cannon fire ceased. It seemed you could hear that lone drum beat for miles. Everyone on both sides stood—in plain view—and stared. The officer was whisked off to Washington's headquarters."

Dramatically Oliver allowed his hand to fall to the dirt. "And that was it. The fightin' was over. Surrender talks began. Next afternoon we all spiffed up for the ceremony. We stood in ranks of proud, fierce victors as the defeated British shuffled out and dropped their muskets in a huge pile. No one laughed or hooted. It felt solemn, almost sacred . . . "

Marcus broke into a howl of laughter, kicking his heels on the ground. "*Solemn*? *Sacred*? That afternoon you said the lousy uniforms itched like a torment and that it was a silly waste of your time to make you stand out in the sun gettin' hot."

Oliver glared. "Marcus, hush up! Some of these tadpoles is new recruits and ain't got no experience with the proper feel of big battles."

"Well *I* heard 'bout 'em more than I ever wants to. I had to live through 'em and that was already more than I wanted."

"Have you really been in battle?" asked one of the new recruits. "I mean on a real firing line against Redcoat regulars, slugging it out, volley for volley?"

"Have I been in battle?" repeated Oliver, seeming to light with an inner glow at this opportunity for more stories.

Marcus muttered, "Oh, brother. They won't shut him up 'til midnight now."

"What battle you want to hear 'bout? I been in mos' all of 'em," Oliver continued. "Long Island, I was under Stirling. We lost over half our regiment that day. Trenton. Ummm-hum. I was in the big charge at Trenton."

Marcus shook his head. "That mornin' you was mostly worried 'bout your feet freezin' off and 'bout Captain Herfanger wantin' to get you killed 'cause you's black."

"Naw," complained Oliver. "It's was a great charge! The day was so wet an' cold gun powder wouldn't light. We had to charge straight into the British lines with bayonets only!"

"Wow!" whispered the recruits.

"Brandywine. I was in the *thick* of things at Brandywine. And Monmouth. I was at Monmouth."

"You was there, all right," laughed Marcus. " 'Cept our company didn't get there 'til the battle was over."

Oliver snapped, "Hush up, Marcus!" Then he pouted and crossed his arms. "Maybe you got a *better* story to tell?"

An awkward moment of silence followed while Marcus slowly rubbed his forehead. "Well, I gots one that's a long sight more important." He said it quietly with an edge of bitter fear in his voice. "I hear we're going to be throwed out of the army."

Night settled soft and gentle over the rows of wooden cabins for the veteran units and canvas tents of the new recruits. With the cooking over, some of the camp fires died to glowing embers. Songs floated into the night air around some of the fires—some raucous and some mournful and filled with sad longings. At some fires men sat quietly. At some men tried to pen letters by the unsteady firelight.

Oliver sniffed and wiped the back of his hand across his mouth. Then he tried to smile. "You think you the only soldier got ears? I hear'd that rumor, too. I say, who cares? This place is looking a mite too settled for my taste. I liked it better when we were a trampin' army roving across New Jersey."

The circle of recruits grew quiet. "I just enlisted," said one small voice. "They gonna' throw me out *already*?" Distant crickets sounded uncomfortably loud as the soldiers drifted into their own thoughts and fears.

"Naw, not you young scrappers. You still gots your enlistment term to serve. It's us old-timers gettin' throwed out."

Major Sherman Herfanger wandered by, his uniform jacket unbuttoned and hanging rumpled over his shoulders. His white shirt and collar were permanently yellowed by years of ground-in dirt, dust, and sweat. "Yer not bein' thrown out. Our entire regiment is being *furloughed*." Just saying the word seemed to cause him pain. Herfanger, who had been promoted to major in 1780, was a blacksmith by trade out of North Carolina. He joined the army in the summer of 1776 and was elected captain of his company because he could read and write. It was the most responsible position he had ever held and he took it seriously, serving faithfully as a line commander without grumbling for almost six years.

The new recruits snapped to attention. Oliver and Marcus lounged where they were. "What in tarnation is a *furlough*, Cap'n?" asked Oliver. "I don't want no hardship duty."

Marcus's eyes widened. "Is that like bein' discharged? I heard discharged was when you finally gets yer back pay." He rubbed his hands together. "I'll be rich, sure 'nuff, with five years' back pay comin'."

Herfanger shifted his weight, ignoring the recruits who were seemingly awed by the presence of a field officer and unable to figure out why the sergeants got by without showing trembling respect for the rank of major. "That's the rub. Furlough just means we get to go home. But we're still technically in the army, so they don't have to pay you nothin. Just goin' to give us a voucher."

Oliver scratched his forehead. "Furlough. Voucher. What kind of gibberish you talkin', Cap'n?"

Herfanger growled. "It's *Major* Herfanger to you. . . . At least, for three more days it is."

Oliver laughed. "You always been da' Cap'n. You always gonna be da' Cap'n to us, Cap'n."

Marcus's teeth flashed in the firelight as he smiled in agreement.

Herfanger had resented having blacks in his command when he took charge. He tried to drive Oliver and Marcus out by giving them the worst work assignments he could. When that didn't work, he tried to get them killed by always placing them in the front rank and greatest danger. Herfanger gave up trying to get rid of Marcus and Oliver in 1780 and promoted them to sergeants. Out of an original 95 soldiers in his company back in 1776, only these three were still alive, in the army, and together.

Herfanger turned to leave, then paused. "Your squads start out-processing tomorrow. Schedules and orders will be available after breakfast."

Marcus asked, "What we s'posed to do after that, Cap'n?"

Herfanger's face twisted in bitter anger, exaggerated by the glowing firelight. "*You*? What am I gonna do? My business is gone—and that was just a small-town blacksmith shop. I've been a *somebody* in this army. I'm a Major! When I leave this place, I'm an out-o'-work, no-good blacksmith. I hain't heard from my wife and kids in over two years . . . "

Oliver said, "You's an officer. There's always jobs for officers."

Herfanger's face glowed with anger as his beefy finger jabbed toward the two sergeants. "We won their dirty war and now Congress is trying to brush us off like an embarrassing stain. Well, I ain't goin' that easy, and I ain't goin' peaceful. They can't throw *me* out!" And he stomped off into the night.

Instead of finishing the defensive redoubts, Herfanger's regiment spent the next three days standing in long, snaking lines outside supply tents turning in army-issued equipment—a musket in this tent, a blanket in the next, an overcoat in the one beyond that.

"I am gonna miss this here overcoat," sighed Oliver. "It is surely the first decent coat I got since Long Island back in '76."

"Think of all da' freezin' winters we would o' killed for a fine coat like this," Marcus agreed. "Shame not to let us keep it."

"They ain't lettin' us keep nothin," said Oliver. "Yesterday I would have had to turn in my britches 'cept I didn't have anything else to wear!"

"Keep moving," barked the supply officer. "Next!"

The lines were made painfully slow because each missing piece of equipment had to be reported on a separate form that stated where the item had been lost and why.

"Where you goin' when we leave tomorrow?" Oliver asked.

"Goin'? I didn't know we was *goin'* anyplace."

"We'll be on *furlough*. You gots to go someplace."

"Then I guess I don't rightly know. I never thought 'bout it afore."

Oliver snapped, "What *else* you got to think about standing in these endless lines?"

Marcus shrugged.

"You's a free man, Marcus. Got no master any more. Now you *gots* to think 'bout what you gonna' do."

Marcus shrugged and grunted.

"Why don't you go back home to South Carolina?" Oliver asked.

Marcus grunted. "I left there a slave. If'n I go back, they'll try to make me a slave again, sure 'nuff. 'Sides, I hear'd both my parents was killed during the riots and attempted revolt in 1779. Nothing to go back to except memories of being a slave." He hung his head and pawed at the ground. "I sure would like to see my mama again. . . . Guess I'm glad she died trying to be free."

Then Marcus shook his head hard to rid himself of the thoughts. "No. I *can't* go back to Carolina." He nudged Oliver. "What 'bout you?"

"West, I think," Oliver answered with the same tone of bravado he used when telling stories. "Maybe Ohio. Maybe all the way to Illinois and find me a nice woman and 'bout 80 acres of nice easy land."

"Maybe I'll tell 'em I want to stay in the army," said Marcus. "It's the only home I've known as a free man."

"In the army!? This ain't no home. 'Sides, you *can't* stay. They're closin' the door. Good-by. Get out o' here. Don't need us anymore. 'Sides, they don't have any money to pay you."

"That's okay. They never paid me yet. But they give me food most of the time and fine coats to wear in winter."

They reached the front of the next line and turned in belts and cartouche boxes as an officer checked their names off a long roster sheet.

"I feel kind o' naked without this stuff," Oliver groused. "I had it on every day fo' as long as I can remember."

Marcus brightened with a sudden idea. "I got it! Think I'll head for that city we hiked through after Yorktown. Everyone was smilin' and cheering. An' everyone was handin' out sweet baked pies and such. . . . What was the name o' that place?"

"You mean Baltimore?"

"Oh, yeah. Baltimore," Marcus smiled. "Right friendly town, Baltimore."

"Ain't gonna be friendly now."

"Who says?" Marcus snapped. "They liked me just fine five months ago. They still gonna' like me and give me pies and sweet cakes now."

Oliver shook his head. "You remember when Philip Rother's regiment was discharged last month? He hiked out thinkin' the same thing. No one gave him nothin. Had hisself no place to live and nothin' to eat. They called him a bum and a free-loader of a ex-soldier. So he decided he'd just have to *borrow* some of this and that—just to get by 'til he found a friendlier place. Got hisself arrested and slapped in irons. He was drug back here and is in the stockade."

"Lawd have mercy!" whispered Marcus. "Rother even got hisself a medal. He was a hero. An' they gave *him* nothin'? What would they do to *me*?"

For the first time in his life Marcus felt the terror of loneliness. As a slave, as a soldier, he had always felt needed and had always known what he was supposed to do. This new image of a future all on his own in an indifferent world felt overwhelmingly frightening. His voice shrank to a trembling whisper. "What am I gonna' do, Oliver? I got no family. I got no skills. All I ever done was work fields and soldier. What am I s'posed to do tomorrow?"

The indifferent silence of the West Point plain was the only answer he received.

Major Herfanger wandered by the campfire that night carrying a bottle of rum and plopped down next to Oliver and Marcus. "Now that the war's over, the country don't need us, the cities don't need us, the people don't need us. So we're thrown out like garbage. Not even a thank you. Just a worthless voucher."

Songs drifted into the pale evening sky from those clustered around a dozen campfires.

One circle roared with laughter as a singer warbled, "Do your ears hang low? Do they wobble to and fro? . . . "

Marcus said, "I never understood that song. Whose ears ever hanged low like that? An' what's it got to do with bein' a Continental soldier?"

Another campfire answered the first with an off-key howl of Yankee Doodle.

"Or that Yankee Doodle song neither," added Marcus. "It makes no sense."

"It's a song," answered Oliver. "Ain't supposed to make sense. S'posed to keep your mind occupied so you don't hear your feet complainin' about too many miles of marchin'."

"Naw. They gotta mean somethin'," insisted Marcus.

Herfanger grunted, "Well, *my* ears are hanging pretty low this night, I tell you."

All three laughed and settled into the silence of close friends sitting comfortably around a fire as they had for almost 2,000 nights. Men can't help growing close when they've shared fires and dinner for 2,000 nights, and when they've shared the repeated danger of battle. They don't plan it. It just happens.

Herfanger hemmed and hawed, toeing the dirt. "I'll miss you two. You're the best soldiers I ever had."

"Does that mean you're startin' to like us, Cap'n?" asked Oliver, flashing a wide smile.

"Don't get sentimental on me," barked the major. "If we was back home in Carolina, I wouldn't admit I know you. But here it's . . . different."

Marcus asked soft and solemn. "So what you gonna do, Cap'n?"

"Head home, I guess. And see what's still there. Don't know what else to do."

Oliver said, "I still gots a sister and brother, I think. Ain't seen 'em since I was 14. They moved out west into New York. I guess I'll try to find them. They the only family I got—after tomorrow."

Marcus struggled to find the right words. "I never knew a fella' could have everything and nothin' before. Everyone says I'm free and I gots everything out there to choose from. 'Cept, none of its mine an' don't seem like anyone's willing to give me any. All I ever done in my life was take orders. It's all I knows how to do. And now everyone says I'm s'posed to be happy that I won't have to take orders ever again. 'Cept I don't know what else to do." He shrugged and poked a stick at the embers in the fire. "I guess, I'll head for a city and see what happens—though I'd rather stay here, get yelled at and face the British." With a final sigh he added. "I envy those new Ranger recruits. They just startin' to build their families. Tomorrow we throwin' ours away."

Herfanger grunted and stormed off to his cabin.

The regiment mustered one last time on the parade ground next morning. General Washington was mounted on his light-gray horse, blue cloak flapping gently in the breeze, face expressionless, unflappable. With a final salute, the regiment was dismissed. All aimlessly walked away from camp, slowly splintering into smaller groups as the roads branched toward different states, different homes, different futures.

Marcus and Oliver paused at a junction of mud and ruts—one heading west into frontier New York, one turning south toward the city. They nodded and started to part. Then both hesitated, needing more. "Take care, Marcus."

"Say 'hi' to your brother and sister, Oliver."

After another awkward pause, the two men turned their backs and walked into a brave new world.

Aftermath

Most of the officer corps saw through the despicable congressional furlough maneuver and refused to leave until paid in full. Some threatened to take over the country. Many threatened to march the army west and set up their own country and leave the fledgling United States defenseless. Some threatened to surround Philadelphia and attack Congress.

One of Washington's finest hours was the speech he made to the officers to keep them from mutinying against the country. One of his crowning achievements was to maintain a fragile peace and sense of mutual respect between Congress and the army officer corps. When the army finally disbanded in 1783, Washington supported the congressional shell game, which allowed them to use promissory notes to avoid paying officers in hard cash. The officers threatened, they muttered, they rattled sabers, but Washington made sure they got just enough to keep them from starting a new war.

Follow-up Questions and Activities

1. **What Do You Know?**

   - What was the Continental Army doing in the closing year of the war? Why?

   - Why did the Revolutionary War grind to a halt? Neither army had defeated the other, yet the fighting stopped. Why?

   - What monumental problems did Congress face as the war ended? Why was the army one of their biggest problems?

   - Why did Congress want to disband the army? Why couldn't they do it?

   - What is the difference between a discharge and a furlough?

2. **Finding Out More**. Following are four important topics from this story for you to research in the library and on the Internet. The reference sources at the back of this book will help you get started.

- How are victorious and losing soldiers treated after a war? Are winning soldiers treated better than losing ones? Research specific examples. Do civilian populations tend to treat all soldiers badly after they have fought a war for their country? Research first American wars and then wars in other countries to see whether what happened to American Revolutionary War soldiers was an exception or commonplace.

- Use the library and Internet to research Revolutionary War songs and their original meanings. How many Revolutionary War songs could you find? What sorts of events and ideas were put into song?

- This story starts shortly after Cornwallis's surrender at Yorktown. Why did Cornwallis have to surrender? Where, and by whom, was the battle fought that actually determined Cornwallis's fate? What was the outcome of the Battle of Yorktown?

- In early 1783, the army officer corps threatened to revolt if Congress didn't pay them their back wages and severance pay. Several officers marched their units to Philadelphia and laid siege to Congress Hall. Research the officer corps' unrest at the end of the war. Who kept them from revolting? How? What affect did that have on Congress when they later searched for someone to nominate as the first president?

3. **Make It Real**

- In this story Marcus, Oliver, and Sherman Herfanger all refer to the army as "family." Why do you think they felt that way about their fellow soldiers? Try to interview veterans of World War II, Vietnam, and the Gulf War. Did they develop these same feelings? What do they think did (or did not) create the sense of family closeness for them? Has anything like that ever happened to you? When? What happened?

- Learn and sing several of the songs popular during the Revolutionary War. "Yankee Doodle" was first written in 1755 by British doctor Richard Shuckburg to ridicule the Colonists. "Do your ears hang low?" was also penned by a British soldier for the same purpose after the Battle of Long Island. Both later became popular children's songs in this country.

4. **Points to Ponder**

- American soldiers were heroes during the war. As soon as it was clear that the war was won (late spring of 1782), both the population and the government of the country turned their backs on those same soldiers and treated them terribly. Why do you think that happened? See how many reasons you can find.

- Did Congress promise to pay soldiers money they didn't have (and knew they wouldn't be able to get) to convince soldiers to continue to fight in the war? Was that an ethically acceptable thing for Congress to do? Why do you think they did it?

Glossary of Terms and Definitions

A number of terms occur in story after story in this book that are not common terms today. It is important to students' understanding of the stories that they first understand these terms. The most important are defined below.

The American Independence Supporters

Committees of Correspondence. Samuel Adams formed the first Committee of Correspondence as a local, informal committee in Boston on November 2, 1772, to "facilitate the spread of propaganda and to coordinate the actions of the Patriot party." By summer 1773 Governor Hutchinson had reported to Parliament that there existed Committees of Correspondence in over 80 Massachusetts communities.

On March 12, 1773, Virginia organized the first official state-level Committee of Correspondence, which became a standing committee of the legislature. Formal county-level committees sprang up from South Carolina to Massachusetts (Maine didn't yet exist as a separate colony.) beginning in late 1773. These formal committees were vastly important in their ability to sway and shape public opinion. These committees also carried out many government functions (judicial, legislative, and executive) in 1782 and 1783 as the British abandoned the various colonies.

Each of these different types of committee was called a "Committee of Correspondence."

The Mechanics. This was the code name for a Boston-based group of message riders. There were no telephones, fax machines, or even regular postal service. If messages were to be safely delivered between Committees of Correspondence or between Sons of Liberty groups, someone had to carry them. These messengers who were willing to carry Patriot correspondence between towns and colonies were called The Mechanics.

Minutemen. Minutemen were members of New England-area Patriot militia groups who had pledged to drop everything else and respond instantly to the call to arms. Minutemen were called out several times for confrontations with the British in the months before Lexington and Concord, but none of those encounters was violent. After Lexington and Concord, the Minutemen melted into the militia units surrounding Boston and then became soldiers in the army. After Lexington and Concord, there was no need to call Minutemen to arms. They already held their arms and would not lay them down until the war was over.

Patriot. Patriots favored American independence. The term grew to mean "one who actively supports independence with deeds." Patriots fought, spied, and carried messages. Patriots darned socks, made gun powder, and grew grains for the army. They joined militia units and actively opposed British control.

Sons of Liberty. "Sons of Liberty" groups (or clubs) developed independently in scattered communities throughout the Colonies after Parliament passed the Stamp Act (1765). Always radical groups that operated in secret and on the fringe of (or outside) the law, the separate Sons of Liberty began to join together and conform to a single mold between 1772 and 1775.

The Boston and New York Sons were the biggest and best organized groups. Boston became the organizational and operational model for other groups.

Acting as the enforcement arm of the early independence movement, the Sons of Liberty distributed legal and illegal flyers and pamphlets, started brawls, tarred and feather pro-British officials and businessmen, threatened and intimidated opponents, and generally undertook every action they could think of to inflame anti-British sentiments and promote liberty.

Whig. This term referred to a political party started in Scotland in the mid-1600s. Whigs opposed the succession to the English throne of James II because of his Catholic sympathies. The Whig party controlled Parliament from 1714 to 1760, when they were ousted by the Tory party. Whigs were an opposition party in England during the time of the American Revolution. Whigs evolved into the Liberal Party in English politics.

Those in America who opposed the British government during the Revolution called themselves Whigs to show their opposition to England and Parliament. Soon, "Whig" and "Patriot" both came to mean "one who supports American Independence and opposes British rule." However, "Whig" usually meant simply the political leanings of a person. "Patriot" implied more of a willingness to *act* in support of the Revolution.

The British and Supporters

Loyalist. A Loyalist favored continued British rule. Many in America were inwardly Loyalists but took no overt action to promote continued British rule. Thus, "Loyalist" referred not to what people did but rather to their political leanings.

Redcoat. The British army and soldiers were called Redcoats because the British infantry wore crimson-red wool waistcoats, cut at the waist in front with thigh-length tails in back. Soldiers were also called "lobster backs" and "bloody backs."

However, not all English military wore red. Many of the cavalry units wore green coats (as did most American cavalry). The Hessian mercenaries wore green or white coats. Some of the Irish and Scottish units wore green or blue coats. The British forces were not a one-color army, but the classic British infantry soldier did wear a bright, easy-to-spot red coat.

Tory. The English Tory party was the conservative political party in Britain. The Tory party struggled until 1760, when they were swept into power with the new king, George III. Tories in Parliament referred to themselves as "Friends of the King."

Any American in the 1770s who wanted to proclaim himself a "friend of the king," took on the political label of "Tory" even though, as a colonist, he could not officially join an English political party. In common usage, "Tory" came to imply one who fought for the Crown. Thus, "Tory" was a stronger term than the milder "Loyalist."

Revolutionary Fortifications

Fort. Forts were large, thick-walled structures that men lived in. Sizes and shapes varied drastically, but all had high walls to keep the enemy out, ramparts (platforms just behind the wall for the defenders to stand on while shooting over the wall), mounted cannons, and walls thick enough so that enemy cannon balls couldn't smash through them.

Redoubt. Redoubts, fortified places smaller than forts, were often star-shaped. They had walls and ramparts, but the walls were often lower than those of a fort. Some had cannon mounts. Redoubts did not contain living quarters, cooking areas, or storage room for supplies and ammunition. They were simply protected areas from which soldiers could fire on attacking enemies. Often a fort would have three or four redoubts around it to hinder the enemy's attack on the fort.

Redoubts were sometimes built as small, temporary fortifications—often in the midst of battle because they could be built far more quickly than a complete fort. The "forts" on Breeds Hill that started the famous Battle of Bunker Hill were actually redoubts. In a practical sense, if soldiers dug trenches and built dirt or log walls to use during a fight, they would generally call it a redoubt.

Weapons

Brown Bess. The Brown Bess was the standard-issue musket for British soldiers. Most French units used a smaller, lighter musket called a Charleville. American soldiers most often provided their own muskets so there was little or no uniformity in American units.

Cartouche Box. Cartouche boxes were small, lined leather boxes that held powder, musket balls, and small strips of wadding cloth—the ammunition for a soldier's musket. Cartouche boxes were attached to a waist belt (or, occasionally, to a shoulder belt). French in origin, these boxes were virtually waterproof and so kept a soldier's powder dry. If a soldier's powder got even a little damp, it would not ignite, and that soldier was worthless in battle. The frontier American equivalent was a powder horn, strung on a leather strap over one shoulder.

Flintlock. Early muskets were built using flintlock design. This term referred to the way the gun was fired. A piece of flint in the musket's hammer struck a metal surface, creating a spark, which ignited a powder trail that led to the main pocket of powder trapped in the barrel. Flintlocks took longer to load and were slower to fire than were other kinds of muskets. By the time of the Revolutionary War, flintlocks were used primarily by old trappers and Indian fighters who had had the weapons for many years.

Musket. A musket is a handheld, shoulder-fired, muzzle-loaded firearm with a long, smooth barrel. The lead musket ball, powder, and wadding were rammed down the barrel with a ramrod before each shot could be fired. Muskets were the most common weapon until the time of the Civil War. Revolutionary War muskets were reasonably accurate up to 100 yards.

Rifle. *Rifling* was a great step forward in weapon accuracy. The term refers to spiral grooves cut into the inside of the weapon's barrel. These grooves forced the ball to spin as it sped down the barrel. A spinning ball flew much farther and straighter, so rifles were accurate to over three times a musket's maximum distance.

Rifles, however, were slower to load and much more expensive than muskets. Each army had small "sharpshooter" units that used rifles, but rifles did not play a major role in the Revolutionary War.

Military Terms

Court martial. A court martial is the military equivalent of putting a soldier on trial for a crime. Officers take the roles of judge and jury and pass sentence according to military rules rather than civilian law.

Fife. A fife is a flute-like instrument, commonly used by eighteenth-century armies as a source of marching music. Fifes and drums led almost every marching regiment.

Flank. *Flank* is a military term for "side." An army of soldiers in a firing line can fire forward. They can turn around and fire backward. But they can't effectively fire to the side because most would be firing into their own soldiers. Thus, armies are always trying to maneuver to attack the enemy on its flank. To "outflank" someone means to get around his side and attack from the side and rear.

Rear guard. A marching army is spread out for miles. The weakest spot in this marching column is the very end, or rear. It is the easiest spot to attack and defeat. Thus, every marching column has to place a strong force—called a "rear guard"—at the end of the column to fend off enemy attacks.

References

There are hundreds of published references on virtually every aspect of the Revolutionary War. These are backed by hundreds more unpublished papers, essays, and letters. Those listed here are ones that I found worthwhile, interesting, compelling, and trustworthy and that are generally available through libraries and Internet searches. Some are older, some are brand new, but all are carefully written history. Many of these sources were consulted in the writing of the stories in this book.

The first section includes nonfiction reference sources. The second section includes the best historical fiction that accurately portrays revolutionary era life and Revolutionary War events. The last section includes Internet sites I found to be reliable, informative, and backed by unbiased, stable organizations.

Nonfiction Resources

Abbott, Edward. *Revolutionary Times*. Boston: Roberts Brothers, 1876 (reprinted in 1984 by Scheer and Rankin).

    Best as a description of rural and urban life during colonial and revolutionary times. A good information source on political action and organization during the war.

Adler, Jeanne. *In the Path of War: Children of the American Revolution Tell Their Stories*. Peterborough, NH: Cobblestone Publishing, 1998.

    First-hand accounts by New England children of their experiences during the war. Good for understanding their perspective and their daily concerns and pattern of life. Not as good for describing major events of the war.

Bacon, Paul, ed. *The Uncommon Soldier of the Revolution*. Harrisburg, PA: Eastern Acorn Press, 1986.

    Brief accounts of the actions of a number of women, children, and a few elderly people during the Revolutionary War. Many spied or carried messages through enemy territory. Some fought in skirmishes, many against frontier Indians. Better as a collection of stories about unheralded Patriots than as a flowing narrative of events during the war.

Bakeless, John. *Turncoats, Traitor, and Heroes*. New York: Lippincott, 1969.

    A fascinating look at the subversive actions of Patriots and Tories to undercut the efforts of the opposition and to bolster their own side of the conflict.

Baker, Charles. *The Struggle for Freedom*. Peterborough, NH: Cobblestone Publishing, 1990.

    One of the comprehensive, chronological reviews of the revolutionary period. This one is good for its coverage of the political struggles more than for the military actions.

Balderston, Marion, and David Syrett. *The Lost War: Letters from British Officers during the American Revolution.* New York: Horizon Press, 1979.

    A collection of extensive quotes from letters penned by more than 50 British officers during the war. Some are represented by many letter entries; some by only a few. Collectively they provide a perspective on the war that Americans rarely get to see.

Benson, Mary. *Women in Eighteenth Century America.* New York: Columbia University Press, 1965.

    An authoritative look at ordinary life for women in the Colonies during the colonial and revolutionary periods. The emphasis is not on the war itself, but rather on the role and function of different classes of women during the period.

Bliven, Bruce. *American Revolution, 1760–1783.* New York: Random House, 1981.

    An excellent and comprehensive chronological tour of the events of and forces that shaped the Revolution. A good basic book for understanding the flow of events during the war. An updated and expanded version was published by Random House in 1986.

Boatner, Mark. *Encyclopedia of the American Revolution.* Harrisburg, PA: Stackpole, 1994.

    Contains brief but very informative entries on most individuals and events of significance during the war. Arranged alphabetically by topic rather than chronologically. A good reference book.

Booth, Sally. *The Women of '76.* Boston: Hastings House, 1973.

    An engaging description of Patriot women in America before and during the Revolutionary War. Good source for information on women's contributions to the war and for descriptions of actions and events featuring American women.

Botting, Douglas. *The Pirates.* Alexandria, VA: Time-Life, 1978.

    A short book providing information on pirates and privateers. The section on privateers directly applies to the Revolution. The rest provides an overview of life on the seas for these adventurers.

Bracken, Jeanne Munn, ed. *Women in the American Revolution.* Carlisle, MA: Discovery Enterprises, 1997.

    Another excellent and accurate description of the lives of women during the revolutionary period and of their efforts to support the war.

Buel, Joy Day, and Richard Buel. *The Way of Duty.* New York: W. W. Norton, 1984.

    A good description of the life of a Continental soldier during the Revolutionary War.

Canon, Jill. *Heroines of the American Revolution.* Santa Barbara, CA: Bellerophon Books, 1994.

    Brief biographical sketches of many of the prominent women who contributed to the Revolution.

Carlo, Joyce. *Trammels, Trenchers and Tartlets: A Definitive Tour of the Colonial Kitchen.* Old Saybrook, CT: Peregrine Press, 1982.

> Not specifically a book on the Revolution; rather, it is the definitive guide to the design, structure, and operation of a colonial kitchen and contains excellent discussions of the cooking styles and preferences of the day as well as the typical diet of colonists of different classes.

Chidsey, Donald. *The Tide Turns: An Informal History of the Campaign of 1776 in the American Revolution.* New York: Crown, 1976.

> A detailed, in-depth discussion of the events (political, social, and military) that led up to and occurred during the pivotal year 1776.

Clyne, Patricia Edwards. *Patriots in Petticoats.* New York: Dodd, Mead, 1976.

> Very readable, short biographies of more than 20 women who made significant contributions to the war effort.

Crary, Catherine. *The Price of Loyalty: Tory Writings from the Revolutionary Era.* New York: McGraw-Hill, 1983.

> Letters and diary excerpts from a variety of Tories (mostly northern) showing the ebb and flow of their fate during the seven years of the war.

Danenbery, Barry. *The Journal of William Thomas Emerson.* New York: Scholastic, 1998.

> A detailed, regular account of the life of one colonist. Good for color and a sense of citizen concerns and life.

Davis, Burke. *Black Heroes of the American Revolution.* New York: Harcourt Brace Jovanovich, 1976.

> One of the best books focusing almost exclusively on black participants and black accomplishments during the Revolution.

Egger-Bovet, Howard, and Marlene Smith-Baranzini. *Brown Paper School US Kids History: Book of the American Revolution.* Boston: Little, Brown, 1994.

> A brief picture book format summary of the most important forces and events of the war.

Eisenberg, Bonnie. *Women in Colonial and Revolutionary America.* Windsor, CA: National Women's History Project, 1989.

> An excellent review of documented information about the life of women during the Revolution, and of the concerns, burdens, and daily schedules of women.

Evans, Elizabeth. *Weathering the Storm: Women of the American Revolution.* New York: Paragon House, 1989.

> A good reference on events affecting and actions by women during the war. A good description of the contributions of women to the war effort.

Felton, Howard. *Mumbet; the Story of Elizabeth Freeman.* New York: Dodd, Mead, 1970.

> A good biography of Elizabeth Freeman, an important black woman during the revolutionary period.

Feradin, Dennis. *Samuel Adams, The Father of American Independence*. New York: Clarion Books, 1998.
> A strong biography of Samuel Adams, in many ways the father of the Revolution.

Fichel, Leslie, and Benjamin Quarles. *The Black American: A Documentary History*. Glenview, IL: Scott, Foresman, 1986.
> Compelling stories and anecdotes about the black experience throughout American history. There is a small section dealing directly with the Revolutionary War. Best as an overall history of black life and accomplishment in America.

Fisher, Leonard. *Picture Book of Revolutionary War Heroes*. Harrisburg, PA: Stackpole, 1970.
> Short, easy-to-read biographical sketches of many of the most prominent figures in the war.

Fleming, Thomas. *Liberty: The American Revolution*. New York: Viking, 1997.
> A good general history of the events of the Revolution. Includes lots of valuable interpretation and discussion of major events.

Freeman, Lucy, and Alma Bond. *America's First Woman Warrior*. New York: Paragon House, 1992.
> A detailed biography of Deborah Sampson.

Fritz, Jean. *Can't You Make Them Behave, King George?* New York: Putnam, 1978.
> Easy-to-read version of the causes for discontent and of the early events of the war. Focuses mostly on Boston and events in that area.

———. *Cast of a Revolution: Some American Friends and Enemies*. New York: Houghton Mifflin, 1972.
> Another excellent collection of short, easily readable biographical entries on the major figures on both sides of the war.

———. *Where Was Patrick Henry on the 29th of May?* New York: Putnam, 1975.
> The story of the framing of the Declaration of Independence and of congressional debate during the early phases of the war.

Gerson, Noel. *The Swamp Fox, Francis Marion*. New York: Crowell, 1983.
> A detailed biography of Francis Marion. Creates an excellent portrait of this important military leader.

Graymont, Barbara. *The Iroquois in the American Revolution*. Syracuse, NY: Syracuse University Press, 1982.
> An excellent documentation of the role of the Iroquois in the war and of the reasons for their participation. Good insights into the thinking of the Iroquois leaders and of the British who used them.

Greenberg, Judith, and Helen McKeever. *In Their Own Words: Journal of a Revolutionary War Woman*. New York: Franklin Watts, 1996.
> Extracted diary, journal, and letter entries written by women during the war. Provides an excellent look at major events from women's perspective as well as the daily lives of women and children.

Gregery, Kristiana. *Winter of Red Snow*. New York: Scholastic, 1996.
    A detailed, diary-like description of Washington's winter camp at Valley Forge during the winter of 1776–1777.

Haven, Kendall. *Amazing American Women*. Englewood, CO: Libraries Unlimited, 1996.
    Includes accurate, powerful stories on four revolutionary era women in 40 separate stories.

———. *New Years to Kwanzaa*. Golden, CO: Fulcrum Publishing, 1999.
    Includes an excellent, historically accurate version of the signing of the Declaration of Independence.

Herbert, Christopher. *Redcoats and Rebels*. New York: Avon Books, 1990.
    A detailed and complete history of the revolutionary period.

Hirsch, S. Carl. *Famous American Revolutionary War Heroes*. New York: Rand McNally, 1974.
    Detailed and complete accounts of the major Revolutionary War figures and of their actions during the war.

Hoffman, Ronald, and Peter Albert. *Women in the Age of the American Revolution*. Charlottesville: University Press of Virginia, 1979.
    A more academic assessment of the role and life of women during the Revolution. Presents extensive research.

Holbrook, Stewart. *The Swamp Fox of the Revolution*. New York, Random House, 1988.
    An excellent biography of Francis Marion. Detailed and complete.

Irving, Washington. *Life of George Washington*. 5 vols. Chicago: Darby Books, 1983.
    Detailed, definitive, and well-researched biography of George Washington. As reliable as any that has been written.

Kaplan, Sidney. *The Black Presence in the Era of the American Revolution*. Washington, DC: Smithsonian Institution, 1993.
    A definitive account of the black population in the 13 Colonies at the time of the start of the Revolutionary War: their status, demographic distribution, culture, work, and social life.

Keener, Cynthia. *Southern Women in the Revolution*. Columbia: University of South Carolina Press, 1998.
    A short work that focuses on the role and contributions of Southern Patriot women. Told primarily through first-person accounts, this book provides an excellent glimpse of colonial life in the South and the bitter civil fighting from 1779 through 1782.

Kerber, Linda. *Women of the Republic*. Chapel Hill: University of North Carolina Press, 1980.
    A good account of prominent women during the mid-eighteenth century, covering their lives and accomplishments.

Ketchum, Richard. *The World of George Washington*. New York: Crown Books, 1984.
      An excellent biography of Washington. This one includes numerous references to events surrounding Washington himself.

Knight, James. *Boston Tea Party: Rebellion in the Colonies*. New York: Troll, 1982.
      A good account of the events leading to war. Centered primarily on Boston and the Massachusetts Colony.

Lancaster, Bruce. *The American Revolution*. Boston: Houghton Mifflin, 1971.
      One of Lancaster's two detailed accounts of the Revolution. Good explanation of and detail for most major events. This volume is more heavily weighted toward political and social events.

———. *From Lexington to Liberty*. New York: Doubleday, 1975.
      Lancaster's second book on the Revolutionary War, this one focuses more on military events and campaigns than does his other book.

Larrabee, Harold. *Decision at the Chesapeake*. New York: Clarkson Potter, 1984.
      Analysis of the decisions made by British, American, and French political and military leaders that led to the battle between French and English fleets at the Chesapeake and, eventually, to Cornwallis's surrender.

Latham, Jean. *Carry On, Mr. Bowditch*. New York: Houghton Mifflin, 1955.
      A detailed account of life on merchant and privateer ships during the colonial and revolutionary periods. Also excellent descriptions of life in port cities and along the waterfront.

Leone, Bruno, ed. *The American Revolution: Opposing Viewpoints*. San Diego, CA: Greenhaven Press, 1992.
      Individual issues and events are discussed in a pro and con format. This book features prominent writings from the period as well as modern analysis. Better used as a review of major decisions and political debates than for events and battles of the war.

MacKenzie, Frederick. *The Diary of Frederick MacKenzie*. New York: New York Times, 1968.
      A detailed account of one man's struggle in the Patriot-Tory civil fights and military service during the Revolution. Hard to read, but loaded with good background and detail.

Marshall, Douglas, and Howard Peckham. *Campaigns of the American Revolution: An Atlas of Manuscript Maps*. Ann Arbor: University of Michigan Press, 1976.
      One of the best and most detailed reviews of military movements, campaigns, and battles of the Revolutionary War.

Martin, Joseph. *Yankee Doodle Boy*. New York: Holiday House, 1995.
      A factual account of a small group of Continental soldiers, tracking their experiences through the war.

Mayer, Jane. *Betsy Ross and the Flag*. New York: Random House, 1972.

> A very patriotic biography of Betsy Ross, this book does not question her role in creating the first flag but does present a complete and accurate accounting of that version of the story.

McCormick, Richard. *New Jersey from Colony to State*. Newark: New Jersey Historical Society, 1981.

> Although the section describing the Revolutionary War is a relatively small part of this book, it is an excellent resource for studying the reactions, feelings, and thoughts of New Jersey citizens in the critical years 1776 and 1777.

McCusker, John, and Russell Menard. *The Economy of British America, 1607–1789*. Chapel Hill: University of North Carolina Press, 1985.

> This book deals primarily with colonial America. It provides a wonderful look at colonial economic life and shows how economic forces and decisions helped propel the Colonies into conflict with England.

McGovern, Ann. *The Secret Soldier*. New York: Scholastic, 1985.

> An excellent biography of Deborah Sampson.

McManis, Douglas. *Colonial New England: A Historical Geography*. New York: Oxford University Press, 1975.

> This book provides an excellent picture of the growing population and economy of New England. It provides social, cultural, and economic profiles of the region and lays the background for the resentments and concerns that sparked the war.

McManus, Edgar. *Black Bondage in the North*. Syracuse, NY: Syracuse University Press, 1973.

> This is one of the few books to provide extensive, accurate information on black slavery in Northern colonies. It traces Northern slavery form its beginnings into the early nineteenth century, when the institution was abolished in all Northern states.

Meltzer, Milton. *The American Revolutionaries: A History in Their Own Words*. New York: HarperCollins, 1987.

> An excellent collection of writings by Adams, Paine, Hancock, and many others showing the progression of social and political thought from 1770 through the Revolutionary War period.

———. *George Washington and the Birth of Our Nation*. New York: Franklin Watts, 1986.

> This is an excellent and scholarly biography of George Washington, with extensive side notes on other historical figures prominent in the founding of the country.

Meyer, Edith. *Petticoat Patriots of the American Revolution*. New York: Vanguard Press, 1986.

> Excellent short biographies of 15 prominent Patriot women. The stories provide good background and scenic detail.

Morris, Richard. *The American Revolution*. Minneapolis, MN: Lerner, 1985.

> A well-written, relatively easy-to-read and understand history of the revolution Broad based in its coverage and relatively unbiased in its presentation.

Morris, Robert. *The Truth about the Betsy Ross Story*. Beach Haven, NJ: Wynnehaven Publishing, 1982.
> A good account of the evidence on both sides of the Betsy Ross-and-the-first-flag story. This book is reliable and believable.

Neumann, Goerge. *Collector's Illustrated Encyclopedia of the American Revolution*. Harrisburg, PA: Stackpole, 1975.
> A good summary of the major events of the war, this book is almost as valuable for its illustrations and visuals as for its text.

———. *Swords and Blades of the American Revolution*. Harrisburg, PA: Stackpole, 1973.
> A good description of the weapons of the mid-eighteenth century and of their use. This book includes discussion of who used which types of arms and why.

Osborne, Mary. *George Washington: Leader of a New Nation*. New York: Dial Books for Young Readers, 1991.
> A good account of the life of George Washington, written to be accessible to younger readers.

Pearson, Jim. *Women of the American Revolution: A Unit of Study for Grades 5-8*. Los Angeles, CA: National Center for History in the Schools, 1997.
> Both good information and lots of study questions and activities for students.

Perics, Esther. *The American Woman: Her Role During the Revolutionary War*. Monroe, NY: Library Research Associates, 1981.
> A scholarly analysis of the role and life of women during the colonial and revolutionary periods. Lots of detail on the normal lives and functions of women.

Purcell, Edward, and David Burg, eds. *World Almanac of the American Revolution*. New York: World Almanac, 1992.
> Brief, encyclopedia-like entries on virtually all events and persons of significance during the Revolution.

Raimo, John. *Biographical Directory of American Colonial and Revolutionary Governors: 1607–1789*. Westport, CT: Meckler Books, 1980.
> Brief, factual accounts of the lives and accomplishments in office of the colonial governors in all 13 American Colonies. Only the last 20 percent of the entries deal with governors active during the pre-war and war years.

Rankin, Hugh. *The American Revolution*. New York: Putnam, 1974.
> A general, readable history of the flow of major social, cultural, military, and political events during the war years.

———. *Francis Marion, the Swamp Fox*. Garden City, NY: Doubleday, 1977.
> An excellent, detailed account of the life and career of Francis Marion.

Richards, Norman. *The Story of the Declaration of Independence*. Chicago: Children's Press, 1968.
> This book traces the origins and development of the ideas, concepts, and wording that appear in the Declaration. It also traces the development of, and debate about, that document.

Scheer, George, and Hugh Rankin. *Rebels and Redcoats*. New York: Da Capo Books, 1967.
    An excellent, authoritative history of the major events of the war. Not many side issues and events are covered, but it is still one of the best for its coverage of the major themes and moments of the war.

Smith, Richard. *Patriarch: George Washington and the New American Nation*. New York: Houghton Mifflin, 1993.
    An in-depth, scholarly biography of Washington and his war and post-war accomplishments.

Sobel, Robert. *The American Revolution: A Concise History and Interpretation*. New York: Ardmore Press, 1967.
    An excellent general history of the war and of its major events. One plus of this book is the interpretive discussions of the significance and effect of events and decisions.

Sosin, Jack. *The Revolutionary Frontier*. New York: Holt, Rinehart & Winston, 1977.
    A good source for understanding wartime attitudes, struggles, plans, and events, from 100 miles inland from the Atlantic all the way to the Great Lakes.

Stein, R. Conrad. *The Story of Lexington and Concord*. Chicago: Children's Press, 1983.
    A good account of the background events leading up to April 19, 1775, and of the hour-by-hour happenings on that day.

Spencer, Eve. *A Flag for Our Country*. Austin, TX: Raintree-Steck-Vaughn, 1993.
    A picturebook version of the Betsy Ross story. Not as detailed as some, but easily readable and a good summary of that version of the origin of our national flag.

Stevens, Bryna. *Deborah Sampson Goes to War*. Minneapolis, MN: Carolrhoda Books, 1984.
    An excellent biography of America's first fighting woman. This book pays particular attention to Deborah's wartime experiences, feelings, and reactions.

Stevenson, Augusta. *Molly Pitcher: Young Patriot*. New York: Aladdin Books, 1980.
    A picturebook format biography of Molly Pitcher. It is best as general background and for its descriptions of Molly's role at the Battle of Monmouth. Not as detailed as other sources for her life at Valley Forge or for her efforts after the Battle of Monmouth.

Stewart, Gail. *The Revolutionary War*. San Diego: Lucent Books, 1991.
    A good summary version of the major events and characters of the Revolution. Not as lengthy and detailed as some histories of the period, this book is still an excellent overview and summary.

Taylor, Dale. *Everyday Life in Colonial America*. Cincinnati, OH: Writers Digest Books, 1997.
    Not specifically a Revolutionary War reference, this book is a factual storehouse of information about daily life in colonial America. The book includes encyclopedia-like entries on all major aspects of colonial life: cooking, commerce, farming, and politics.

Tebbel, John. *Turning the World Upside Down.* New York: Orion Books, 1993.

An excellent history of the Revolutionary War. This book places particular emphasis on the final two years of fighting, that is, on the Southern Campaign. It also features excellent descriptions of British thoughts, reactions, feelings, and decisions.

U.S. National Park Service. *Boston and the American Revolution.* Washington, DC: U.S. National Park Service, 1998.

An excellent summary of the events in Boston from 1770 through 1776.

———. *Morristown: Official National Park Handbook.* Washington DC: US National Park Service, 1994.

Factual, detailed summary of Washington's three winter camps at Morristown, New Jersey, and a quick summary of the Morristown Mutiny carried out by many of Washington's officers.

Weil, Ann. *Betsy Ross: Designer of the Flag.* Indianapolis, IN: Bobbs-Merrill, 1983.

Although it wholeheartedly supports Betsy's claim as the maker of the first flag and ignores flaws and holes in the evidence to support that claim, this book is a detailed, complete version of the Betsy Ross legend.

Weir, Robert. *Colonial South Carolina: A History.* Millwood, NY: KTO Press, 1983.

Although focusing primarily on colonial life in South Carolina, this book does contain excellent summaries of the pivotal wartime events in South Carolina from 1779 through 1781.

Wheeler, Richard. *Voices of 1776.* New York: Meridian Books, 1972.

Excerpts of letters and journals written by participants in the major events and battles of the war. There is little analysis and interpretation, but the book is rich with the flavor, sound, and emotion of the period.

Wilbur, Keith. *Pirates and Patriots of the Revolution.* Old Saybrook, CT: Globe Pequot Press, 1994.

A good sourcebook for life aboard privateer ships, covering the typical construction, weaponry, and compliment of a privateer ship and many of the significant engagements by privateers during the war.

———. *Revolutionary Medicine.* Old Saybrook, CT: Globe Pequot Press, 1997.

An excellent summary of medical knowledge, training, equipment, theory, and practice during the eighteenth century. There are also several entries describing major battles from the perspective of attending physicians.

Wister, Sally. *Sally Wister's Journal.* Bedford, MA: Applewood Books, 1995 (reprint of original 1902 manuscript).

Sally Wister was a Philadelphia girl sent into the country to escape the British occupation. She wrote a detailed diary of her life during this period. It is primarily an account of the social engagements and dreams of a 16-year-old colonial girl.

Zall, P. M. *Becoming American: Young People in the American Revolution.* Hamden, CT: Linnet Books, 1993.

Short, biographical entries describing the lives and Revolutionary War actions of a number of primarily New England youths.

Historical Fiction

Avi. *The Fighting Ground*. New York: Harper & Row, 1984.

Benchley, Nathaniel. *George the Drummer Boy*. New York: Harper & Row, 1977.

Collier, James, and Christopher Collier. *My Brother Sam Is Dead*. New York: Scholastic, 1974.

Forbes, Esther. *Johnny Tremain*. New York: Dell, 1970.

————. *Paul Revere and the World He Lived In*. New York: Houghton Mifflin, 1962.

Lawson, Robert. *Ben and Me*. Boston: Little, Brown, 1988.

O'Dell, Scott. *Sarah Bishop*. New York: Scholastic, 1980.

Web Sites

The Internet contains tens of thousands of sites that provide information on the Revolutionary War. I have included selected sites here. Some are general information sites that cover substantial portions of the war period, and others are site-, event-, or person-specific. Most include good links to related sites. All sites were accessed in July 2000.

Use these sites as starting points for online research, or use keywords from the stories in this book with your favorite search engine to locate the sites you need. A number of sites referenced for a particular person or event contain similar information on related people and events; for example, usahistory.com/wars is listed only for the Battle of Trenton (www.usahistort.com/wars/trenton.htm), but by changing the last element of the URL, this site can provide information on other battles and war-related events.

All the sites listed include the prefix http://; it has been omitted here for convenience.

205.161.11.2/student/revwar/revwar.html
  General information and good links to other sites.

209.54.40.178/towncrier/towncrier3.html
  General information.

americanhistory.about.com/msub24.htm
  Information on the war along the frontier.

battle1777.saratoga.org
  Battle of Saratoga and Burgoyne's surrender.

classicals.com/federalist/TheRevolutionaryWar/messages/109.html
  Battle of King's Mountain, South Carolina.

classicals.com/federalist/GeorgeWashingtonhall/messages/21.html
  Battle of Trenton.

databank.oxydex.com/compendium_bibliographium/american_focus/
Benjamin_Franklin.html
  Biographical information about Benjamin Franklin.

earlyamerica.com
  General information site.

earlyamerica.com/review/fall97/arnold.html
  Information on the career of Benedict Arnold.

home.earthlink.net/gfeldmeth/chart.rev.html
  Information on revolutionary events.

jeffline.tju.edu/archives/phdil
  Letters and commentary from the war period.

lcweb2.loc.gov/const/declar.html
  Development of the Declaration of Independence.

lcweb.loc.gov/exhibits/declara/declaral.html
  Development of the Declaration of Independence.

lcweb2.loc.gov/ammem/bdsds/bdsdhome.html
  History of the Continental Congress.

lil.org
  Click on "History Guide."

memory.loc.gov/ammem/amlaw
  Colonial and revolutionary period legal developments.

memory.loc.gov/ammem/gwhtml/gwhome.html
  General site plus detail on Washington and Mt. Vernon.

memory.loc.gov/ammem/rbpehtml
  General site.

revolution.h-net.msu.edu
  General information.

se94.ameslab.gov/tour/gwash.html
  Biographical information about George Washington.

sin.fi.edu/franklin/rotten.html
  Biographical information about Benjamin Franklin.

userpages.aug.com/captbarb/femvets.html
  Information on female soldiers.

Vroads.virginia.edu/~CAP/ROTUNDA.sara_1.html
  General Burgoyne's history and his surrender.

www.cr.nps.gov/seac/chpi
  Information on colonial Charleston.

www.dell.homestead.com/revwar/files/ARNOLD.htm
  Information on the career of Benedict Arnold.

www.discoveryschool.com/fall98/programs/revwar4/resources.html
  Information on colonial Charleston.

www.dohistory.org
  General information.

www.encyclopedia.com/articles/07698.html
  Battle of Long Island.

www.english.udel.edu/lemay/franklin
  Biographical information about Benjamin Franklin.

www.geocities.com/Pentagon/Bunker/8757/revvirtual.html
  Virtual battlefield tours (in this case, Bunker Hill).

www.greeceny.com/arm/welch/weapons.htm
  Revolutionary War weapons.

www.historictowns.com/Boston/teaparty.com
  Boston Tea Party events.

www.historyplace.com/unitedstates/revolution/index.html
  General revolutionary period site.

www.historyplace.com/unitedstates/revolution/teaparty.html
  Boston Tea Party.

www.incwell.com/biographies/Franklin.html
  Biographical information about Benjamin Franklin.

www.itt.colombia.edu/history/lexcon.html
  Information on the battles of Lexington and Concord.

www.kidpost.com/reflib/usahistory/AmericanRevolution/YorktownBattle.htm
  Battle of Yorktown and Cornwallis's surrender.

www.johnpauljones.com
  Information on John Paul Jones.

www.kargatane.com/crossroads/newyorkcity.html
  New York City in the Revolutionary War.

www.liberty.net.org/iha/march
  Good general information.

www.lihistory.com/4/gbatt281.htm
  Long Island Patriot letters and other documents during the war.

www.lpitr.state.sc.us/marion.htm
  Information on Francis Marion.

www.multieducator.com/revolt
  Battle information.

www.nps.gov
  National Park Service home page. Includes information on a dozen Revolutionary War sites.

www.nps.gov/gewa
 Biography of George Washington.

www.nps.gov/moor
 History of the Continental Army's winters at Morristown, New Jersey.

www.odci.gov/cia/ciakids/history/nathan/html
 Story of Nathan Hale.

www.ovta.org/main.html
 Battle of King's Mountain, South Carolina.

www.pbs.org/ktea/liberty/chronicle
 Colonial life and times.

www.pbs.org/ktea/liberty/chronicle/lexington.html
 Information on the battles of Lexington and Concord.

www.pbs.org/ktea/liberty/chronicle/weekly/aaloo497.htm
 History of the Continental Congress.

www.pcs.sk.ca/sjk/sjkcolon.htm
 General information.

www.rockingham.k12.va.us/EMS/RevWar/AmRevolution.htm
 General information.

www.seacoastnh.com/jpj
 Information on John Paul Jones.

www.semo.net/suburb/dlswoff
 Military history of the war.

www.shelby.net/jnkmnmp/cornwal.htm
 Information on General Cornwallis.

www.si.umich.edu/spies
 Letters from and about revolutionary period spies.

www.snowerest.net/jmike/amrevmil.html
 Military history ofthe war.

www.universitylake.org/primarysources.html
 Good source of original period documents.

www.usahistory.com/wars/trenton.htm
 Battle of Trenton.

www.ushistory.org/valleyforge
 Information on Washington's winter at Valley Forge.

www.usmm.org/revolution.html
 Information on privateer action.

www.valleyforge.org
 Information on Washington's winter at Valley Forge.

www.virginia.edu/gwpapers
Records of Washington's papers and correspondence.

www.wappingerschools.org/oakgrove/class/revwar.html
Information on the war in upstate New York.

www.whitehouse.gov/wh/glimpse/presidents/html/gwl.html
Biographical information about George Washington.

www.wpi.edu/Academics/Depts/MilSci/BTSI/abs_sar2.html
Battle of Saratoga and Burgoyne's surrender.

www.wpi.edu/Academics/Depts/MilSci/BTSI/abs_bostea.html
Boston Tea Party.

www2.cr.nps.gov/abpp/revlist.htm
Battles and events by state.

Index

353

from LIBRARIES UNLIMITED

More American History

AMAZING AMERICAN WOMEN
40 Fascinating 5-Minute Reads
Kendall Haven

Haven tells the stories of the first American woman doctor, the first woman social worker, the first American woman to fly, the first U.S. congresswoman, and 36 other women of note. **All Levels.**
xxii, 305p. 6x9 paper ISBN 1-56308-291-8

EXTRAORDINARY PEOPLE IN EXTRAORDINARY TIMES
Stories of Unsung American Heroes
Patrick M. Mendoza

Dozens of unsung heroes and unusual characters, from the first woman to receive the Congressional Medal of Honor to the black man who broke precedence to fire a gun during the attack on Pearl Harbor, take center stage in this intriguing work. Also contains little-known facts about well-known personalities. **Grades 4–9.**
x, 142p. 6x9 paper ISBN 1-56308-611-5

AMERICA IN HISTORICAL FICTION
A Bibliographic Guide
Vandelia L. VanMeter

Portrayals of America's people, places, and events in historical fiction make an exciting supplement to U.S. history classes. This book helps educators and students locate the best in classic and contemporary fiction in this subject area. **Grades 6–Adult.**
xvi, 280p. 6x9 cloth ISBN 1-56308-496-1

LITERATURE CONNECTIONS TO AMERICAN HISTORY
Resources to Enhance and Entice 7–12
Lynda G. Adamson

Identifying thousands of historical fiction novels, biographies, history trade books, CD-ROMs, and videotapes, these books help you locate the best resources on American history for students. Some books with more illustration than text will be valuable for enticing slow or reticent readers. **Grades 7–12.**
xii, 624p. 7x10 paper ISBN 1-56308-503-8

For a free catalog or to place an order, please contact
Libraries Unlimited/Teacher Ideas Press.
800-237-6124 • Fax: 303-220-8843 • www.lu.com
Mail to: Dept. B045, P.O. Box 6633, Englewood, CO 80155-6633